GRAPHIC DESIGN REFERENCED

A VISUAL GUIDE TO THE LANGUAGE, APPLICATIONS, AND HISTORY OF GRAPHIC DESIGN

ROCKPORT

First published in the United States of America by
Rockport Publishers, a member of
Quayside Publishing Group
100 Cummings Center
Suite 406-L
Beverly, Massachusetts 01915-6101
Telephone: (978) 282-9590
Fax: (978) 283-2742
www.rockpub.com

Library of Congress Cataloging-in-Publication Data
Gomez-Palacio, Bryony.
  Graphic design, referenced : a visual guide to the language, applications, and history of graphic design /
Bryony Gomez-Palacio and Armin Vit.
     p. cm.
  Includes index.
  ISBN-13: 978-1-59253-447-0 (hardcover)
  ISBN-10: 1-59253-447-3 (hardcover)
  1. Graphic arts. 2. Commercial art. I. Vit, Armin. II. Title. III. Title: Visual guide to the language,
applications, and history of graphic design.
  NC997.G565 2009
  741.6--dc22

                                                                        2009007126

  ISBN: 978-1-59253-742-6

GDR

DESIGN, LAYOUT AND PRODUCTION
UnderConsideraton, LLC: Bryony Gomez-Palacio, Armin Vit

PRODUCTION COORDINATOR
Regina Grenier

COVER IMAGES
The full images and their corresponding credits can be found
on the following pages:

Front cover, TOP TO BOTTOM
209, 377, 205, 256, 238, 58, 95, 383, 312, 194

Back cover, TOP TO BOTTOM
240, 199, 380, 200, 199, 141, 97, 176, 57, 94, 100, 369, 49, 46

TYPOGRAPHY
Graphic Design Referenced is typeset in Mercury Text by
Hoefler & Frere-Jones and Stag Sans by Christian Schwartz,
who also created an all-caps stencil edition for this book.

10 9 8 7 6 5 4 3 2

Printed in China

REFERENCED GRAPHIC DESIGN REFERENCED GRAPHIC DESIGN REFERENCED GRAPHIC DESIGN REFERENCED GRAPHIC DESIGN

BEVERLY MASSACHUSETTS

A VISUAL GUIDE TO THE LANGUAGE, APPLICATIONS, AND HISTORY OF GRAPHIC DESIGN

ROCKPORT PUBLISHERS

Bryony Gomez-Palacio and Armin Vit

ACKNOWLEDGMENTS

First and foremost, we want to thank every single person who answered our emails and phone calls and took the time to provide the materials and information that are the essence of this book.

Graphic Design, Referenced would most likely not exist had it not been for the vision of Rockport's Winnie Prentiss, publisher, and Emily Potts, acquisitions editor, who approached us with the idea of creating an ambitious tome about graphic design. Most important, we thank them for their patience as we extended our delivery dates months—and months. Also at Rockport, we would like to thank Regina Grenier, art director and senior design manager, for her support in the design of this book, and Tiffany Hill and Cora Hawks for their apt management skills.

For helping us avoid major embarrassments we extend our deep gratitude to Aaris Sherin, assistant professor of graphic design at St. John's University, for her indefatigable fact-checking, and to Madeline Gutin Perri, for making us sound like better writers with her acute copyediting.

The early advice and suggestions of Michael Bierut, Tobias Frere-Jones, Jonathan Hoefler, Adrian Shaughnessy, and our readers at Speak Up were integral to getting us on the right track. Preliminary research by Nikita Prokhorov helped ease the burden, and suggestions of design projects to illustrate some of the entries by Joe Marianek unearthed true gems. Extended appreciation to Steven Heller, Michael Johnson, and Patrick Burgoyne for their consistent help in matters large and small through this project.

Many thanks to all these wonderful individuals who helped us with the most simple and complex requests (appearing in the chronological order they assisted us): Stephen Coles, Michael Pieracci, and Yves Peters, FontShop International; Rich Kaplan, Finlay Printing; Kurt Koepfle, Susannah McDonald, Tamara McKenna, Adi Wise, Simon Beresford-Smith, Pentagram; Bob Zeni, STA; Dmitry Utkin, designyoutrust.com; Emmet Byrne, Walker Art Center; Design Maven; Elaine Lustig Cohen; Laetitia Wolff; Markus Rathgeb; Derrick Schultz and Katie Varrati; Emily Roz and Mike Essl, Herb Lubalin Study Center; Marian Bantjes; Stephen Eskilson; Joe Kral; Kari Horowicz and David Pankow, Cary Graphic Arts Collection, RIT; Michael Evamy; Marc J. Frattasio; Thomas Phinney, Adobe; Jennifer Bass; Louise Sandhaus; Grant Hutchinson; Robert Jones and Jordan Crane, Wolff Olins; Ian Lynam; David Pearson; Heather Strelecki, AIGA; Sarah Coffman; Michelle French; Mark Kingsley; Maaike de Laat; Allan Haley; Steff Geissbuhler; Jose Nieto; Joe Miller; Kevin Reagan; Richard R. Anwyl, The Center for Design Study. Apologies if we left anyone out.

To our parents and brothers, our most fervent cheerleaders—without their support and confidence in us, this would have been a constant uphill challenge.

And, above all, to our daughter, Maya, whose unbridled sense of curiosity and discovery fuel our own.

INTRODUCTION

It is both painful and cathartic to admit this in print and in the very first sentence of our introduction: This book is one of the hardest, most challenging, and most stressful projects we've undertaken. One part was simply the physical and logistical implications we experienced—writing close to 115,000 words, gathering more than 2,500 images and their respective release forms, and keeping track of the 3,500 emails we wrote, not to mention facing the writing deadlines we embarrassingly had to push back time and again. The other part of this gestational burden—and the one that bears most heavily on us despite the joy of finishing the project—is that the book is, relatively speaking, incomplete.

At the outset, we established that *Graphic Design, Referenced* would serve as a metaphorical clearinghouse for graphic design information, covering its basic principles, formative history, seminal projects, and influential practitioners.

But, as we soon found out, it was impossible to cover everything, be it for time constraints, the limitations of our already generous page count, the availability of reproducible images, or the participating consent of designers or those holding the rights to the work, putting us in a position where for every dozen successful inclusions there were a handful of upsetting omissions—and we realize the latter are as significant as the former in a field as rich and diverse as graphic design. These conditions, however, don't exempt us from criticism on the conscious exclusions we made. If asked politely, we will be happy to explain our position, whether it was blissful ignorance or premeditated judgment. Of course, this is not all irremediable: Pending the success of this first edition (*wink, wink*), many of these gaps could be mended.

The final content of the book is the result of a constantly fluctuating whirlpool of names, terms, typefaces, methods, events, brands, magazines, and numerous other verbs, nouns, and proper nouns that act as reference points for graphic designers—hence the title. Adopting the word *reference* allowed us to look at graphic design in two ways: first, as an acknowledgment of how graphic designers colloquially reference their own history, constantly pointing to particular designers or specific projects as sources of inspiration or comparison; and, second, as a challenge to create a book that serves as an authoritative reference of both textual and visual information, documenting and chronicling the scope of contemporary graphic design. Perhaps a better way to explain the book is with our elevator pitch: If you find yourself in the sole company of graphic designers, this book will likely address every professional subject that might arise, giving you enough information to laugh at an inside joke or nod in knowing agreement at a thoughtful reference.

Because the material of this book treads territory similar to that of Philip B. Meggs's *A History of Graphic Design*, Richard Hollis's *Graphic Design: A Concise History*, and even the latest entry

Notes about the book and how to use it

STRUCTURE

Each chapter (for example, "Principles") is composed of subchapters (for example, "Principles of Typography"), and within those are broad labels that cover several entries (for example, "Black Letter" is one entry under the label "Classification" in "Principles of Typography"). The broad labels are explained on each subchapter page, establishing the context and criteria of the entries.

Text

Most entries range from 150 to 300 words. This is not much. So we bluntly admit that many details have been left out and certain stories might feel incomplete. We made every effort to include the most relevant information, but it wasn't always possible. When available, we have made further reading recommendations.

Recommended Reading

This icon appears at the bottom of some entries; it points you to page 390, where you can find accessible suggestions.

Bibliography and Footnotes

Sorry, there are none. This is not to imply we did not consult vast numbers of books, journals, magazines, and video and radio interviews. We did. And, surprisingly, most of these reference materials are easily accessible through online searches. When they are not fully available online, the original sources can be acquired at bookstores, libraries, or from acquaintances who hoard design literature. We take this opportunity to praise Google Books and Amazon.com's "Look Inside" feature, which gave us access to many books that would have made for much costlier research had we bought them.

into the historical survey category, Stephen J. Eskilson's *Graphic Design: A New History*, we sought to differentiate our content—which wholeheartedly builds on these giants' shoulders—by offering a new organizational perspective through which we can parse our past and present while offering new inclusions from the growing canon of our profession. In "Principles," we look at the foundations of graphic design to establish the language, terms, and relatively objective concepts that govern what we do and how we do it. In "Knowledge," we explore the most influential sources through which we learn about graphic design, from the educational institutions we attend to the magazines and books we read. With "Representatives," we attempt to gather those solo or group practitioners who, over the years, have been the most prominent or have steered the course of graphic design in one way or another. Finally, through "Practice," we highlight the iconic work that both exemplifies best practices and illustrates the potential legacy of the work we produce.

With this framework in place, we forged ahead in filling in the nearly 500 blanks through a combination of comprehensive (although admittedly not exhaustive) bursts of text and—testing our puzzle-solving skills—as many images as the layout was willing to accommodate. Despite the aforementioned stress and challenges, this has been a thrilling book to define, research, write, and visualize. While this may not be everyone's idea of a good time, we loved immersing ourselves in the world of graphic design. Design books, sporting dozens of Post-it notes, are scattered through our office; our scanner always has a queue of materials waiting to be digitized; our Web browser history is miles long; the U.S. Postal Service, UPS, and FedEx are constantly delivering packages containing original design artifacts that designers have sent us or that we have purchased on eBay; our transfer server is endlessly active with uploads and downloads of files; and we have used this project as an excuse to visit graphic design archives in our vicinity. It may sound corny and perhaps paradoxical to the opening paragraph, but this has been an unexpectedly enriching experience.

The result is a book we believe—or, at the very least, hope—provides an informative, energetic, and nimble point of view on the many facets of our profession. We are neither historians nor critics, simply practicing designers who acknowledge the importance of being aware of the path our profession has taken so it can be steered in new directions. This book is ultimately a reflection of our own formative experiences, and its content represents what we have found important, relevant, and influential over the course of many years. We are anxiously confident and eagerly unsure about the relevance and reception of *Graphic Design, Referenced*—but we trust it will serve as a worthy stepping-stone, for us and the profession, to forge a new history and practice in the twenty-first century.

Bryony Gomez-Palacio and Armin Vit

Related

One goal we wanted to achieve with this book was to show the web of connections in our industry, and in the spirit of the Internet we have created links between related items. These are made evident in the running text by a gray underline and arrow gently pointing you to the appropriate page, like this › 10.

Historical Images

To our dismay, design projects dating to the 1950s and earlier are painfully expensive to acquire from universities, museums, and special collections. If money and time were not at issue, this book would be flooded in them. Given our time constraints and budget, we have limited their inclusion, and for our two timelines we have made our own interpretations of some of the most iconic and best-known images.

Contemporary Images

For entries that did not require specific design projects, we made a conscious effort to find fresh and previously unpublished work from around the world. Much of it was harvested from websites like ffffound.com, manystuff.org, monoscope.com, and thedieline.com. Some, however, you may have seen before.

For Further Consideration

In the course of the book are ten entries we singled out through a different design and longer narratives. These are projects or topics we feel deserve extended consideration and attention.

Feedback

We look forward to receiving corrections, questions about omissions, or any other kind of feedback. Please visit underconsideration.com/gdr.

1869 / USA

The first advertising agency, N. W. Ayer & Son, is founded

1880 / USA

Edward J. Hamilton founds the Hamilton Company in Two Rivers, Wisconsin, it becomes the largest producer of wood type

1886 / USA

Ottmar Mergenthaler invents the first typesetting machine, the Linotype

1887 / USA

Tolbert Lanston invents the Monotype typesetting machine

1896 / GREECE

The Games of the I Olympiad present the first Summer Olympics › 356

KEY REPRESENTATIVES

GERMANY **Peter Behrens** / UK **William Morris** / USA **Dard Hunter, Bruce Rogers**

c. 1880 – c. 1910

Arts and Crafts

1891 / UK

William Morris founds the Kelmscott Press

1895 / USA

Elbert Hubbard establishes the Roycroft community

1876 / USA

Handbill poster using wood type

KEY REPRESENTATIVES

GERMANY (JUGENDSTIL) **Peter Behrens** / FRANCE **Jules Cheret, Alphonse Mucha, Théophile Steinlen, Henri de Toulouse-Lautrec** / UK **Aubrey Beardsley, The Beggarstaff Brothers: William Nicholson, James Prydel** / USA **William Bradley** / VIENNA (SECESSION) **Gustav Klimt**

c. 1890 – c. 1915

Art Nouveau

1896 - 1926 / GERMANY

Georg Hirth publishes *Jugend* ("Youth") magazine

A Humble, Illustrated Timeline

A truly exhaustive timeline of graphic design would begin thousands of years B.C., taking the reader through the Renaissance and the industrial and digital revolutions, and covering the Art Nouveau, Constructivism, and Bauhaus movements, to name just a few key milestones. Luckily, this approach was already taken in Philip B. Meggs' *A History of Graphic Design*, which remains the cornerstone of graphic design history.

It was clear from the beginning that we would not be able to add anything new to the early chapters of design history. Even the first half of the twentieth century proved beyond our reach. We are again fortunate in that Richard Hollis'

Graphic Design: A Concise History is a fulfilling overview of the evolution of the graphic arts into graphic design and its development in Europe and the United States. We heartily recommend these two books to readers clamoring for an in-depth survey.

Our own timeline, which follows, is an abridged summary of some of the most relevant events, hubs, designers, and design work from the end of the nineteenth century and into the beginning of the twenty-first. It tells only a fraction of the story, but perhaps just enough to provide a sense of the foundation on which the representatives in this book have built upon.

NOTES

All illustrations are one-color interpretations of the original design and are not exact replicas.
Due to space and layout structure the position of some of the years is not perfect and sometimes the same years will not align.
Some significant entries are not included in the timeline because they are covered in-depth throughout the book.

1903 / USA

Frederic W. Goudy founds
the Village Press

1904 / USA

Dard Hunter, *Little
Journeys to the Homes
of Great Businessmen*
book cover

1907 / GERMANY

Behrens is appointed industrial designer for
the Allgemeine Elektrizitäts-Gesellschaft
/ SHOWN *AEG Lamp* poster, 1910

World War I
1914 - 1918

**Russian
Revolution**
1917

1917 / USA

James Montgomery Flagg, *I Want You for
U.S. Army* poster

1896 / FRANCE

Théophile Steinlen, *Cabaret du
Chat Noir* poster

1897 / GERMANY

Thomas Heine, *Simplicissimus* poster

KEY REPRESENTATIVES

AUSTRIA **Julius Klinger** / GERMANY **Lucian Bernhard, Ludwig
Hohlwein, Hans Rudi Erdt** / SWITZERLAND **Otto Baumberger**

c. 1905 - c. 1920

Sachplakat ("Object Poster")

1905 / GERMANY

Lucian Bernhard, *Priester Matches* poster

1910 / GERMANY

Hans Josef Sachs publishes
Das Plakat ("The Poster")

KEY REPRESENTATIVES

ITALY **Fortunato Depero, Filippo Marinetti**

c. 1910 - c. 1930

Futurism

1909 / FRANCE

Filippo Marinetti publishes
his "Futurist Manifesto"
in the French newspaper
Le Figaro

1914 / ITALY

Filippo Marinetti, *Zang Tumb
Tumb* Edizioni Futuriste de Poesia
page detail

1927 / ITALY

Fortunato Depero, *Depero
Futurista* book

KEY REPRESENTATIVES

GERMANY **Raoul Hausmann, John Heartfield, Kurt Schwitters,
Theo van Doesburg** / SWITZERLAND **Jean Arp, Hugo Ball,
Tristan Tzara** / USA **Marcel Duchamp, Man Ray**

c. 1915 - c. 1925

Dada

1918 / SWITZERLAND

In the third number of *Dada*
magazine Tristan Tzara publishes
"Dada Manifesto 1918"

1919 / GERMANY

Raoul Hausmann, *Der Dada* No. 1 cover

1922 / USA

The term "graphic design" is used for the first time by W. A. Dwiggins › 141 in an article for the *Boston Evening Transcript*

1923 - 1932 / GERMANY

Kurt Schwitters publishes *Merz* journal / SHOWN *Merz*, no. 11 cover

FRANCE Jean Carlu, A.M. Cassandre / UK E. McKnight Kauffer

c. 1925 - c.1940

Art Deco

1923 / FRANCE

A.M. Cassandre, *Au Bucheron* poster

KEY REPRESENTATIVES

RUSSIA Gustav Klutsis; El Lissitzky; Alexander Rodchenko; Stenberg Brothers: Georgii Stenberg, Vladimir Stenberg; Varvara Stepanova; Vladimir Tatlin

Georgii and Vladimir Stenberg, *The Man with the Movie Camera* poster

c. 1920 - c. 1930

Constructivism

1919 / RUSSIA

El Lissitzky, *Beat the Whites with the Red Wedge* poster

1923 / RUSSIA

Alexander Rodchenko, *Dobrolet Airline* poster

1929 / RUSSIA

KEY REPRESENTATIVES

NETHERLANDS Piet Mondrian, Gerrit Rietveld, Bart van der Leck, Theo van Doesburg

c. 1920 - c. 1930

De Stijl

1917 - 1931 / NETHERLANDS, GERMANY

Theo van Doesburg publishes *de Stijl* ("the Style") magazine until his death in 1931

1919 / NETHERLANDS

Theo van Doesburg ("De Stijl" wordmark) and Vilmos Huszar (woodcut), *de Stijl* art journal cover detail

KEY REPRESENTATIVES

GERMANY Josef Albers, Herbert Bayer, Max Bill, Walter Gropius, Johannes Itten, Wassily Kandinsky, Ludwig Mies van der Rohe, László Moholy-Nagy, Oskar Schlemmer, Joost Schmidt

c. 1920 - c.1940

Bauhaus

1919 / GERMANY

Walter Gropius establishes the Staatliches Bauhaus Weimar ("State House of Building Weimar") school and publishes the Bauhaus Manifesto

1923 / GERMANY

The Bauhaus holds its first public exhibition of student work

1923 / GERMANY

Joost Schmidt, exhibition poster

1925 / GERMANY

The school relocates to Dessau

KEY REPRESENTATIVES

GERMANY Herbert Bayer, El Lissitzky, László Moholy-Nagy, Jan Tschichold

c. 1920 - c. 1930

New Typography

1923 / GERMANY

Herbert Bayer, 2 Million Mark banknote for the Thuringian state government in Weimar

World War II
1939 - 1945

Heinz Schulz-Neudamm,
Metropolis poster

1925 / FRANCE

The Exposition
Internationale des
Arts Décoratifs
et Industriels
Modernes is held
in Paris

1926 / GERMANY

1932 / FRANCE

A.M. Cassandre, *Dubonnet* poster

1927 / USA

Sol Cantor and Dr. Robert L.
Leslie found The Composing
Room, a typesetting company

1929 / USA

M.F. Agha joins Condé Nast and
becomes art director of *Vogue*,
Vanity Fair and *House and Garden*

1934, 1986 /
SWITZERLAND, USA

Herbert Matter, Swiss travel poster; Paula Scher, Swatch watches poster

1930 / USA

Fortune magazine founded by Henry Booth
Luce / SHOWN John F. Wilson (illustration),
Fortune cover, October 1940

1934 - 1942 / USA

Dr. Leslie publishes *PM* (Production
Manager), later renamed *A-D* (Art
Director) magazine / SHOWN Lester
Beall, *PM* cover, November 1937

1936 / USA

My Man Godfrey opening title sequence

1935 / GERMANY

The Nazi swastika flag is decreed the
new German national flag

1925 - 1934 / GERMANY

The Deutscher Werkbund publishes
Die Form journal / SHOWN Joost
Schmidt, *Die Form* cover, 1926

1932 / GERMANY

The school
relocates to
Berlin

1933 / GERMANY

Under Nazi
pressure the
Bauhaus closes

1937 / USA

Upon emigration, László Moholy-Nagy
establishes the New Bauhaus School
(renamed Institute of Design in 1944)
in Chicago

1937 / USA

Lester Beall, *Rural Electrification—
Running Water* poster

1937 / USA

William Golden joins CBS

1924 / GERMANY

Herbert Bayer, business card

1928 / GERMANY

Tschichold publishes *Die Neue Typographie:
Ein Handbuch für Zeitgemäss Schaffende*
("The New Typography: A Handbook for the
Contemporary Designer")

1935 / SWITZERLAND

Two years after fleeing Germany, Tschichold
publishes *Typographische Gestaltung*
("Typographic Form") in which he writes,
"To my astonishment I detected most
shocking parallels between the teachings of
Die Neue Typographie and National Socialism
and fascism"

World War II
1939 - 1945

1942 / USA

Jean Carlu, *America's Answer! Production* poster

1941 / USA

Charles and Ray Eames marry

1941 / USA

Walter Landor founds Landor Associates in San Francisco, California

1942 / USA

J. Howard Miller, *We Can Do It!* poster

1942 / UK

Abram Games, *Grow Your Own Food* poster

GERMANY **Max Bill, Otl Aicher** / ITALY **Max Huber** / SWITZERLAND **Theo Ballmer, Max Bill, Karl Gerstner, Armin Hofmann, Richard Paul Lohse, Josef Müller-Brockmann, Hans Neuburg, Emil Ruder, Carlo Vivarelli** / USA **Rudolph de Harak**

c. 1950s – EARLY 1970s

International Typographic Style

1945 / USA

Georg Olden joins CBS

1947 / USA

Paul Rand publishes his first design book, *Thoughts on Design*

1947 / UK

Tschichold joins Penguin Books › 274

1943 / USA

The weekly *Saturday Evening Post* magazine publishes, through four consecutive issues, Norman Rockwell's *Four Freedoms* posters

1946 / SWITZERLAND

Armin Hoffman and Emil Ruder establish the Basel School of Design › 128

1953 / GERMANY

Max Bill and Otl Aicher establish the Hochschule für Gestaltung (HfG) in Ulm

1948 / ITALY

Max Huber, *Gran Premio dell' Autodromo* poster

1949 - 1971 / USA

As design consultant for the Upjohn Company, Burtin becomes art director of its magazine, *Scope* / SHOWN *Scope* cover, vol. IV, no. 2, Summer, 1954

POLAND **Roman Cieślewicz, Wiktor Górka, Tadeusz Gronowski, Wojciech Fangor, Jan Lenica, Eryk Lipiński, Jan Młodożeniec, Józef Mroszczak, Franciszek Starowieyski, Waldemar Świerzy, Henryk Tomaszewski, Tadeusz Trepkowski, Wojciech Zamecznik, Bronisław Zelek**

c. 1940s – c. 1960s

Polish School of Posters

1946 / POLAND

Henryk Tomaszewski begins creating movie posters for the Polish Film Department

Armin Hofmann, *Die Gute Form* poster

Joseph Muller-Brockmann, *Musica Viva* poster

1954 / SWITZERLAND

1955 / USA

Hoffman begins teaching at Yale School of Art › 129

1957 / SWITZERLAND

Edouard Hoffman and Max Miedinger release Neue Haas Grotesk—renamed Helvetica › 373 in 1960

1958 / SWITZERLAND

1958 – 1965 / SWITZERLAND

Richard Paul Lohse, Josef Müller-Brockmann, Hans Neuburg, and Carlo Vivarelli publish *Neue Grafik* › 97

KEY REPRESENTATIVES

GERMANY Otl Aicher / UK F.H.K. Henrion, Wolff Olins / US Saul Bass, Lester Beall, Ralph Eckerstrom, Chermayeff & Geismar, John Massey, Paul Rand, Elinor Selame, Unimark, Massimo Vignelli, Lance Wyman

MID 1950s – EARLY 1980s

Rise of Corporate Identity

1950s – 1980s / USA

Under the patronage and leadership of Walter Paepcke the Container Corporation of America (founded in 1926) establishes a cohesive corporate identity with Ralph Eckerstrom and John Massey as sequential design directors

1954 / USA

Herbert Matter, New Haven Railroad › 350 identity

1956 / USA

Paul Rand begins working on the identity of IBM › 341

1954 / FRANCE

Adrian Frutiger releases the Univers › 372 type family

1951 / USA

Paepcke establishes the International Design Conference in Aspen (ICDA)

1952 / USA

The Massachusetts Institute of Technology (MIT) establishes its Office of Publications headed by Muriel Cooper › 188 until 1958 and Jacqueline S. Casey from 1972 to 1989

1954 / USA

Robert Brownjohn, Ivan Chermayeff and Tom Geismar get playful with *Watching Words Move* booklet

1962 / USA

Stephen O. Frankfurt, *To Kill a Mockingbird* opening title sequence

1952 / POLAND

Tomaszewski and Józef Mroszczak join the Academy of Fine Arts in Warsaw as faculty and co-directors

1952 / POLAND

Trepkowski Tadeusz, *Nie!* poster

1957 / POLAND

Tomaszewski, *Symfonia Pastoralna* poster

1964 / POLAND

Jan Lenica, *Alban Berg Wozzeck* poster

1958 / UK

The Campaign for Nuclear Disarmament
› 348 and the Direct Action Committee
Against Nuclear War organize a rally
and march to Aldermaston in protest of
nuclear weapon testing

1960 / USA

Ben Shahn, *Stop H-bomb
Tests* poster

1962 / USA

Andy Warhol paints
Campbell's Soup Cans

› 348

KEY REPRESENTATIVES

USA Rick Griffin, Alton Kelly, Bonnie MacLean,
Peter Max, Victor Moscoso, Stanley "Mouse"
Miller, Wes Wilson / UK Hapshash and the
Coloured Coat: Michael English, Nigel
Waymouth; Osiris Visions

MID 1960s – MID 1970s

Psychedelia

1967 / USA

Victor Moscoso, *The Steve Miller
Blues Band* poster

Vietnam War
1959 – 1975

◄ **MID 1950s – EARLY 1980s**

Rise of Corporate Identity

1960 / US

Chermayeff & Geismar,
Chase Manhattan Bank
identity

1960 / UK

F.H.K. Henrion, KLM
identity

1964 / USA

Ralph Eckerstrom
and Massimo Vignelli
establish Unimark
International

1967 / USA

Massimo Vignelli, Unimark,
American Airlines identity

1967 / UK

Wolff Olins, Bovis
identity using a hum-
mingbird to identify a
construction company

1963 / FRANCE

A.M. Cassandre, Yves Saint Laurent logo

1967 / USA

Landor Associates, Levi's logo

1960 / USA

Saul Bass, *Psycho* opening title sequence

1968 / FRANCE

From within the student- and faculty-occupied École des Beaux-Arts in
Paris, the Atelier Populaire creates hundreds of silkscreen protest posters

Paris, May 1968 Student and Labor Revolts
1968

1962 / UK

Maurice Binder, *Dr. No* opening title sequence
introducing the James Bond gun barrel sequence

1964 / USA

Pablo Ferro, *Dr. Strangelove or: How I Learned
to Stop Worrying and Love the Bomb* opening
title sequence

1966 / POLAND

The first International Poster Biennale
in Warsaw takes place

1968 /USA

Stewart Brand
publishes the first
issue of the *Whole
Earth Catalog*

1968 /SWITZERLAND

Wolfgang Weingart › 178
becomes a teacher in the
newly established Advanced
Class of Graphic Design
at Basel School of Design

› 178

1967 / USA

Bonnie MacLean, *Eric Burdon & the Animals, Mother Earth, Hour Glass* poster

1969 / USA

Woodstock Music & Art Fair takes place

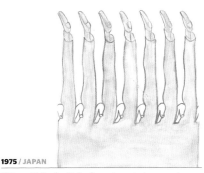

1975 / JAPAN

Shigeo Fukuda, Keio department store poster

1979 / USA

Tibor Kalman, with Carol Bokuniewicz and Liz Trovato, establish M&Co. › 183

1979 / GERMANY

Erik Spiekermann › 226 establishes MetaDesign

1971 / USA

Carolyn Davidson, Nike logo › 343

1972 / USA

Paul Rand, IBM logo gets its stripes

1974 / USA

Danne & Blackburn, NASA logo

1977 / USA

Rob Janoff, Apple logo

1970s / NETHERLANDS

Co-founded in 1963 by Ben Bos, Wim Crouwel, Friso Kramer, Dick and Paul Schwarz (brothers), and Benno Wissing, Total Design establishes a minimalist, standardized identity approach that permeates the country's corporations

1976 / USA

Editor Leonard Koren publishes the first issue of the avant-garde magazine *Wet*

1978 – 1982 / NETHERLANDS

Rick Vermeulen, Willem Kars, Henk Elenga, Gerard Hadders and Tom van den Haspel publish *Hard Werken* magazine—they later adopt Hard Werken as the name of their collective

1970 - 1990 / FRANCE

Pierre Bernard, François Miehe and Gérard Paris-Clavel form the socially conscious design collective Grapus—all three were members of the Atelier Populaire and had previously studied with Henryk Tomaszewski in Poland

1971 / USA

Katherine and Michael McCoy are appointed co-chairs of the two-dimensional/three-dimensional program at Cranbrook Academy of Art › 130

1972 / UK

Pentagram › 162 is established

KEY REPRESENTATIVES

UK Barney Bubbles, Mark Perry, Jamie Reid / USA Frank Edie, John Holmstrom, Winston Smith

MID 1970s - EARLY 1980s

Punk

1977 / UK

Jamie Reid, *Never Mind the Bollocks, Here's the Sex Pistols* album back cover

1970 / UK

Bernard Lodge, *Doctor Who*, season 7 opening title sequence

1970 - 1972 / SWITZERLAND

American designers Dan Friedman and April Greiman study with Weingart

1972 / UK

MIT Press publishes *Learning from Las Vegas: The Forgotten Symbolism of Architectural Form* by Robert Venturi, Steven Izenour and Denise Scott Brown

1978 / USA

R/GA, *Superman* opening title sequence

1981 / USA

August 1, at 12:01 a.m.
MTV › 352 **launches**

KEY REPRESENTATIVES

USA Dan Friedman; April Greiman; Willi Kunz;
"The Michaels" (San Francisco): Michael Mabry,
Michael Manwaring, Michael Patrick Cronan,
Michael Vanderbyl; Jayme Odgers, Deborah Sussman

LATE 1970s – MID 1980s

New Wave

1979 / USA

April Greiman, CalArts Viewbook

1986 / USA

Paul Rand, Next logo

1987 / USA

With the support of editor-
in-chief Sonny Mehta, Carol
Devine Carson establishes
an in-house design group
at Random House's Knopf
Publishing Group that includes
Barbara deWilde, Archie
Ferguson and Chip Kidd › 192

KEY REPRESENTATIVES

NETHERLANDS / Hard Werken, Studio Dumbar / UK Jonathan Barnbrook,
Neville Brody, Peter Saville, Why Not Associates / USA Andrew Blauvelt,
David Carson, Elliott Earls, Ed Fella, Allen Hori, Tibor Kalman, Jeffery
Keedy, Laurie and P. Scott Makela, Katherine McCoy

1984 / USA

Rudy VanderLans
publishes the first issue
of *Emigre* › 100 magazine

1986 - 2002 / UK

Mark Holt, Simon Johnston and Hamish Muir,
founders of design firm 8vo, publish *Octavo*,
an international journal of typography

LATE 1970s – LATE 1990s

Postmodernism

1981 / UK

Neville Brody
becomes art director
of *The Face* › 332

1983 - 1985 / USA

Jeffery Keedy attends
Cranbrook Academy
of Art

1985 / USA

Lorraine Wild joins the California
Institute of the Arts (CalArts) › 131 to
renew its graphic design program

1985 - 1987 / USA

Ed Fella › 185 attends
Cranbrook Academy
of Art

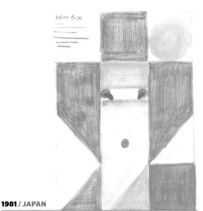

1981 / JAPAN

Ikko Tanaka, *Nihon Buyo* poster

**Adobe creates
PostScript language**
1982

**Apple introduces
the Macintosh**
1984

1987 / USA

Tibor Kalman, November menu board at
Restaurant Florent

1981 / USA

Paul Rand, *Eye-Bee-M* poster

1983 / USA

Philippe Apeloig, *Chicago, Birth of a
Metropolis 1872 – 1922* poster

1987 / USA

Gail Anderson and Fred Woodward join
Rolling Stone magazine › 328

1989 / USA

Mildred Friedman curates the exhibit *Graphic
Design in America: A Visual Language History*
at the Walker Art Center › 120

1989 - 2002 / USA

The American Center for Design grows from a transformation of The Society of Typographic Arts—it eventually closes due to economic stress

1996 / USA

Paul Rand, Enron logo

His last logo before passing away was for Doug Evans + Partners—Evans was a former employee

1994 / UK

Neville Brody holds the first FUSE conference, followed a year later with a sequel in Berlin

1993 / UK, USA

The essay "Cult of the Ugly" by Steven Heller is published in *Eye*

1995 / USA

Elliot Earls, *The Conversion of Saint Paul* poster

The Dot-com Bubble
1995 - 2000

1996 / WORLD

Being some of the few typefaces installed in nearly every computer allowing for proper online rendering, Arial, Times New Roman, Verdana, and Georgia rise to typographic prominence

1998 / USA

Sergey Brin and Larry Page launch the Google search engine

1995 / USA

P. Scott and Laurie Haycock Makela are appointed designers-in-residence after the McCoys

2003 / USA

Jeffrey Zeldman authors *Designing With Web Standards*

2000 / USA

Allen Hori, *Not Yet the Periphery* poster

1990 / USA

Sheila Levrant de Bretteville is appointed director of studies in graphic design at Yale School of Art › 129

1990 / UK

Rick Poynor launches *Eye* › 103

1991 / UK

Steve Baker, Dirk Van Dooren, Karl Hyde, Richard Smith, Simon Taylor, John Warwicker, and Graham Wood establish Tomato

1992 / USA

With David Carson as art director, editor Marvin Scott Jarrett launches *Ray Gun* › 330

1993 / USA

Publisher Louis Rossetto with John Plunkett as art director, launches *Wired* magazine

1995 / USA

Kyle Cooper, *Seven* opening title sequence—founds Imaginary Forces one year later

1997 / GERMANY

Steffen Sauerteig, Svend Smital and Kai Vermehr establish eBoy, specializing in complex pixel illustrations

1999 / NETHERLANDS, UK, USA

First Things First 2000 manifesto › 48 is published

2000 / USA

Stefan Sagmeister takes a year off without clients

2003 / USA

Futurebrand redesigns Paul Rand's logo for UPS › 342 —initiating a coincidental flurry of high-profile coporate identity redesigns

2005 / USA

Emigre ceases publication

1997 / USA

Milton Glaser, *Art is Whatever* poster

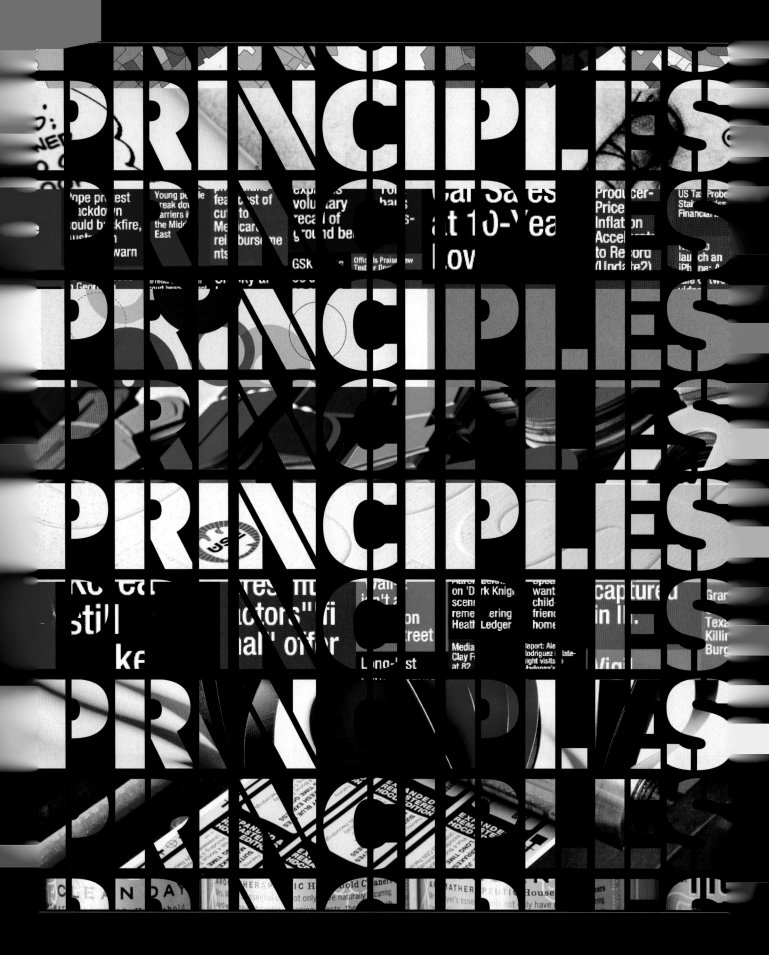

Graphic design has been evolving for more than one hundred years and across three centuries—from its early recognition as commercial art in the late nineteenth century, to the coinage of the term by W.A. Dwiggins in 1922, to its current standing as a visual communication discipline encompassing myriad specialties. Over the decades, the profession has changed through academic, practical, and technological shifts that have gradually established a series of principles through which graphic design can be taught, understood, categorized, and practiced. Grasping the breadth of terms, definitions, techniques, and processes, is essential to understanding graphic design.

zeit
genö
ssi
sche

chi
ne
si
sche

Bilder

Schrift

sch
rift
pla
kate

Museum

POST
ERS

14.September-06.November.2005
Mo.-Fr.: 09.00-21.00 Uhr, Sa.: 09.00-12.00 Uhr
Rössligasse 12, HGK Luzern
Organisiert von Posters Lucerne
Vernissage: Kornschütte im Rathaus Luzern
14. September 2005 um 18 Uhr

PRINCIPLES
Of Design

24
Disciplines

It's a running joke that not even designers' parents know what their sons and daughters do. "Something with computers" is one of the most accurate responses. This uncertainty may be caused by the wide range of specialties and disciplines in which designers can engage—designing logos, book covers, food packaging, film titles, museum exhibits—blurring the potential for a clear definition. The possibility of working in different mediums and contexts, through different means of production, for a varied range of clients and end-users is one of the greatest allures of graphic design.

50
Layout

Throughout the myriad disciplines in graphic design and its numerous manifestations, one fundamental remains constant: layout. No matter what the project is—big or small, online or printed, single- or multi-page, flat or three-dimensional, square or round—images and/or text must be placed and organized consciously. Layout can be objectively described as the physical properties (spacing, sizing, positioning) and arrangement of the design elements within a determined area and, ultimately, as the finished design. This leads to the subjective assessment of how effectively those properties are arranged within that area—and to heated discussions among designers. While a layout can be executed in infinite ways, a few principles must be taken into consideration so informed decisions can be made on how to exploit it.

56
Color

Apart from typography, color may be the most indispensable and influential variable in graphic design, as it has the power to convey a wide range of emotions, signal specific cues, and establish an immediate connection with the viewer. Because of the sweeping extent of interpretations and associations that colors trigger, a definitive assessment of its influence and meaning is impossible. The most sensible and beneficial task for designers is to understand how color is composed and categorized, and to practice how colors behave—alone or in combination—in their intended contexts.

Detail of *BILDER-SCHRIFT, THE CHINESE POSTER IN SWITZERLAND* **EXHIBITION POSTER FOR POSTER LUCERNE ASSOCIATION** / Hesign International / Germany, 2005

Identity Design

The process of identifying a product, service, or organization, identity design is more than simply creating a logo—even if there is nothing simple about that. Through a concise and consistently applied set of distinctive elements—colors, typography, and other visual cues in unison with a logo—identity designers create a visual system that makes a product, service, or organization easily identifiable. The identity can be manifested in business cards, uniforms, marketing materials, and other communication materials. Identity design is broadly divided into corporate identity and brand or retail identity. The former specializes in design for corporations and businesses, while the latter focuses on design meant for direct contact with consumers. In both cases, identity design is an influential aspect of our profession because it generates tangible manifestations of the intangible values of any given product, service, or organization, no matter how big or small.

DELTA AIR LINES IDENTITY REDESIGN / Lippincott / USA, 2007 / Airport photo: Albert Vecerka/Esto

BUTTERFIELD MARKET IDENTITY PROGRAM / Mucca Design: creative direction, Matteo Bologna; art direction, Christine Celic; design, Christine Celic, Lauren Sheldon / USA, 2007

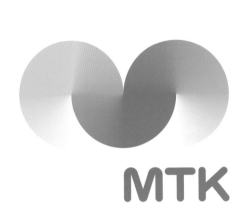

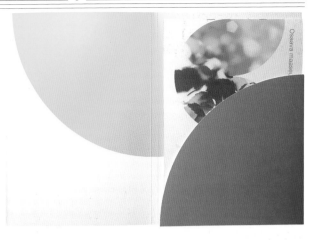

Maa- ja metsätaloustuottajain Keskusliitto MTK ry

MTK, THE CENTRAL UNION OF AGRICULTURAL PRODUCERS AND FOREST OWNERS IDENTITY PROGRAM / Porkka & Kuutsa / Finland, 2007

Branding

Typically related to consumer products and services—although the same principles apply to corporations and businesses, even personalities—the goal of branding is to form an overall perception of any product, service, or organization in the consumer's mind through a variety of means. These range from the behavior of staff to lighting conditions in a store, to the music that plays in a TV commercial, to the photography in a print campaign, to the tone of voice in which something is communicated. Branding is usually the result of collaboration among graphic designers, strategists, researchers, and writers, where every discipline—web, advertising, public relations, identity design—comes together cohesively to position and deliver the aspirations, values, and benefits of the product, service, or organization. Successful branding creates positive associations and establishes consistent expectations for the consumer. And, yes, successful branding also generates revenue.

BRIGADE QUARTERMASTERS BRANDING / Thomas W. Cox / USA, 2002–2003

NEW YORK'S BID FOR THE 2012 SUMMER OLYMPICS BRANDING / BIG, Ogilvy & Mather Worldwide: creative direction, Brian Collins; design direction, Jennifer Kinon; design, Kristin Johnson, Erika Lee, Christine Koroki, Abigail Smith, Luis Moya; design consulting, Rick Boyko, RG/A, TwoTwelve Associates, Giampetro + Smith, Stuart Rogers, Bobby C. Martin Jr.; writing, Charles Hall, Sophia Hollander / USA, 2004 / Images: courtesy of NYC2012

Collateral Design

All products, services, and organizations must communicate beyond what branding, identity, and advertising can offer and, in this regard, collateral design can be one of the most varied and active disciplines in graphic design. Through an unlimited range of approaches, designers create brochures, pamphlets, manuals, catalogs, and annual reports of all sizes, page counts, and production techniques, with singular regularity. Ranging from lavish to low-end productions, from oversized to compact, from informational to emotional, collateral design offers infinite communicative and expressive possibilities—maybe too many.

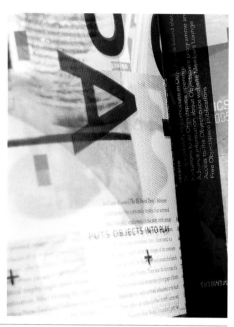

JUST HOLD ME, **OBJECTSPACE EXHIBITION BROCHURES** / Utilizes multiple paper stocks left over from previous jobs / Inhouse Design Group Ltd.: design, Alan Deare / New Zealand, 2006

LEGRAIN THÉÂTRE DE LA VOIX PROGRAM FOR THE STUDIO OF MICHEL BOUVET / Ellen Tongzhou Zhao / Paris, 2007

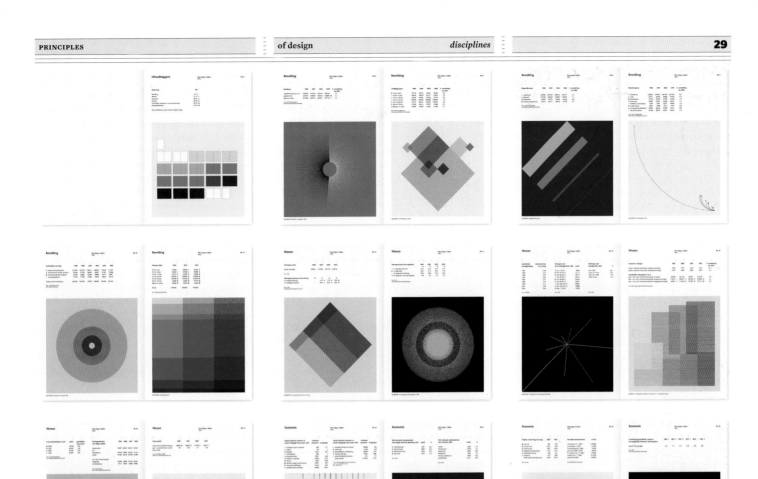

***THE HAGUE IN FACTS AND FIGURES: CITY OF THE HAGUE* ANNUAL REPORT** / Toko: design, Eva Dijkstra / The Netherlands, 2004

***SQUARE FEET*, INTERFACE CATALOG** / Valentine Group / USA, 1998

Environmental Design

Despite its name, environmental design is not necessarily concerned with ecological initiatives; instead, it refers to the application of design to a specific environment. Whether in service of a museum, an airport, a train or subway station, an amusement park, a movie theater, a shopping mall, or an entire neighborhood, environmental design aids and enriches the way in which the destination is experienced, navigated, and understood. Taking the shape of directional and informational signage (or wayfinding systems), exhibit design, retail and restaurant graphics, and even interior decoration, among other manifestations, this discipline provides a rich output for design as it interacts with the built environment and benefits from the diversity of materials and textures in which it can be produced at various scales—any environmental designer will tell you that Helvetica Bold (or any other typeface) is much more amazing when specified in feet rather than points.

BROOKLYN SUPERHERO STORE CO. STOREFRONT SIGNAGE FOR 826NYC / Sam Potts, Inc.: Sam Potts / USA, 2004

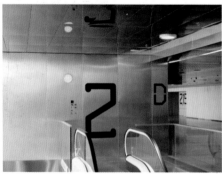

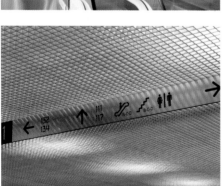

CINCINNATI CONVENTION CENTER ICONOGRAPHY, SIGNAGE, AND INTERIORS / Sussman/Prejza & Company, Inc.; architecture, LMN Architects / USA, 2006 / Photos: J. Miles Wolf

CENTRO DE CONVENCIONES INTERNACIONAL DE BARCELONA SIGNAGE AND MURAL / Mario Eskenazi, Ricardo Alavedra / Spain, 2003–2004

NATIONAL GALLERY OF VICTORIA ENVIRONMENTAL GRAPHICS AND WAYFINDING / emerystudio / Australia, 2003

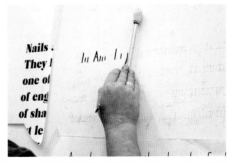

***OUT OF THE ORDINARY: SPECTACULAR CRAFT*, VICTORIA AND ALBERT MUSEUM EXHIBITION GRAPHICS IN THE PORTER GALLERY** / Sara de Bondt / UK, 2007 / Photos: V&A Museum

Iconography

The intricate difficulties of creating cohesive systems of dozens of icons that must communicate an extensive amount of varying information in a unified style and with the least number of visual elements possible make iconography a rare specialty. Icons are developed for a range of applications—user interfaces for computers and handheld devices, software applications, instructional manuals, warning signs on equipment, signage, weather information, and more—and must be adaptable to the various mediums in which they are deployed, from pixel-based graphics on a wristwatch to metal-cast identifiers in an airport. Iconography plays a major role in large graphic programs as well, like the Olympic Games › 356 or a zoo, because no one likes to confuse fencing with javelin throwing, or bears with lemurs.

COLOGNE BONN AIRPORT IDENTITY AND SIGNAGE SYSTEM FOR FLUGHAFEN KÖLN BONN GMBH / Integral Ruedi Baur Paris, Berlin, Zürich: Ruedi Baur, Chantal Grossen, Eva Kubinyi, Toan Vu-Huu, Simon Burkart, Axel Steinberger / Germany, 2000–2004

NEW YORK TIMES ICONOGRAPHY AND GRAPHIC USER INTERFACE FOR
IPHONE APPLICATION / Felix Sockwell, LLC; The *New York Times*: creative
direction, Khoi Vinh; design, Caryn Tutino / USA, 2008

2004 SUMMER OLYMPIC GAMES PICTOGRAMS / k2design: creative direction, Yiannis Kouroudis;
design, Yiannis Kouroudis, Dimitra Diamanti, Chrysafis Chrysafis / Greece, 2003

wines
we love

cult
wine

female
winemaker

critics'
choice

local
wine

organic or
biodynamic

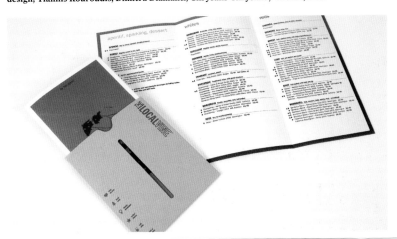

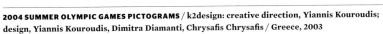

THE LOCAL VINE BRAND ICONOGRAPHY AND MENU / Turnstyle: art direction, Ben Graham; design, Jason Gómez, Ben Graham, Lesley Feldman / USA, 2007

TOILETS SYMBOL SIGN

Soon after World War I ended, Viennese social scientist and philosopher Otto Neurath was appointed secretary-general of the Austrian Association of Cooperative Housing and Garden Allotment Societies and tasked with disseminating information in a country whose working class was broadly uneducated. One of his first public exhibits used charts with simple drawings; for example, the increase in poultry production was represented through a pile of

bird drawings. The exhibition was a success, and in 1924 Neurath established the Social and Economic Museum in Vienna to further his research and develop the potential of pictorial display of quantitative information requiring minimum involvement of language.

Over the next decade, along with his wife, Marie Neurath, he developed the International System of Typographic Picture Education (ISOTYPE), which consists of thousands of pictograms—most

of them drawn by Gerd Arntz—symbolizing industrial, demographic, political, and economic data. ISOTYPE also suggested the proper display of these pictograms, and many newspapers and magazines adopted this visualization method. Further evolution of a universal archetypal human figure came in the pictograms, following a strict angled grid, that Otl Aicher ›166 designed for the 1972 Summer Olympic Games ›356 in Munich. These icons then served as the foundation for

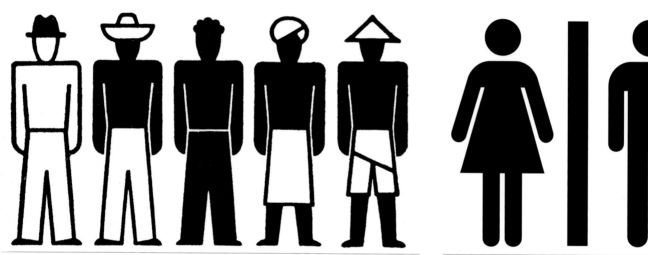

SAMPLE ISOTYPE OF MEN / Gerd Arntz / Austria, c. 1936

TOILETS ICON FROM THE SYMBOL SIGNS COLLECTION / AIGA|The Professional Association for Design; U.S. Department of Transportation / USA, 1974

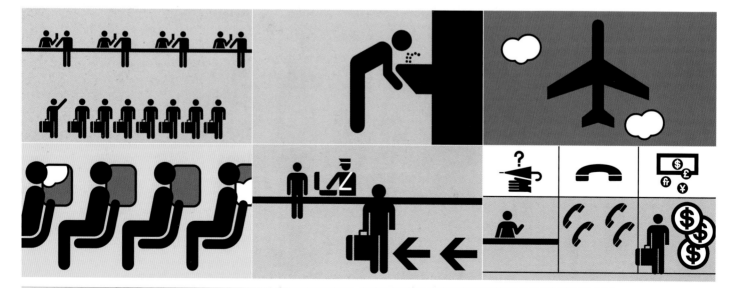

***AIRPORT*, A SHORT FILM INCORPORATING AIGA'S PUBLIC DOMAIN SYMBOL SIGNS** / Iain Anderson / Australia, 2005

other comprehensive pictorial systems by Aicher for ERCO and the Munich airport. It's in public environments like airports, hospitals, and large complexes that pictorial communication can breach language barriers and even illiteracy.

Throughout the world, pictorial systems were constantly developed, usually from the ground up, resulting in different visual interpretations of the same concept. In the United States, under the Federal Design Improvement Program of 1972, the U.S. Department of Transportation (DOT) engaged the American Institute of Graphic Arts (AIGA) › 244 to oversee the development of a cohesive and universal set of "symbol signs" that could become the default solution for way-finding projects. Designers Roger Cook and Don Shanosky worked with a committee comprising Tom Geismar › 156, Seymour Chwast › 171, Rudolph de Harak, John Lees, and Massimo Vignelli › 160 to create an initial set of 34 symbol signs. These were released in 1974 and followed by 16 more in 1979.

While all 50 symbol signs serve important functions, none appear to have achieved the popularity and ubiquity of the toilet symbol sign. A clear evolution from Neurath's ISOTYPE, the man and woman are stripped to their bare-minimum details, with only their clothes as differentiators—pants for him and dress for her. Due to their sheer simplicity, they are prone to cooptation for humor and satire or for political, social, and cultural commentary; because they represent everyone, they offend no one. And despite the clarity of the toilets symbol sign, designers and establishment owners alike have continually found clever alternatives to indicate rest room gender.

RACE 2 THE 2DAY SALE **TV ADVERTISEMENT FOR TARGET** / Lobo / Brazil, 2007

FUNDÇÃO SERRALVES MUSEUM / Portugal, 2008 / Photo: Flickr user Riddle

MUSEUM OF MODERN ART, NEW YORK / USA, 2008 / Photo: Kate Shanley

SOHO LONDON PUBLIC RESTROOM / UK, 2008 / Photo: Leah Buley

BROOKLYN MUSEUM / USA, 2006 / Photo: J. Brandon King

Information Design

While designers manage and organize information in every project, one specific discipline deals with presenting complex information—statistics, research findings, data comparisons, forms, and more—in the most efficient and easily understood way possible. Through innovative, allusive, and engaging diagrams, charts, graphs, iconography, and illustration or photography, information design visually presents facts, figures, events, and data that aid in the understanding of any given topic. Typically used in editorial contexts, as supporting elements for articles in newspapers, magazines, and journals, information design thrives in the interactive realm. The Internet has fostered a new breed of information design that can parse both live and static data from various sources and present a dynamic view of how this data is changing and evolving by the second. With the added layer of user interactivity, information design can now engage users in ways few other disciplines can.

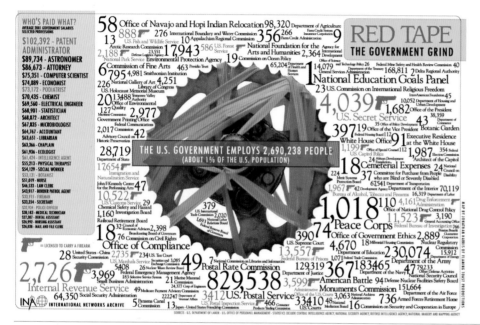

PRINCETON UNIVERSITY'S INTERNATIONAL NETWORKS ARCHIVE INFORMATION MAPS ILLUSTRATING THEIR EXPERIMENTAL MAPPING PHILOSOPHY / Number 25 / USA, 2003

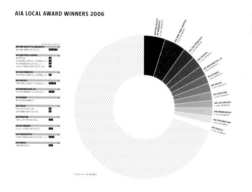

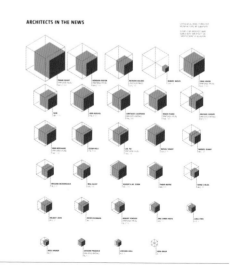

THE FIRST ANNUAL EDUCATION SURVEY INFOGRAPHICS FOR *Architect* MAGAZINE / Catalogtree / Netherlands, 2007

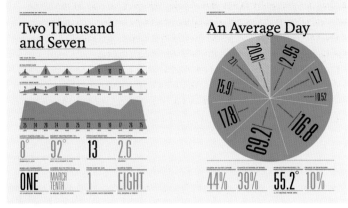

Two Thousand and Seven

8° 92° 13 2.6

ONE · MARCH TENTH · 1 · EIGHT

An Average Day

44% 39% 55.2° 10%

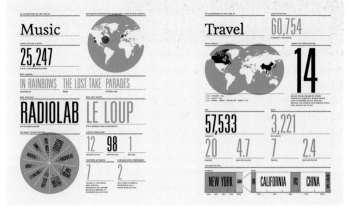

Music

25,247

IN RAINBOWS · THE LOST TAKE · PARADES

RADIOLAB · LE LOUP

12 98 1

7 2

Travel

60,754

14

57,533 · 3,221

20 4.7 7 2.4

NEW YORK · CALIFORNIA · CHINA

AN ACCOUNTING OF THE YEAR IN

Dining

EATING LOCATIONS

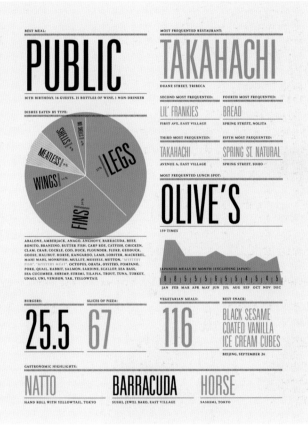

BEST MEAL:

PUBLIC

30TH BIRTHDAY, 16 GUESTS, 15 BOTTLES OF WINE, 1 NON-DRINKER

DISHES EATEN BY TYPE:

LEGS · SHELLS · MEATLESS · WINGS · FINS

ABALONE, AMBERJACK, ANAGO, ANCHOVY, BARRACUDA, BEEF, BONITO, BRANZINO, BUTTER FISH, CARP ROE, CATFISH, CHICKEN, CLAM, CRAB, COCKLE, COD, DUCK, FLOUNDER, FLUKE, GEODUCK, GOOSE, HALIBUT, HORSE, KANGAROO, LAMB, LOBSTER, MACKEREL, MAHI MAHI, MONKFISH, MULLET, MUSSELS, MUTTON, "MYSTERY FISH" "MYSTERY MEAT" OCTOPUS, ORATA, OYSTERS, POMPANO, PORK, QUAIL, RABBIT, SALMON, SARDINE, SCALLOP, SEA BASS, SEA CUCUMBER, SHRIMP, SURIMI, TILAPIA, TROUT, TUNA, TURKEY, UNAGI, UNI, VENISON, YAK, YELLOWTAIL

BURGERS: · SLICES OF PIZZA:

25.5 · 67

MOST FREQUENTED RESTAURANT:

TAKAHACHI

DUANE STREET, TRIBECA

SECOND MOST FREQUENTED: · FOURTH MOST FREQUENTED:

LIL' FRANKIES · BREAD

FIRST AVE, EAST VILLAGE · SPRING STREET, NOLITA

THIRD MOST FREQUENTED: · FIFTH MOST FREQUENTED:

TAKAHACHI · SPRING ST. NATURAL

AVENUE A, EAST VILLAGE · SPRING STREET, SOHO

MOST FREQUENTED LUNCH SPOT:

OLIVE'S

159 TIMES

JAPANESE MEALS BY MONTH (EXCLUDING JAPAN):
JAN FEB MAR APR MAY JUN JUL AUG SEP OCT NOV DEC

VEGETARIAN MEALS: · BEST SNACK:

116 · BLACK SESAME COATED VANILLA ICE CREAM CUBES

BEIJING, SEPTEMBER 26

GASTRONOMIC HIGHLIGHTS:

NATTO · BARRACUDA · HORSE

HAND ROLL WITH YELLOWTAIL, TOKYO · SUSHI, JEWEL BAKO, EAST VILLAGE · SASHIMI, TOKYO

FELTRON 2007 ANNUAL REPORT / Nicolas Felton / USA, 2008

Editorial Design

Shaping the layout and pacing of magazines, newspapers, and books—items bought, read, and collected by millions of people—across dozens and hundreds of pages in collaboration with editors, writers, photographers, illustrators, and information designers is the task of editorial designers. With newspapers and magazines, the challenge and joy is creating unique layouts under a consistent style, governed by strict grids, and determined by impending deadlines. For books, the schedules may seem more relaxed, but the demands of extensive content, the need for consistent pacing, and the imperative to maintain an even visual execution that permits the material inside to be the protagonist provide the framework for book designers. Regardless of the end product, one goal is constant in editorial design: To design a successful visual hierarchy of information punctuated by bold graphic treatments—like a double-page, full-bleed photograph, to mention just one example—that lead readers from beginning to end, maintaining their attention and sparking their curiosity.

LE MONDE DIPLOMATIQUE NEWSPAPER PREVIOUS DESIGN

LE MONDE DIPLOMATIQUE **NEWSPAPER REDESIGN** / SpiekermannPartners / Germany, 2005

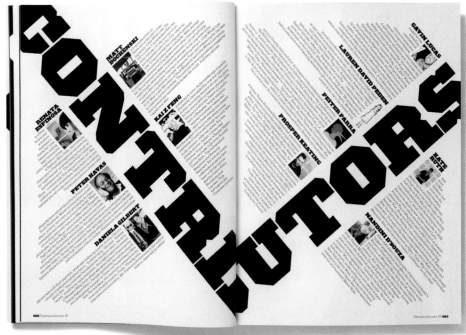

PLASTIQUE MAGAZINE / Studio8 Design: art direction, Matt Willey; design, Matt Willey, Matt Curtis / London, 2007

FLORAS SCHÖNSTE BLÜTEN BOOK DESIGN FOR PRESTEL / LIQUID Agentur für Gestaltung / Germany, 2007

Poster Design

As a highly celebrated form of design and because of the sheer size of the blank canvas offered, poster design is a coveted endeavor. Whether they are announcing concerts, films, products, or sporting events, or serving causes of activism or public awareness, posters have tremendous impact and resonance. The poster's guises: a utilitarian device for conveying information, a provocative voice for calling to action, or a seductive lure for selecting a specific product or service. Included in permanent collections of museums, shown in galleries, and organized in biennales worldwide, posters are ambassadors for the design profession, public beacons of the creative and communicative potential this profession offers.

UNIVERSITÀ DEGLI STUDI DI MACERATA CONFERENCE POSTERS / Iceberg: art direction and design, Marcello Piccinini, Simona Castellani, Paolo Rinaldi / Italy, 2002–2006

SOUND OPTIONS RADIO SHOW POSTER / 2007

SHELLAC POSTER / 2007

CHICAGO SHORT FILM BRIGADE POSTER / 2008

The Bird Machine: Jay Ryan / USA

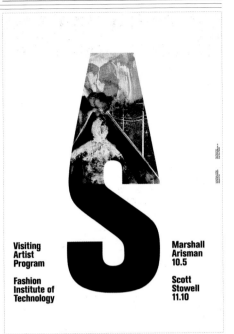

FASHION INSTITUTE OF TECHNOLOGY VISITING ARTISTS POSTERS / Piscatello Design Center: design, Rocco Piscatello / USA, 2004–2007

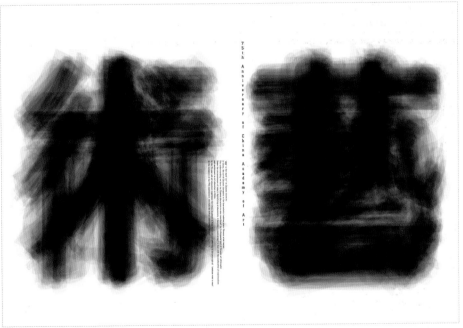

***NEW GRAPHIC* POSTER FOR *NEW GRAPHIC* MAGAZINE** / Hesign International / Germany, 2004

75TH ANNIVERSARY OF CHINA ACADEMY OF ART POSTER / Hesign International / Germany, 2003

Packaging

More than other disciplines, packaging is intimately tied with the general consumer because it occupies almost every moment of everyone's day. It manifests in the endless array of products people purchase or use, from shampoo bottles to milk cartons, paint buckets, soda cans—every conceivable item available for consumption. At its widest application, packaging serves to unify large families of products, abiding by strict legal requirements through consistent visual systems that allow variety (different sizes, flavors, quantities, etc.) and create a unique and recognizable presence on store shelves across regions and even countries. Packaging can also serve smaller stores or boutiques through limited-distribution products offering a differentiating identity. Regardless of the volume or reach of any given product, packaging offers the possibility to enrich each design through the use of different materials, finishes, and production techniques that interact with the three-dimensional presence of the product. The challenge of packaging, to persuade the consumer to pick the product it embodies over another or a dozen others, is its driving force.

BLOSSA GLÖGG ANNUAL EDITION WINE BOTTLE SERIES FOR VIN & SPRIT / BVD: creative direction, Catrin Vagnemark; design, Susanna Nygren Barrett, Mia Heijkenskjöld / Sweden, 2003–2008

MACK BREWERY PACKAGING / Tank Design / Norway, 2006

SULA FRAGRANCES PACKAGING FOR SUSANNE LANG PARFUMERIE / Concrete Design Communications, Inc.: creative direction, Diti Katona, John Pylypczak; design, Agnes Wong, Natalie Do / Canada, 2007

THREE OF THE 25,000-PLUS PRODUCTS OFFERED BY THE JAPANESE MAIL ORDER COMPANY ASKUL / StockholmDesignLab / Sweden, 2006–ongoing

Interactive Design

As the youngest discipline, interactive design has been redefining itself since the mid-1990s, evolving energetically along with technology and the growing embrace of the Internet—although interactive work has been practiced since long before the advent of the Internet in the form of interactive kiosks, CD-ROMs, and earlier forms of user interface. While websites may be the most common expression of interactive design, the discipline takes form as user interfaces for electronic equipment (digital cameras, handheld and mobile devices, computers), software applications, electronic ticketing kiosks; as onscreen menus for DVDs and cable or satellite guides; and as electronic displays of information. Key to interactive design is consideration for the end-user. The designer focuses on the usability and accessibility of the design, striving for the least obstructive and most intuitive interaction with the information. Interactive design relies on the collaboration of graphic designers, front-end and back-end programmers, and information architects—or a really smart person who can do all these things.

THE ART OF DINING AND BOOK OF THE DEAD, INTERACTIVE INTERPRETIVE INSTALLATIONS FOR DETROIT INSTITUTE OF ARTS / Pentagram: Lisa Strausfeld / USA, 2007

THE CHICAGO MANUAL OF STYLE ONLINE / The University of Chicago / USA, 2007

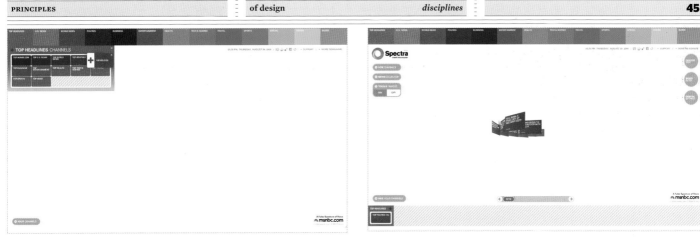

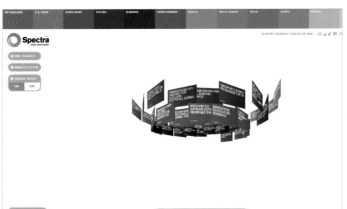

MSNBC SPECTRA VISUAL NEWSREADER, AN ALTERNATE METHOD FOR RETRIEVING NEWS FROM MSNBC.COM / SS+K / USA, 2008

AIGA CONTENT MANAGEMENT SYSTEM USER INTERFACE REDESIGN / Weightshift: art direction and design, Naz Hamid / USA, 2007

Motion Graphics

Affordable, powerful, and easy-to-use software, coupled with an increasing number of output channels—the web, mobile devices, hundreds of TV channels, outdoor digital displays, buildings with fancy screens in their lobbies—have brought increased attention and interest to motion graphics, a discipline practiced as far back as the 1920s. Whether it's the opening (or closing) titles of a movie or TV show, the two-second animation of a logo, the full composition of a short film or music video, the graphics over live-action footage, or the coveted identifiers for TV channels, motion graphics thrive in the integration and orchestration of typography, imagery, sound, digital effects, and storytelling with movement and time, allowing designers to take on an exciting and glamorous-sounding role other disciplines don't offer—director—even if the cast's biggest star is just Mrs. Eaves › 381.

THE CAT IN THE HAT **OPENING TITLES** / **Universal Pictures** / **Imaginary Forces** / **USA, 2003**

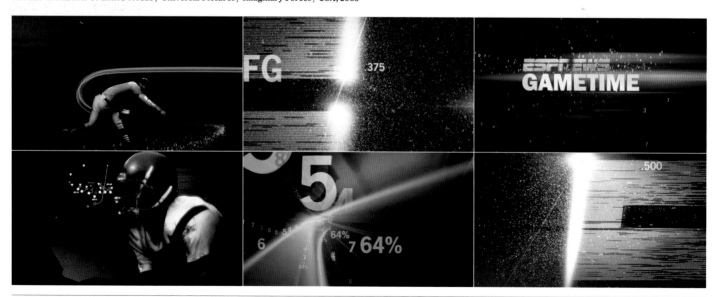

ESPNEWS ANIMATION / **Trollbäck + Company: creative direction, Jakob Trollbäck, Joe Wright; assistant creative direction, Matthew Tragesser; design, Tetsuro Mise, Tolga Yildiz, Paul Schlacter, Lloyd Alvarez, Dan Degloria; animation, Lloyd Alvarez, Dan Degloria, Lu Liu, Fu-Chun Chu, Peter Alfano; production, Danielle Amaral; executive production, Marisa Fiechter** / **ESPN: Rick Paiva, David Saphirstein, Wayne Elliott** / **USA, 2008**

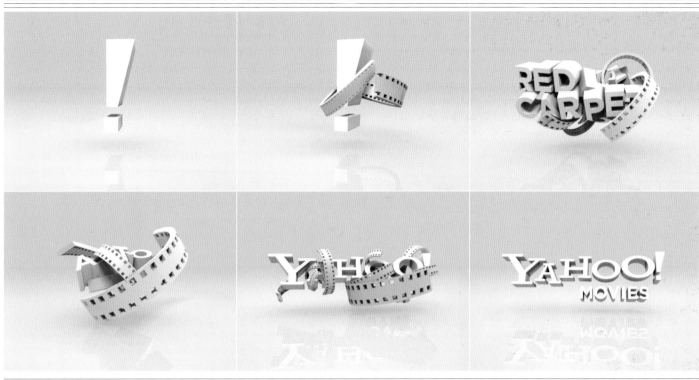

ANIMATION THAT PLAYS WHILE CONTENT IS LOADING FOR YAHOO! / GRETEL: Greg Hahn, Diana Park, Joe Di Valerio / USA, 2006

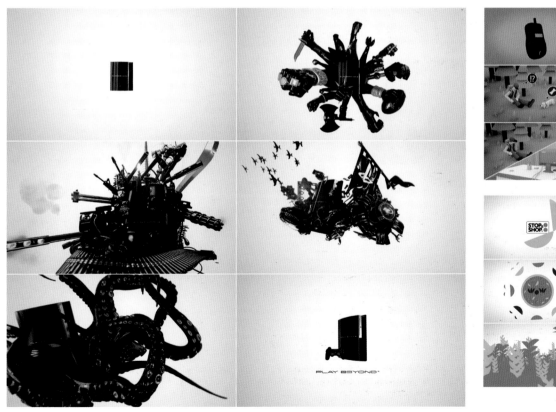

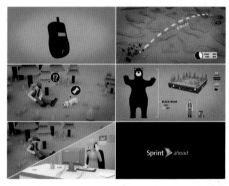

Clockwise *UNIVERSE OF ENTERTAINMENT* FOR PLAYSTATION 3, *IREDELL* FOR SPRINT, *STOP* FOR STOP & SHOP ADVERTISING MOTION GRAPHICS / Superfad / USA, 2007, 2008, 2008

FIRST THINGS FIRST MANIFESTO

During a meeting of the Society of Industrial Artists at London's Institute of Contemporary Arts on November 29, 1963, graphic designer Ken Garland wrote and declaimed the First Things First Manifesto. Facing a booming British economy and a rise in consumerism, Garland reacted against the established notion that the most lucrative application of graphic designers' talent was flogging unnecessary material goods like cat food, deodorants, and cigarettes. He contended that designers should lend their services to more worthy endeavors, like signs for streets and buildings, educational aids, and scientific and industrial publications. The manifesto was signed at that meeting, and it was self-published and distributed in January 1964; its 22 signatories included seasoned designers, photographers, and students. It gathered quick and fervent attention when it was published later that month in the *Guardian* newspaper and mentioned on a BBC TV news show the same day. Publications around the world soon reprinted the manifesto.

In 1998, the rebellious magazine *Adbusters* reprinted the original manifesto in an issue that editor Kalle Lasn and art director Chris Dixon

first things first

A manifesto

We, the undersigned, are graphic designers, photographers and students who have been brought up in a world in which the techniques and apparatus of advertising have persistently been presented to us as the most lucrative, effective and desirable means of using our talents. We have been bombarded with publications devoted to this belief, applauding the work of those who have flogged their skill and imagination to sell such things as:

cat food, stomach powders, detergent, hair restorer, striped toothpaste, aftershave lotion, beforeshave lotion, slimming diets, fattening diets, deodorants, fizzy water, cigarettes, roll-ons, pull-ons and slip-ons.

By far the greatest time and effort of those working in the advertising industry are wasted on these trivial purposes, which contribute little or nothing to our national prosperity.

In common with an increasing number of the general public, we have reached a saturation point at which the high pitched scream of consumer selling is no more than sheer noise. We think that there are other things more worth using our skill and experience on. There are signs for streets and buildings, books and periodicals, catalogues, instructional manuals, industrial photography, educational aids, films, television features, scientific and industrial publications and all the other media through which we promote our trade, our education, our culture and our greater awareness of the world.

We do not advocate the abolition of high pressure consumer advertising: this is not feasible. Nor do we want to take any of the fun out of life. But we are proposing a reversal of priorities in favour of the more useful and more lasting forms of communication. We hope that our society will tire of gimmick merchants, status salesmen and hidden persuaders, and that the prior call on our skills will be for worthwhile purposes. With this in mind, we propose to share our experience and opinions, and to make them available to colleagues, students and others who may be interested.

Edward Wright
Geoffrey White
William Slack
Caroline Rawlence
Ian McLaren
Sam Lambert
Ivor Kamlish
Gerald Jones
Bernard Higton
Brian Grimbly
John Garner
Ken Garland
Anthony Froshaug
Robin Fior
Germano Facetti
Ivan Dodd
Harriet Crowder
Anthony Clift
Gerry Cinamon
Robert Chapman
Ray Carpenter
Ken Briggs

Published by Ken Garland, 13 Oakley Sq NW1
Printed by Goodwin Press Ltd. London N4

RECENT REPRINT OF THE ORIGINAL MANIFESTO PUBLISHED IN 1964

later showed to Tibor Kalman › 183, who suggested they update the manifesto for the end of the century. Along with Rick Poynor › 237, and with Garland's approval, *Adbusters* drafted a revised text that addressed the changes of more than 30 years. At a time when the rise of the Internet economy and the consumerism it engendered—Hummers and Herman Miller Aeron chairs, among other excessive luxuries—reached an unapologetic crescendo, First Things First 2000 called for a "reversal of priorities" away from

the advertising, marketing, and branding of such products to focus instead on environmental, social, and cultural causes. With 33 signatories from around the world, the manifesto was published jointly by *Adbusters*, *AIGA Journal of Graphic Design* › 105, *Blueprint*, *Emigre* › 100, *Eye* › 103, *Form*, and *Items* between 1999 and 2000.

Through both incarnations, First Things First triggered hearty debate in the industry and shed light on professional choices graphic

designers must make. They can choose from a wide variety of disciplines, each providing its own technical and conceptual challenges and resulting in a diverse range of tangible outcomes, but just as important is choosing who and what the work is done for.

ADBUSTERS, NO. 27 / Canada, Autumn 1999 / Image: Courtesy Adbusters Media Foundation

JOURNAL OF GRAPHIC DESIGN, CULT, AND CULTURE ISSUE: POP GOES THE CULTURE 17, NO. 2 / USA, 1999 / Image: Courtesy of AdamsMorioka Vault, AIGA

EMIGRE, NO. 51 / USA, Summer 1999

EYE 33, VOL. 9 / UK, Autumn 1999

Grid

The immediate reaction to the notion of a grid might be to feel constrained, limited, and bound to a boring set of modular columns and horizontal axes. Luckily, nothing could be farther from the truth. Grid-based design is intimately tied to the International Typographic Style (or, more colloquially, Swiss Design) from the early 1950s, which sought visual simplicity and uniformity through the deployment of design elements on a mathematically constructed grid, resulting in extremely precise layouts—to the subjective delight or horror of designers over time. The grid is, at its best, an infrastructure upon which to build both complex and austere layouts that enable hierarchy and accessibility through flexibility and consistency.

Through its most avid proponents, including Max Bill, Karl Gerstner, and Josef Müller-Brockmann ›152, the International Typographic Style typifies the grid-based approach, but its use may be traced to Constructivism and de Stijl, followed by the Bauhaus, building up to a more vocal and practical statement of its importance in Die Neue Typographie ("The New Typography"), as expressed by Jan Tschichold's ›140 influential "Elementare Typographie."

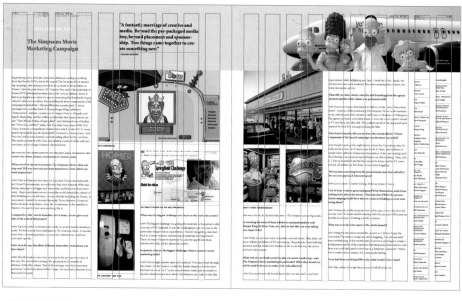

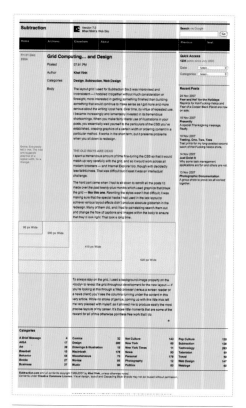

SUBTRACTION EXPOSED GRID (in pink) / Khoi Vinh / USA, 2005

CREATIVITY **MAGAZINE** / art direction, Jeanine Dunn / USA, May 2008

This 24-page treatise explained and demonstrated the use of asymmetrical typography set in multiple columns vying for the alignment of all elements on the page while rejecting the antiquated notion of central-axis type compositions. Tschichold's 1928 book, *Die Neue Typographie*, further cemented the necessity of this new approach.

The use of the grid became more entrenched with the rise of corporate identity in the 1950s and 1960s, when design firms like Unimark and Chermayeff & Geismar › 156 and designers like Lester Beall › 146 and Paul Rand › 159 created identities for national and global corporations, relying on its power to establish strict corporate design programs that specified, sometimes to the sixteenth of an inch, where and how every design element should be placed and how it should be used through corporate manuals that were, themselves, manifestations of the grid. In 1972, Otl Aicher's design for the Summer Olympics › 356 in Munich gave the grid a global audience, while Wim Crouwel › 153 in the 1980s and Experimental Jetset in the 1990s gave the grid a sense of cool. Above all, the grid has evolved into an indispensable structure enabling designers to produce rationalized layouts. Ignoring the grid use is akin to professional suicide.

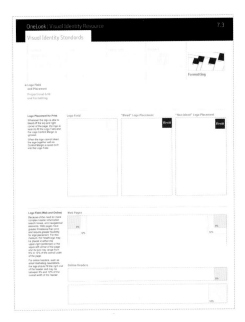

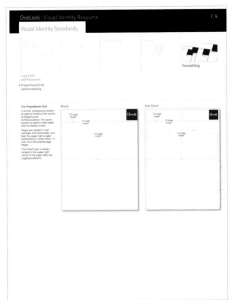

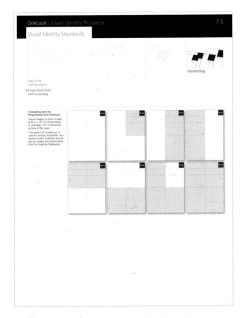

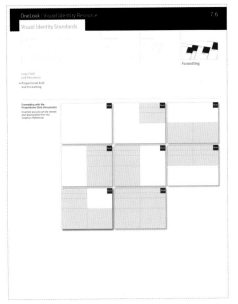

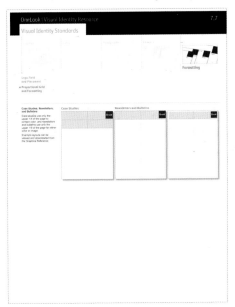

HEWITT ASSOCIATES, INC., ONELOOK VISUAL IDENTITY RESOURCE WEB-BASED PAGE LAYOUT CONCEPT DEMONSTRATION PAGES / Crosby Associates / USA, 2007

Anatomy of a Layout

Whether of a magazine spread, a packaging label, or a website, a layout can be built through a common set of elements that aid and support its design. By manipulating the values of margins, column count and their width, gutterspace, and horizontal guides—basically, the elements of a grid—each layout can adapt to its context and produce innumerable variations primed for each designer's creativity.

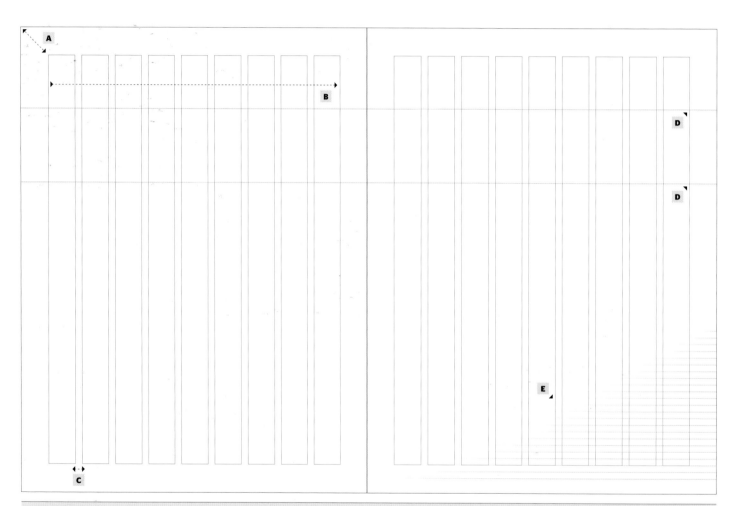

After defining the size of the layout, one should start by defining the margins (**A**), the space within the layout that buffers the content and the edge of the final product. Margins can be as small or large as desired (and should not be seen as unbreakable, as full-bleed layouts can be powerful), but printing considerations should be taken into account so key design elements aren't dangerously close to mutilation. Within the margins, a number of columns (**B**) should be specified to help organize, align, and distribute the content efficiently, consistently, and logically.

The number of columns is a personal decision; it can be 1, 12, or 33, as long as attention is paid to the gutters (**C**), the space between columns that defines how far apart they are set. Once vertical decisions are made, horizon lines (**D**) that define key horizontal positions in the layout should be established. These are especially helpful in creating consistency in multiple-page projects. Finally, an underlying baseline grid (**E**) that allows consistent horizontal spacing can add a deeper level of cohesion to the layout.

Hierarchy

Establishing a hierarchy that is easy to navigate and understand may sound like a simple premise, but most failed designs are the result of necessary elements being improperly emphasized, prioritized, or presented—for example, the confusing ballots in Florida during the 2000 U.S. presidential elections that offered no visual cues to making the desired selection and instead obfuscated the process. Successful hierarchy empowers end-users and enables them to interact suitably with any given design. This is achieved through the proper and conscious implementation of visual prompts that emphasize significant content within the design while gradually minimizing the attention needed for other elements, whether by exaggerating the size of text or image, by isolating a design element, or by employing additional graphics that call attention to a specific place in the layout. A design without hierarchy is flat, unmemorable, and, as in the example mentioned here, potentially dangerous.

Above left **ORIGINAL 2000 COOK COUNTY BUTTERFLY BALLOT**
Above right **PROPOSED REDESIGN OF THE CHICAGO COOK COUNTY BUTTERFLY BALLOT** / Marcia Lausen / USA, 2000

SHEILA JAM PACKAGING SYSTEM / Company, London / UK, 2008

SKI-CLUB TRAMELAN: 100 ANS D'HISTOIRE ET DE SPORT / Onlab: Nicolas Bourquin, Linda Hintz / Germany, 2008

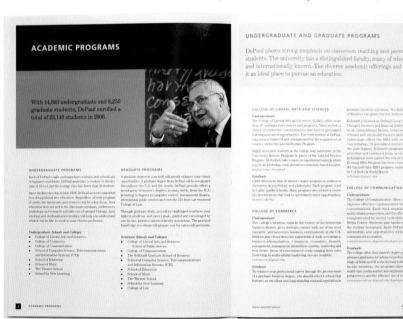

DE PAUL UNIVERSITY INTERNATIONAL STUDENT VIEWBOOK / End Communications: design, Kyle Eertmoed, Kyle Romberg / USA, 2007

White Space

Somewhat comparable to the elusive white whale in *Moby-Dick*, white space (technically, *negative space*) is the eternal quest of graphic designers who struggle to justify to clients or higher ranks the blank real estate in brochures, websites, stationery, and other design projects. White space is, in essence, the space where no image or text exists. The gut urge—designers will say it's the client's—is to fill those voids, yet it's imperative to recognize that the negative space between images and text is as important as the placement and sizing of images and text itself. Legitimate use of white space, objectively addressed, enables hierarchy and pacing by allowing the end-user to rest while navigating the design or by isolating an element that demands attention. Subjectively, it can add tension or even dramatic effect. In a visual environment where most advertisements, consumer products, and posters express a need to fill in all the blanks, designs that employ white space communicate best.

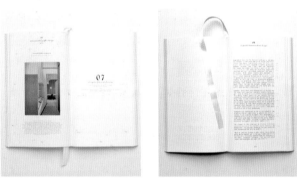

365: THE AIGA IN DESIGN 23 / Rigsby Hull: illustration, Andy Dearwater; photography, ProGraphics / USA, 2002

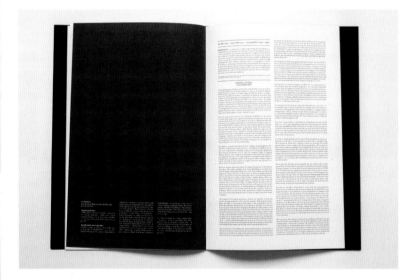

DOMINION BOOKLETS FOR JOAN MOREY / Albert Folch Studio / Spain, 2005

Contrast

The concept of contrast in a layout operates on two levels: first, how the elements within the layout contrast, and, second, how the layout itself contrasts with its context. Both scenarios respond to utilizing opposing forms of comparison that can be executed visually—big or small, empty or full, black or white, purple or orange, and so forth—forcing distinction between one thing and another as a way to communicate a message. Within a layout, this permits the design to make one or more points of distinction, while in context it allows the end product to stand apart in its surroundings. An added tangent to contrast is that it can go in two directions: low contrast and high contrast. Each has advantages and disadvantages, and both approaches can solidify the intention and mood of any given design.

OWP/P ARCHITECTS OFFICE PROSPECTUS / Debossed and foil-stamped on Plike, a plastic-like material / End Communications / USA, 2008

DRY SODA PACKAGING / Turnstyle: art direction, Steve Watson, Ben Graham; design, Steve Watson / USA, 2004–2006

MICHAEL HANEKE: NOW, YOU CAN LET GO **FILM PRESENTATION MATERIALS** / Nikolay Saveliev / USA, 2007

Color

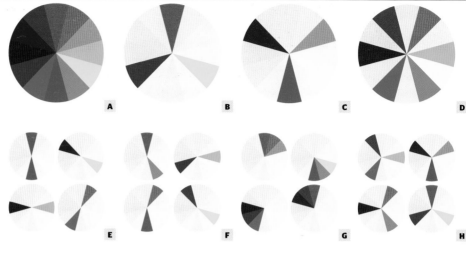

Summarizing color theory on a single page, when dozens of books have been composed on the subject, is impossible. Consider the following as a primer on this complex and rich subject. The basic structure of color can be represented through the color wheel (**A**), which consists of twelve units: three primary colors (**B**), three secondary colors (**C**), and six tertiary colors (**D**). Common combinations can be derived from this structure: complementary (**E**) by choosing colors on direct opposites of the wheel; clashing (**F**) by selecting a color on either side of its complementary color; analogous (**G**) by selecting three adjacent colors; and triad (**H**), where the selected three colors are equidistant from each other on the wheel. Unlimited combinations can be made through the choice of any hue (**I**), tint or saturation (**J**), and shade or brightness (**K**). This, of course, should not stop anyone from combining pink with red with teal.

BIENNALE DE LA JEUNE CRÉATION POSTER /
Fanette Mellier / France, 2006

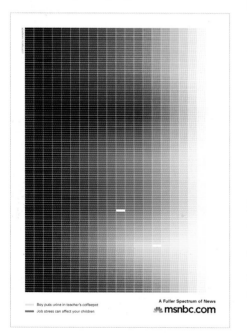

MSNBC SPECTRUM CAMPAIGN LAUNCH / 1 of 39
ads created / SS+K: creative direction, Sam Mazur,
Matt Ferrin; art direction, Matt Ferrin; writing,
Sam Mazur / USA, 2007

ROCK MY WORLD CCA WATTIS INSTITUTE FOR CONTEMPORARY ARTS EXHIBIT CATALOG / Volume, Inc.: creative
direction, Adam Brodsley, Eric Heiman; design, Eric Heiman / USA, 2007

Color Palette

Selecting a range of colors to apply to a design is integral to its success, impact, and appropriateness, as different color combinations suggest, trigger, and signify a diverse range of moods, references, and associations—all relative to context and audience. Color palettes can be as simple as the pairing of two colors and as complex as a system of multiple colors broken down by primary and secondary sets of colors ranging in the dozens. Palettes can also extend from monochromatic combinations to wildly assorted selections. It is not uncommon to assign loose adjectives to color palettes, like "warm," "trendy," or "sophisticated," but if color itself is subjective, communicating what a color palette is meant to imply is even more so: What may feel like a "warm" color palette to one person may feel "rustic" or "earthy" to others. There is no right or wrong when defining a color palette—as long as no retinas are burned in the process.

COLUMBUS BREWING COMPANY IDENTITY AND PACKAGING / Element: creative direction, John McCollum, Meg Russell; design, Jeremy Slagle / USA, 2007

UTS SCHOOL OF ARCHITECTURE SUB-BRANDING, CATALOG, POSTERS, AND WEBSITE / Toko: design, Michael Lugmayr / Australia, 2008

Gradient

Providing a sense of depth, texture, and movement beyond what a flat color can achieve, a well-conceived gradient can make a powerful visual statement or add an audacious and playful sheen. The beauty—and the danger—of gradients is their unlimited iterations; whether they comprise all the colors in the rainbow slowly transitioning into each other or any color disappearing into white, deepening into black, or segueing into another, gradients can quickly turn into visual crutches that compensate for lack of stronger design intentions. The versatility of gradients make them especially attractive because they can be reproduced on a variety of mediums. They render perfectly in screen and online applications, and almost every print technique can render them as well, including silkscreen and letterpress. Few things are more endearing than a finely crafted split fountain poster.

SELF-PROMOTIONAL PORTFOLIO / Individual booklets contain each project, while the cover gradients reflect the color palettes held within / Abi Huynh / Canada, 2008

CREATING WELLNESS LOGO AND PACKAGING / End Communications: design, Kyle Eertmoed, Kyle Romberg / USA, 2003

Split Fountain

Whether rendered in offset, silkscreen, or letterpress printing, a split fountain effect is achieved by putting two or more colors in the press' fountain, or repository of ink. In offset, this means the colors, separated by fountain splitters, are blended by the oscillation of the press; in silkscreen and letterpress, the colors must be carefully blended by hand.

FOUR-COLOR SPLIT FOUNTAIN WITH WOOD-BLOCK TYPE / Tom Rowe / UK, 2007

Color Rendition

Grasping the ephemeral subtleties of color is essential to practicing design, but just as important is understanding how to translate these into functional designs that are reproducible in a variety of formats. The clear divide is print and screen, where CMYK and RGB color models, respectively, reign over each medium. Screens emit color, so they rely on RGB as an additive model, where the combination of red, green, and blue equal white. Paper absorbs color, so it relies on CMYK as a subtractive model, where the combination of cyan, magenta, and yellow equals black. Mysteries of the human brain's color perception aside, the important lesson is that CMYK does not belong on screen and RGB does not perform in print.

In a design for screen, the main consideration is ensuring that all work is rendered as RGB so it is properly interpreted. When it comes to print, however, the CMYK model is only one of a variety of methods through which to render color. CMYK, or four-color printing, utilizes a plate for each color to produce any color combination—from flat fields of color to photographs and illustrations. If a highly specific color is desired, CMYK is not necessarily the most accurate or easiest to procure consistent results with; for these cases, spot colors are the most precise by using color matching systems like Pantone (also referred to as PMS), which is widely used in America and Europe, or Toyo, used mostly in Asia. The downfall to spot colors is that full-color photographs are not possible. Finally, grayscale or single-color (which applies to spot color) printing is another option; this approach relies on the interpretation of color, light, and shadow values as shades of a single color, from light to dark, reproduced in the form of a halftone using dots of varying sizes.

Often, the scope and specifications of a project as well as its final use will determine the color rendition chosen, but they can also be selectively chosen to achieve specific communication goals that support a designer's concept.

CMYK: Subtractive

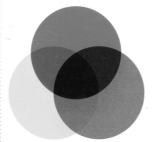

RGB: Additive

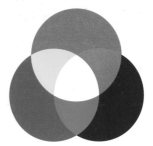

CMYK and RGB compared in print

4-color printing

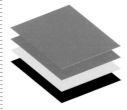

Photograph construction

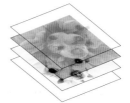

Flat color construction

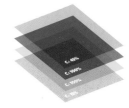

1-color printing

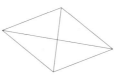

Grayscale

Spot color

Halftone

Detail of halftone, exaggerated for display

2004 Annual Report

Society of Graphic Designers of Canada

British Columbia Chapter

President

Yves Rousselle, MGDC

president.bc@gdc.net

Gadzooks, another year! This past year we got back to the **business** of design.

We delivered more programming focused on **small business concerns** expressed by our members, covering topics of copyright, taxation and business management.

We improved our Chapter as a business, strengthening membership, budget controls and financial stability, which was one of our goals in 2003. With some additional funds, we hope to be able to provide our members with more **free stuff and events** in 2005.

Our Society **spoke out** to the media and the business community when the Vancouver Olympic committee worked towards grossly devaluing our profession's contribution to our country and economy.

A dialogue has begun with this province's **consumer taxation branch** in hopes of improving government's understanding of our profession and how we conduct business.

And the **fun stuff**. We met some of our profession's **heroes**, including Amy, Cameron and Molly from Infinite Scale Design, who are now preparing the look and feel for the upcoming NFL Superbowl; Debbie Millman, who talked to us about managing small clients like Burger King and Hershey's; and Casey Hrynkow, who's been on my hero list for a long time, shared her vast knowledge with us.

Thanks to all members for your participation and another **big thanks** to our loyal sponsors who are integral in helping us reach our goals. Again, I encourage all members to work with our sponsors and **share the love**. And finally a group hug to my fellow board members whose energy, creativity and dedication has overwhelmed me throughout the year.

READ ME

Yves is the owner of the design firm Bau-Wow, as well as a partner in Orange Dog.

www.bauwow.com

Secretary

Sigrid Albert, MGDC

secretary.bc@gdc.net

This was a fun year to be on the GDC/BC executive. While everyone on the committee is responsible for their own duties, input from all execs into any area is encouraged. For example, due to our lack of an Events Executive this past year, we all took turns organizing events. I took on the **Xmas Tease Party** organization which had me consulting with bar owners, magicians, jazz singers and burlesque dancers.

The Secretary position, which I have held for these past 2 years, is a great starting position for anyone who wants to get involved with the GDC/BC at the executive level. It has a well-defined set of recurring duties, making it relatively easy to incorporate into a work schedule, while providing an opportunity to contribute to and learn about other executive positions.

I look forward to taking on the **Education Executive** position in 2005-2006.

Sigrid is the owner of Echelon Design.

www.echelondesign.com

Membership

Judy Snaydon, MGDC

membership.bc@gdc.net

Members come and members go, but the opportunities and challenges facing the GDC/BC remain mostly unchanged. We are the **largest** GDC Chapter in the country by a considerable margin, but our ability to alter the face of the design industry in our province is always dependant on the volunteer executives' ability to juggle GDC business with making a living.

Positive changes in 2004 included the arrival of a group of new members eager to step up to the plate and become involved in the Chapter. Enthusiastic new faces are always a huge encouragement to all of us on the board. In 2005 we hope to involve more members in manageable volunteer roles which will greatly benefit the organisation and members alike. Membership is an area where committed volunteers can make a real difference.

Another **positive trend** is a sense of greater overall curiosity about the GDC and the services and opportunities it provides. This year we received 279 requests for information about membership. There has been a notable increase in inquiries about volunteering opportunities. We currently have 73 member and non-member volunteers listed in our database.

Disappointing changes in 2004 included a **drop in membership** numbers over 2003. Although we received little feedback from members, membership numbers may have been affected by January's rate increase. It is an ongoing struggle for the GDC to understand **what motivates members** to join and to keep supporting the society.

I welcome any **feedback** from members about what makes you renew your membership every year and what you think would make GDC membership even more desireable.

After 6 great years of freelancing, Judy felt the need for a change, and is now heading up the graphic design department at Mountain Equipment Coop. Change is good!

READ ME

Association Liaison

Serge Bédard, MGDC

liaison.bc@gdc.net

Here, at the end of my 2-year term as Association Liaison, I find I've gained a great appreciation of the Society's endevours to provide a communication network between its members and businesses for the exchange of information and ideas pertinent to the development of the profession. I also appreciate the new relationships that I have made that have enabled me to be part of a network of great people. The Society is only as effective and productive as its individual members make it and in my term I have seen, first hand, many volunteer's efforts ensure that the goals of the society are maintained.

This, 2004, was a quiet year for this position. There was the usual liaising with other associations but most of the promotion of the GDC was made through events, communications, membership and the commitment of a great volunteer board.

I will be stepping down from my position on the board, but I encourage members to get more involved. The position of Association Liaison presents a good opportunity to **network** and meet members of other professions and business. Our friends in architecture, photography, advertising and other related professions are often hosting events that could benefit all of us. We really need someone to keep in touch with them, and encourage working together.

If you are interested, please contact Yves at president.bc@gdc.net

Serge is an independent designer.

READ ME

Sponsorship

Riley Maslinger, MGDC

sponsorship.bc@gdc.net

Our sponsors have given us much more than financial support. They have shown their loyalty year after year, they have been enthusiastic members of our community, and they have helped with their time and resources in every way.

I am very excited about my **new role** as the Sponsorship Chair because maintaining and building the relationships we have with our sponsors is crucial to maintaining the activities, services and events that we enjoy. My **primary objective** in this role is to ensure the sponsors get the most from their participation the GDC/BC.

This year we will be looking for sponsors to help us with accommodation for speakers (hotels), catering, venues and other event sponsors so that we can continue to bring in speakers like **Rick Valicenti**, keep the **Salazar** and **Grapher Awards** going and provide more events for our community of designers. It is important, while looking for sponsors, that we find companies that are interested in being involved with BC's graphic design community so they will benefit from their on-going participation.

You can **help build our sponsorship** by letting your suppliers know that you are a GDC member and that sponsoring the GDC locally or nationally is a great opportunity to reach the graphic design market.

You can help maintain our sponsorship by using sponsor services and, when you do, **tell them** how much you appreciate their involvement.

Please contact me if you have any questions about sponsorship or if you think your company or one of your contacts may be interested in becoming a GDC sponsor.

A Vancouverite who loves skiing and her two little girls, Riley runs Honeycomb Creative and photosphere.com with her husband.

READ ME

events

JANUARY 2004 Annual General Meeting ft Infinite Scale Design Group	This was when we first got the brilliant idea of luring you out to our AGM with the draw of someone more interesting than our humble selves. **Infinite Scale** wowed us with their **Look of the Olympic Games Story**. **Metropolitan Fine Printers** sponsored. And don't forget how much fun we had singing that song ... c'mawn, you enjoyed it.
APRIL The Paper Bash	Thanks to **Peter Eller**, for spearheading this bashful event with volunteers **Peter Romich, Paulo Alvarez, Rene Quijada, Jason Lau** and **Quentin Harris**.
MAY Olympic Summit	The **Pow Wow** in the middle of the **Foofaraw**. Vancouver's senior designers agreed.
JUNE New York Stories: Debbie Millman	The business design of the design business? **Debbie Millman** showed us how; **Casey Hrynkow** hugged her for it.
JUNE Salazar Student Awards	See the Education report for details.
SEPTEMBER Copyright Law: David Wotherspoon	Expert advice from a charming lawyer on all those sticky copyright issues.
OCTOBER Beer ft Taxes	Our version of "Octoberfest" ... or was it "Bitchfest"? Fun and educational, whatever it was. Thanks to our tax experts from **Berk & Associates**.
NOVEMBER The Business of Design: Casey Hrynkow	There's no-one better in this town to give us advice about running a design firm than our very own **Casey Hrynkow**.
DECEMBER Xmas Tease	Seasonal feather boas & Burlesque: what more can we say? **Jim Skipp** enjoyed himself!

2004 New Members

MGDC	8
LGDC	2
Associate	3
Graduate	5
Student	16
Total	34

Includes 4 transfers from other Chapters.

There were 13 member resignations in 2004. An additional 21 memberships were cancelled as a result of unpaid dues. Total change in membership: 34 member decrease over 2003.

New Members 2004

Student

Kimberley Ang
Sarah Balakshin
Diane Bozic
Sanjit Singh Fernandes Bakshi
Lisa Kemingway
Kristin Kubbard
Melissa Irving
Sandy Jakkavanrangsei
Scott Laurie
Xu-Xuan Lin
Veronica Mak
Nina Palmer
Christopher Paxton
Luvlina Sanghera
Shannon Zelland
Christine Joltof

Graduate

Cameron E. Jantzen
Keith Leinweber
Gale Leitch
Sonya Pacfiniuk
Shannon White

Associate

Adam Blasberg
Uta Nagel
Darcy Paterson

Professional

Matthew Clark
Byron Dowler
Lisa Edward
Bozena Kacro-Buckley
Felicia Lo
Santiago J. Salazar
Daniela Wood
Nancy Wu

Licentiate

Amanda Daly
Julie Lavoie

Resignations 2004

Lisa Birrell
Simon Beitchford
Steven dwayne Beyl
Lily Chow
Mariah Hamilton
Corrie Keeinga
Natasha Lafos
Kimberley Norcott
Adrienne Noyes
Chloe Perron
Nigel Procter
Steve Reny
Lindsay Simmonds

Total GDC/BC paid Membership

	2003	2004
FGDC	3	3
MGDC	109	118
LGDC	15	16
Associate	13	20
Graduate	18	21
Student	39	54
Total	197	231

Education

Terrance Fines

education.bc@gdc.net

For the past two years, I have had the privilege of being involved with the GDC/BC as a student executive member. This past year in particular was a very gratifying one, as I was able to witness the BC Chapter transform into a new, and exciting entity. With a group of dedicated executives and sponsors, a new era of the Chapter is now evolving.

Joining the GDC as a student member has had immense benefits for me as a young designer, and I would urge others to experience this for themselves.

As an executive team, we are always encouraging GDC members at every level to become involved, as member input and participation are the essence of what we are trying to accomplish. Member participation is our greatest asset.

As Education Chair for the past two years, I will be passing the education torch to fellow executive, **Sigrid Albert**, whose experience will greatly benefit our student members. I am looking forward to my continued involvement with the GDC, and will continue to contribute in any way I can.

READ ME

Terry is a local independent designer, husband, dad, printer, film buff & dog lover who enjoys long walks at Spanish Banks with good coffee and good conversation.

GDC/BC Salazar Student Awards

This year's judges were:
Regan Burns, MGDC (Kaldor Design Group),
Derek Hepburn, MGDC (Tekton Creative)
Christopher Clark, MGDC (Serengeti Design Group).

Thank you to all of the judges for their dedication and hard work.

Platinium Sponsor, Metropolitan Fine Printers is the founding sponsor of the GDC/BC Salazar Student Awards which include scholarships created in support of graphic design development in British Columbia.

We would also like to thank this year's **supporting sponsor Eres, UBC Robson Square** and our guest speaker, **Matthew Clark** of Subplot Design for his wonderfully informative presentation.

2004 GDC/BC Salazar Student Award Winners

4-Year Programme Winner	**Nina Palmer**, Emily Carr Institute
3-Year Programme Winner	**Todd Chapman**, Capilano College
2-Year Programme Winner	**Daniele Maria Rudischer**, Malaspina University College
4-Year Honourable Mention	**Kimberly Ang** Emily Carr Institute
3-Year Honourable Mention	**Eyan Miller** Capilano College
2-Year Honourable Mention	**Nicole Gaboury**, Malaspina University College

sponsors

2004 Platinum Sponsors

Metropolitan *fine* PRINTERS

In 2004 **Metropolitan** started off the year by sponsoring our AGM in January, subsidizing the cost of bringing the design group **Infinite Scale** to talk to us about designing for the Olympics. Met also printed **The Point** 3, and the materials for the **Salazar Awards**, for which they are the founding sponsor.

Hemlock PRINTERS LTD.

Hemlock Printers upgraded themselves to Platinum Sponsorship this year with their additional contribution to the 2003 **Grapher Catalogue**. In November they saved our heinies by printing **The Point** 4.

2004 Gold Sponsor

Teldonprintmedia

Teldon Print Media printed the materials for the **Paper Bash**, and will be printing **The Point** 5 in March 2005, to complete their Gold Sponsorship for 2004.

2004 Silver Sponsors

WESTERN | PRINTERS & LITHOGRAPHERS

Western Printers did a lovely job of printing last year's Annual Report. Remember it?

True Colours

True Colours was a new sponsor for us this past year, and they supplied those fabulous banners you see at all our events.

2004 Bronze Sponsors

Cascades

Cascades Paper, a long-time sponsor of the GDC, provided paper for last year's **Annual Report**, **The Point** 3, and the **Paper Bash**.

COAST PAPER

Coast Paper also continues to keep us in print with their paper donations; in 2004 for the **Salazar Awards** and **The Point** 4.

RepArt

RepArt contributed some fabulous illustrations to **The Point** 3.

SYDNEY

Sydney Sales handles our mailings, the assembly of our membership kits, and provided the lovely machine sewing for **The Point** 5.

Treasurer

Patricia Ku, MGDC

treasurer.bc@gdc.net

As treasurer, on behalf of the GDC/BC, I would like to say thank you to all the board members for their hard work which made our Chapter financially sound, and made 2004 a great year.

It is certainly great that we further strengthened the Chapter's financial position this past year! Compared with some previous years when there was no surplus, or there was a deficit. **We are in very good shape**. But, when we think about what we want to do, it seems that the funds are still not sufficient. Many great international designers are too far away from us. It is too expensive to invite them here to meet our members. There are many great design shows around the world, we could hardly afford to bring them here either. The GDC's 50th anniversary is right around the corner. Celebrations have been long-awaited by our members, especially those who have loved and devoted so much to their Society. There are also many great ideas not yet in progress and still to be realized because they are too costly.

With a stronger financial position we might possibly make things happen gradually. For those who are satisfied with what we have done, I would say that next year

financials

Unaudited Statement of Revenue & Expenses

January 1–December 31, 2004 [in dollars]

Income	Event Income		
	BC Chapter AGM	$	3,820.74
	Business Basic Event		1,480.00
	Christmas Party		1,360.00
	Copyright Event		815.00
	Grapher '03 Catalogue		350.00
	New York Stories		1,175.00
	Paper Bash		405.00
	Total Event Income	$	9,405.74
	Interest Income		8.29
	Membership Dues from National		18,839.30
	Miscellaneous		5.95
	Sponsor Cash Contributions		8,300.00
Total Income		$	36,559.28
Expenses	Accounting Fees	$	490.00
	Administration & Database		3,921.50
	Advertising & Promotion		4,412.77
	Couriers		762.89
	Event Expenses		
	BC Chapter AGM	$	4,935.83
	Business Basic Event		772.77
	Christmas Party		3,276.82
	Copyright Event		649.38
	Grapher '03 Catalogue		40.39
	National AGM		2,831.76
	New York Stories		1,071.08
	Paper Bash		839.29
	Salazar Student Awards		1,243.70
	Strategic Connections Conference		120.14

Ethics & Professional Practices

Linda Coe, FGDC

ethics.bc@gdc.net

Professional practices relating to the business of design are clearly detailed in the GDC Code of Ethics. The VP Ethics offers information and mediation; the role is extensive, and activities pertain to professional, client, supplier, educator and community relations. Where necessary, written grievances may be sent to the National Ethics Committee (via the National Secretariat) for review, to mediate and informally resolve them. The Ethics Committee may refer non-frivolous grievance cases to the National Discipline Committee for a hearing.

In 2004, local queries concerned disputes arising from ill-prepared contractual agreements. Two professional practice events, **Understanding Copyright** with David Wotherspoon and **Design Business Basics** with Casey Hrynkow tackled this and other business issues. The upcoming **Business In Vancouver How To** book includes the article, "**How to Use a Contract for Design Services.**"

Assisting the Ethics Chair provides opportunities to connect with the business community and increase awareness of standard practices within our profession.

Interested volunteers may contact me at the email address above.

Linda has over 25 years of experience as a design practitioner and educator.

E-communications

Mel Buenaventura

ecommunications.bc@gdc.net

Kicking off the 2004 e-news was GDC National launching a **new web site** that transformed the old site into one that addressed the needs of the Society pertaining to enhancement of its public image, improved access to general information and provided better usability for an individual member's page, as an example.

This upcoming fiscal year for 2005, GDC/BC will hope to again transform from its current state to one that will address e-communication objectives of the chapter through the use of various electronic media, such as enhanced web functionality catering to specific chair needs, e-mail template and e-newsletter. Such efforts will better communicate the aspirations of the society pertaining to events, membership, news and any other community-related information of interest.

In addition, if you would like to volunteer and learn valuable experience in research, business, marketing, writing, design and co-ordination of web content—where required—please contact me at the email address above. You can help shape, in small increments, the design community of BC.

I'm looking forward to another fun year.

Mel possesses over a decade of marketing communications experience in the private, public and non-profit sectors.

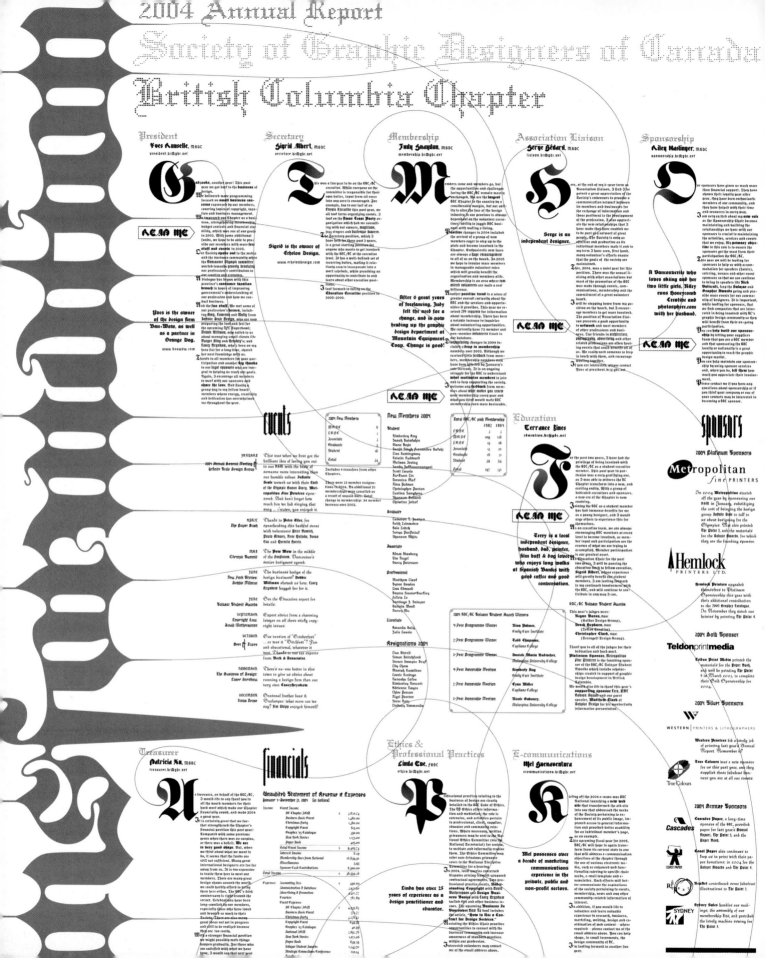

PRINCIPLES
Of Typography

62
Anatomy

It is unlikely that a graphic designer would be fired from a reputable job for referring to the ear of the lowercase letter *g* as "that cute thing that sticks out on top" or for not knowing the difference between a terminal and a finial, but it certainly does no harm to learn the proper terms for the elements from which the characters of the alphabet are constructed.

63
Genealogy

The abundance of type families can sometimes be daunting—a feeling magnified by their myriad weights, styles, and variants, with a semantically confusing collection of terms that are easily misunderstood and repeatedly miscommunicated. Is it *typeface* or *font*? *Italic* or *oblique*? Is this *condensed* or *compressed*? Just how old are old-style figures? Grasping the breadth and alternatives offered within each type family may ease the pain of selecting the most appropriate. Scrolling through the Font drop-down menu and selecting whichever type family is highlighted after you count to ten is also a valid option.

66
Classification

Over the course of the twentieth century, significant efforts have been made to coin the ultimate set of terms to classify the ever-growing collection of typefaces. In the 1920s, French typographer Francis Thibaudeau classified typefaces by the shape of their serifs into Elzevirs, Didots, Egyptians, and Antiques. In 1954, another French typographer, Maximilien Vox, proposed a more comprehensive system based on a historical approach; categories included Classics (subdivided into Humanistic, Garaldic, and Transitional), Moderns (Didonic, Mechanistic, Lineal), and Others (Incised, Script, Manual, Black Letter, and Non Latin). This system was adopted in 1962 by the Association Typographique Internationale (ATypI) and later by Adobe to organize its immense library. Other notable attempts were made by Italian typographer Aldo Novarese in 1956 and Canadian typographer Robert Bringhurst in 1992, as well as by the digital type foundries looking to organize their offerings in a manner more accessible to a growing audience of type buyers. This section features a classification based on the way designers refer to typefaces in daily parlance, because seldom is the occasion when a creative director recommends his or her designer to try a Mechanistic instead of an Elzevir.

74
Typesetting

Perhaps the activity that occupies the largest part of graphic designers' time is typesetting—quite simply, arranging letters into words, words into sentences, sentences into paragraphs, paragraphs into layouts. A few principles and semantics on spacing, organization and proper punctuation use are imperative for competent typesetting.

Detail of **SOCIETY OF GRAPHIC DESIGNERS OF CANADA, BRITISH COLUMBIA CHAPTER, 2004 ANNUAL REPORT** / Typeset in ten different Black Letter typefaces / Marian Bantjes / Canada, 2007

Anatomy

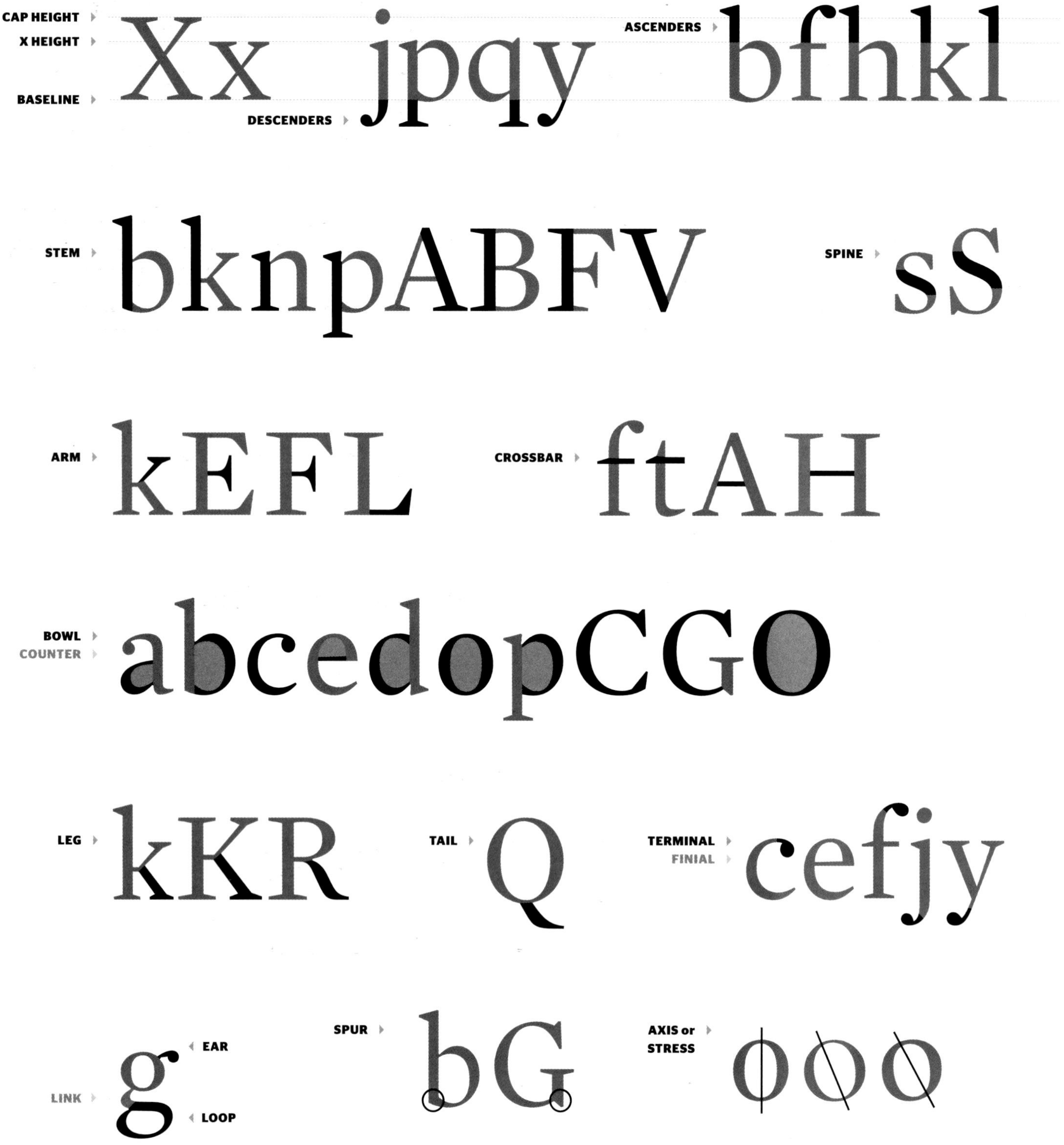

CAP HEIGHT ▸
X HEIGHT ▸
      Xx   jpqy   ASCENDERS ▸ bfhkl
BASELINE ▸
DESCENDERS ▸

STEM ▸ bknpABFV   SPINE ▸ sS

ARM ▸ kEFL   CROSSBAR ▸ ftAH

BOWL ▸
COUNTER ▸ abcedopCGO

LEG ▸ kKR   TAIL ▸ Q   TERMINAL ▸
FINIAL ▸ cefjy

g   ◂ EAR
LINK ▸   ◂ LOOP   SPUR ▸ bG   AXIS or ▸
STRESS   ∅∅∅

Genealogy

During the end credits of a 2007 episode of the game show *Wheel of Fortune*, host Pat Sajak asked co-host Vanna White what her favorite font was—"I use Arial, and I use Geneva," she swiftly replied. Aside from the surprising topic of the banter, it was the choice of words that point to the misunderstandings, even among graphic designers, about the actual semantics of typography, especially as graphic design's language seeps into the mainstream more and more. What Sajak should have asked is "What is your favorite *type family*?" Otherwise, White's response should have been specific to the weight, style, and point size of Arial and Geneva that she favors.

When type was cast in metal, and specific weights, styles, and point sizes were stocked by printers, a *font* referred to a single variant of these alternatives—for example, Helvetica Bold at 55 points. In the realm of digital technology, *font* refers to the digital file that stores the information and scalable characteristics of the *typeface* or, in other words, the design. A typeface is a single weight or style with singular features and aesthetic. The aggregation of typefaces with common design elements executed through a set of weights and styles is a *type family*.

Typeface and *font* are the most commonly misused terms, freely exchanged between each other—a problem enabled, in part, by software applications that lump typographic choices under "Font" menus and palettes.

abcdefghij klmnopqrs tuvwxyz
MERCURY ROMAN

abcdefghij klmnopqrs tuvwxyz
MERCURY SEMIBOLD

abcdefghij klmnopqrs tuvwxyz
MERCURY BOLD

abcdefghij klmnopqrs tuvwxyz
MERCURY ITALIC

abcdefghij klmnopqrs tuvwxyz
MERCURY SEMIBOLD ITALIC

abcdefghij klmnopqrs tuvwxyz
MERCURY BOLD ITALIC

ABCDEFGHIJ KLMNOPQRS TUVWXYZ
MERCURY ROMAN SMALL CAPS

ABCDEFGHIJ KLMNOPQRS TUVWXYZ
MERCURY SEMIBOLD SMALL CAPS

ABCDEFGHIJ KLMNOPQRS TUVWXYZ
MERCURY BOLD SMALL CAPS

TYPE FAMILY

abcdefghijklmnopqrstuvwxyz
MERCURY SEMIBOLD

TYPEFACE: SPECIFIC WEIGHT (SEMIBOLD)

abcdefghijklmnopqrstuvwxyz
MERCURY SEMIBOLD ITALIC

TYPEFACE: SPECIFIC WEIGHT (SEMIBOLD) AND STYLE (ITALIC)

abcdefghijklm nopqrstuvwxyz
MERCURY SEMIBOLD ITALIC, 34PT

FONT: SPECIFIC WEIGHT (SEMIBOLD), STYLE (ITALIC) AND SIZE (34PT)

V
MERCURY SEMIBOLD, 34 PT, LETTER V

GLYPH

Weight

GOTHAM / TOBIAS FRERE-JONES, 2000

abc **EXTRA LIGHT**   abc **LIGHT**   abc **BOOK**   abc **MEDIUM**

abc **BOLD**   **abc BLACK**   **abc ULTRA**

APEX SERIF / CHESTER JENKINS, 2002

abc **LIGHT**   abc **BOOK**   **abc MEDIUM**

abc BOLD   **abc EXTRA BOLD**

MINION / ROBERT SLIMBACH, 1990

abc **REGULAR**   abc **SEMIBOLD**

abc BOLD   **abc BLACK**

The quickest, most efficient, and most traditional way of calling attention to a word, sentence, or paragraph may be the simple act of making it bold—more effective, of course, if there is something less bold to contrast it with. Bold weights, specifically for serifs, did not come into play until the nineteenth century, but they have slowly become de rigueur with the introduction of tightly packaged type families with myriad weights, like Adrian Frutiger's Univers › 372 in the mid-twentieth century. Today, it is rare to encounter a regular- or medium-weight typeface without bolder,

or even lighter, counterparts. While it would be easy to peg this affluence on advancements in font development software, creating different weights of a typeface is far less simple than it would appear, and each weight must be optically redrawn. The examples show the relationship between the various weights and the challenge of maintaining a slightly fluctuating height while altering the widths to redefine the weight—from super-invisible-thin to you-must-be-blind-to-miss-it-black.

Width

TITLING GOTHIC / DAVID BERLOW, 2005

EFV **SKYLINE**   EFV **COMPRESSED**   EFV **CONDENSED**

EFV **NARROW**   EFV **NORMAL**   EFV **WIDE**

EFV **EXTENDED**

INTERSTATE / TOBIAS FRERE-JONES, 1993

EFV **COMPRESSED**   EFV **CONDENSED**   EFV **NORMAL**

BAUER BODONI / LOUIS HOLL, HEINRICH JOST, 1926

EFV **CONDENSED**   EFV **ROMAN**

It's hard to imagine how the endless lists of credits crammed onto today's movie posters would look if no one had dabbled in condensing the alphabet. So it's fitting that, in the late nineteenth century, posters for the era's entertainment industry, like the circus, employed an array of wood-carved typefaces that were produced in a dizzying variety of condensed and extended widths. These weren't necessarily thought of as type families with shared design features; instead, they were grouped rather objectively by the printer to fit longer words with condensed typefaces and shorter words with extended ones. It wasn't until the 1900s that typefaces like Morris Fuller Benton's Cheltenham were designed in various widths from the start and billed as a type family.

Today's multiwidth type families are significantly more purposeful in their design and construction. As shown, the key to maintaining uniformity is keeping the width of the stems consistent while extending horizontally, allowing for minor adjustments in height and weight—as opposed to the recurring crime of simply scaling an existing typeface horizontally, mangling the proportions of the original design. While condensed/compressed and wide/extended are the most common widths, no law prohibits designing a typeface as narrow as a pencil or as wide as a ferry.

Style

aefmvx   aefmvx   aefmvx   aefmvx

ROMAN   **ROMAN**

                            ITALIC   **OBLIQUE**

aefmvx   *aefmvx*   *aefmvx*   *aefmvx*

WHITMAN / KENT LEW, 2003   GALAXIE POLARIS /   TRADE GOTHIC /   ITC LUBALIN GRAPH /
                           CHESTER JENKINS, 2005   JACKSON BURKE, 1948   HERB LUBALIN, 1974

Like peanut butter and jelly, roman and italic typefaces work together for a seamless combination of distinctive flavors. While the oldest italic can be traced to Francesco Griffo at the end of the fifteenth century, it wasn't until the seventeenth century that combining roman with italic (sometimes from different typefaces) in the same line blossomed as a way to make distinctions within text, and it wasn't until the early twentieth century that roman typefaces were drawn hand in hand with their italic counterparts. Italics, as shown, are a flowing interpretation of the roman characters, with a more pronounced start and end of the penstrokes. They are drawn at angles as subtle as 2 degrees or as precipitous as 25. Some of the characters in italics are drawn differently—for example, the lowercase *a*, drawn as a double-story in roman and single story in italic, or the *f* with an extension of its stem—and italics are commonly 5 to 10 percent narrower than roman characters. Obliques, in contrast, are simply the roman characters sloped, with no optical corrections or modifications, resulting in wider characters and a lack of design intent. In other words, using obliques is akin to combining peanut butter with pickle relish.

ROMAN ◀ ▶ SMALL CAPITALS   **TITLING FIGURES ◀ ▶ OLD-STYLE FIGURES**

Fruk|kurF   1234567890 | 1234567890

                                 SCALA / MARTIN MAJOOR, 1988

Fruk|kurF   **1234567890 | 1234567890**

                                 SECTION / GREG LINDY, 2003

Small capitals and old-style figures carry a sophisticated air of tradition and Old World charm—the former with its dollhouse furnishings size, the latter with its playful ascenders and descenders. Old-style figures were the most commonly used form of numbers from the sixteenth to the early nineteenth century, when titling figures, as tall as the uppercase letters, slowly displaced them. Not until late in the twentieth century did digitally produced typefaces embrace this style once again.

Small caps, on the other hand, have always been part of the visual lexicon of typography; they were common companions to their roman counterparts since the sixteenth century, and they have survived the butchering of their proportions by desktop publishing and software applications that deceivingly shrink uppercase letters to fit the lowercase *x*-height at the push of a button. Small capitals, titling, and old-style figures all must be drawn individually to achieve the proper structural relationships between them.

VAW   **ROMAN ◀ ▶ DISPLAY**   VAW   VAW   **ROMAN ◀ ▶ DISPLAY**   VAW

VAW|VAW   VAW|VAW

H&FJ DIDOT / JONATHAN HOEFLER, 1991   REQUIEM / JONATHAN HOEFLER, 1992

Making typography big—big as in display sizes like 100-point, 160-point, 300-point—in the computer is not difficult whatsoever, and there is nothing wrong about doing so. However, with infinitely scalable typography, design elements drawn to function at small sizes will appear gargantuan, even unsightly, when blown out of proportion. When typefaces were cast in metal and each individual font size was created independently, it was possible to modulate the contrast of the design elements to maintain a similar texture through different point sizes, but with digital typography, all sizes are created equal. Some type families, like the ones shown, include display styles drawn specifically for reproduction at larger point sizes by exaggerating the contrast of the design. Vice versa, it's important to avoid using a display style at small point sizes.

Serif

Moving beyond the admittedly cute moniker of "little feet," serifs are the finishing strokes in all letters other than *O*, *o*, and *Q*. Serifs are either unilateral, protruding in one direction only, like the top left serif on *F*; or they are bilateral, as when they protrude in two directions, like the bottom serifs on *F*.

Since the fifteenth century, the shape of these little feet has defined the evolution of serif (or Roman) typefaces as typographers reacted to the work of their predecessors and adapted to new printing technologies. Humanist serifs, developed during the Renaissance, represent a shift away from the black letter used in the first decades of movable type. In the sixteenth century, Garaldes—taking their name from Claude Garamond and Aldus Manutius—featured more contrast between thick and thin strokes. Transitionals, with more defined serifs and a more vertical structure, paved the way for a distancing from calligraphic letterforms with the introduction of the Didones—the name derives from Firmin Didot and Giambattista Bodoni—or Moderns in the eighteenth century, with their simplified serifs and high contrast. And in the nineteenth century the New Transitionals were an evolved blend of the typefaces before them, produced to meet the new processes enabled by the Industrial Revolution.

Certainly, the origin of many of these typefaces can't be ignored: Roman inscriptional texts dating to the first century, like the famed Trajan › 368 column. These serifs, Glyphic or Incised, are representative of chisel on stone, as opposed to pen on paper—although one theory suggests these incisions were first drawn with a brush and then chiseled, leaving the true origins of the serif unclear. The result can be subtle, as in the flared serifs of the namesake Trajan, or it can be robust, with big, triangular serifs and abrupt joints within each character, like this book's Mercury.

HUMANIST

Quick Fox, Lazy Dog: Jumped.

ADOBE JENSON / ROBERT SLIMBACH, 1996 / *Based on Nicolas Jenson's work in the fifteenth century*

TRANSITIONAL

Quick Fox, Lazy Dog: Jumped.

BASKERVILLE / JOHN BASKERVILLE, CIRCA 1754

NEW TRANSITIONAL

Quick Fox, Lazy Dog: Jumped.

CENTURY SCHOOLBOOK / MORRIS FULLER BENTON, 1924

GARALDE

Quick Fox, Lazy Dog: Jumped.

BEMBO / STANLEY MORISON, 1929 / *Based on Francesco Griffo's work in the fifteenth century*

DIDONE or MODERN

Quick Fox, Lazy Dog: Jumped.

DIDOT / FIRMIN DIDOT, 1784

GLYPHIC or INCISED

QUICK FOX, LAZY DOG: JUMPED.

TRAJAN / CAROL TWOMBLY, 1989 / *Based on the inscription in Rome's Trajan column, erected in the first century*

Sans Serif

In the typographic equivalent of circumcision, sans serifs are stripped to the bare minimum by losing the serif appendages. They first appeared broadly in the mid-nineteenth century (they are referred to as Gothics) with the introduction of typefaces carved from wood. The increased production of sans serifs in all widths and sizes remains today, as sansserifs prove to be quite malleable.

While it wasn't the very first sans serif, Akzidenz Grotesk ›369, released in the 1890s, represents the mechanic structure of the Neo-Grotesques, which featured nearly even widths, as opposed to the Grotesques, which retained some characteristics of pen-drawn typefaces through slight contrast of thicks and thins. Geometric sans serifs, like Futura ›371 and Kabel from the 1920s, represent even more logic-driven letterforms peeled of any possible decoration. Humanist sans serifs were rooted in the calligraphic traits of fifteenth-century serifs rather than the evolution of woodtypes.

NEO-GROTESQUE

Quick Fox, Lazy Dog: Jumped.

AKZIDENZ GROTESK / BERTHOLD TYPE FOUNDRY, 1898

GROTESQUE

Quick Fox, Lazy Dog: Jumped.

FRANKLIN GOTHIC / MORRIS FULLER BENTON, 1904

GEOMETRIC

Quick Fox, Lazy Dog: Jumped.

FUTURA / PAUL RENNER, 1927

HUMANIST

Quick Fox, Lazy Dog: Jumped.

GILL SANS / ERIC GILL, 1927

Some Notes on Possibly Confusing Terms

Grotesque, from the German word *Grotesk*, was, indeed, from a lack of compliments and the abrupt change in the status quo these typefaces represented. *Gothic* was the American term for sans serifs, even though *Gothic* also refers to Black Letter ›68, which in turn is sometimes wrongly labeled as *Old English*, a style all its own. *Lineale* is another term for sans, and (just for trivia) in Spain it is referred to as *Palo Seco* ("dry stick"). For some time, slab serifs were referred to as *Clarendons* and later as *Egyptians*, but as more slabs have been developed, certain design characteristics have helped group them.

Slab Serif

While slab serifs are typically classified within serifs, their different visual attitude—defined by their thick, square-ended serifs—begs for its own category. Also a popular style during the mid-nineteenth century (Clarendon ›375 was first produced in 1845), slabs have evolved into a combination of structures, like the Clarendons and Egyptians, which are constructed more like serifs, and the Geometrics, which are based on sans serifs designed to sport slabs. And not all slabs are created equal: Geometrics and Egyptians lack brackets, the curvy connectors that segue stems and arms with the serifs, like the Clarendons.

CLARENDON (BRACKETED SLABS)

Quick Fox, Lazy Dog: Jumped.

CLARENDON / ROBERT BESLEY, 1845

EGYPTIAN (UNBRACKETED SLABS)

Quick Fox, Lazy Dog: Jumped.

ZIGGURAT / JONATHAN HOEFLER, 1991

GEOMETRIC (EVEN, UNBRACKETED SERIFS)

Quick Fox, Lazy Dog: Jumped.

ITC LUBALIN GRAPH / HERB LUBALIN, 1974

Black Letter

Newspaper nameplates, beer labels, religious scriptures, and tattoos, as well as heavy metal bands, hip-hop moguls, and pop starlets, all employ Black Letter, a typographic style used for more than 600 years. Its first use is hard to pinpoint, as Black Letter was a gradual and diverse evolution of varied sources like Carolingian, Old English, and the handcrafted work of scribes dating as far back as the ninth century in France, Italy, and Germany. Black Letter became de rigueur between the fifteenth and sixteenth centuries, especially after Johannes Gutenberg's momentous printing of the Bible in 1452, with the introduction of movable type in Germany—and even though the style spread and evolved from this country, the link between the two has been inextricable, possibly for the worse.

During the 1930s, Black Letter—the fraktur style specifically—was appropriated by the Nazi regime and used in its propaganda. In 1941, however, Adolf Hitler, through his secretary Martin Bormann, decreed that fraktur was not to be used anymore for its alleged Jewish origins. Complaints of illegibility may have played a bigger role. Despite this dark period, Black Letter remains one of the most used and versatile typographic choices, and it has enjoyed modern-day revivals by some of the industry's most celebrated type designers.

RECOMMENDED READING › 390

BASTARDA or SCHWABACHER

Quick fox, Lazy Dog: Jumped.

LUCIDA BLACKLETTER / CHARLES BIGELOW AND KRIS HOLMES, 1992 / *Based on fifteenth century black letter*

ROTUNDA

Quick Fox, Lazy Dog: Jumped.

SAN MARCO / KARLGEORG HOEFER, 1990 / *Based on fifteenth century black letter*

FRAKTUR

Quick Fox, Lazy Dog: Jumped.

FETTE FRAKTUR / LINOTYPE / *Based on nineteenth century black letter*

TEXTURA

Quick Fox, Lazy Dog: Jumped.

ENGRAVERS OLD ENGLISH / MORRIS FULLER BENTON, 1907 / *Based on nineteenth century black letter*

Black Letter version 2.0

...is the new Black   **A**

...is the new Black   **B**

...is the new Black   **C**

...is the new Black   **D**

...is the new Black   **E**

Underware's Fakir, 2006 (**A**); Miles Newlyn's Sabbath Black and Ferox, 1992 and 1995 (**B,C**), Jim Parkinson's Avebury, 2005 (**D**); and Corey Holms's Brea, 2003 (**E**)

Script

Just like handwriting, script letterforms are infinitely different and have been around since humans have put pen to paper with the intent of writing—doodling came along when they were forced into meetings. Script typefaces have long strived to translate the inherently dynamic, fluid, and imperfect act of writing into metal, wood, photo, and digital typefaces, amounting to an inordinate amount of choices in a dizzying number of approaches.

Script typefaces run a wide gamut of characteristics, and classifying them can be a frustrating task. They can be divided by their subjective aesthetics (formal versus casual); by the connections, or lack thereof, of its letters (flowing versus nonflowing); by the tool used (felt pen, quill pen, or brush, among others); and by other variables, such as upright, reverse, and handwritten scripts. In their variety, scripts have been pigeonholed for specific uses—formal scripts for wedding invitations, casual scripts for diners, and handwritten scripts for get-well cards, for example.

But scripts have enjoyed a renaissance in the twenty-first century, with young type designers like House Industries › 228, Underware › 232, and Alejandro Paul breathing new life and vibrancy into them with the help of OpenType. This format allows fonts to react to character placement—so a word like *feel* is rendered with two different glyphs for the letter *e*, or by having a dozen ways of connecting the *e* to other letters, giving the text the cadence of handwriting, where no two characters are drawn exactly alike. Pointing to the popularity of scripts are font retailers like Veer › 233, whose inventory of exclusive and stock scripts are top sellers over serif and sans serif typefaces.

FLOWING

CASUAL

Fox, Dog: Jumped

BRUSH SCRIPT / ROBERT E. SMITH, 1942

FORMAL

Fox, Dog: Jumped

BICKHAM SCRIPT / RICHARD LIPTON, 1997

UPRIGHT (FORMAL)

Fox, Dog: Jumped

FRENCH SCRIPT / MONOTYPE DESIGN STUDIO, 2003

BRUSH

Fox, Dog: Jumped

MISTRAL / ROGER EXCOFFON, 1953

HANDWRITTEN (CASUAL)

Fox, Dog: Jumped

SCHOOL SCRIPT / MONOTYPE

egg gobble look matter LIGATURES ACTIVE

egg gobble look matter LIGATURES INACTIVE

BELLO / UNDERWARE, 2004

OPENTYPE LIGATURES IN ACTION

NON-FLOWING

CASUAL

Fox, Dog: Jumped

SINCLAIR / PAT HICKSON, 1992

FORMAL

Fox, Dog: Jumped

LIBERTY / WILLARD T. SNIFFIN, 1927

UPRIGHT (CASUAL)

Fox, Dog: Jumped

SONORA / PROFONTS, 2005

BRUSH

Fox, Dog: Jumped

CHOC / ROGER ESCOFFON, 1954

HANDWRITTEN (FORMAL)

Fox, Dog: Jumped

VOLGARE / STEPHEN FARRELL, 1996

Bitmap

Bitmap fonts, made out of black on white pixels set in a grid, are designed to render appropriately at specific sizes on screen. Originally, these were developed to meet the coarse resolutions rendered by early operating systems (OS) and printers in the 1980s, and as technology allowed for type to render more smoothly—at least at sizes bigger than 9 points—their use was slowly discontinued in the mid 1990s. But later that decade, bitmap fonts experienced a resurgence through their use in web design, as they appeared sharp and clear no matter which monitor or OS the end-user had. In less than ten years, designers and type dabblers have generated a large sum of bitmap fonts, as they are comparatively easy to develop and distribute. And despite the intended use of some bitmap fonts at 5 points, 7 points, or 9 points on screen, designers have felt compelled to use them in print applications at vertiginous three-figure sizes.

QUICK FOX,
LAZY DOG:
JUMPED.

SILKSCREEN / **JASON KOTTKE, 1999** / *Designed on a 5 × 5 pixel grid*

QUICK FOX,
LAZY DOG:
JUMPED.

SUPERMAGNET / **SVEN STÜBER, 2001** / *Designed on a 5 × 5 pixel grid*

Quick Fox,
Lazy Dog:
Jumped.

UNIBODY / **UNDERWARE, 2002** / *Designed on a 10 × 10 pixel grid*

QUICK FOX,
LAZY DOG:
JUMPED.

FIXED V2 / **ORGDOT, 2001** / *Designed on a 12 × 12 pixel grid*

The Fuzzy World of Anti-Aliasing

Type on screen looks smooth and curvaceous, following the carefully crafted twists and turns of each character that typeface designers agonize over. But don't trust your eyes—all you are seeing are square pixels rendered at grayscale values that simulate those curves. Aliasing is the natural bitmap state in which graphics are rendered on screen; it yields a jagged collection of black pixels incapable of rendering smooth curves, so anti-aliasing is the feature that corrects this on screen. Bitmap typefaces are meant to be used aliased so the pixels render sharp, while regular typefaces must use anti-aliasing to display as intended.

Monospace

Monospace typefaces take their cue from typewriters, where all letters conform to a specific physical width, resulting in letterforms that must expand or condense to make the best use of the allotted space—hence the wide *is* and tight *ms*. They are also referred to as *nonproportional*, in contrast to typical proportional typefaces, where each character is a different width. Another feature of monospace typefaces—which can be seen as a pro or a con—is that they are spaced perfectly evenly, creating nicely aligned columns of text. This is helpful for creating the financial tables of an annual report, and has proven to be the best practice among programmers for writing code. The odd spacing, unusual letterforms, and a propensity for futuristic and typewriter designs limit the applications of monospace fonts.

Quick Fox,
Lazy Dog:
Jumped.

COURIER / **HOWARD "BUD" KETTLER, 1955**

Quick Fox,
Lazy Dog:
Jumped.

OCR A / **AMERICAN TYPE FOUNDERS, 1968**

QUICK FOX,
LAZY DOG:
JUMPED.

ORATOR / **JOHN SCHLEPPER, 1962**

Quick Fox,
Lazy Dog:
Jumped.

OCR B / **ADRIAN FRUTIGER, 1966**

Spacing
non-proportional

Spacing
proportional

Grunge

Somewhere at the intersection of Kurt Cobain's unkempt appearance, the wide availability of the type design software Fontographer, and the mainstream climax of postmodernism and deconstructive typography from the 1980s, a new breed of amalgamated, scratchy typefaces populated the 1990s and early 2000s, in parallel with the increased (and eventually decreased) popularity of the Grunge musical movement, from which these typefaces got their label. There are no clear definitions for Grunge typefaces, but they share a jarring aesthetic and philosophy that contrasts with the conventions of classic typography. They also have in common the appropriation of existing typefaces as well as the visual vernacular to generate new designs. Early examples in 1990, like Barry Deck's Template Gothic › 382, based on a sign in his local laundromat, and P. Scott Makela's Dead History, a fusion of the serif Centennial with the bubbly sans VAG Rounded, cemented the feasibility of creating a new hybrid, imperfect language developed through the emerging font development software that could turn anyone into a type designer. This led to a boom of amateur type designers and digital type foundries—including Emigre › 224, [T-26] › 229, GarageFonts, Plazm, and Thirstype › 200—whose work defined much of the look of the 1990s.

Quick Fox, Lazy Dog: Jumped.

DEAD HISTORY / P. SCOTT MAKELA, 1990

QUICK FOX, LAZY DOG★ JUMPED.

MC AUTO / BRIAN STUPARYK, 2002

Quick Fox, Lazy Dog: Jumped.

ESCALIDO STREAK / JIM MARCUS, 1994

FALLEN THYME / FONTOSAURUS TEXT, 2001

TURBO RIPPED / GYOM SÉGUIN

QUICK FOX LAZY DOG JUMPED

LAUNDROMAT 1967 / LAST SOUNDTRACK, 2006

Undeclared

If comedian Jerry Seinfeld had a typographic sense of humor, he would surely ask, "What's the deal with Optima? I mean, is it a serif? or is it a sans serif?" These two typefaces, Optima and Copperplate Gothic, have long baffled designers with their flared serifs attached to sans serif structures.

Quick Fox, Lazy Dog: Jumped.

OPTIMA / HERMANN ZAPF, 1958

QUICK FOX, LAZY DOG: JUMPED.

COPPERPLATE GOTHIC / FREDERIC W. GOUDY, 1901

AMERICAN WOOD TYPE

In the middle of the nineteenth century, an alternative to metal typesetting and printing arrived in the form of wood type. Less costly and more versatile, wood type prompted an influx of new display typeface designs ranging from sans serifs to slab serifs and Tuscans that were eagerly used for posters and broadsides in wild assemblages of widths, weights, and sizes. Enthusiasm for this print method waned toward the end of the century, especially as metal typesetting evolved into a more mechanized practice with the introduction of Linotype and Monotype machines. However, wood type alphabets lingered in print shops around the United States, and one of their most ardent collectors was Rob Roy Kelly, a prolific and influential graphic design educator and historian. A graduate of Yale School of Art and Architecture, Kelly taught for more than 30 years at Minneapolis College of Art and Design (MCAD), Kansas City Art Institute, Carnegie Mellon University, Western Michigan University, and Arizona State University. At MCAD he established a printmaking course where he used his wood type collection with the students, who queried him about its origins and uses. In 1957, Kelly began to organize his

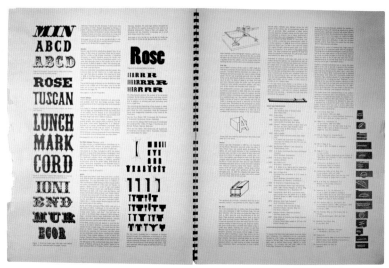

FOLIO OF AMERICAN WOOD TYPE, VOL. 1 / Rob Roy Kelly / USA, 1965

collection. He delved deeper into the topic, documenting the role of wood type in the history of printing and typography.

Working primarily from a 1906 type specimen issued by the Hamilton Manufacturing Company, one of the largest producers of wood type in the United States, and from other specimens at Columbia University, the Henry E. Huntington Library and Art Museum, the Newberry Library, and the New York Public Library, Kelly created a comprehensive classification system and established the date and manufacturing origins of most typefaces in his collection. In 1963 he published an early version of his findings in the Walker Art Center's *Design Quarterly no. 56*, and in 1967 he published *American Wood Types 1828–1900, Volume One*, an imposing 17 × 22-inch publication. Its acclaim was followed by the 1969 publication of *American Wood Type, 1828–1900: Notes on the Evolution of Decorated and Large Types and Comments on Related Trades of the Period*, which was reprinted in 1977. The publication's broader availability helped it find its way into the hands of graphic designers who, facing the unflinching dominance of Helvetica ›373, parlayed Kelly's research into a revival of a visual language long forgotten. Toward the end of the 1960s Kelly sold his collection to the New York Museum of Modern Art ›121, which then sold it to the University of Texas at Austin, where it now resides as a research collection ›124 available to students once more.

Typesetting

ALIGNMENT

A few principles and semantics on spacing, organization and proper punctuation use are imperative for competent typesetting.

A few principles and semantics on spacing, organization and proper punctuation use are imperative for competent typesetting.

A few principles and semantics on spacing, organization and proper punctuation use are imperative for competent typesetting.

A few principles and semantics on spacing, organization and proper punctuation use are imperative for competent typesetting.

FLUSH LEFT / RAGGED RIGHT　　**CENTERED**　　**FLUSH RIGHT / RAGGED LEFT**　　**JUSTIFIED**

LEADING or LINE SPACING

A few principles and semantics on spacing, organization and proper punctuation use are imperative for competent typesetting.

8/12

A few principles and semantics on spacing, organization and proper punctuation use are imperative for competent typesetting.

8/15

A few principles and semantics on spacing, organization and proper punctuation use are imperative for competent typesetting.

8/18

A few principles and semantics on spacing, organization and proper punctuation use are imperative for competent typesetting.

8/21

The space between lines of text is typically referred to as *leading*—pronounced like the metal, *lead*, not like *leader*—which comes from the days of metal typesetting when bars (also called *strips* or *slugs*) of lead of different thicknesses were placed between lines of text to create spacing. Colloquially, leading is defined by saying

"8 over 12" or writing 8/12, meaning 8-point type size with 12-point leading. As the example shows, when using equal increments in leading, in this case 3-point, it is possible to horizontally align paragraphs with different leading values.

TRACKING or LETTER SPACING

typesetting
typesetting
typesetting

typesetting
typesetting
typesetting

TYPESETTING
TYPESETTING
TYPESETTING

TYPESETTING
TYPESETTING
TYPESETTING

NORMAL, LOOSE, AND LOOSER TRACKING

Tracking is the overall spacing between each letter. It is possible to track as tight or as loose as the heart desires but, as the example shows, Goudy and Spiekermann may be right. Small caps and uppercase letters do benefit from more generous letterspacing.

"Men who would letterspace lower case would shag sheep."
American typographer
Frederic W. Goudy

"Anyone who would letterspace lower case would steal sheep."
German typographer
Erik Spiekermann
paraphrasing
American typographer
Frederic W. Goudy

KERNING

Top
Top
o -80

Wet
Wet
E -80

MAVERICK
MAVERICK
V -80　R -20　C -40　K -20

FIRST LINES SHOW NO KERNING ADJUSTMENTS, BOTTOM LINES ARE ADJUSTED. NUMERIC VALUES ARE BASED ON ADOBE INDESIGN.

Kerning is the space between two specific letters. It is adjusted independently from the tracking. Digital typefaces are equipped with thousands of kerning pairs that provide a good start, but invariably tweaking must be performed, especially on text set at bigger sizes, where the spacing is more pronounced. In some circles, good kerning skills are what separate the true professionals from the dabblers.

Keming. (kĕm'ĭng).
n. The result of improper kerning

TERM INTRODUCED IN JANUARY OF 2008 BY DAVID FRIEDMAN OF IRONICSANS.COM

ORPHANS and WIDOWS

Perhaps the activity that occupies the largest part of graphic designers' time is typesetting— quite simply, arranging letters into words, words into sentences, sentence into paragraphs, paragraphs into layouts.

A few principles and semantics on

> Orphans, above, occur when the first line of a paragraph begins at the end of a column or page. Widows, below, occur when the last line of a paragraph is the first in a column or page. To paraphrase Robert Bringhurst in *The Elements of Typographic Style*, orphans have no past, but they do have a future, and widows have a past but not a future. Typically, however, a single word left alone at the end of a paragraph is referred to as an *orphan*.

Perhaps the activity that occupies the largest part of graphic designers' time is typesetting— quite simply, arranging letters into words, words into sentences, sentence into paragraphs, paragraphs into layouts.

A few principles and semantics on spacing, organization, and proper punctuation use are imperative for

spacing, organization, and proper punctuation use are imperative for competent typesetting.

Perhaps the activity that occupies the largest part of graphic designers' time is typesetting— quite simply, arranging letters into words, words into sentences,

competent typesetting.

Perhaps the activity that occupies the largest part of graphic designers' time is typesetting— quite simply, arranging letters into words, words into sentences, sentence into paragraphs, paragraphs into layouts.

HANGING PUNCTUATION

Perhaps the activity that occupies the largest part of graphic designers' time is typesetting— quite simply, arranging letters into words, words into sentences, sentence into paragraphs, paragraphs into layouts. "A few principles," he said "and semantics on spacing, organization, and proper punctuation use are imperative for competent typesetting."

> The default setting for paragraphs in layout programs is to begin every line of text at the same vertical edge, whether the alignment is flush left or right, but when a line of text begins with a quotation mark the vertical texture of the text is broken by a smaller glyph, as above. The alternative is to hang the punctuation outside of the vertical edge so all the words are aligned to the origin of the edge, creating a smoother texture, as below. With justified alignment, this also applies to commas and periods on the right edge.

Perhaps the activity that occupies the largest part of graphic designers' time is typesetting— quite simply, arranging letters into words, words into sentences, sentence into paragraphs, paragraphs into layouts. "A few principles," he said "and semantics on spacing, organization, and proper punctuation use are imperative for competent typesetting."

PUNCTUATION

 "Funny," he said.

QUOTATION MARKS

> One of the biggest peeves in proper typesetting is the widespread misuse of quotation marks, which are typically substituted by prime marks, more dismissively called *dumb quotes*. Quotation marks have an opening and a closing glyph and can be distinguished by their curliness in serif typefaces and their angularity in sans serif typefaces.

 I am 5′6″ tall

PRIME MARKS

> A single prime mark denotes feet, and a double prime mark inches. Nothing more, nothing less.

— A man-eating shark

HYPHEN

> Hyphens join words and break syllables. In this case, the absent hyphen in "a man eating shark" would indicate a culinary experience rather than a threat.

— Open 1:00–2:00 p.m.

EN-DASH

> En-dashes indicate ranges and can usually be read as "to." They are the width of an *n*.

— Then—shyly—they kissed.

EM-DASH

> Em-dashes break, interrupt, or punctuate a sentence with additional narrative. Lazy typists use two hyphens instead of a proper em-dash. Make sure your design does not suffer from this. They are the width of an *m*.

● ● ● And...Action!

ELLIPSIS

> In typesetting, ellipses have their own glyph with slightly compact spacing, which tends to look more natural than three periods in a row.

Legibility

Beyond the physical, optical ability to better distinguish between 24-point-type and 6-point-type, legibility relates to the ease or complexity required to decipher, distinguish, and understand a visual message, taking into consideration its context, its environment, and the audience for which it is intended: A prickly 1970s flyer for a punk band is as legible as a formal engraved wedding invitation set in a Spencerian script; it is simply a matter of context. There are indeed cases where legibility can be hindered or exalted by the designer; every choice, from type size to tracking, leading, color selection, and layout, has the potential to influence legibility. The trouble, however, has always been defining what is good and bad.

Designers and typographers have long battled about the appropriateness of certain design mannerisms. Most notable was the legibility haze from the 1980s and 1990s, starting with the avant-garde layouts of *Emigre* › 100 magazine and its novel typefaces that were neither, say, a Helvetica › 373 or a Garamond › 364. Parallel to *Emigre* was the robustly layered and deconstructed work coming out from Cranbrook Academy of Art › 130 as a reaction to modernism. Joining the fray in the 1990s was David Carson › 186, whose work for *Beach Culture* and *Ray Gun* › 330 magazines literally neglected legibility in favor of aesthetics. Steven Heller › 238 questioned *Emigre*'s impact, calling it a "blip in the continuum" in his 1993 essay "Cult of the Ugly," and proponents of clarity and functionality met these manifestations of design with ardent opposition, with Massimo Vignelli › 160 as the most vociferous. Of course, these visual (and verbal) confrontations had neither winner nor loser, but the accompanying dialog and the extremes to which legibility was pushed and pulled demonstrated the malleability of typography in the hands of graphic designers.

Imagine that you have before you a flagon of wine. You may choose your own favourite vintage for this imaginary demonstration, so that it be a deep shimmering crimson in colour. You have two goblets before you. One is of solid gold, wrought in the most exquisite patterns. The other is of crystal-clear glass, thin as a bubble, and as transparent. Pour and drink; and according to your choice of goblet, I shall know whether or not you are a connoisseur of wine. For if you have no feelings about wine one way or the other, you will want the sensation of drinking the stuff out of a vessel that may have cost thousands of pounds; but if you are a member of that vanishing tribe, the amateurs of fine vintages, you will choose the crystal, because everything about it is calculated to reveal rather than hide the beautiful thing which it was meant to contain.

This spread THROUGH MORE THAN 2,000 WORDS, BEATRICE WARDE, AN AMERICAN SCHOLAR, WRITER, AND TYPE ENTHUSIAST, DREW AN ASTUTE METAPHOR BETWEEN A CRYSTAL GOBLET AND TYPOGRAPHY IN HER 1955 ESSAY "THE CRYSTAL GOBLET, OR PRINTING SHOULD BE INVISIBLE." TALKING ABOUT BOOK TYPESETTING AND PRINTING, WARDE ARGUED THAT DESIGN AND TYPOGRAPHY SHOULD BE INVISIBLE, ALLOWING FOR THE CONTENT TO SHINE AND COME THROUGH UNFILTERED, LIKE A CLEAR, UNADORNED CUP OF WINE. THE OPPOSITE, A CUP THAT IS DECORATED AND EXTRAVAGANT, STANDS IN THE WAY OF APPRECIATION OF ITS CONTENTS, A CATASTROPHE NO SMALLER THAN A DESIGN THAT INDULGES IN ITS OWN AESTHETICS. AND TO THINK THAT NEITHER PUNK, NOR GRUNGE, NOR BITMAP TYPEFACES WERE AVAILABLE IN THE 1950S.

Printing demands a humility of mind, for the lack of which many of the fine arts are even now floundering in self-conscious and maudlin experiments. There is nothing simple or dull in achieving the transparent page. Vulgar ostentation is twice as easy as discipline. When you realise that ugly typography never effaces itself; you will be able to capture beauty as the wise men capture happiness by aiming at something else. The "stunt typographer" learns the fickleness of rich men who hate to read. Not for them are long breaths held over serif and kern, they will not appreciate your splitting of hair-spaces. Nobody (save the other craftsmen) will appreciate half your skill. But you may spend endless years of happy experiment in devising that crystalline goblet which is worthy to hold the vintage of the human mind.

Despina Curtis
Set Design
Styling
Design Consultancy
+44 (0)7958 031 668
studio@despinacurtis.com
www.despinacurtis.com

PRINCIPLES
Of Print Production

80

Print Methods

Between a designer's imagination and the final designed project lies the broad, sometimes intimidating process of bringing it to fruition through different print methods. With unique advantages and disadvantages—in cost, quality, availability, and appropriateness—each method yields distinct results through specific processes. Being aware of how each method works can only enhance the original concept of a design so it is optimized to make the best use of its print method.

86

Finishing

As significant as the quality and method of the printed material is the way in which it all comes together for its final presentation through choices in binding, folding, and any additional special techniques that can help define the physical presence of the finished piece—be it a lavish 80-page perfect-bound annual report with an embossed, laser-cut, spot gloss-varnished cover and a gatefold centerfold with diecuts, or a humble 12-page saddle-stitched brochure.

Detail of **DESPINA CURTIS IDENTITY AND PORTFOLIO CARDS** / Multistorey / UK, 2008

Offset (Sheetfed, Web)

As the most commonly used method, offset, also called *offset lithography*, offers versatility, quality, and speed. Offset presses can be small, printing one or two colors at a time on small paper sheets (around 18″ wide), or large, accommodating up to eight colors at the same time and printing on large paper sheets (up to 55″ wide). In any of the configurations, CMYK, spot colors, varnishes and coatings can be deployed through available units. One typical offset job—say, an annual report—would print on a six-color press where four of the color units are used for CMYK, a fifth unit for a spot color, and the last unit for a varnish or coating.

There are two kinds of offset presses: sheetfed and web. Sheetfed presses are most commonly used for brochures, stationery suites, posters, and other printed materials that benefit from accuracy and quality and for print runs not exceeding an average of 20,000 units (single sheets of paper are fed individually to the press). Web presses can print larger volumes—up to hundreds of thousands of units of newspapers, magazines, and catalogs—by running at faster speeds and feeding the paper from a huge roll that is continually unspooling. The downside to web printing is that quality and detail are harder to control.

The process begins by transferring digital files to plates, typically made of metal, on which an image is impressed. Within the press itself, these plates are wrapped around a roller that interacts as an intermediary with two sets of rollers: above, ink rollers that supply ink from the wells; and below, a blanket roller that transfers the ink to the paper. The blanket roller is important because it adapts to different paper surfaces. This aspect of the method gives it its name, as the roller offsets the original plate from the paper.

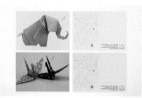

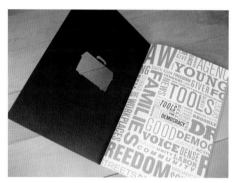

IORI HOTEL GLOBAL BRANDING, INCLUDING TWO-COLOR OFFSET STATIONERY, CARDS, MENU, NOTEBOOKS, AND POSTCARDS / Tea Time Studio / Spain, 2008

PUZZLES, Alexis Cuadrado / bjurecords / Hyperakt: Deroy Peraza / USA, 2008

TOOLS FOR DEMOCRACY, **NORTH STAR FUND 2007 ANNUAL REPORT** / Hyperakt: creative direction, Julie Vakser; design, Julie Vakser, Matthew Anderson / USA, 2008

Letterpress

The origins of letterpress printing can be traced to the eleventh century in China, when wood and clay blocks were carved, leaving the desired character in relief to be inked and pressed onto paper. The premise has not changed much to this date, just the means, which has progressed since the advent of movable type printing that relied on metal-cast typography in the fifteenth century in Europe through the large broadsheets using woodcut designs of the nineteenth century to the mechanized printing press in the Industrial Revolution. Today, letterpress enjoys a renaissance with the availability of vintage presses, metal and wood type collections, and craftspeople who have brought this method into the twenty-first century—specifically with the appearance of photopolymer plates that can render any digital file into a raised plate for use in restored nineteenth-century rotary presses. The tactile imprint of the raised design on paper gives some designers joyful goosebumps.

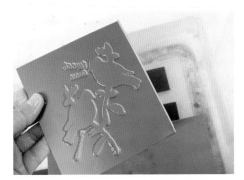  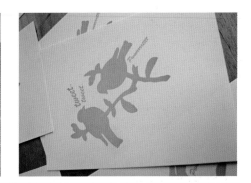

FROM POLYMER PLATE TO PRESS / USA, 2007 / Photos: Flickr user Sarah is me

MUSEUM OF INDUSTRIAL ARCHAEOLOGY AND TEXTILE WORKSHOP METAL TYPE AND STUDENT POSTER / Armina Ghazaryan / Belgium, 2008

  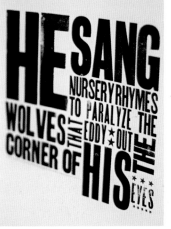

LETTERPRESSED BUSINESS CARDS / design and printing, Dolce Press / USA, 2008

EMILY SERVAIS (EARLY MISSIVE PRESS) PRINTING AT THE CRANKY PRESS / Canada, 2008 / Photos: Emily Servais, Sue Globensky

Silkscreen Printing

Popular for its versatility and its bright and solid color reproduction, silkscreen printing (also referred to as *silkscreening*, *screen printing*, and *serigraphy*) is a reliable method for producing work affordably and handsomely. Throughout the years it has served the likes of Andy Warhol, aspiring rock bands, and tchotchke makers who produce limited-edition prints, affordable low-volume T-shirts, and mass-produced branded pens, to name a few examples. Many designers have their own silkscreen setups to produce small-run designs, thus maintaining complete control of the piece from concept to finish and producing quality as good as that of vendors with big, loud automated machines. The ability to print on paper, fabric, metal, wood, concrete, and plastic is a major benefit of silkscreen printing.

The silkscreen printing process begins with the impression of a design applied to a nylon or polyester mesh—originally it was a silk mesh, hence the name—by coating it with photo emulsion, subjecting it to light while blocking out the artwork that will be printed. This stage creates a stencil for each color of the design. Ink is applied to the final surface—T-shirt, CD, paper, what have you—with the help of a squeegee onto the final surface, over and over and over.

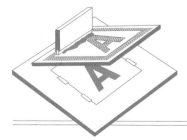

AUTOMATIC SILKSCREEN PRINTING MACHINE / USA, 2008 / Photo: Flickr user Conor Keller

MANUAL SILKSCREEN SETUP AND ACCOUTERMENTS / UK, 2007 / Photo: Flickr user richt

TABLETOP SILKSCREEN SETUP / USA, 2008 / Photo: Flickr user karpov the wrecked train

GREEN INK GETS A PASS ON A SCREEN / Photo: Aesthetic Apparatus

***THE SUBMARINES DECLARE A NEW STATE!* POSTER** / Aesthetic Apparatus: design, Michael Byzewski, Dan Ibarra / USA, 2006

Engraving

Engraving, the caviar of printing techniques, is an expensive, specialized, and time-consuming printing process resulting in a softly raised surface, dense color saturation, and sharp reproduction worth salivating over, perfect for invitations to black-tie affairs. Engraving is achieved by carving an image—by hand, or, thanks to modernity, through automated machinery—out of a metal plate (usually copper), filling the resulting hollow spaces with ink, and then placing paper on top while applying forceful pressure so the paper picks up the ink.

ENGRAVING PLAQUE FOR BUSINESS CARD

RESULTING BUSINESS CARD FROM PLAQUE

DETAIL OF ENGRAVING WITH GOLD INK

USA, 2004 / Materials: Courtesy of Lehman Brothers, Inc.

Thermography

The final result of thermography—a raised surface and glossy finish—is similar to that of engraving, and to someone unbothered by the intricacies of printing, they are exactly alike. Unlike engraving, however, thermography is neither expensive nor refined, and its process is completely different. Thermography is achieved by using slow-drying ink, typically on an offset press, coating it with thermography powder, and finishing it by applying heat that fuses the powder with the ink and causes the image to rise. Typographic and design details are usually lost due to the inflation process of the ink—not ideal for those concerned with attention to detail.

RAISED-INK DETAIL ON A WEDDING INVITATION / Kristen Jackson / USA, 2008 / Photo: Flickr user CryBabyInk

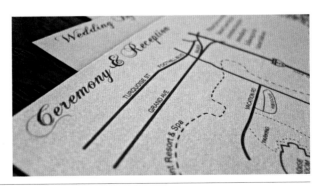

SANDRA AND THOMAS THREE-PIECE WEDDING INVITATION / Rolaine Llanes / USA, 2008

Flexography

Operating typically through a web press, flexography uses rubber or soft plastic plates with a slightly raised image and, instead of the oil-based inks used in offset, water-based inks that dry faster. This method is used for materials that are not as porous as paper, like plastic, kraft, or labels—so it is commonly used for packaging purposes like bread wrappers, plastic grocery bags, and milk cartons. Because it runs on a web press and the plates are made from soft material, the fidelity of the image, registration between color plates, and density of color are far from optimal.

STICKER PRESS CHECK AT THE IVY HILL PLANT / USA, 2007 / Photos: Steve Silvas

EXAMPLE OF FLEXOGRAPHY PRINTING ON A MASS CONSUMER PRODUCT PLASTIC BAG / USA, 2008

Foil Stamping

When a sophisticated detail of glitter and panache is desired, foil stamping provides the delicate, luxurious, and even dazzling effect that has been used since the first and second centuries in illuminated manuscripts—this later term arose from the result of this process—which involved grinding gold into a thin powder and then hammering it onto a page to yield the illuminating result. Today, the process is not as grueling: A relief plate (or die) is created with the design, it is heated and placed on a letterpress, and a piece of foil paper is used on top so as the paper goes through the press, the foil adheres to the raised image. Foil stamping can be done on a variety of materials, including cloth, leather, and wood, and is opaque enough to stand out in any color material—gold on black cloth is a classic.

NOTTINGHAM TRENT UNIVERSITY LIMITED-EDITION POSTCARDS / Un.titled / UK, 2007

PLAYSTATION3 LAUNCH MATERIALS / RGB Studio: design, Rob Brearley; Love Creative / UK, 2007

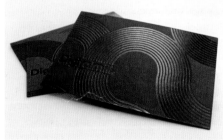

DIGITALMILL IDENTITY / RGB Studio: design, Rob Brearley / UK, 2008

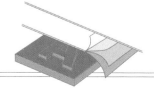

Digital Printing

Slowly but steadily, digital printing has evolved into a print method that designers are comfortable with. Unlike offset printing › 80, digital printing does not require plates; rather, it uses toner (powder) instead of ink (liquid) that lies on top of the paper instead of being absorbed. It can accommodate small print runs (in the hundreds and low thousands) at an affordable price. The quality of the images, type, and solid blocks of color has increased enormously, but digital printing still can't match the fidelity of offset nor match PMS colors consistently. Since the late 1990s, Xerox, Hewlett-Packard, and Heidelberg have made complex digital printers available—with each version improving capabilities and quality—that can accommodate a wider range of paper choices. These machines can collate and bind, but perhaps their biggest asset is their ability to produce variable data—that is, each printed unit can display unique data without much hassle. The quick turnaround time, low cost (relative to offset), and improved quality are no longer ignored by designers.

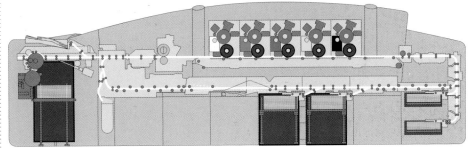

Photos: Heidelberger Druckmaschinen AG

Inkjet

For very small print runs (in the hundreds) or even single prints, inkjet printing is the optimal method—and, with the right equipment, designers can do the job from the comfort of their office or home. Producing richly saturated images—including a black blacker than any black before it—and sharply defined type on a wide range of papers, including heavily textured specialty papers, inkjet printing is ideal for art prints, posters, and mockups for client presentations. Inkjet is also used in commercial printing as a method for imprinting addresses and other variable information for magazines and catalogs. Otherworldly pricing for the consumer inks aside, inkjet printing is an excellent way for photographers, illustrators, small design firms, and independent designers to present their work.

Photos: Epson America, Inc.

Binding and Folding

Several ways, the choice of which is typically determined by budget and page count, are available to bring together printed material. Projects requiring no more than 6, 8, or even 12 pages can usually be fulfilled through folding, creating a piece that is easy to mail and distribute and providing enough pacing in how it unfolds to give the reader a sense of direction to engage with the content. Projects that climb between 20- and 40-page counts are best bound, be it an affordable saddle-stitch or a more expensive perfect binding. Any project over 40 pages can't be sustained by saddle-stitching, making perfect binding the economic choice and case binding the more costly choice. Certainly, these are only the basic starting points, and, for the right price, projects can be bound or folded in innovative ways—but until that elusive patron arrives, it's best to grapple the basics.

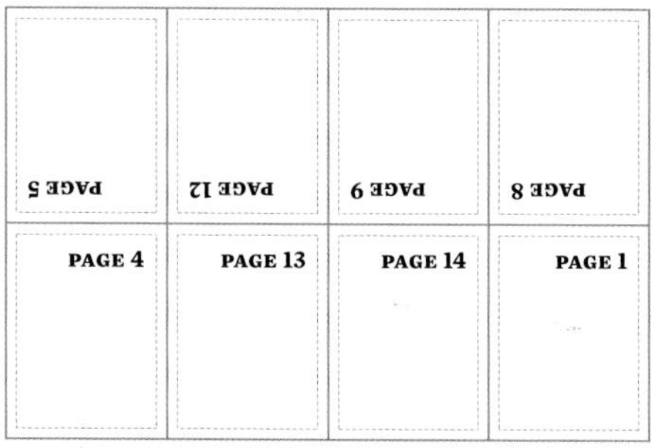

PAGE 5	PAGE 12	PAGE 9	PAGE 8
PAGE 4	PAGE 13	PAGE 14	PAGE 1

Almost all printed pieces—simple letterheads, envelopes, and posters designed to fit standard sheet sizes excluded—are executed in large sheets of paper, resulting in the signatures where pages are arranged in a seemingly topsy-turvy way (officially called *imposition*). These are folded and trimmed to meet correctly when seen as spreads. Common signature sizes are as small as 4 pages per sheet or as large as 32 pages per sheet.

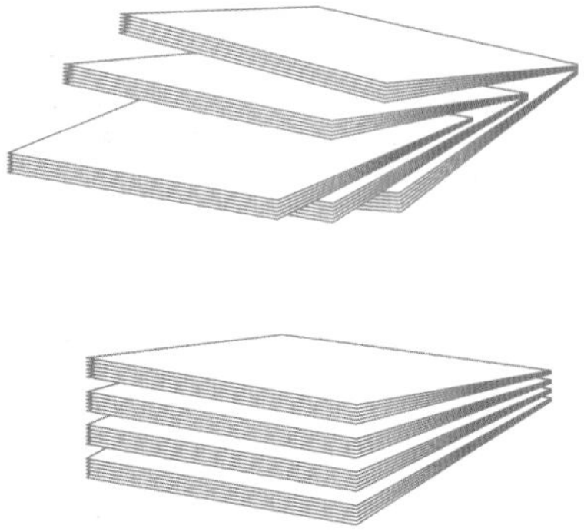

When the necessary signatures are folded and trimmed, they can be nested for saddle-stitching or gathered for perfect and case binding.

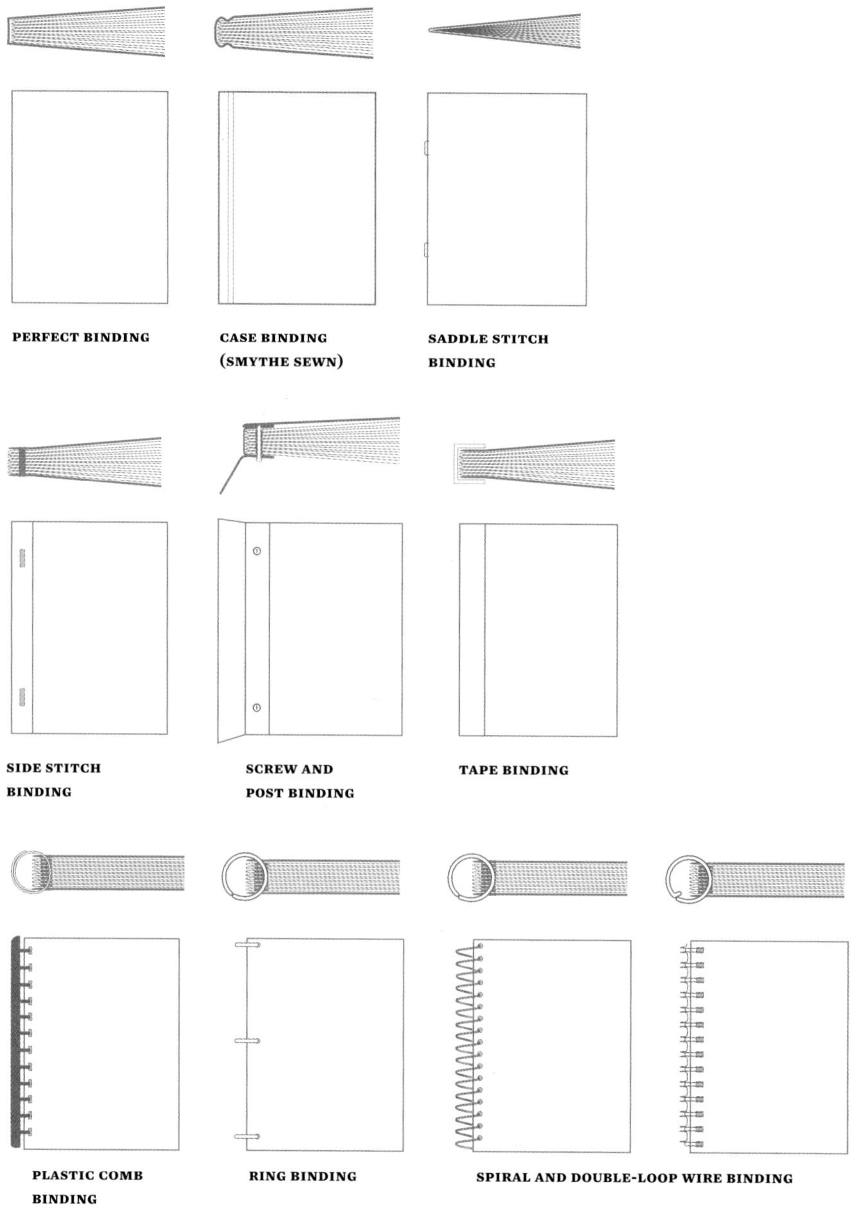

PERFECT BINDING

CASE BINDING (SMYTHE SEWN)

SADDLE STITCH BINDING

SIDE STITCH BINDING

SCREW AND POST BINDING

TAPE BINDING

PLASTIC COMB BINDING

RING BINDING

SPIRAL AND DOUBLE-LOOP WIRE BINDING

A SAMPLE OF AVAILABLE BINDING METHODS

THE OLYMPICS IS THE WEDDING OF SPORT AND ART / French fold binding, with the insides printed, adding an additional layer of interest (and cost(/ Thompson Design / RGB Studio: design, Rob Brearley / UK, 2006

BOOMBOX / Richard Mortimer in association with M.A.C. Cosmetics / Eat Sleep Work | Play / UK, 2007

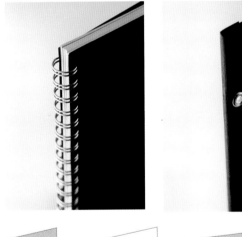

Left to right **DETAILS OF DIFFERENT BINDING METHODS** / Double-loop wire binding, side grommet binding, perfect binding with glued covers, case binding (Smythe-sewn)

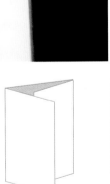

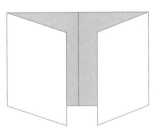

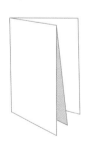

FOUR-PAGE SIMPLE FOLD

SIX-PAGE ACCORDION FOLD

SIX-PAGE BARREL OR ROLL FOLD

EIGHT-PAGE GATEFOLD

EIGHT-PAGE FRENCH FOLD/ SIXTEEN-PAGE SIGNATURE

EIGHT-PAGE PARALLEL FOLD

For pieces that are folded, imposition is also necessary, although in a less complicated manner than binding. However, the imposition varies greatly among the numerous folding methods. With a large sheet that folds down to a small size, the twists and turns can be confusing.

Varnishes

Applied as a protective measure to keep the ink from rubbing off, as an aesthetic finish to bring attention to specific design elements, or as a combination of both tasks, varnish comes in a variety of finishes and can be applied in several ways. Glossy, satin, dull, and matte are common offerings applied either in line as an additional ink when the job is going through the press or in a second pass through the press. Varnish can be applied as a flood, covering the entire sheet, or as spot, hitting only a few areas of the design. For increased protection and sheen there are ultraviolet varnishes, where a plastic coating is applied and then dried using ultraviolet light, and film laminates in thicknesses from 0.001 to 0.010″ that allow the end-user to, if desired, submerge the final product in water without damage.

RICHARD MORAN PHOTOGRAPHY IDENTITY / RGB Studio: design, Rob Brearley / UK, 2008

UN.TITLED BUSINESS CARD / Un.titled / UK, 2008

Emboss / Deboss

Formed using two matching molds, a male and a female (snicker if you must), called a *die*, embossing and debossing create raised and suppressed images respectively that add texture and dimensionality to an otherwise flat surface. Impressions can be as thick as 1/8″ and can contain multiple levels for a layered effect. A common method of embossing/debossing, referred to as *blind embossing*, is to create the texture without adding ink; this is done in part because it looks great but also because registering a die with pre-printed design is difficult and often yields poor results. As embossing/debossing is a relatively costly technique, an alternative is to use letterpress and ask for a deep impression.

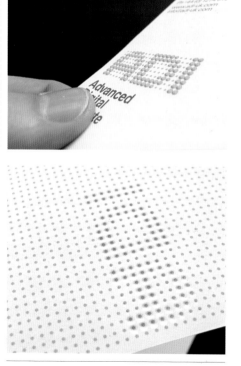

ADVANCED DIGITAL INSTITUTE IDENTITY / RGB Studio: design, Rob Brearley / UK, 2006

CHEK GROUP IDENTITY / Hyperakt: creative direction, Deroy Peraza; design, Deroy Peraza, Matthew Anderson / USA, 2008

DYSON EMPLOYEE BRAND BOOK / Thirteen / UK, 2005

Die-Cutting

Just like a cookie-cutter, with equally delicious results, die-cutting can give a unique contour such as rounded corners, angled edges, or tabs, or it can punch out specific shapes within the edges of a piece. Thin metal strips are bent and molded in the desired shape and pressed in place onto a wooden block, creating a die on which paper is pressed for cutting. If the press is gentle enough, labels can be kiss die-cut so the backing remains intact. Dies are also used for creating perforations and for scoring; sometimes all three functions are performed at the same time on the same die. Because dies are costly to make, it is canny to ask printers if they have existing dies from previous jobs that can be recycled. Some printers keep a stock of common dies for items like pocket folders.

SALT RESTAURANT BUSINESS CARD / Flux Labs / USA, 2003

PUB DEPARTMENT STORE RELAUNCH PARTY INVITATION / 25ah / Sweden, 2007

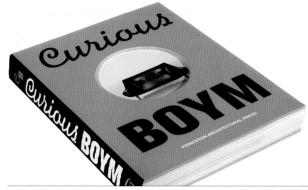

CURIOUS BOYM: DESIGN WORKS, Constantin Boym, Peter Hall, Steven Skov Holt / Die-cut from cover doubled as a coaster and invitation to the book party / Princeton Architectural Press / KarlssonWilker, Inc. / USA, 2002

Laser-Cutting

Because die-cutting is done by hand and re-quires bending strips of metal that have finite malleability, the intricacy and detail of a design is limited. Laser-cutting, however, provides exponential freedom in the kind of artwork that can be, literally, burned away from paper surfaces to create complex and highly detailed designs with more holes than a colander. Work-ing from a digital file, the laser cuts through the paper; it can either vaporize the material or cut the contour of a shape and air-scoop the remaining knocked-out material. If there is one drawback to laser-cutting, it is that it leaves a burn mark around the edges where it cuts, but this is nothing a dark paper stock can't fix while vast improvements are being made on this issue.

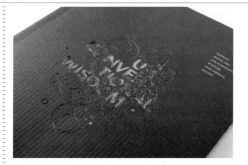

NEENAH PAPER, INC. *UNCONVENTIONAL WISDOM* **2006 ANNUAL REPORT** / Addison / USA, 2007

ACADEMY FOR EDUCATIONAL DEVELOPMENT *DESIGN IGNITES CHANGE* **POSTER** / Marian Bantjes / Canada, 2008

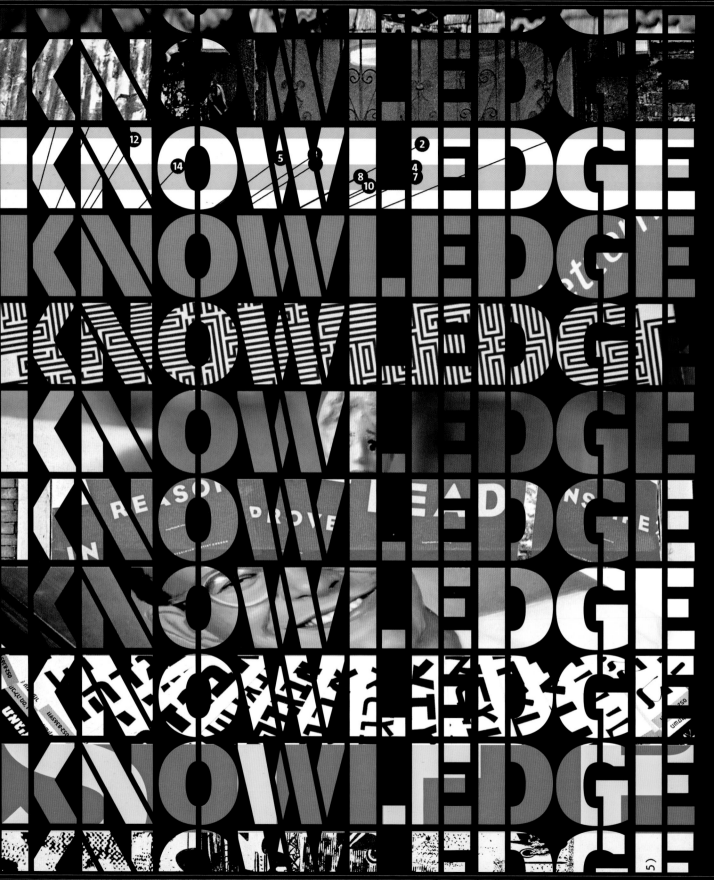

Imperative as it is to stay abreast of world news, cognizant of other disciplines, and interested in a variety of topics, delving fully into the world of graphic design is essential. A sustained interest in the trade publications, books, blogs, and exhibits that catalog and trace the evolution of graphic design helps broaden one's understanding of how it is practiced, talked about, and showcased. As a whole, the knowledge found in printed publications, online resources, cultural organizations, and educational institutions forms a snapshot of the vast and varied practice of graphic design that helps cement its status as a legitimate profession with a deep history and an extensive reach into every imaginable field in business, culture, commerce, and politics.

Neue Grafik
New Graphic Design
Graphisme actuel

Internationale Zeitschrift für Grafik und verwandte Gebiete
Erscheint in deutscher, englischer und französischer Sprache

International Review of graphic design and related subjects
Issued in German, English and French language

Revue internationale pour le graph et domaines annexes
Parution en langue allemande, anglaise et française

Ausgabe September 1958

Issue for September 1958

Fascicule septembre 1958

Inhalt

Einführung
Der Einfluß der modernen Kunst auf die zeitgenössische Grafik
Industrie-Grafik
Foto-Experimente für die Grafik

Die besten neuzeitlich gestalteten Schweizer Plakate 1931-1957
Experiment Ulm und die Ausbildung des Grafikers
«Die unbekannte Gegenwart.» Eine thematische Schau des Warenhauses Globus, Zürich

Chronik
Buchbesprechungen
Hinweise
Pro domo

Einzelnummer Fr. 15.–

Contents

Introduction
The Influence of Modern Art on Contemporary Graphic Design
Industrial Design
Experimental Photography in Graphic Design
The best recently designed Swiss Posters 1931-1957
The Ulm Experiment and the Training of the Graphic Designer
"The Unknown Present." An Exhibition with a special theme for the Globus store, Zurich

Miscellaneous
Book Reviews
Memoranda
Pro domo

Single number Fr. 15.–

Table des matières

Introduction
L'influence de l'art moderne sur la phique contemporaine
Graphique industrielle
Photo expérimentale pour la graphi

Les meilleures affiches suisses actuelles 1931-1957
L'expérience d'Ulm et la formation graphiste
« L'actualité inconnue.» Exposition thématique des Grands Magasins Globus, Zurich

Chronique
Bibliographie
Indications
Pro domo

Le numéro Fr. 15.–

. Lohse SWB/VSG, Zürich

uburg SWB/VSG, Zürich

uburg SWB/VSG, Zürich

neidegger SWB, Zürich

SWB, Zürich

ber und Redaktion
nd Managing Editors
t rédaction

rlag
Publishing

Richard P. Lohse SWB/VSG, Zürich
J. Müller-Brockmann SWB/VSG, Zürich
Hans Neuburg SWB/VSG, Zürich
Carlo L. Vivarelli SWB/VSG, Zürich

Verlag Otto Walter AG, Olten

KNOWLEDGE

On Paper

94

Journals and Magazines

Despite the rise of up-to-the-minute, largely free content sprouting continuously online since early 2000, design journals and magazines have maintained their relevance even when the trend was to pronounce their imminent death. Since the mid-twentieth century, design publications have maintained graphic designers informed, engaged, and challenged through an evolving stream of content that covers the most relevant practices and representatives in graphic design through the deft guidance of their editors and cadre of willing writers.

106

Books

Love them or hate them, graphic design books provide comprehensive insight into the myriad subjects they cover, from exhaustive monographs to helpful how-to manuals to inspirational compendiums to educational resources to any number of other specialty topics. Proudly displayed on designers' bookshelves around the world, graphic design books form a large library that chronicles the history and practice of the profession—lovingly designed, to boot. The selections here are only indicative of the numerous books found in each category; a visit to the bookstore is highly encouraged to discover the rest.

Detail of *NEUE GRAFIK*, ISSUE 1 / Carlo L. Vivarelli / Switzerland, 1958–1960 / From the collection of Joe Kraal

Print

As the earliest American design publication, first published in 1940, *Print* was originally a technical journal for professionals in the printing and publishing industries, and it slowly grew into a general graphic design magazine. Its focus and ambition changed dramatically when Martin Fox, an aspiring playwright and hesitant design aficionado, became editor in 1963. Under Fox's editorship, *Print* chronicled the burgeoning field of graphic design as it came of age in the 1960s and 1970s, publishing with equal fervor American designers and their European counterparts while establishing a precedent for design criticism with its introduction of the column "A Cold Eye" in the late 1980s. After Fox's 40-year stay, Joyce Rutter Kaye took the helm of the magazine in 2003, where she has continued the international bent of the magazine. She also delved into touchier subjects—like sex, with a full issue devoted to the subject in 2004, the best-selling issue of that year, of course. *Print* is a four-time winner (1994, 2002, 2005, and 2008) and ten-time nominee in the General Excellence category of the Ellie Awards, presented by the American Society of Magazine Editors.

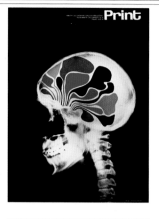
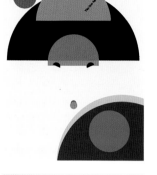

PRINT MAGAZINE / 1940–2008

Graphis

Under the selective direction of its founding editor and designer, Walter Herdeg, *Graphis* quickly established itself as a commanding arbiter of taste after its first issue was published in 1944. Based in Zurich, Herdeg compiled issues with exhaustive profiles of designers and illustrators from around the world, establishing a truly international publication that exposed work seldom seen by professionals in their respective continents. Beyond its periodic publication, *Graphis* has published numerous annuals—the first in 1952, becoming one of the most revered compendia of work—as well as individual volumes devoted to a single discipline or topic. In 1986, seasoned graphic designer B. Martin Pedersen acquired *Graphis* from Herdeg and moved its headquarters to New York. In the two decades since, Pedersen has maintained the thoroughness of the magazine and produced luscious annuals and compendia that continue to flank the walls of designers' libraries around the world.

GRAPHIS MAGAZINE / USA

Typographica

In contrast to the seemingly narrow range of topics its name implies, the British publication *Typographica* was one of the most eclectic design publications of its time. It blended serious observations about the practice of typography and graphic design in modernism and the New Typography with photographic essays and adventurous assessments and collections of found typography, graphic ephemera, and other varied creative outlets that interested its founder, editor and designer Herbert Spencer. In 1949, at the young age of 25 and with publishing and printing support from Lund Humphries and its chairman, Peter Gregory, Spencer published the first issue of *Typographica*. He continued to do so for 18 years and 32 issues, which were divided in two groups, the Old Series and the New Series, each one starting at number one. The design of the magazine itself—typically laden with different papers and tactile production methods—reflected Spencer's paradoxical interests, adding to the allure of the publication. *Typographica* remains an object of obsession today: The starting price for an auction of a collection of issues 1–16 on eBay is US$4,000.

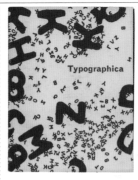

NEW SERIES, NO. 1 / UK, 1960

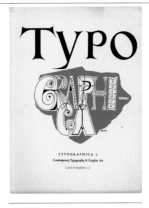

OLD SERIES, NO. 2 / UK, 1950

OLD SERIES, NO. 3 / UK, 1950

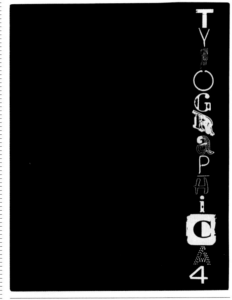

NEW SERIES, NO. 4 / UK, 1961

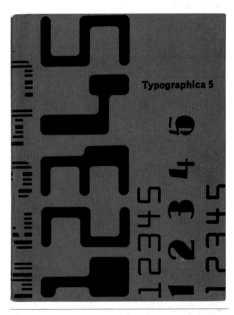

NEW SERIES, NO. 5 / UK, 1962

NEW SERIES, NO. 7 / UK, 1963

OLD SERIES, NO. 13 / UK, 1957

OLD SERIES, NO. 14 / UK, 1958

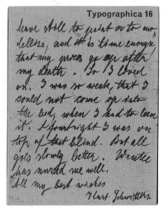

NEW SERIES, NO. 16 / UK, 1967

RECOMMENDED READING › 390

Size proportions across issues respected

Communication Arts

Beckoning from within the white covers of *Communication Arts* since 1959, when it was launched by Richard Coyne and his partner, Bob Blanchard (it garnered an initial circulation of 5,000 in its first six months and now has an audited paid circulation over 63,000), is a consistent torrent of work produced in the fields of graphic design, advertising, photography, and illustration presented in a flatteringly austere format that continually puts the work front and center. Richard Coyne's wife, Jean Coyne, later joined the magazine full-time, and, in 1986, their son Patrick Coyne joined the staff; both remain as editors of the magazine and continue the legacy of Richard Coyne, who passed away in 1990. *Communication Arts* is perhaps best known for its brutally competitive and widely browsed design annuals. The first annual, in 1960, received 5,000 entries; today it receives more than 8,000 entries and requires three days and nine judges to narrow the list down to fewer than 200 winners. Besides bragging rights, the winners look great against white.

PREMIER ISSUE / design, Lloyd Price / USA, August 1959

THE ART ANNUAL / design, Jean Coyne / USA, 1976

Design, Jean Coyne; photography, William Arbogast / USA, 1967

Design, Richard Coyne; photography, William Arbogast / USA, 1968

Design, Dugald Sterner; photography, William Arbogast / USA, 1972

Illustration, James Marsh / USA, May/June 1991

DESIGN ANNUAL / design, Patrick Coyne / USA, November 2003

COMMUNICATION ARTS MAGAZINE / USA

Industrial Design (I.D.)

In 1954, publisher Charles Whitney launched *Industrial Design* to cover its namesake growing field, with Jane Fisk and Deborah Allen, staff members from another Whitney publication, *Interiors*, acting as editors. The debut featured some of the last art direction and design by Alvin Lustig › 144, who succumbed to diabetes the following year. Over its existence, the magazine has experienced multiple changes, with different owners taking responsibility as well as different editors taking the magazine in varied directions—notable among them Ralph Caplan › 238 in the 1960s, Steven Holt and Chee Pearlman in the 1990s, and, most recently, Julie Lasky. The very name of the publication was changed—to *International Design* in 1988—to reflect the broadening interest and coverage of the magazine. Through it all, *I.D.* has surfaced as a thoughtful publication covering the numerous fields and professionals that fall under the label of design, always through a global scope. With their annual "I.D. 40" special issue, the magazine brings together some of the most influential designers in diverse industries and locations, demonstrating the richness and variety of design.

I.D. MAGAZINE, ISSUES 1–3 / Alvin Lustig / USA, 1954

I.D. MAGAZINE / USA, 1993–2007

Neue Grafik

Officially and plainly titled, in its English translation, as *New Graphic Design: International Review of Graphic Design and Related Subjects* Issued in German, English, and French language, *Neue Grafik* was first published in 1958 by its Zurich-based editors and active proponents of the International Typographic Style, Richard Paul Lohse, Josef Müller-Brockmann › 152, Hans Neuburg, and Carlo L. Vivarelli. The latter designed the iconic four-column cover as well as the page layout, all set in Akzidenz Grotesk › 369, which came to represent the strict philosophy of Swiss design. Through its 18 issues in nearly seven years of publication, *Neue Grafik* published the work and writing of its editors, usually signed collectively as "LMNV," along with that of other Swiss designers, including Max Bill and Emil Ruder. In the twenty-first century, more than 50 years since it was first published, the covers of *Neue Grafik* remain bastions of a singular approach to design.

NEUE GRAFIK, **ISSUES 1–6** / Carlo L. Vivarelli / Switzerland, 1958–1960 / **From the collection of Joe Kraal**

U&lc

At the forefront of phototypesetting was the International Typeface Corporation (ITC) › 220, started by Herb Lubalin › 167, Aaron Burns, and Ed Rondthaler in 1970, an ever-growing collection of expressive typeface designs aimed squarely at advertising agencies and the burgeoning graphic design profession. To promote its typefaces, instead of simply advertising in trade publications or mailing type samplers, ITC introduced in 1973 *U&lc* (*Upper & lowercase*), a free tabloid magazine printed in one color, on newsprint, designed exclusively with ITC typefaces, and content developed solely for this quarterly publication. In its first eight years and until his death in 1981, Lubalin edited and designed the magazine, offering dramatic and energetic layouts that showcased ITC's products. Edward Gottschall, the editorial successor, maintained this formula until 1990. With Margaret Richardson as editor, each issue was guest-designed by lucky designers given a free hand.

The amalgam of exuberant design and relevant content that combined work from designers, illustrators, and typographers with playful collections of ephemera and typographic experiments made *U&lc* one of the most widely circulated and ogled design publications in the 1980s and 1990s. At its peak, the magazine's circulation reached 200,000, and it even came to include advertising from related businesses very much aware of its reach and influence.

In the mid-1990s, things started to change as the typeface industry was revolutionized by digital production and distribution—a new environment that ITC quickly embraced. With new editor John D. Berry, ITC launched *U&lc Online* in 1998, a companion to the magazine that was about to undergo a radical transformation. Celebrating its twenty-fifth anniversary, the first issue of 1998 was redesigned as a glossy and measly (by comparison) letter-sized magazine, and the following issue introduced a new logo and layout designed by Mark van Bronkhorst that abruptly distanced itself from its original incarnation. Needless to say, the change was not welcome. In the fall of 1999, *U&lc* published its last issue. Today, designers hold on to the brittleness of its newsprint heyday.

VOL. 3, NO. 2 / USA, July 1976

VOL. 5, NO. 3 / USA, September 1978

VOL. 5, NO. 4 / USA, December 1978

VOL. 7, NO. 4 / USA, December 1980

U&LC: THE INTERNATIONAL JOURNAL OF TYPOGRAPHICS / International Typeface Corporation / design, Herb Lubalin

U&LC: THE INTERNATIONAL JOURNAL OF GRAPHIC DESIGN AND DIGITAL MEDIA / International Typeface Corporation / design, Mark van Bronkhorst

VOL. 25, NO. 1 / USA, Summer 1998

VOL. 25, NO. 2 / USA, Fall 1998

VOL. 25, NO. 3 / USA, Winter 1998

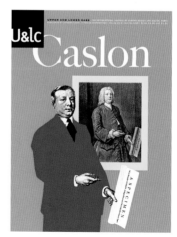

RECOMMENDED READING › 390

Baseline

First published in London in 1979 by TSI (Typographic Systems International Ltd.), a member of the Letraset Group of Companies, and founded by Mike Daines, *Baseline*—produced irregularly, only when material and time were available—served initially as a vehicle to promote new typeface designs. After years of inconsistent yet fulfilling publication and Letraset's increasing business problems, Daines and Hans Dieter Reichert, who was appointed art director in 1993, purchased the magazine from Letraset in 1995. Since then, Bradbourne Publishing Limited, formed by Daines and Reichert, has published *Baseline* independently. *Baseline* has been financed, edited, designed, and produced through Reichert's London-based design firm, HDR Visual Communication, three times a year amid the rest of their client work. In January 2007, Daines resigned from *Baseline* and Bradbourne Publishing Ltd. Since spring of that year, HDR Visual Communication is solely responsible for the content and the design and production of the magazine.

BASELINE MAGAZINE LOGOS / 1993–2007, 2007–present

BASELINE MAGAZINE ISSUE 53 / Autumn 2007

BASELINE ISSUES

HDR Visual Communication / UK

Creative Review

Creative Review was launched as a quarterly in London in 1980. Its owner, Centaur, was already publishing *Marketing Week* and saw an opportunity for a magazine aimed at the growing community of creative professionals. *Creative Review* soon developed into a monthly, its readership drawn chiefly from the graphic design and advertising industries and supplemented by crafts such as photography, illustration, and commercials production. As these fields have grown and diversified, so has the magazine's scope—in the hands of Patrick Burgoyne, editor since 1999, and, previously, Lewis Blackwell ›239, who held the position for ten years—so it now encompasses all forms of visual communication, whether commercially produced or self-initiated. Its geographical reach has also widened, with subscribers in over 80 countries and, through the *CR Blog*, readers in 190 countries and counting. Since 1990, *Creative Review* has supported the growth of young designers with their annual celebration of "Creative Futures": designers under the age of 28 who will one day take your clients and jobs.

Art direction, Gary Cook; design, Substance / August 1983

Art direction, Gary Cook; design, Substance / January 1995

Art direction, Nathan Gale; photography, Jenny van Sommers / March 2002

Art direction, Paul Pensom; photography, Andy Barter / March 2002

Art direction, Paul Pensom; design, Karlsson Wilker / June 2008

CREATIVE REVIEW MAGAZINE / UK / Photos: PSC Photography

Emigre

The first and subsequent handful of issues of *Emigre* in 1984 were not the cathartic design publication it would eventually become in the hands of its founder, editor, and designer, Rudy VanderLans. It was first conceived—by VanderLans, with fellow Dutch natives and California residents Marc Susan and Menno Meyjes—as a publication to showcase the work of photographers, writers, designers, and artists who live, or had lived, outside their countries of origin: émigrés. Three issues in, Meyjes and Susan pursued their own interests—the former wrote *Indiana Jones and the Last Crusade*—and VanderLans found himself with a magazine all his own that he could mold as desired. It was the right time and place for a groundbreaking publication. Just as the Macintosh was introduced and the majority of designers shied away from its potential, *Emigre* exploited its early quirks and limitations to produce a new design language that was out of the ordinary.

Replacing the typewriter bodies of text used in the first two issues of *Emigre* were coarse, bitmap digital typefaces created by Zuzana Licko › 225, VanderLans' wife, setting a precedent for the magazine to be designed exclusively in the dozens of typefaces that Emigre Fonts › 224—the duo's digital type foundry—would develop over the next three decades. As *Emigre* gained notoriety for its design and the work it showcased—like a full issue in 1988 devoted to the album covers designed by Vaughan Oliver for London-based music label 4AD › 301—it began its deep and tumultuous affiliation with the design industry. It aligned itself, perhaps unconsciously, with a fledgling cadre of students, teachers, writers, and practitioners who consistently challenged, through writing and practice, the existing tenets of graphic design, at the same time the profession was polarized by the Macintosh and experienced momentous shifts.

The first collaboration between *Emigre* and Cranbrook Academy of Art › 130 was in 1988, with issue 10 being fully edited, designed, and produced by the students—among them future collaborators like Ed Fella › 185, Andrew Blauvelt, Allen Hori, and Jeffery Keedy. Over the magazine's lifespan, *Emigre* and Cranbrook sinuously came together regularly, as other members like Katherine McCoy › 185, Lorraine Wild, Laurie Haycock Makela, P. Scott Makela, and Elliot Earls contributed to the canon of design with their writing, typeface designs, or both. As Wild, Keedy, and Fella became teachers at CalArts › 131, that institution also became part of the unofficial fold. What these institutions and *Emigre* had in common—in retrospect, a sense of

EMIGRE MAGAZINE / Emigre design, Rudy VanderLans / USA

giddy exploration—manifested on the surface as a visually wild aesthetic that made many of their contemporaries uncomfortable. In the pages of *Print* › 94 in 1992, Massimo Vignelli › 160 described *Emigre* as "a national calamity" and "an aberration of culture," while Steven Heller › 238 deemed it nothing more than a "blip in the continuum" in the 1993 essay "Cult of the Ugly" in *Eye* › 103. Even David Carson › 186 had an ongoing spat with the magazine. Despite the unpleasantness, accompanied by the ongoing challenge of self-publishing a magazine, VanderLans's mettle carried *Emigre* as it continually evolved.

Unlike that seen in other design magazines, VanderLans' editing approach allowed for extensive interviews, exhaustive profiles, reprints of older texts, and the publication of lengthy essays packaged in designs that changed completely from issue to issue, all while parading the growing collection of exclusive typefaces—sometimes to an extreme, like 1991's issue 19, set solely in Barry Deck's Template Gothic › 382. Until 1997 and issue 41, *Emigre* was produced as a tabloid, making it expensive to print and ship, even at small quantities of 3,000 to 5,000. With issue 42, the magazine underwent one of its biggest transformations: It shrank to letter size, upped its circulation to 43,000, and was distributed free. The change was drastic, but so was the increased readership and attention *Emigre* received—including the legendary letters to the editor, titled "Dear *Emigre*," which ranged from brief, expletive-filled missives to essay-length submissions that ran unedited and generated heated back-and-forths between writers and readers. It continued in this form, publishing central writings and eclectic collections of material—from VanderLans' own photographs of the California desert to Experimental Jetset's pictographic ode to lost formats like cassette tapes—until 2001, when issue 60 was an audio CD, and so were the following three issues, with the exception of issue 62, which contained Earls' confounding *Catfish* DVD. In a final iteration, now with only 6,000 units, *Emigre* was co-published with Princeton Architectural Press, and focused completely on writing. The first in this pocket book format, issue 64, *Rant*, was an acknowledged provocation to challenge young designers and writers "to develop a critical attitude toward their own work and the design scene in general." It worked. Lengthy discussions on blogs like Speak Up › 113, representing the new generation, and retorts from young and previously unpublished designers and writers printed in the following issues of *Emigre* demonstrated there was indeed a fire to be lit. Despite this resurgence of engagement with design criticism and writing, *Emigre* ceased publication in 2005 with issue 69, boldly titled *The End*.

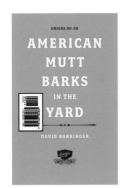

Size proportions across issues respected

HOW

Conceived as an offshoot of *Print* › 94 in 1985, *HOW* was originally billed as "The Magazine of Ideas and Technique in Graphic Design," and its primary focus was how-to articles. In 1989, when it was purchased by Cincinnati-based F + W Publications and Laurel Harper became editor, the magazine shifted to a more general focus on business and creativity.

Since then—and with a change of the editorial guard in 1998 to Bryn Mooth, who had been a staff member since 1990—*HOW* has established itself as a lively resource for business and career advice as well as some of the most energetic work from the United States. It has been able to extend that attitude and persona to the popular Design, Mind Your Own Business, and In-HOWse Designer conferences.

HOW **MAGAZINE** / cover art direction, Tricia Bateman / Photos: Hal Barkan

STEP inside design

With more than six years in its second incarnation as *STEP inside design*, it might be easy to forget that, from 1985, when it was first published, to 2002, it was called *Step-by-Step Graphics*, and its content was primarily a literal interpretation of its name, highlighting the skills and techniques of graphic design. Originally intended to serve designers looking to embrace desktop publishing and the possibilities of the computer, the scope of

content became less relevant as the industry matured, leading to changes in name, design, and editorial approach to cover the creativity behind the design and the professionals who make it happen. Overseeing this transition was Emily Potts, the magazine's editor from 1998 to 2006; she established a dynamic publication later headed by Tom Biederbeck. One of the magazine's most popular and unique issues was the "*STEP* 100 Design Annual," a selective compendium chosen from up to 3,000 entries. In 2009 *STEP* ceased publication.

STEP-BY-STEP GRAPHICS **MAGAZINE** / USA, 1990, 1999

STEP INSIDE DESIGN **MAGAZINE** / USA, 2002, 2008, 2008

@Issue

Around 1986, writer Delphine Hirasuna and Pentagram › 162 partner Kit Hinrichs attempted to find a publisher for a proposed magazine. They envisioned a bridge between designers and corporate clients, addressing the ever-present perception that neither party clearly understands what each other contributes to their intended collaboration. Not until 1994, when Hinrichs mentioned the idea to the new marketing manager of Potlatch papers, did they find someone to underwrite the project. The Corporate Design Foundation, founded in 1985, got involved as the official publisher of *@Issue: Journal of Business and Design*. Since 1995, with Hirasuna as editor and Hinrichs as creative director, *@Issue* has been publishing real-life case studies that bring to life the original concept with incisive interviews and overviews of designers and clients working together. Offered by subscription only, its circulation is a remarkable 100,000 as of its latest issue. With the success of the magazine, a spinoff conference was started in 2006, with designers and clients speaking jointly about specific projects and further cementing the relationship between business and design.

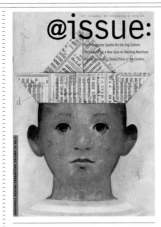

Illustration, Gerard DuBois / 2005

Photography, Gerald Bybee / 2001

Illustration, John Hersey / 1998

Photography, Stephen Smith / 2006

Illustration, Michael Schwab / 2002

@ISSUE MAGAZINE / Pentagram: Kit Hinrichs / USA

Eye

Through two decades of publishing, starting with its founding in 1990 by British writer and critic Rick Poynor › 237, *Eye* has established itself as one of the most diverse design publications. It continually delves deeply into the past, present, and future of graphic design with incisive, critical, and challenging writing from a multitude of writers around the world. In 1997, Dutch writer and editor Max Bruinsma › 237 took on the editorial responsibilities, and in 1999, music industry writer John Walters became the editor. Comparable in attitude to its writing, the design of the magazine has rarely settled for conventions, with a unique editorial design approach developed quite boldly between 1997 and 2005 by creative director Nick Bell and now extended by art director Simon Esterson. In 2008, Walters purchased the magazine from Haymarket Brand Media, the latest of four publishers and owners of the magazine, now self-publishing through Eye Magazine Ltd, a new company established with Esterson and business director Hannah Tyson.

EYE MAGAZINE / UK

Critique

"The charter of *Critique*," wrote Marty Neumeier in its inaugural Summer 1996 issue, "is simply this: to share insight of the craft's greatest practitioners, so that nothing is lost on the journey forward." For five years, Neumeier Design Team designed, edited, and financed a finely crafted design publication, offered quarterly, that kept pace with the immense changes the design profession faced in the late 1990s and into the 2000s—perhaps too closely. After 18 issues, *Critique* folded in 2001, due to financial reasons: the economic climate, the lack of subscribers, and the limited amount of paid advertising in the magazine. Despite its short run, *Critique* left an indelible mark in its readers, who mourn its absence.

CRITIQUE MAGAZINE / Published by Marty Neumeier / USA, 1996–2001

Dot Dot Dot

As an independent magazine, published and financed by its two Amsterdam-based founding editors, Stuart Bailey and Peter Bilak, *Dot Dot Dot* has remarkably persevered since 2000 with a publication that feels completely different from issue to issue—and from anything else on the market—with content that straddles every fine (and not so fine) line between art, design, architecture, music, and literature. With a proudly loose editorial and aesthetic approach that serves the magazine's title, *Dot Dot Dot* is, as noted in the pilot issue, "a magazine in flux" and "ready to adjust itself to content." Perhaps what makes this publication so remarkable is that it is only one project among many the editors undertake, allowing a fluctuation of interests without being occupied with *Dot Dot Dot* full time. Bilak, based in The Hague, Netherlands, is a typeface designer with the large family Fedra to his credit, while Bailey, who moved to New York in 2006, operates Dexter Sinister, a "Just-In-Time Workshop and Occasional Bookstore" with designer and writer David Reinfurt. Like their magazine, their careers are open-ended.

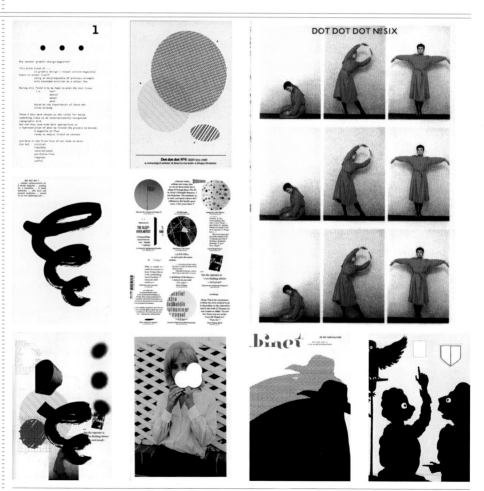

DOT DOT DOT MAGAZINE / USA, 2000–2008

AIGA Journal of Graphic Design

Between the early 1920s and World War II, the American Institute of Graphic Arts (AIGA), founded in 1914, published a newsletter (called *News-Letter*) that resurfaced in 1947 as the *A.I.G.A. Journal*. Over the next six decades the journal was published regularly, adapting to different editors, volunteers, staff, and board members and changing its name to *Journal of AIGA* in 1965 and then to *AIGA Journal of Graphic Design* in 1982. The journal had its greatest impact during the late 1980s and the 1990s. Steven Heller ›238, its editor since 1985, gathered insightful and provocative essays from practitioners around the industry chronicling the profession's ongoing evolution. In this form, the journal's last issue was published in 2000. The following year, a followup effort, *Trace: AIGA Journal of Design*, was published for four issues, and in 2004 the journal took its latest form as VOICE: AIGA Journal of Design ›113, an online publication edited by Heller and enhanced by reader comments.

AIGA JOURNAL 1, NO. 1 / masthead illustration, Reynard Biemiller / USA, June 1947

AIGA JOURNAL 2, NO. 1 / decorative initials, Mr. Valenti Angelo / USA, May 1949

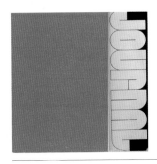

JOURNAL OF THE AMERICAN INSTITUTE OF GRAPHIC ARTS, NO. 19 / design, Antupit & Others / USA, 1971

AIGA JOURNAL OF GRAPHIC DESIGN 11, NO. 1 / illustration, Mirko Ilic / USA, 1993

JOURNAL OF GRAPHIC DESIGN, CULT AND CULTURE ISSUE: POP GOES THE CULTURE 17, NO. 2 / writing, Ken Garland / USA, 1999

IDEA

Founded by Kikumatsu Ogawa in 1912, the publishing house of Seibundo Shinkosha created publications on themes as diverse as popular science and gardening. One of its magazines was *Koukoku to Chinretsu* (*Advertising and Display*), first published in 1926 and covering the world of advertising in Japan, ceasing publication in 1941 due to World War II. A successor came in 1953—*IDEA*, headed by editor-in-chief Takashi Miyayama and art director Hiroshi Ohchi—with an editorial policy to bridge Japan and the world in the context of modern graphic design. Miyayama and Ohchi established *IDEA*'s exhaustive and authoritative display of work, with whole issues devoted to single designers from around the world. The two founders left in 1964 and 1974 respectively. *IDEA* remains active today under the leadership of Kiyonori Muroga and Toshiaki Koga.

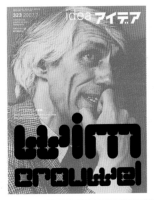
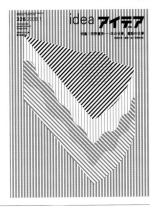

IDEA MAGAZINE IN RECENT YEARS / Japan

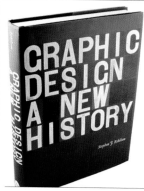

A HISTORY OF GRAPHIC DESIGN, By Philip B. Meggs / John Wiley & Sons, 1983 (1st ed.), 1992 (2nd ed.), 1998 (3rd ed.), 2005 (4th ed.)

Now that it is in its fourth edition (2005), with translations into Chinese, Hebrew, Japanese, Korean, and Spanish, it's safe to say that Philip B. Meggs' detailed and exhaustive narrative of graphic design is perhaps the most influential tract on the impressively broad history of the profession and the numerous social, cultural, political, and economical shifts that have contributed to its development since humans first drew a horse on a cave's wall. While it's not a book to sit with next to a fireplace on a rainy weekend, Meggs should be found on the bookshelf of every designer for continued reference.

GRAPHIC DESIGN: A CONCISE HISTORY, By Richard Hollis / Thames & Hudson, 1994 (1st ed.), 2001 (2nd ed.)

Written as a narrative, where characters intertwine and one event leads to the other, Richard Hollis' take on design history is brisk and detailed. As its title suggests, the scope is smaller than that of *A History of Graphic Design*. Hollis begins in the late nineteenth century, and as the decades and book progress, he moves swiftly between countries to establish the areas of greatest influence at any given time. The book is peppered with small, mostly black and white illustrations that aid the story and pique the taste of readers for further research.

GRAPHIC DESIGN: A NEW HISTORY, By Stephen J. Eskilson / Yale University Press, 2007

Also beginning at the end of the nineteenth century is the lusciously illustrated book by Stephen J. Eskilson, the latest entry in the historical survey category—a fact that allows the author to weave the developments of the late 1990s and the beginning of the twenty-first century more organically than his predecessors, who made amendments with each edition. Eskilson's book came under heavy criticism for factual errors—none that cannot be easily and understandably corrected in a second edition—and received subjective complaints about its approach and selection criteria, but its positive value to an increasingly authoritative design history is undeniable.

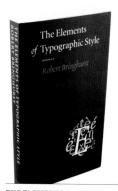

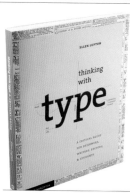

THE ELEMENTS OF TYPOGRAPHIC STYLE, By Robert Bringhurst / Hartley and Marks Publishers, 1992 (1st ed.), 1996 (2nd ed.), 2002 (3rd ed.)

The subjective question of what constitutes good typography has always concerned designers, and as a subjective point of discussion it's best to start with an objective question: What constitutes *proper* typography? Canadian typographer, book designer, and poet Robert Bringhurst provides a passionate and elucidating rulebook with this industry-anointed bible, establishing an etiquette for the use of typography. With florid language and a vast knowledge of historical material, tying together digital typography with its origins, Bringhurst explains everything from how to space dashes to the placement of quotation marks. Typography can be good or bad, but it should always be proper.

TWENTIETH-CENTURY TYPE, By Lewis Blackwell / Rizzoli, 1992 (1st ed.); Gingko Press, 1999 (remix ed.), Laurence King Publishing, 1998 (2nd ed.); Yale University Press, 2004 (3rd ed.)

The history and development of graphic design is intimately tied to the evolution of typography, and Lewis Blackwell engagingly traces this symbiosis. Decade by decade, Blackwell presents the defining typefaces, their designers, and their implications for and repercussions in the aesthetics of visual communication. A concise and clear glossary, classification system, and anatomy analysis complement the rest of the content.

THINKING WITH TYPE, By Ellen Lupton / Princeton Architectural Press, 2004

If one does not know typography (and all the term implies), Ellen Lupton's book is an ideal place to start learning. Divided into three chapters—"Letter," "Text," and "Grid"—this book gives readers the tools to understand what typefaces are, how they function, and how they operate in context. Lupton offers clear diagrams, enticing examples from print and interactive design, and accessible language. Deployed throughout the book are "Type Crimes" that gleefully illustrate common pitfalls in typography; the appendix of "helpful hints" and "dire warnings" alone is worth the price of the book.

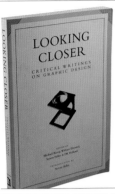 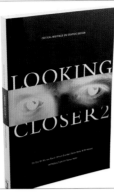   

LOOKING CLOSER: CRITICAL WRITINGS ON GRAPHIC DESIGN 1–5, Edited by Michael Bierut (1–5), William Drenttel (1–2, 4–5), Jessica Helfand (3), Steven Heller (1–5), DK Holland (1–2), and Rick Poynor (3) / Allworth Press, 1994 (1), 1997 (2), 1999 (3), 2002 (4), 2007 (5)

A book about graphic design with a resounding zero number of images and a lot (*a lot*) of text sounds far-fetched, but that was the scope for the first *Looking Closer* in 1994, an anthology of design writing and criticism that had been slowly and vehemently emerging over the years in trade magazines and journals. Now with five volumes and comprising 254 essays by 165 writers, *Looking Closer* presents a clear sampling of the kind of criticism art and architecture have enjoyed for a long time, arguably cementing their importance—and now it's graphic design's turn.

  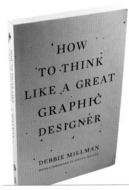

WHAT IS A DESIGNER? THINGS, PLACES, MESSAGES, By Norman Potter / Studio Vista, 1969 (1st ed.); Hyphen Press, 1980 (2nd ed.), 1989 (3rd ed.), 2002 (4th ed.)

It may seem surprising that some of the soundest advice and most grounded descriptions of what a designer is and does originated in the late 1960s with a cabinetmaker. Of course, that is not to belittle Norman Potter's professional underpinnings or to gloss over his success as a teacher and writer but rather to emphasize that the fields of architecture, graphic, interior, and product design, and, yes, even cabinetmaking share a set of ethical, practical, and intellectual principles that govern its practitioners—all sternly and vividly presented in this book.

HOW TO BE A GRAPHIC DESIGNER WITHOUT LOSING YOUR SOUL, By Adrian Shaughnessy / Princeton Architectural Press, 2005

Although there is no bullet list on how to hold on to the proverbial designer soul, Adrian Shaughnessy, drawing from two decades of running his own design firm, exposes all the less glamorous aspects of becoming a graphic designer, and staying one. Without sugarcoating, Shaughnessy writes about going on interviews, delving into a freelance career, setting up a new studio, running said studio, acquiring clients, and the wobbly act of self-promotion. Supported by interviews with a cadre of international designers, this book may be as significant as a bachelor's degree in the education of graphic designers.

HOW TO THINK LIKE A GREAT GRAPHIC DESIGNER, By Debbie Millman / Allworth Press, 2007

This isn't really a how-to book, as the title would have you think—and, perhaps, using almost all of the same words in a different order, *How Great Graphic Designers Like to Think* would be a better one. Inside, Debbie Millman offers rare insight into the lives, minds, fears, dreams, and processes of some of the profession's most successful practitioners. She interviews her subjects with an empathy that extracts answers about the realities of being a graphic designer, moving beyond their achievements or aesthetics to reveal the people behind the work.

DESIGN DICTIONARY, Edited by Michael Erlhoff, Timothy Marshall / Birkhäuser, 2008

As its name implies and as its subtitle, *Perspectives on Design Terminology*, elaborates, the *Design Dictionary* is a comprehensive tome covering more than 250 definitions extracted from the world of design, each written by one of 110 contributors from around the globe. Relentless, the book covers extremely specific terms like *flyer*, *gimmick*, and *intellectual property* as well as boundlessly broad subjects like *design process*, *look and feel*, and *responsibility*. Excluding arrows and little decorative birds, the book is a dense 472 pages' worth of definitions. Sometimes a thousands words *is* worth more than an image.

DESIGN WRITING RESEARCH, By Ellen Lupton, Abbott Miller / Kiosk, 1996; Phaidon 1999

Named for the eponymous firm established by Ellen Lupton and Abbott Miller in 1985, *Design Writing Research* is a collection of essays on a head-spinning range of topics like deconstruction, iconography, Andy Warhol, and stock photography—lucidly written and designed. It also includes an unconventional timeline of design history. In addition to its enthusiastic content, the book demonstrates the effectiveness of the designer-as-author model, where both text and layout benefit from a parallel and combined point of view.

NO MORE RULES: GRAPHIC DESIGN AND POSTMODERNISM, By Rick Poynor / Laurence King Publishing, Yale University Press, 2003

As one of the most recent *isms* in graphic design history, postmodernism lacks the clarity of a conventional and agreed-upon definition that other *isms* now enjoy. With *No More Rules*, Rick Poynor wades through the deconstructed and the theorized to find the common, or perhaps uncommon, thread that ties the tumultuous years of the mid-1980s and mid-1990s. But rather than taking a chronological view of the subject, Poynor addresses it by looking at its defining characteristics: deconstruction, appropriation, technology, authorship, and opposition. Illustrated with some of the most polarizing work of the period, *No More Rules* is a critical snapshot of this time.

MARKS OF EXCELLENCE, By Per Mollerup / Phaidon, 1997

The memorable simplicity of most logos belies the complexity of their creation as well the infinite possible directions in which any given logo can be developed. Per Mollerup's analytical book celebrates the power of this simplicity while presenting an assertive taxonomy, providing a solid ground for designers' discussion of logo design. After establishing historic background, Mollerup organizes some of the world's most recognized logos according to motif—animals, hearts, mythology, waves, and so on—yielding a comprehensive view of the rich practice of corporate and brand identity design.

THE PUSH PIN GRAPHIC, By Seymour Chwast, edited by Steven Heller and Martin Venezky / Chronicle Books, 2004

For many designers, particularly those who began practicing at the dawn of the 1980s and after, the eclectic *Push Pin Graphic*, published by Push Pin Studios from 1957 to 1980, is a collection of legendary and influential status—and mostly impossible to experience in person anymore. In this 256-page ode to the periodical, all 86 issues are represented through their covers and some of the most memorable spreads, allowing new generations to relish on the successful mixture of illustration, design, writing, and editing that made the *Push Pin Graphic* such a coveted publication.

THE CHEESE MONKEYS, By Chip Kidd / Scribner, 2001; Perennial, 2002; Harper Perennial, 2008

As a source of information—especially in contrast to the monographs, surveys, and anthologies gathered in this section—a novel might not seem an appropriate selection, yet the world Chip Kidd created around his main character, Happy, and his experience attending art school at a state university in the late 1950s is a vicarious thrill as he and his fellow students suffer the whims of the tyrannical commercial art teacher, Winter Sorbeck, and the loony tendencies of the drawing teacher, Dorothy Spang. The anxiety-laden critiques in Sorbeck's class should bring back memories and give goosebumps to any designer.

Monographs focusing on the work of a single graphic designer or design firm suffer from a love-hate relationship with readers—and nonreaders. At extreme ends of the appreciation spectrum, monographs can be considered insightful or self-congratulatory, comprehensive or self-indulgent, and, basically, necessary or unnecessary. Regardless of personal feelings, monographs, if done well, are carefully edited collections of work that exemplify the best a designer or design firm has to offer while providing insight into the process and confirming the need for their publication.

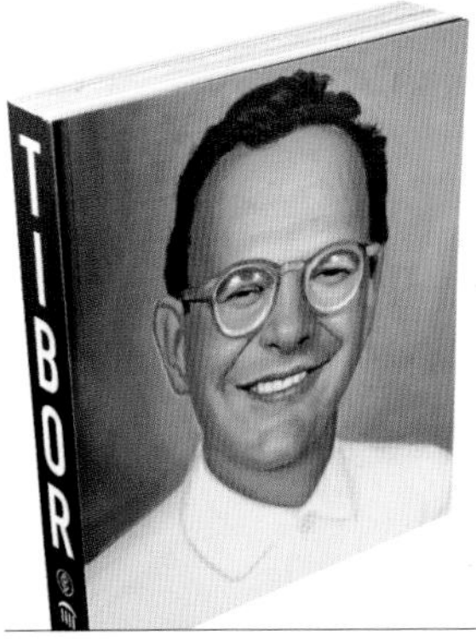

TIBOR KALMAN, PERVERSE OPTIMIST, **Edited by Peter Hall and Michael Bierut / Booth-Clibborn Editions, Princeton Architectural Press, 1998**

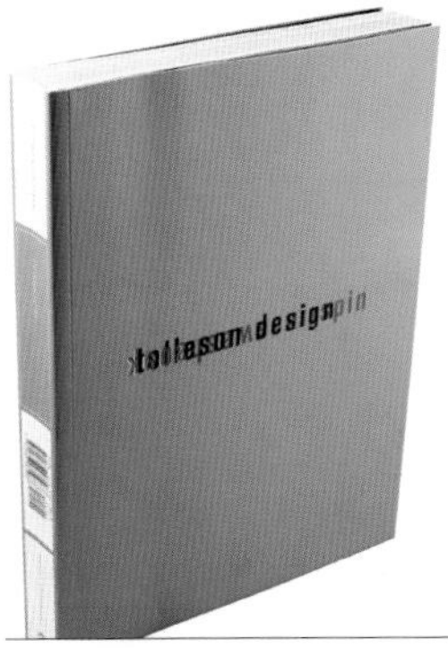

SOAK WASH RINSE SPIN, **By Tolleson Design / Princeton Architectural Press, 2000**

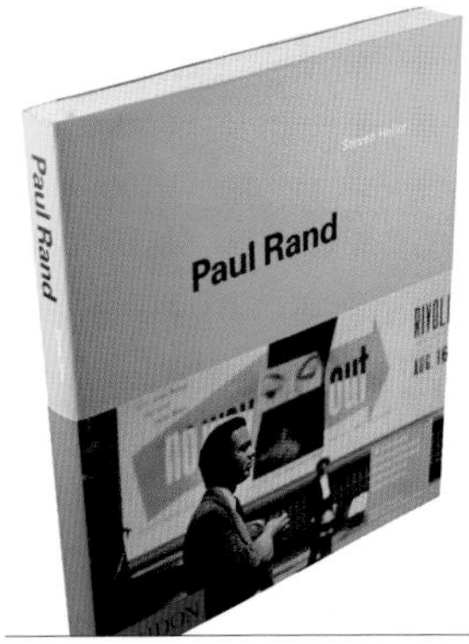

PAUL RAND, **By Steven Heller / Phaidon Press, 2000**

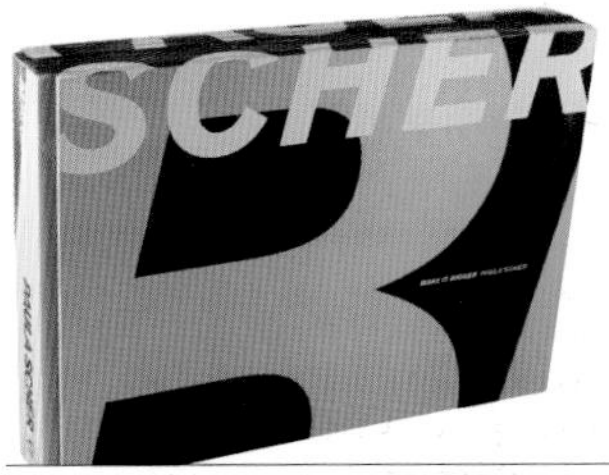

MAKE IT BIGGER, **By Paula Scher / Princeton Architectural Press, 2002**

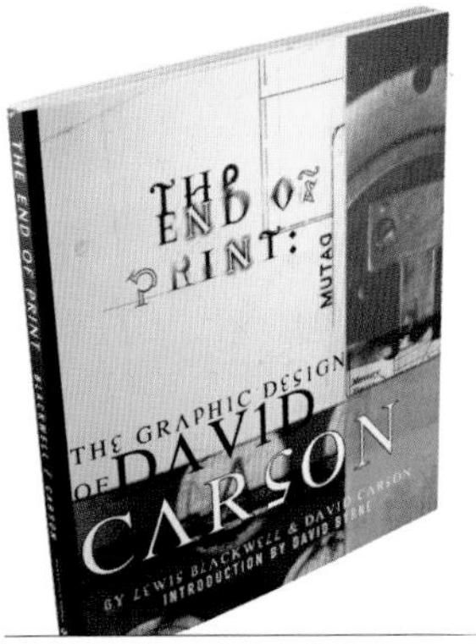

THE END OF PRINT, **By Lewis Blackwell and David Carson / Chronicle Books, 1995 (1st ed.), 2000 (2nd ed.)**

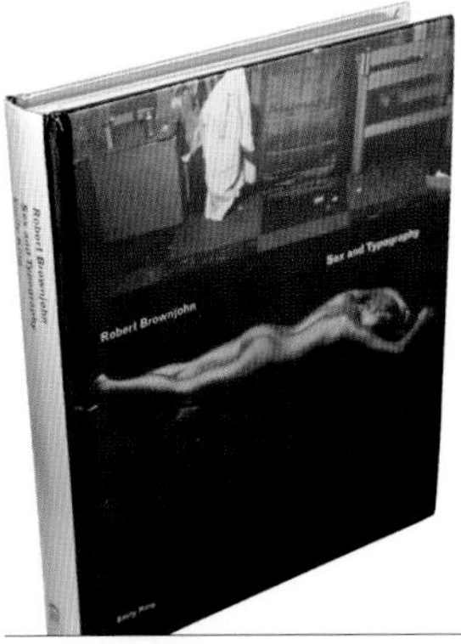

ROBERT BROWNJOHN: SEX AND TYPOGRAPHY, **By Emily King / Laurence King Publishing, Princeton Architectural Press, 2005**

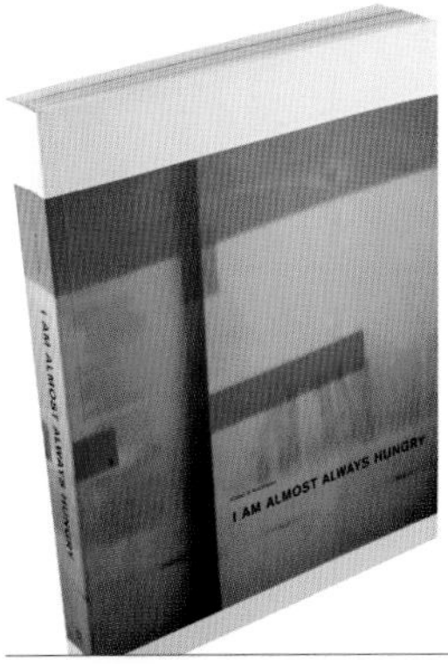

I AM ALMOST ALWAYS HUNGRY, **By Cahan & Associates / Princeton Architectural Press, 1999**

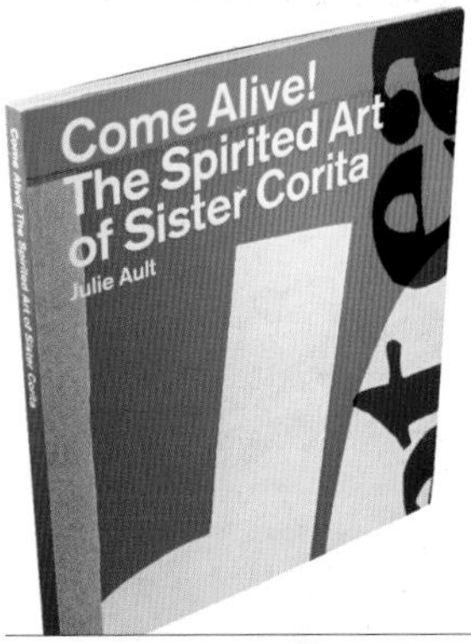

COME ALIVE! THE SPIRITED ART OF SISTER CORITA, **By Julie Ault / Four Corners Books, 2007**

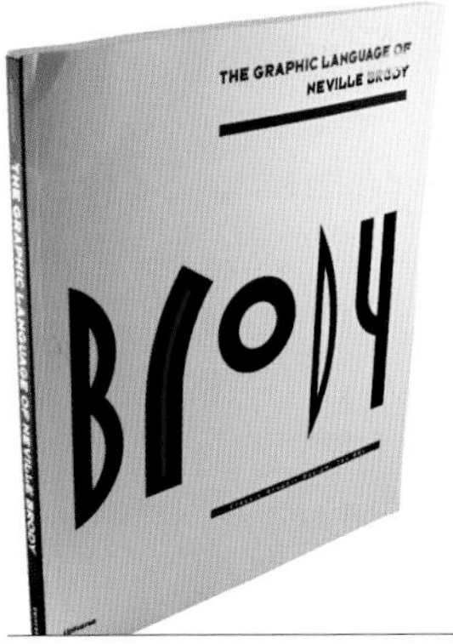

THE GRAPHIC LANGUAGE OF NEVILLE BRODY, **By Jon Wozencroft / Universe, 1988**

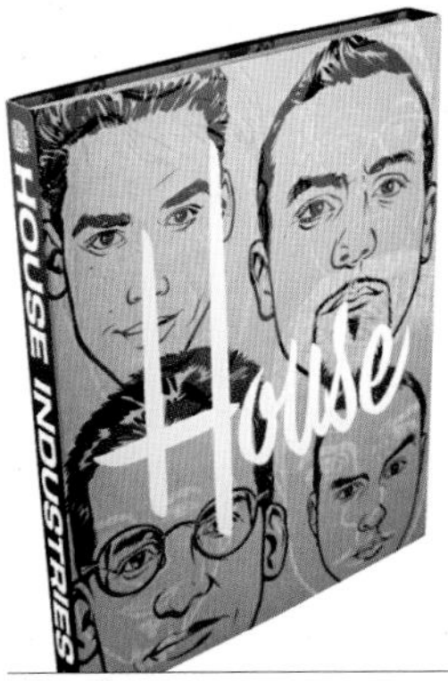

HOUSE INDUSTRIES, **By House Industries / Die Gestalten Verlag, 2003**

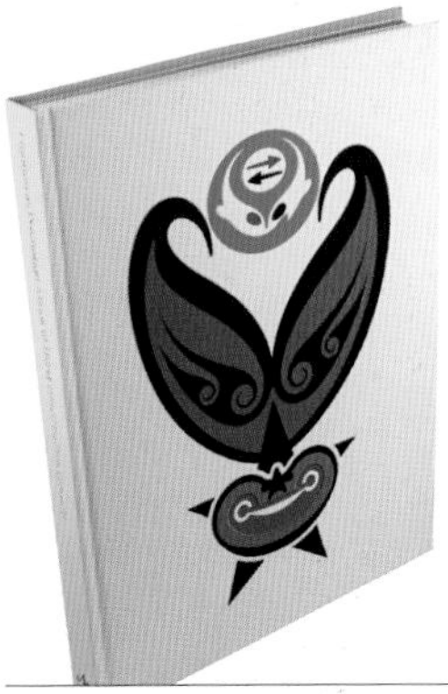

EMOTION AS PROMOTION, **By Rick Valicenti / Monacelli, 2005**

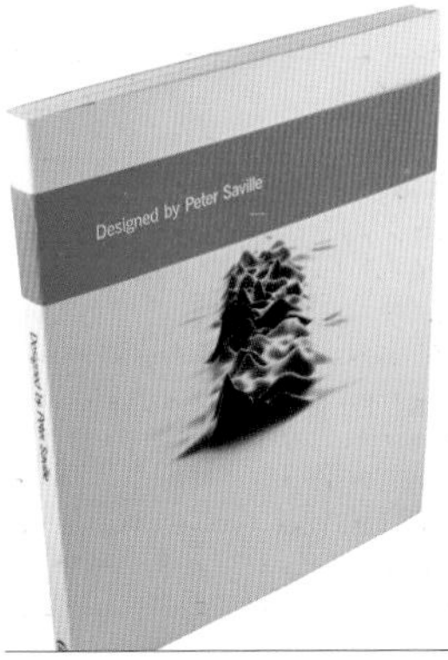

DESIGNED BY PETER SAVILLE, **By Peter Saville, Edited by Emily King / Princeton Architectural Press, 2003**

Q▾

lustig

about alvin lustig   books & periodicals   architecture & interiors   ads, ide

alvin lustig 1915 - 1955 modern design pioneer

---

devoted to good design

Alvin Lustig believed in the power of design when applied to all aspects of life.

Born Modern by S. Heller

abstract & playful design

Each New Classics book jacket Lustig created had its own unique character.

New Classics Gallery

no design boundaries

Lustig immersed himself in all aspects of design, including architecture.

Office Interiors Gallery

design with typ

Early in his caree created geometr using type ornam

Typographic Gall

KNOWLEDGE
Online

112
Blogs, Forums, and Journals

While the interactivity and immediacy of blogs, forums, and other comment-driven journals and magazines did not kill the printed magazine, book, or newspaper, as was feared—it just scared them silly—it did instigate a new form of dialog between authors and readers that, within the proper context, yields conversations augmented by differing points of view. In graphic design, where the means of communication are mostly visual, the propagation of the written word urged a new generation of designers to develop a voice that could easily find an audience, and it provoked the older generation to adapt their experience to a new medium, creating a level field on which to find out who has the last word about design. Luckily, no one does.

115
Archives, References, and Repositories

With bottomless servers that can host an infinite number of images and documents—granted, as long as someone takes responsibility for feeding them the data, paying the hosting fees, and renewing the domain names—the Internet is an endlessly blossoming environment where collections of design ephemera, out-of-print articles and essays, or archives of a designer's work can be globally shared with relative ease, whether curated by individuals or generated by hundreds of users. These generous gestures—more often than not, this content is free to passersby—offer the opportunity to delve into visuals or words that would otherwise remain inaccessible or, worse, forgotten.

117
Online Radio and Podcasts

The unique intonations, acoustics, and cadences of the spoken word can bring most subjects to life, including graphic design. With the improbability of a live AM or FM radio show solely devoted to graphic design offset by the ease and accessibility of generating digital audio files that can be archived, shared, and downloaded, a slew of interviews with designers has been broadcast over the Internet, providing designers with a relatively fresh content form through which to learn about their industry and practitioners. Plus, words like *Helvetica*, *Spiekermann*, and *kern* sound more exotic spoken than written.

Typo-L
LISTSERV.HEANET.IE/LISTS/TYPO-L.HTML

Prior to the rise of blogs and forums, a now seemingly prehistoric mode of group discussion was through email—a discussion list—where a group of people would sign-up and send queries and replies through their own email applications. In 1992, to support the development of TeX, a typesetting system popular for computer science, mathematics, and physics books, Peter Flynn started Typo-L to discuss the minutiae of typeface design and the practice of typesetting. As the list outgrew its initial niche audience, typeface and graphic designers, developers, and other interested parties subscribed to Typo-L. There they shared reading lists and discussed everything from ligatures to accents, modernism, and David Carson › 186 with the unbridled energy permitted by this new mode of global communication. A large majority of subscribers migrated to blogs and forums in the early 2000s, but Typo-L continues—one email at a time.

Typophile
TYPOPHILE.COM

In April 2000, San Francisco-based designers Jared Benson and Joe Pemberton launched Typophile as a host to exclusive, interactive articles on typography developed by Jonathan Hoefler › 230. Alongside it were the increasingly popular forums, where anyone with a subscription could start a discussion (usually heated), upload ongoing development of a typeface for public critique, or challenge the growing readership to identify typefaces in use. Since its inception, Typophile has engaged the relatively small community of type designers and developers through an endless barrage of discussions attracting its most fervent practitioners. Benson and Pemberton launched the Typophile Film Festival in 2004 to coincide with that year's TypeCon › 249 conference in San Francisco, and the collection of type-driven films and animations gathered in the three years it ran were received by sold-out crowds.

Typographica
TYPOGRAPHICA.ORG

Originally edited by both Joshua Lurie-Terrell and Stephen Coles, the latter of whom retains sole editorship, Typographica—no relation to Herbert Spencer's journal of the same name › 95—was launched in 2002, one of the first industry blogs to operate with multiple authors from around the world talking about typography and typeface design. Dozens of authors have contributed over time, most effusively during its first three years, as Typographica deployed post after post after post to an enthusiastic crowd learning the good manners and bad behaviors of blogging. To further engage its readers, Typographica encouraged them to submit designs for the blog's rotating nameplate, wowing fellow readers. Since 2006 Typographica has been, to the sadness of many, briefly active, only offering an annual review of typefaces where readers sing the praises of their favorites through conscientious reviews.

Speak Up

UNDERCONSIDERATION.COM/SPEAKUP

While it wasn't the first blog to focus on graphic design, nor the last, Speak Up was the first to engage a broad following from the industry through its no-holds-barred, heated discussions fueled by the fluctuating group of authors that would light them and the growing congregation of commenters that would fan them. Launched in 2002 by Armin Vit—who was exposed to blogging as one of the authors on Typographica—and Bryony Gomez-Palacio, Speak Up grew over the years as it chronicled and critiqued the news, events, books, and general output of graphic designers. Continually looking to engage its readership, Speak Up has hosted a number of contests, it provides a monthly word that readers can illustrate through the Word It feature, and its has served as a launching pad for events like seriouSeries and publications like *Stop Being Sheep*.

Design Observer

DESIGNOBSERVER.COM

As traditional writers and journalists pondered the benefits and detriments of blogs, four of the graphic design industry's leading writers and practitioners with many years of experience—Michael Bierut › 203, William Drenttel, Jessica Helfand, and Rick Poynor › 237—unexpectedly launched Design Observer in 2003. Broadly addressing the topics of business, culture, art, politics, and architecture as they intersect with design, the four writers quickly gathered a wide following with typically long and considerate writing. For the most part, the ensuing discussions follow a similar path, although explosive interchanges are not rare. Over the years, other seasoned writers who otherwise do so for professional fees—like Steven Heller › 238, Alice Twemlow › 241, and Tom Vanderbilt—have joined Design Observer to strengthen the quality of writing and research that is rarely associated with blogging.

VOICE: AIGA Journal of Design

VOICE.AIGA.ORG

As the AIGA sought a new critical writing outlet to reach its membership it seized the growing acceptance of online design writing and launched VOICE in 2004 with Steven Heller › 238 as editor. Unencumbered by the costs and logistics of a printed journal, VOICE has been able to publish as articles become available and attract a changing number of contributors, including veteran writers and critics like Ralph Caplan › 238, Ellen Lupton › 240, Phil Patton, and Véronique Vienne. While not an immediate comment catalyst like its fellow blogs and forums, VOICE fosters an authoritative tone lent by its organization and extends the tradition of design writing and criticism first established in 1947 with the *AIGA Journal of Graphic Design* › 105, long before the "post" button was even an idea.

Core77

CORE77.COM

In 1995, as students in the Industrial Design graduate program at Pratt Institute, Stuart Constantine and Eric Ludlum presented Core77 as their thesis: embracing the nascent medium of websites and interface design to consolidate information and resources about their future profession. From the outset, Core77 attracted a wide and loyal following that avidly contributed articles, resources, job openings, and more, and fueled its growth to become a de facto destination for industrial designers. Allan Chochinov joined in 2000 as a partner and has overseen the consistent development of Core77's editorial voice and community, including a popular blog, feature articles, special publications, and offline events. Found in its accompanying forums is the 1 Hour Design Challenge, where readers are invited to come up with concepts and sketches for things like cycling shoes or bettering the rainshower experience. Despite a focus on industrial design, much of its content is relevant to any creative endeavor.

A List Apart

ALISTAPART.COM

More than just the 1534-0295 International Standard Serial Number (ISSN) that identifies it as an electronic periodical publication, A List Apart is a hub that has influenced the way web design is practiced. Launched as a mailing list in 1997 by web developer Brian M. Platz and web designer and writer Jeffrey Zeldman, it amassed a following of 16,000 subscribers within months. In 1998, it moved to the web to establish a consistent stream of knowledgeable articles vetted and edited by Zeldman and his team and organized in the broad topics of Code, Content, Culture, Design, Process, and User Science, under the long-running premise of developing content "for people who make websites." Leading by example, A List Apart was one of the first websites to migrate to a Cascading Style Sheet (CSS) layout in 2001—in other words, a big deal, for those who may flinch at web talk.

Typotheque

TYPOTHEQUE.COM/ARTICLES

To complement the online presence of Typotheque, the type foundry run by Peter and Johanna Bilak from The Hague, a comprehensive and growing selection of articles has been easily available on their website since 2001— perhaps the only online curated anthology of critical writing on typography. While some articles are reprints from old magazines and journals—including the infamous 1993 "Cult of the Ugly" (*Eye*) by Steven Heller › 238— Typotheque offers previously unpublished material culled from presentations and lectures as well as a generous serving of book reviews and interviews. With more than 140 articles in English, Spanish, French, German, Italian, and Korean, Typotheque offers a global view of design writing and criticism.

Rene Wanner's Poster Page
POSTERPAGE.CH

The world of poster design is an international one, and each locale has its share of heroes, exhibitions, and competitions. Chronicling this world, in detail, is Rene Wanner, a PhD in experimental physics who happens to be a poster collector. Now in early retirement in a small town in Switzerland, Wanner started his website in 1997 as a way of showcasing the sizable poster collection he began in 1977 on a trip to Warsaw, Poland. Maintaining the site himself, Wanner mounts web exhibitions showcasing the work of a specific poster designer, or exhibitions shown in parallel to bricks-and-mortar shows, and keeps score of biennial winners, publications of books and catalogs, and photo galleries that readers submit of exhibit openings across the world. It all adds up to a massive archive of poster work that would otherwise have remained unseen except by a few individuals.

BibliOdyssey
BIBLIODYSSEY.BLOGSPOT.COM

In 2005, Paul K—or peacay, or PK, or anything that downplays his own persona in the benefit of the content he presents—launched BibliOdyssey, a blog gathering some of the most remarkable rare book illustrations, graphic art, illuminated manuscripts, lithographs, and Renaissance prints found online, creating a stimulating dichotomy of centuries-old work presented through a two-decade-old medium. Paul ventures into the web with inquisitive zeal, treading through digital libraries, cultural archives, and social bookmarking sites. He is aided by illustrators, librarians, historians, bibliophiles, archivists, and other bloggers who provide help and tips. Along with the addictive images, Paul provides insightful commentary on the artist as well as the source collection. After only two years, Paul published the aptly titled *BibliOdyssey: Amazing Archival Images from the Internet* book, bringing a large percentage of its content full circle to the printed page.

Grain Edit
GRAINEDIT.COM

Focusing on the graphic design work produced between the 1950s and 1970s as well as on modern-day work influenced by its aesthetics, Grain Edit provides a constant stream of visual nostalgia in the form of type specimens, posters, postage stamps, books, album covers, and other ephemera from across the world. Edited by California-based David Cuzner since 2007, the site also conducts interviews with designers who revel in the same visual frequency and regularly provides galleries of their work. Cuzner draws from his own library as well, offering photographs of rare books, catalogs, maps, magazines, and other materials that rarely fail to extract a sigh of longing for this kind of work.

The Design Encyclopedia

THEDESIGNENCYCLOPEDIA.ORG

Conceived by Bryony Gomez-Palacio and Armin Vit of UnderConsideration and built by Chicago-based House of Pretty, The Design Encyclopedia was launched in 2003 to piggyback on the growing interest, both positive and negative, in Wikipedia, itself launched in 2001. Using and acknowledging the same premise of users being able to create and modify content, The Design Encyclopedia aims to funnel as much information and imagery found online as well as references to print materials and publications to create a clearinghouse of resources and information about the broad practice of design. Despite a slow evolution, The Design Encyclopedia offers more than 600 entries covering everything from Dungeons and Dragons to *Emigre* › 100, Herb Lubalin › 167 to Steve Jobs. A special section is devoted to archiving student thesis projects and other articles that have not benefited from wide publication.

Alvin Lustig

ALVINLUSTIG.ORG

In an ideal twenty-first-century world, every historic character from the annals of graphic design would have a domain name pegged to his or her legacy, the site hosting a detailed collection of the work, exhaustive biographical details, bibliographical references, and any other materials that would act as an expanding archive, educational resource, or, even, mere inspiration. An example of this approach is at alvinlustig.org, a website launched in 2005 by Patricia Belen and Greg D'Onofrio of Brooklyn-based Kind Company, that gathers the work and writings of Alvin Lustig › 144. With the help of Lustig's widow, Elaine Lustig Cohen, and Steven Heller › 238, Kind Company has built the definitive online presence for this designer, whose work has been highly celebrated and influential—now, even more so.

AIGA Design Archives

DESIGNARCHIVES.AIGA.ORG

As of this writing, more than 19,000 entries have been dutifully cataloged in the online AIGA Design Archives, a dynamic website launched in 2005 that contains the winners of AIGA's national juried competitions from as far back as 1925. Designed and built by Portland, Oregon-based Second Story, the archives are accessible through an extremely friendly Flash interface that skitters to bring up results organized by category or special collection and responds swiftly to detailed searches for anything from typefaces used, to firm and designer names, to client industries. A welcome bell-and-whistle device is a powerful zooming tool that allows exploration of all the tiny 4-point type that was all the rage in the 1990s, to mention one example.

FFFFOUND!
FFFFOUND.COM

One of the many promises of the Internet is the ability to harness the interests of hundreds and thousands of users to create a single whole. Through FFFFOUND! a social image bookmarking website developed by online trailblazer Yugo Nakamura in 2007, users "find" images they like and, with the press of a button, add that image to the infinitely updatable home page. The bent is decidedly toward the graphical, with hundreds of book covers, posters, logos, illustrations, photography, typefaces, and type experiments gracing the alternatively sparse design of FFFFOUND! itself. The endless and random barrage of images provides unprecedented exposure to a variety of work from all over the world, generating an evolving snapshot of global visual culture.

Design Matters
STERLINGBRANDS.COM/DESIGNMATTERS.HTML

The image of a graphic designer in the twenty-first century eagerly carving an hour out of each Friday afternoon to listen to a radio show, as if it were the only means of communication, doesn't sound quite plausible. But so was the debut of Design Matters on Internet talk radio network VoiceAmerica in 2005, hosted by brand fiend Debbie Millman. Broadcast live on Fridays—and handily available for future download—Design Matters presents lively conversations between Millman and her increasingly engaging list of guests, including design luminaries like Michael Bierut › 203, Milton Glaser › 170, and Paula Scher › 182 as well as mainstream talents like writer Malcolm Gladwell, Nobel Prize-winner Eric Kandel, and artist Lawrence Weiner. Establishing the mood through a thoughtful monolog, Millman leads her guests through properly researched questions, extemporaneous banter, and, an overall sassy attitude that keeps her listeners tuned in.

Typeradio
TYPERADIO.ORG

Attendees of the 2004 TypoBerlin conference were treated to the introduction of Typeradio, a live show transmitted from a makeshift studio and broadcast as a "micro FM station"; anyone within 5,000 feet, or within distance of the 20 Typeradio-endorsed radios placed throughout the venue, could tune in to 92.7 FM and listen to interviews with Stefan Sagmeister › 202 and Peter Saville › 180, among others. Typeradio—a collaboration of Donald Beekman, Liza Enebeis, and Underware › 232 (Akiem Helmling, Bas Jacobs, Sami Kortemäki)—has since traveled to other conferences around the world to capture interviews and conversations, while at the same time developing original shows and content independent of conferences. Their full library, available for streaming online or as iTunes podcasts, provides a bounty of dialogs with more than 150 designers, writers, and educators worldwide.

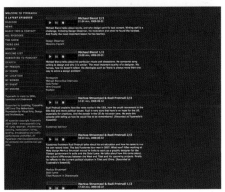

Summer's Cool

 Encourage your child's love of learning! Register now for a summer filled with awesome adventures in contemporary art.

KNOWLEDGE
In Halls

120
Museums

In many of its guises, graphic design has only intermittently been the subject of exhibits or on display in the permanent collections of museums around the world, but as the profession's fame grows and the value of its historic artifacts comes to light, more and more contemporary art museums are displaying posters, logos, packages, and brochures with the same reverence and care afforded to other artists. Through retrospectives of individual designers or themed exhibitions, museums offer the pleasure of seeing original pieces of work more typically experienced at small sizes in books and catalogs. Equally encouraging are the growing acquisitions of design work these museums make, to be preserved and handled with white gloves.

124
Archives

Preserving graphic design is a fraction of the concern at larger museums, so the importance of smaller archives and study centers strongly focused on graphic design is paramount to maintaining physical samples of graphic design, which is fleeting by nature. Housed within universities, design schools, and museums, such archives offer researchers and curious designers the rare opportunity to leaf through 40-year-old annual reports and centuries-old type specimens, or to stand next to 6-foot-tall posters.

Detail of **2006 SUMMER CLASSES BROCHURE FOR THE WALKER ART CENTER, MINNEAPOLIS SCULPTURE GARDEN** / Walker Art Center: design, Scott Ponik / USA, 2006

Cooper-Hewitt National Design Museum

As the only museum in the United States completely devoted to historic and contemporary design, the Cooper-Hewitt, founded in 1897, is one of the industry's most ardent champions, presenting the importance of design to a wide public. Its ambitious National Design Triennial series, started in 2000, is paramount in weaving the different manifestations of design. The annual National Design Awards, launched in 1997 to celebrate the best practitioners in a variety of creative fields, have attracted a healthy dose of media attention. With Ellen Lupton › 240 as curator of contemporary design since 1992, the museum has produced tightly focused exhibitions on graphic design, like *The Avant-Garde Letterhead* (1996), *Mixing Messages: Graphic Design in Contemporary Culture* (1996–1997), and *Graphic Design in the Mechanical Age* (1999), among others. A visit just to experience contemporary design in the historic Andrew Carnegie Mansion in New York is well worth the price of admission.

Walker Art Center

Minneapolis' Walker Art Center, founded in 1927, offers a rich array of experiences in the form of exhibitions, lectures, performances, and workshops, and has long been associated with graphic design; *Design Quarterly*, published from 1946 to 1993, regularly featured the work of graphic designers; *Insights*, an ongoing lecture series in collaboration with the Minnesota chapter of the AIGA › 244, has been running since 1986; a landmark exhibit curated by Mildred Friedman in 1989, *Graphic Design in America: A Visual Language History*, further cemented its consideration for the profession; and, perhaps most notably, its in-house design group has produced all the catalogs, exhibit graphics, collateral, and identity components of the organization under the guidance of design directors Mildred Friedman (1979–1990), Laurie Haycock Makela (1991–1996), Matt Eller (1996–1998), and Andrew Blauvelt (1998–present), garnering acclaim and building goodwill with the industry.

New York Museum of Modern Art

The New York Museum of Modern Art (MoMA), founded in 1929, is known for its impressive permanent art collection, certainly with good reason, and while product design is a more common sight, graphic design has briefly seeped onto its walls. Most recently, it has been entwined in the elaborate and comprehensive *SAFE: Design Takes on Risk* (2005–2006) and *Design and the Elastic Mind* (2008) exhibitions curated by Paola Antonelli, the museum's senior curator in the department of architecture and design. Past exhibitions include *The Graphic Designs of Herbert Matter* (1991), *Typography and the Poster* (1995), *Stenberg Brothers: Constructing a Revolution in Soviet Design* (1997), *The Russian Avant-Garde Book, 1910–1934* (2002), and *Fifty Years of Helvetica* (2008). MoMA has also acquired the work of Irma Boom › 193, Massimo Vignelli › 160, and Willi Kunz › 257, as well as a set of lead Helvetica › 373 Bold 36-point type from 1956.

San Francisco Museum of Modern Art

With a versatile mix of media making up the exhibits at the San Francisco Museum of Modern Art (SFMOMA), it is exalting that graphic design has continually been included in the rotation. Drawing from its permanent collection of architecture and design, SFMOMA regularly features the work of West Coast designers like Rebeca Méndez, AdamsMorioka, Jennifer Morla, Jennifer Sterling, Martin Venezky, and Lorraine Wild. In 1999 it presented *Tiborcity: Design and Undesign by Tibor Kalman, 1979–1999*; it has displayed editorial work from the pages of *Emigre* › 100 and *Wired* magazines, and *Belles Lettres: The Art of Typography*, was shown in 2004.

Victoria and Albert Museum

Somewhere within the more than 500,000 square feet of London's Victoria and Albert Museum (V&A), founded in 1852, and amid its voluminous collections and exhibitions of paintings, ceramics, sculpture, textiles, and furniture, glimpses of graphic design shine brightly. Aside from its iconic logo, designed by Alan Fletcher in 1988, V&A has wooed the industry with exhibitions like *Brand.New* (2000–2001), *Paper Movies: Graphic Design and Photography at* Harper's Bazaar *and* Vogue, *1934–1963* (2007), and the momentous *Modernism: Designing a New World, 1914–1939* (2006) and *China Design Now* (2008). To coincide with the Beijing Summer Olympic Games in 2008, the V&A organized *A Century of Olympic Posters*, which will go on tour until the 2012 games in London.

Design Museum

Before the Design Museum opened its halls in a renovated 1940s banana warehouse in 1989, it had a previous iteration as the Boilerhouse, a gallery located in the basement of the Victoria and Albert Museum, established by Terence Conran and directed by Stephen Bayley. Both incarnations aimed to bring attention to the practice of design. In its brief history, the museum has already experienced its share of controversy as resignations and inside spats have become public—and not worth relating here—oddly distracting from the content it offers. For graphic designers, the tenure of director Alice Rawsthorn › 241 (2001–2006) may be the most fruitful, as she fostered exhibitions on Peter Saville › 180, Saul Bass › 158, and Alan Fletcher; recent exhibitions on Robert Brownjohn › 155, Jonathan Barnbrook, and Helvetica › 373 have fared substantially well. Since 2003, the museum has bestowed a £25,000 prize to a *Designer of the Year*, an initiative that regularly ends in controversy.

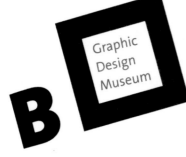

Wolfsonian–Florida International University

Originally founded in 1986 to exhibit and document the decorative and propaganda arts collection of Mitchell Wolfson Jr., the Wolfsonian became a part of Florida International University (FIU) in 1997 when Wolfson donated the collection and its historic Miami Beach building, a now-renovated seven-story, 56,000-square-foot museum. The Wolfsonian-FIU is home to an enviable collection of twentieth-century political propaganda, including prints, posters, drawings, and books from Germany, Italy, and the United States, as well was material from the United Kingdom, Spain, Russia, Czechoslovakia, and Hungary. Other collections that may cause designers to salivate are holdings of posters, catalogs, and other ephemera from the transportation and travel industry—ocean liners, airplanes, zeppelins, and trains—and from the World Fairs and Expositions. In 2008, the museum presented *Thoughts on Democracy*, an exhibition that showcased the work of 60 designers who reinterpreted Norman Rockwell's *Four Freedoms* posters.

Graphic Design Museum

Iconic urban design hubs like New York, San Francisco, London, and The Hague lack one thing that Breda, a small city of approximately 200,000 in the south of the Netherlands, has: a museum devoted solely to graphic design. Opened in 2008, the Graphic Design Museum, Beyerd Breda, is the first of its kind, as much for its content and focus as for its approach to providing exhibitions and resources targeted toward adults, kids, and an in-between category simply labeled "young." One of the main attractions upon its inauguration was the retrospective show *100 Years of Graphic Design in The Netherlands*. Fingers crossed, this museum will have many imitators.

St Bride Library

Opened in 1895, the St Bride Library in London specializes in printing and its supporting specialties of typography, calligraphy, photography, book binding, and printmaking, among dozens of others. With approximately 50,000 books, 3,500 periodicals, catalogs and directories, a collection of metal and wood type from the seventeenth to the twentieth century, and special collections holding the work of W.A. Dwiggins › 141, Eric Gill, and Beatrice Warde, the St Bride Library is, literally, a treasure trove.

Herb Lubalin Study Center

Established within the Cooper Union for the Advancement of Science and Art › 131 in 1985—curated by Ellen Lupton › 240 until 1992, and now headed by Mike Essl and Emily Roz—the Herb Lubalin Study Center of Design and Typography contains a vast collection of work from the twentieth century. Its most significant collection is a comprehensive archive of the logo, editorial, and packaging work, along with hordes of sketches, of Herb Lubalin › 167, a Cooper Union alumnus. Smaller collections of Lou Dorfsman › 173, Herbert Bayer, Bradbury Thompson, Alvin Lustig › 144, and Alexey Brodovitch › 143, as well periodicals and posters, complement the archives.

AIGA Design Archives

If browsing lauded graphic design through a web-based Flash interface › 116 does not satisfy a designer's curiosity, a visit to the AIGA Design Archives, housed since 2006 in the Daniel Libeskind-designed Denver Art Museum, probably will. The archive holds the winning selections from the AIGA's national design competitions since 1980. In 2007, Darrin Alfred was assigned as the AIGA Assistant Curator for Graphic Design, overlooking the collection as well as managing additional acquisitions like the 875 psychedelic rock posters and 20 works by Art Chantry › 184 it acquired in 2008.

Type Directors Club Library

The library of New York's Type Directors Club (TDC) › 247 is replete with type specimens, foundry catalogs, broadsides, and calligraphic works. A rare item in the Type Directors Club collection is a 15-minute videotape culled from reels of the great American type designer Frederic W. Goudy.

Rob Roy Kelly American Wood Type Collection

For his seminal publication, *American Wood Types 1828–1900, Volume One* › 72, Rob Roy Kelly amassed a large collection of wood type that, as it became hard to manage, he sold to MoMA's › 121 head librarian, Dr. Bernard Karpel, in the 1960s. In turn, Karpel sold it to the Harry Ransom Humanities Research Center at the University of Texas at Austin (UT) within six months. The collection languished there until 1991, when the Center was about to toss it as it reorganized its space but instead contacted the university's art department to see if anyone would be interested, and professor Gloria Lee adopted it. In 2004, as part of his tenure research at UT, David Shields unofficially took over the collection and started to work with students to unpack the 40 boxes and explore their contents. By printing and digitizing the entire collection, they arrived at 135 type families (close to 170 unique typefaces), many of which had not been published in Kelly's book—and, most promising, Shields encourages visitors to come in and use the type, as it was meant to be.

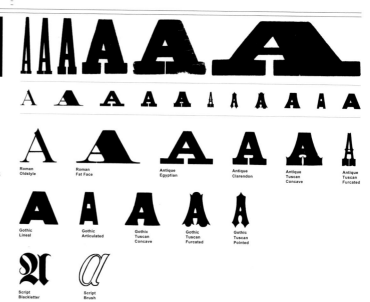

Analysis of the American Wood Type Collection showing the range of the styles and the different widths found

Graphic Design Archives at Rochester Institute of Technology

Established by R. Roger Remington under the administrative care of the broader Cary Graphic Arts Collection at the Rochester Institute of Technology (RIT), the Graphic Design Archives focus on the work of American graphic designers working from the 1920s to the 1950s, including Saul Bass, Lester Beall, Alexey Brodovitch, Tom Carnese, William Golden, Rob Roy Kelly, Alvin Lustig, Cipe Pineles, Ladislav Sutnar, and Bradbury Thompson. Complementing the design artifacts are sketches, correspondence, and other materials that help paint a broader picture of each designer.

The Doris and Henry Dreyfuss Study Center Library and Archive

On the third floor of New York's Cooper-Hewitt National Design Museum › 120 is a 70,000-volume array of books, periodicals, catalogs, and trade literature dating from the fifteenth through the twentieth centuries, including work from graphic designers like Ladislav Sutnar › 150 and Paula Scher › 182 and the design firm M&Co. › 183. For those looking for more depth, a collection of 750 pop-up and movable books is also available.

Arts of the Book Collection at Yale

As part of the Yale University Library system, the Arts of the Book Collection contains close to one million bookplates, a large collection of design ephemera, advertising cards, and volvelles (graphic wheels), among other material. It also provides access to the masters theses of graphic design program students since 1952. Parallel to a donation from Marion Rand of her late husband's work to the Department of Manuscripts and Archives in the Sterling Memorial Library, the Arts of the Book Collection holds around 200 books from Paul Rand's › 159 personal library.

Archival boxes used to store each font individually

KNOWLEDGE
In Classrooms

128

While students can and should make use of
the very best of the higher education available to
them, it is difficult to deny that some educational institutions consistently deliver results
by offering access to an effective faculty roster
and facilities as well as by continually producing
graduates brimming with professional preparation. And just as graphic design can manifest
in an infinite number of ways—as opposed to,
say, accounting, where there is a right or wrong
answer—an education in graphic design is as
varied and peculiar, with each program taking
on the personalities and beliefs of its directors
and faculty, giving students ample choice among
the theories and methodologies that will best
help them develop their own.

BV (BEAULIEU VINEYARD) WINE / Jin Young Lee;
instructors, Bryony Gomez-Palacio, Armin Vit /
USA, 2007

Basel School of Design

In 1942, Emil Ruder was hired by the Allgemeine Gewerbeschule (General Vocational School) to teach typography to typesetting and printer apprentices, and in 1946 Armin Hofmann ›152 joined the faculty to help establish the graphic design program, the Schule für Gestaltung Basel (Basel School of Design), that would become influential for students like Steff Geissbuhler ›157, Karl Gerstner, Hans-Rudolf Lutz, Yves Zimmerman, and numerous other designers. Hofmann's approach—a foundation in the basics as explored through exercises of "repetition, intensification, contrast, and dispersion"—was documented in *Graphic Design Manual: Principles and Practice*, published in 1965, and many of those exercises can now be found in numerous schools.

In 1968, after more than a decade of Ruder conducting informal postgraduate study in typography with two or three students a year, the Advanced Class of Graphic Design (*Weiterbildungsklasse für Graphik*) was established as an official international graduate design program with seven new students. It introduced Wolfgang Weingart ›178, a former student, as one of the teachers, who took the program into new directions as he questioned established typography practice and the rules that governed it. His effervescent approach to teaching typography attracted a new generation of designers like Americans Dan Friedman and April Greiman ›179, who imported this typographic impetus. In 2000, a split left two Basel schools of design, one now affiliated with the University of Applied Sciences Northwestern Switzerland as an accredited program, the other remaining a vocation school. This vocational school has also hosted the Basics in Design and Typography summer program since 2005, with Weingart as one of the teachers and the intention of keeping the legacy of the *Weiterbildungsklasse* alive.

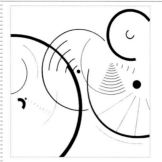 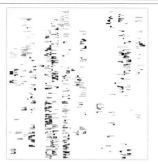 

BLACK AND WHITE EXERCISES EXPRESSING A SERIES OF THEMES: BICYCLE TRAFFIC, BIRCH TREES, MUSIC / Steff Geissbuhler; instructors, Armin Hofmann, Verlag Arthur, Niggli AG / Switzerland, 1958–1964

POSTAGE STAMPS HIGHLIGHTING THE SWISS FOLK SPORTS OF HORNUSSEN (A LOOSE CROSS BETWEEN GOLF AND BASEBALL), STEINSTOSSEN (STONETHROW), AND SCHWINGEN (FOLK WRESTLING) / Joachim Müller-Lancé; instructor, Max Schmid / Switzerland, 1982–1986

NO ALCOHOL AT THE WHEEL POSTER FOR THE CITY OF BASEL / Joachim Müller-Lancé; instructor, Armin Hofmann / Switzerland, 1982–1986

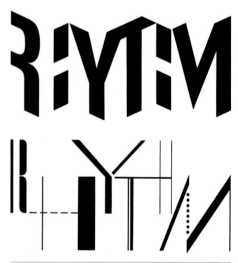

RHYTHM IN JAZZ AND IN NEW WAVE WORDMARK / Joachim Müller-Lancé; instructor, Christian Mengelt / Switzerland, 1982–1986

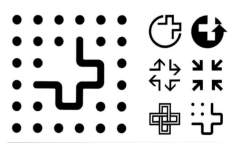

SWISS SOCIETY FOR INTER-REGIONAL COOPERATION LOGO / Joachim Müller-Lancé; instructor, Armin Hofmann / Switzerland, 1982–1986

Yale School of Art

As a book designer and avid typographer, Alvin Eisenman was offered a position with Yale University Press and a supplemental teaching position at the university's art school, leading to the establishment of the first graduate studies program in graphic design (graphic arts, as it was first called) in the United States in 1950 in New Haven, Connecticut. Under Eisenman, who held the position of program director until 1990, the graduate program attracted some of the leading practitioners of the time, including Armin Hofmann (who taught there for 30 years and helped established strong ties with the Basel School of Design › 128), Alexey Brodovitch › 143, Alvin Lustig › 144, Herbert Matter, Bradbury Thompson, and, of course, Paul Rand › 159, who started as a visiting critic in 1956 but soon after became a faculty member and stayed until 1993.

While the program had just a handful of full-time faculty members, its affluent influx of visiting designers and critics enrich the student experience and is a model that continues today. In 1990, Sheila Levrant de Bretteville, a 1964 graduate of the program, was appointed Eisenman's successor—with an unfortunate dose of controversy, as Rand and other members resigned in disapproval of the decision. She has fostered a new generation of visiting designers and critics including Michael Bierut › 203, Matthew Carter › 221, Jessica Helfand, Allen Hori, and Scott Stowell, as well as foreigners like Irma Boom › 193, Armand Mevis, and Linda van Deursen. With an inquisitive approach fostered by de Bretteville, students explore topics of personal interest, and their ideas become part of the work—indeed a harsh distancing from the modernist and functional underpinnings of the previous generation. Regardless of era, Yale's graduate program prepares its students to excel in the changing climate of graphic design.

RECORD COLLECTION MAPPING / Dmitri Siegel; instructor; Barbara Glauber / USA, 2002

YALE UNIVERSITY AND SWERVEDRIVER BAND SIMULTANEOUS EVENT POSTER / Dmitri Siegel; instructor; Armand Mevis / USA, 2002

INSPIRED BY AN ITALIAN SPORK AND BASED ON HELVETICA ROUNDED, THE MOSCARDINO TYPEFACE EXPLORES LIGATURES WELL BEYOND THE EXPECTED / Tracy Jenkins; instructors, Sheila Levrant de Bretteville, Susan Sellers / USA, 2003

Cranbrook Academy of Art

No classes. No teachers. No projects. This is the modus operandi of the graduate program in two-dimensional design at Cranbrook Academy of Art in Michigan, where students define their own projects, rely on each other for critiques, and work with an artist-in-residence and visiting designers to realize their self-directed projects. This model and the resulting work of the graphic design students since the 1980s has long attracted the attention, both positive and negative, of the industry. In 1971, Michael and Katherine McCoy › 185 were hired to run a joint two-dimensional/three-dimensional program; their teaching drew from their experience in Swiss design and modernism.

However, in the late 1970s, the notions of postmodernism and the vernacular in architecture started to seep in as influenced by Robert Venturi, and, during the 1980s, the critical theory and the writings of Roland Barthes and Jacques Derrida. These led to the exploration of deconstruction and poststructuralist ideas through design strategies by students like Andrew Blauvelt, Ed Fella › 185, Jeffery Keedy, and Allen Hori. Much of the work was largely bulked as a postmodernism aesthetic without further consideration; nonetheless, there is a fluctuating yet discernable texture to its students' work.

In 1995, two Cranbrook graduates, P. Scott and Laurie Haycock Makela, were appointed designers-in-residence after the McCoys. They continued the legacy of exploration, now accentuated by digital design online and motion graphics, and infused an energy all their own, attracting designers from around the world. Unfortunately, their time at the academy was cut short by Scott's death in 1999, although Laurie continued until 2001. Elliot Earls, another graduate, then took on the position, leading the exploration in a field where boundaries in media and disciplines are easier to cross. Then again, that has never been a limitation.

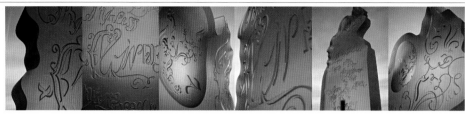

Above and right **TO THE LOSS OF OUR PRINCESS**, THESIS PROJECT / Cinderella's tombstone, handlettered and built with precision-machined resin / Catelijne van Middelkoop / USA, 2001–2002 / Photos: Ryan Pescatore Frisk

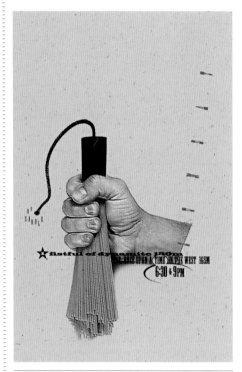

CRANBROOK'S SPAGHETTI WESTERN STUDENT FILM SERIES POSTER / Doug Bartow; instructor, Katherine McCoy / USA, 1994

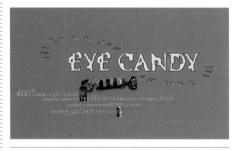

EYECANDY POSTER / Doug Bartow; instructor, Katherine McCoy / USA, 1995

HEY DUTCHIE! TYPE SPECIMEN POSTER / Catelijne van Middelkoop / USA, 2001–2002

California Institute of the Arts

With degrees from Cranbrook Academy of Art ›130 in 1975 and the Yale graduate program ›129 in graphic design in 1982, a brief stint at Vignelli Associates ›160, a teaching position at the University of Houston's architecture and graphic design departments, and a burgeoning interest in design history and education, Lorraine Wild brought a comprehensive background to renew the graphic design program at California Institute of the Arts (CalArts) in Valencia when she was appointed its director in 1985. Soon after, Cranbrook graduates Jeffery Keedy and Ed Fella ›185 joined the faculty, bringing their exploratory outlook into a structured program informed by history and theory. CalArts has benefited over the years by a faculty made up, in part, by active practitioners—as graphic designers, writers, curators—like Caryn Aono, Anne Burdick, Geoff Kaplan (a Cranbrook graduate), Michael Worthington, and Louise Sandhaus and Gail Swanlund, who have both also acted as program directors.

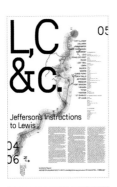

CALIFORNIA INSTITUTE OF THE ARTS GRAPHIC DESIGN DEPARTMENT END-OF-YEAR SHOW / Ryan Corey, Lucas Quigley; instructor, Gail Swanlund / USA, 2005

OCCIDENTAL TYPEFACE SPECIMEN POSTER / Ryan Corey; instructor, Greg Lindy / USA, 2005

A WORK OF SOME AES-THETIC AND SPIRITUAL VALUE POSTER / Ryan Corey; instructor, Gail Swanlund / USA, 2005

.1-10 TYPOGRAPHIC HIER-ARCHY PROJECT: ZAHA HADID LISTENS TO THE MAGNETIC FIELDS / Ian Lynam; instructor, Jeffery Keedy / USA, 2003

ARTIST LECTURE, YEHUDIT SASPORTAS POSTER SET / Ian Lynam; instructor, Ed Fella / USA, 2004

Cooper Union

The Cooper Union School of Art is one of the three schools that make up the Cooper Union for the Advancement of Science and Art, New York's prestigious institution that admits a select group of undergraduates and offers them a full-tuition scholarship for their four-year stay. The rigorous admission process includes an ever-changing "home test" that tasks applicants on a variety of exercises, ensures the seriousness of the candidates, and gives the school the honor of having one of the lowest acceptance rates in the nation. So it must come as no surprise that Cooper Union has proven a fertile ground for the industry. Some of its most iconic practitioners have graduated from its halls, including the founding members of Push Pin Studios ›168 Seymour Chwast, Reynold Ruffins, Edward Sorel, and Milton Glaser, as well as Herb Lubalin ›167, Lou Dorfsman ›173, Ellen Lupton ›240, Abbott Miller, and Stephen Doyle, among others.

SEE EMILY ROZ HERB LUBALIN STUDY CENTER EXHIBITION AT THE COOPER UNION SCHOOL OF ART / Seth Labenz and Roy Rub; instructor, Mike Essl / USA, 2006

TICKET TO DESIGN PRELIMINARY BUSINESS CARDS FOR SETH LABENZ AND ROY RUB / Seth Labenz, Roy Rub; instructor, Mike Essl / USA, 2006

UNITING, GIFT RECEIVED BY EVERY MEM-BER OF THE UNITED STATES CONGRESS IN SUPPORT OF THE UNITING AMERICAN FAMILIES ACT [S.1278] / Seth Labenz, Roy Rub; instructor, Stefan Sagmeister / USA, 2006

School of Visual Arts

Co-founded in 1947 as the Cartoonists and Illustrators School by Burne Hogarth and Silas H. Rhodes, the School of Visual Arts (as it was later renamed in 1955) was, from the beginning, set up so its faculty would be comprised solely of professional, working designers. Hogarth left in 1970, but Rhodes stayed involved with the school—as its president for six years in the 1970s, as a chairman of the board, and as a creative director of both the Visual Arts Press Ltd. and the numerous recruitment posters deployed in the city's subway system for 55 years (see right)—until his death in 2007. The majority of the school's 3,000-plus undergraduate students are enrolled in the graphic design program, where they are taught by more than 100 professional designers including Paula Scher › 182, Carin Goldberg, James Victore, Paul Sahre, Louise Fili › 197, and Debbie Millman.

QUALITY MAGAZINE / Julia Hoffmann; instructor, Carin Goldberg / USA, 2001–2002

IN ON IT POSTER FOR P.S. 122 / Julia Hoffmann; instructor, Carin Goldberg / USA, 2001–2002

CAFÉ PARCO BRANDING / Jin Young Lee; instructors, Bryony Gomez-Palacio, Armin Vit / USA, 2007

School of Visual Arts MFA Designer as Author

In 1997, the Designer as Author graduate program from the School of Visual Arts was co-founded by Steven Heller › 238 and Lita Talarico, both of whom still co-chair the program. As in the undergraduate program, professional designers and writers—like Brian Collins › 204, Milton Glaser › 170, Stefan Sagmeister › 202, and Véronique Vienne—make up the faculty that gathers in the evenings with the dozen or more students to develop a viable concept through any means necessary and take it to a point where it could be commercially produced and marketed or publicly accessible. Because of this focused premise, many of the program's students have the ability to make an instant impact with consumer-ready projects, like Deborah Adler's ClearRX › 318 package for Target and Jennifer Panepinto's beautiful Mesü porcelain bowls for food measuring.

ABYSSINIAN BAPTIST CHURCH OF HARLEM IDENTITY, COLLATERAL, AND ADVERTISING / thesis project turned reality and further aided by the Sappi Ideas That Matter Grant / Bobby C. Martin Jr.; thesis advisor, Paula Scher; instructors, Steven Heller, Brian Collins, Dorothy Globus, Martin Kace / USA, 2003

THE AMAZING PROJECT, WHERE AMAZING PEOPLE DO AMAZING THINGS TO CHANGE THE WORLD / Randy J. Hunt; thesis consulting, Brian Collins, Gail Anderson; thesis adviser, Mark Randall / USA, 2006 / Photo: Adam Krause

School of Visual Arts Subway Posters

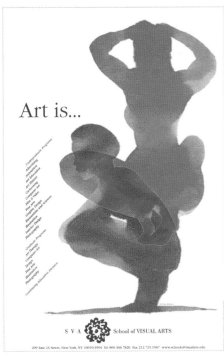

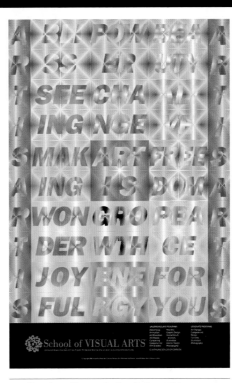

Art direction, Silas H. Rhodes; design, Milton Glaser / USA, 2000

Art direction, Silas H. Rhodes; design, Adrienne Leban / USA, 2002

Art direction, Silas H. Rhodes; design, James Victore / USA, 2003

Art direction, Silas H. Rhodes; design, Frank Young / USA, 2003

Art direction, Silas H. Rhodes; design, Stefan Sagmeister / USA, 2004

Art direction, Silas H. Rhodes; design, James McMullan / USA, 2004

Rhode Island School of Design

BRAZIL FILM POSTER / Kai Salmela; instructor, Dietmar Winkler / USA, 2006

TORINO SUMMER OLYMPIC GAMES SCHEDULE POSTER / Kai Salmela; instructor, Doug Scott / USA, 2007

OHIO BICENTENNIAL CELEBRATION IDENTITY / Joe Marianek; instructors, Douglass Scott, Lucinda Hitchcock / USA, 2003

RISD STICKER 2003 YEARBOOK / Joe Marianek, Adriana Deléo, Wyeth Hansen, Ryan Waller, Lily Williams; instructors, Douglass Scott, Lucinda Hitchcock / USA, 2003

Maryland Institute College of Art

BLACKS IN WAX ARTIST BOOK / Silkscreened on transparent wax-like paper / Bruce Willen; instructor; Jennifer Cole Philips / USA, 2001

WHOLESOME FOODS PACKAGING / Bruce Willen; instructor; Jennifer Cole Philips / USA, 2001

SMALL ROAR GRADUATE THESIS PROJECT / Upon the birth of their daughter, Mike and Stephanie Weikert opened for business / Mike Weikert / USA, 2005

Portfolio Center

DECECCO REBRANDING AND PACKAGING / Sam Potts; instructor, George Gall / USA, 2000 / Photo: Lisa Devlin

EXODUS, PROMOTIONAL PIECE FOR ADOBE'S JOANNA / Sam Potts; instructor, Hank Richardson / USA, 1999 / Photo: Lisa Devlin

CAUSE + EFFECT SELF-CURATED EXHIBITION CATALOG / Sam Potts; instructor, Melissa Kuperminc / USA, 2000 / Photo: Lisa Devlin

IMPACT CHAIR, REFLECTING A PERSONAL EXPERIENCE FROM 9/11 / Dave Werner; instructor, Hank Richardson / USA, 2006

MONDAVI WINE PACKAGING / Dave Werner; instructor, Hank Richardson / USA, 2006

KENNEDY CENTER PROMOTIONAL SUITE / Dave Werner; instructor, Nicole Riekki / USA, 2006

Royal College of Art

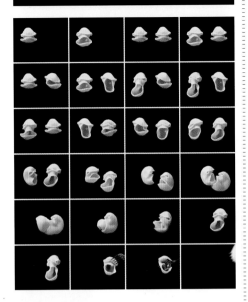

EAT OR BE EATEN **SINGING PASTA ANIMATION** / Tomi Vollauschek / UK, 2000

TRANS-FORM **MAGAZINE** / FL@33: Agathe Jacquillat, Tomi Vollauschek; advisors, Gert Dumbar, Russell Warren-Fisher / UK, 2001

Central Saint Martins College of Art & Design

THE EVOLUTION OF PRINT, **AN INSTALLATION SHOWCAS-ING THE EXPLOSION OF KNOWLEDGE FROM THE START OF LETTERPRESS TO THE TWENTY-FIRST CENTURY** / Diego Ulrich; instructor, Max Ackermann / USA, 2008

THREE-DIMENSIONAL AILERON TYPEFACE FOR USE IN OPEN SPACES / Diego Ulrich; instructor, Max Ackermann / USA, 2008

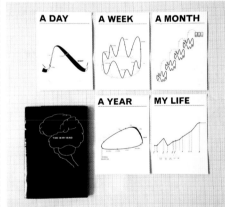

INFORMATION GRAPHICS ON THE REPRESENTATION OF TIME AS IT IS FELT / Clara Brizard; instructor, Sara De Bondt / UK, 2008

BEYOND MY WINDOW, DIE FENSTER **SERIES OF DIE-CUT AND SCREENPRINTED POSTERS** / Clara Brizard; instructor, Sara De Bondt / UK, 2008

University of Reading, MA in Typeface Design

Aufmerksamkeit
Trzecia Sesja Ogólnego Zgromadzenia
Buchgewerbe
Inspirován prací českých typografů
DISCLOSURE
книгопечатание
δημιουργός
N16LE *LOUGHBOROUGH* JUNCTION
Dynamically
The Society of Typographic Aficionados 2005

MAIOLA / Released by FontFont in 2005 / Veronika Burian; instructors, Gerry Leonidas, Gerard Unger / USA, 2003

abcdefghijklmnop qrstuvwxyz:;., ABCDEFGHIJKLMN OPQRSTUVWXYZ& 1234567890

abcdefghijklmnop qrstuvwxyz:;., ABCDEFGHIJKLMN OPQRSTUVWXYZ& 1234567890

Gaoming Beresford Rd
Jiangmen Wellington
Zongsan Hammersmith
Information Rupert
Quarry Bay Heathrow
Schriftgrößen Eas
København Denmark
Ellesmere Port 59
Blackpool Harrowgate
Shamshuipo Canad
Bromborough→
Wanchai Spring Garden

Bibliothéque Trains
Arrondissement
Embankment South
Tsimshatsui Trafalga
Departures Internati
Guangzhou Bebingto
Kowloon Tong 7695
Espergærde Garden
Spadina Domestic Fligh
République Richmond
Birkenhead Hamilton
Expo Line N Vancouver

ARRIVAL TYPE FAMILY FOR UNIVERSITY OF READING / Released in 2005 / Keith Chi-hang Tam; instructors, Gerry Leonidas, Gerard Unger / UK 2001–2002

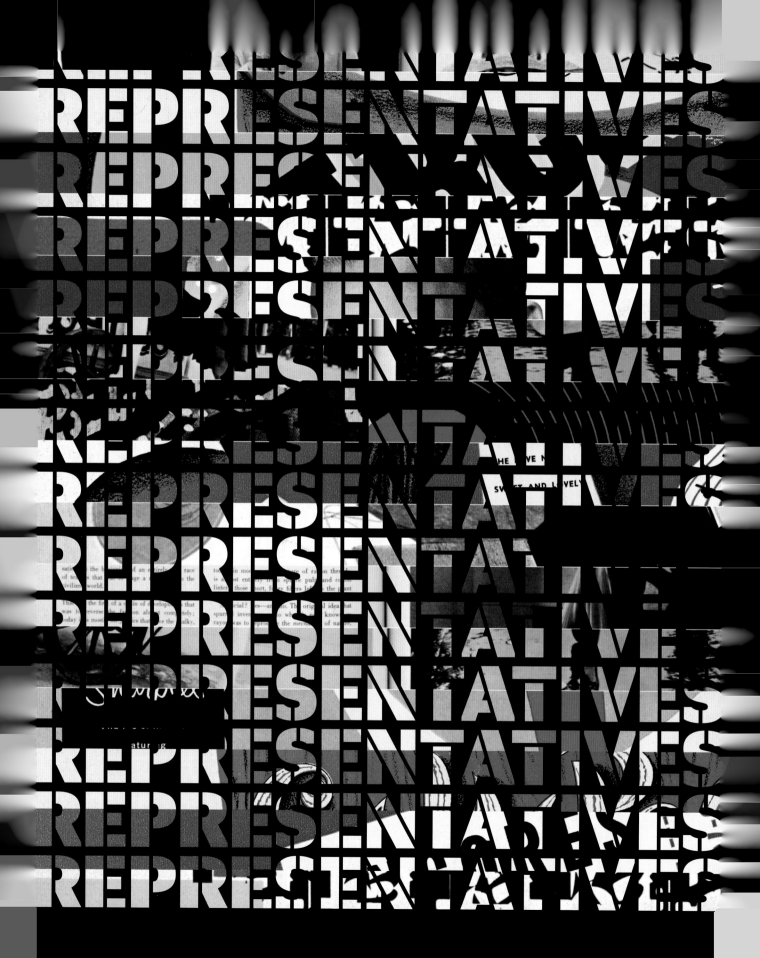

As graphic design has evolved over the course of the twentieth century and into the twenty-first from a craft focusing on the finer aspects of printing and typesetting into a multifaceted profession thriving on the communication of messages through a variety of means and media, numerous individuals and groups of individuals have helped not only define each milestone but propel the next one forward through outstanding and innovative work on which future generations can build. These people are representative of a specific period in the history of graphic design but at the same time transcend any given period or style by being exemplary models of how graphic design can be practiced and of the kind of work that can be produced within any cultural, political, economic, and technological context.

REPRESENTATIVES
Of Design

It's difficult to establish hard-edged boundaries around the years in which designers make an impact, in part because many of the individuals and groups noted in this section stretch across numerous decades. However, certain developments help establish broad timelines where they thrived or made their biggest impact.

140
1920s–1960s

Spurred by the graphic innovations and new visual languages developed through Constructivism in Russia, de Stijl in the Netherlands, and Bauhaus in Germany, it's possible to see the genesis of graphic design, as is known today, with imagery and typography coming together more clearly and with more defined purposes, whether for matters of commerce or protest. In the 1950s, the rise of the International Typographic Style made Switzerland the center of attention; this remains one of the most influential epochs. Meanwhile, in the United States, the influx of European and Russian immigrants and a growing group of Americans gave shape to the publishing and advertising industries from the 1930s onward. What these designers shared, more than geographic location or stylistic approach, was a pioneering spirit that established the potential of graphic design.

155
1960s–1980s

During the late 1950s and 1960s there was a precipitous rise in the discipline of corporate identity, as many of the world's largest corporations began a vigorous growth period fueled by highly industrialized processes and more viable communication and transportation methods. In these early years, individual designers or small design firms were able to tackle these projects, and their output defined the look and feel of business. Toward the end of the 1960s and into the 1970s the world was awash in cultural changes, and graphic designers played a remarkable role in giving visual form to the many incandescent issues of this time, illustrating the communicative potential of graphic design beyond the realm of corporate communication. In parallel, the fields of magazine and book design, music packaging, and advertising reflected a fledgling evolution in the hands of art directors.

176
1980s–2000s

Even before the digital revolution signaled a new era in graphic design, the late 1970s and early 1980s gave way to a reassessment of the tenets of graphic design and typography as New Wave and Postmodernism explored new theories and practices. But, certainly, the introduction of the Macintosh computer in 1984 was an explosive and divisive moment in graphic design history that catalyzed a slew of possibilities that some embraced while others rejected. By the early 1990s, the assimilation of the computer was unquestionable, and this generation of designers—whether in solo practice, small firms, or voluminous offices—has thrust the profession into nearly all other fields. These designers now stand at the verge of the next milestone.

Detail of **WORLDFORMAT KUNSTKREDIT BASEL 1976-1977 POSTER FOR THE CITY ORGANIZATION IN SUPPORT OF THE ARTS** / Wolfgang Weingart / Switzerland, 1977

Jan Tschichold
1902 (LEIPZIG, GERMANY) - 1974

In 1923, after graduating from the Academy for Graphic Arts and Book Production in Leipzig, Jan Tschichold began his comprehensive career as a typeface designer and book designer working freelance for various publishers. A 1923 Bauhaus exhibition in Weimar that same year proved a catalyst, exposing him to the New Typography, an approach that became synonymous with his early work, strongly manifested in the publication, two years later, of *Elementare Typographie*, an insert in the Leipzig journal *Typographische Mitteilungen* (*Typographic News*). This piece explained and illustrated the principles of New Typography. In 1928, Tschichold published the first of many books and manuals he would author, *Die Neue Typographie* (*The New Typography*), laden with visual examples that demonstrated his beliefs as he further rejected decoration and advocated functional and efficient design.

After seven years of teaching in Munich, Tschichold emigrated with his family from Germany to Basel, Switzerland, in 1933, fleeing the Nazi regime. He worked again as a book designer and began to distance himself from the New Typography as he embraced serif typefaces and classic arrangements, realizing that typography was more nuanced and there is more than one way to make successful design. In 1947, he moved to London when he accepted the invitation to standardize the popular Penguin Books › 274. With little consistency across hundreds of titles, Tschichold established authoritative guidelines—cemented in the *Penguin Composition Rules*—to ensure quality from cover to cover and making an indelible mark on the publishing industry. He returned to Basel in 1949 to continue his work for book publishers, and in 1955 he became a consultant for the pharmaceutical firm F. Hoffmann-La Roche, designing their collateral materials during the next 12 years. Straddling the extremes between centered, classic typography and asymmetric modern typography, the work of Jan Tschichold remains a vibrant example of both approaches.

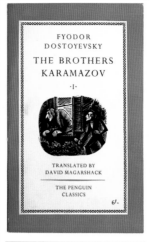

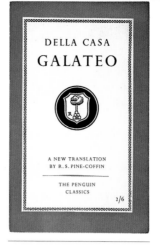

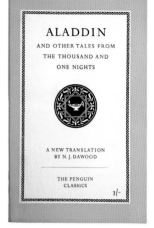

THE BROTHERS KARAMAZOV, Fyodor Dostoevsky, Translated by David Magarshack / Jan Tschichold; roundel artwork, Cecil Keeling / UK, 1958

DELLA CASA GALATEO, Translated by R.S. Pine-Coffin / Jan Tschichold; roundel artwork, Cecil Keeling / UK, 1959

ALADDIN AND OTHER TALES FROM THE THOUSAND AND ONE NIGHTS, Translated by N.J. Dawood / Jan Tschichold / UK, 1960

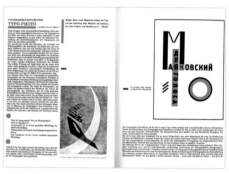

TYPOGRAPHICHE MITTEILUNGEN, Jan Tschichold / Germany, October 1925 / Images: Courtesy of the International Dada Archive, University of Iowa Libraries

Sabon

At the request of German printers looking for a typeface in the vein of Garamond that would perform equally well across different typesetting models, Tschichold designed Sabon in 1964 to be produced simultaneously by three foundries: D. Stempel AG, Linotype, and Monotype. Based on a 14-point Roman typeface attributed to Claude Garamond from a 1592 specimen sheet issued by the Egenolff-Berner foundry, Sabon is named after Jakob Sabon, a student of Claude Garamond and the owner of a type foundry in Germany that was later known as Egenolff-Berner. Since its release, Sabon has been a mainstay in book design as a highly readable and pleasant typeface.

 RECOMMENDED READING › 390

William Addison Dwiggins

1880 (MARTINSVILLE, OHIO, USA) - **1956**

After studying under Frederic W. Goudy at the Frank Holme School of Illustration in Chicago and working briefly in his Village Press in Massachusetts in 1904, William Addison Dwiggins established himself in 1905 as a freelance commercial artist, becoming a prolific letterer, calligrapher, and illustrator for the advertising industry. In 1923, however, when diagnosed with diabetes, he shifted disciplines and turned to book design, a field in which he already had experience, even if not positive: In 1919, after an uninspiring, brief position at Harvard University Press, he wrote, "Extracts from an Investigation into the Physical Properties of Books as They Are at Present Published," a mock (but nonetheless scathing) critique of the field, published by the Society of Calligraphers, an imaginary club run by Hermann Püterschein, one of Dwiggins' many pseudonyms and alter egos. Mwano Masassi, an African designer, was another, and Kobodaishi, the Buddhist patron saint of the lettering arts, whom Dwiggins "visited" in 1935 and gave him the inspiration for his typeface Electra, was likewise a fabrication.

More official writings included "New Kind of Printing Calls for New Design," published in 1922 in the *Boston Evening Transcript*, in which he famously first used the term *graphic design*, and 1928's *Layout in Advertising*, a book compiling his accrued knowledge. Designing jackets and interiors, Dwiggins made his most indelible mark through his long collaboration with Alfred A. Knopf, Inc., where he produced more than 300 works from the late 1920s through the next three decades. In his late forties, Dwiggins began a career in type design when he was asked by Mergenthaler Linotype to develop a sans serif; this, only a year later, resulted in Metroblack. Through a long association he created four other commercial typefaces—Electra, Caledonia, Eldorado, and Falcon—along with dozens of well-catalogued typefaces-in-progress that have inspired many contemporary type designers. Tangentially, Dwiggins had an avid hobby: designing and constructing marionettes, with accompanying miniature theater sets, and writing plays and performing for friends. Dwiggins passed away in 1956 in Hingham, Massachusetts.

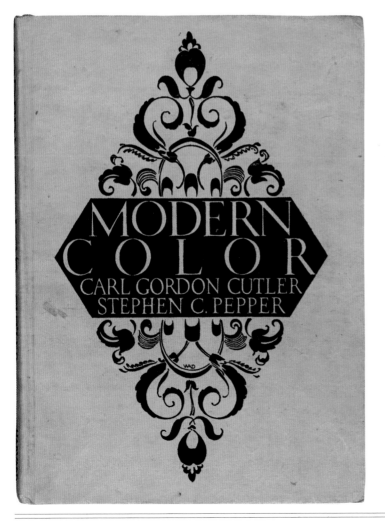

Clockwise **THE OLD MAN'S COMING**, Gosta Gustaf-Janson / W.A. Dwiggins / USA, 1936

THE ANNUAL OF BOOKMAKING / W.A. Dwiggins / USA, 1938

THE GIFT OF THE MAGIC STAFF, Fannie E. Ostrander / W.A. Dwiggins / USA, 1902

MODERN COLOR, Carl Gordon Cutler, Stephen C. Pepper / W.A. Dwiggins / USA, 1923

Alex Steinweiss

b. 1917 (BROOKLYN, NEW YORK, USA)
CURRENTLY SARASOTA, FLORIDA, USA

Alexander Steinweiss attended Abraham Lincoln High in Brooklyn, where he was a member of the Art Squad, a group of students that included Gene Federico, Seymour Chwast › 171, and William Taubin, among other young talents. Guided by their visual arts teacher, Leon Friend, they worked on school publications, posters, and signs, giving them a sense of what it would be like to design once they became professionals. In 1934, Steinweiss attended Parsons School of Art, and upon graduation in 1937 found employment with Joseph Binder, a Viennese poster designer recently relocated to New York. Steinweiss spent approximately three years with Binder and then left to establish his own studio. That venture lasted just a few months because the recently reorganized Columbia Records › 300 needed an art director and its president, William Paley, offered the job to the 23-year-old Steinweiss.

At first, his responsibilities included the design of the label's catalogs, posters, logos, and advertising. But just a few months in, he revolutionized conventional practice: The 78 rpm records were typically placed inside protective, nondescript pasteboard covers with the name of the album and artist simply stamped on the cover and spine; despite concerns of increased costs, Steinweiss took this blank canvas and designed the first album cover with original art and design. With proven success—including a 894 percent increase in sales of a reissue of Beethoven's Ninth Symphony—Steinweiss went on to develop hundreds of covers for Columbia as its art director until 1944, and then, when he joined the U.S. Navy designing posters and booklets in an 8-to-4 job, as a freelancer for Columbia at night. Steinweiss' covers are, in themselves, as influential as the groundbreaking fact of their existence.

SMASH SONG HITS, Rodgers & Hart / After years of albums being packaged in generic sleeves, this was the first consciously packaged album cover design / Columbia Records / 1939

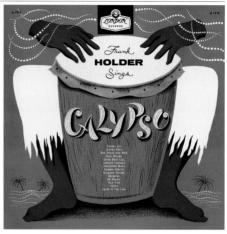

CALYPSO, Frank Holder / London Records / 1957

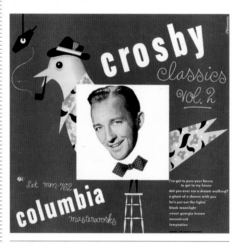

CROSBY CLASSICS VOL. 2 / Columbia Records / 1948

ENCORES, Frankie Carle / Columbia Records / 1947

MARCHES, Edwin Franko Goldman and the Goldman Band / Columbia Records / 1941

CONTRASTS IN HI-FI, Bob Sharples and His Orchestra, featuring the Sandmen / London Records / 1958

Alex Steinweiss / USA

Alexey Brodovitch
1898 (OGOLITCHI, RUSSIA) - 1971

Arriving in Paris in 1920 from revolution torn Russia, Alexey Brodovitch began his career painting sets for Ballet Russes and gradually immersing in design earning recognition through the International Exposition of Modern Industrial and Decorative Arts and by winning a poster competition for Bal Banal, a dance benefit for Russian artists. Approached to establish an advertising art department at the Philadelphia Museum and School of Industrial Art (now the University of the Arts), he moved to the United States in 1930, providing a starting point for his highly influential teachings—among his first group of students was photographer Irving Penn. Brodovitch worked across design and advertising in Philadelphia and New York, but his pivotal career point came in 1934 when Carmel Snow, new editor-in-chief of *Harper's Bazaar* › 327, saw an advertising show hosted by the Art Directors Club › 245 in New York curated by Brodovitch and offered him the art director position that evening.

With an unparalleled sensibility and approach to photography, layout and typography Brodovitch governed the look of *Harper's Bazaar* for the next 24 years. He commissioned work from European artists like Man Ray, Salvador Dalí, and A.M. Cassandre and American photographers like Richard Avedon, Lisette Model, and Diane Arbus—most of whom were Brodovitch's students in his Design Laboratory class at the New School for Social Research in New York that ran from 1941 to 1959. Brodovitch collaborated with art director Frank Zachary to create the short-lived *Portfolio*, a luscious magazine for visual artists published for just three issues. Brodovitch published *Ballet* in 1945, a collection of his own photographs—blurred and full of motion—of the Ballet Russes de Monte Carlo taken between 1935 and 1937. He left *Harper's Bazaar* in 1958 and moved back to France in 1966, he passed away in 1971 in Le Thor, France.

RECOMMENDED READING › 390

PORTFOLIO / Zebra Press / co-edition, Alexey Brodovitch, Frank Zachary; art direction, Alexey Brodovitch / USA, 1950–1951

HARPER'S BAZAAR MAGAZINE / Alexey Brodovitch / USA, 1939, 1952

Alvin Lustig

1915 (DENVER, COLORADO, USA) - **1955**

Investing his energy in practicing magic instead of focusing on his studies, Alvin Lustig's interest quickly shifted when he was introduced to modern art and French posters in high school—soon the posters for his shows got all his attention. Lustig's higher education took place at Los Angeles Community College and the city's Art Center School, punctuated by independent study courses with acclaimed architect Frank Lloyd Wright and French painter Jean Charlot. Lustig established his first design firm in 1937, in Los Angeles; despite a slow start, it signaled the beginning of a prolific body of work that spanned platforms and disciplines—from book covers, advertising, and identity to interior design, textiles, lighting, and furniture.

In 1944, Lustig moved to New York as the director of visual research at *Look* magazine, a position he held for two years before going back to California. During the 1940s and 1950s he designed many book covers, including the New Classics series by New Directions › 278 (1945–1952), in which his abstract solutions represent the creative direction of the author rather than an iconic element of the story itself. His work for Noonday Press (1951–1955) can be identified by its purely typographical work.

Lustig went back to New York in 1950 as his battle with diabetes, which eventually rendered him blind, worsened. During this period he continued to work—most notably on the signage for Philip Johnson's Seagram building in New York and the new *Industrial Design* › 96 magazine—aided by his wife Elaine Lustig Cohen and his studio staff. He succumbed to diabetes at the ripe age of 40.

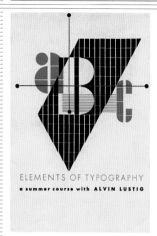

ELEMENTS OF TYPOGRAPHY: A SUMMER COURSE WITH ALVIN LUSTIG FLYER / 1939

AIGA JOURNAL / 1952

WHO BUT YOU, SHEET MUSIC COVER FOR MARK WARNOW / 1945

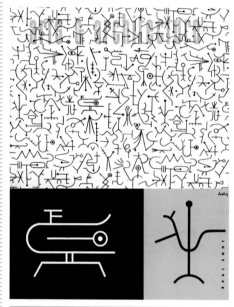

ARTS AND ARCHITECTURE LOGO AND MAGAZINE REDESIGN / 1948

STAFF, IN-HOUSE PUBLICATION FOR *LOOK* MAGAZINE / 1944

ANATOMY FOR INTERIOR DESIGNERS / Whitney Publications / 1946

Alvin Lustig / USA

Cipe Pineles

1908 (VIENNA, AUSTRIA) - 1991

Three years after arriving in the United States from Vienna, in 1926 Cipe Pineles enrolled in Brooklyn's Pratt Institute. After struggling to find employment upon graduation—her portfolio earned her interviews, but the disappointment by employers in seeing a woman did not earn her any jobs—she found employment with Contempora, a small design firm, where one project launched her career: For cotton mill Everfast, Pineles created a series of small boxes with mannequins draped in fabric combinations of her choosing. At a party given by coworker Leslie Foster Nast, wife of publisher Condé Nast, the series caught the latter's attention, and he recommended her for a position under the tutelage of Dr. M.F. Agha, art director for *Vogue*, *Vanity Fair*, and *House and Garden* magazines. Pineles spent 15 years at Condé Nast, earning an increasing charge of responsibility, becoming art director of *Glamour* in 1942, and gaining recognition in a male-dominated industry.

Starting in 1947, she was able to infuse two publications with her own approach and sensibilities. She was art director for *Seventeen* magazine, geared to teenage girls and run by editor Helen Valentine, until 1950, and later for *Charm*, "The magazine for women who work," also headed by Valentine, until 1959. After a short stint at *Mademoiselle*, Pineles joined the design firm of her second husband, Will Burtin—her first husband, William Golden of CBS, passed away unexpectedly in 1959—and began teaching publication design at Parsons School of Design in 1962, where she taught until 1987 and also was director of publications. Pineles broke ground in the field of editorial design and, perhaps more importantly, broke the profession's glass ceiling, becoming the first female member and Hall of Famer of the Art Directors Club › 245. She passed away in Suffern, New York, in 1991.

CHARM MAGAZINE / art direction, Cipe Pineles; photography, William Helburn / USA, April 1956

CHARM MAGAZINE / art direction, Cipe Pineles; photography, Carmen Schiavone / USA, April 1956

CHARM MAGAZINE / art direction, Cipe Pineles; photography, William Helburn / USA, April 1956

SEVENTEEN MAGAZINE / art direction, Cipe Pineles; photography, James Viles / USA, April 1949

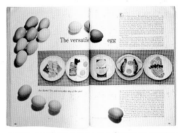

SEVENTEEN MAGAZINE / art direction, Cipe Pineles; photography, Francesco Scavullo / USA, April 1949

SEVENTEEN MAGAZINE / art direction, Cipe Pineles; photography, Francesco Scavullo / USA, April 1949

SEVENTEEN MAGAZINE / The photograph background features Pineles' holiday cards received in 1947 / art direction, Cipe Pineles; photography, Ray Solowinsky / USA, December 1948

VOGUE MAGAZINE / art direction, Mehemed Fehmy Agha, Cipe Pineles; photography, Horst P. Horst / USA, April 1939

PARSONS BREAD BOOK / Through her editorial design course at Parsons School of Design, Cipe Pineles and her students produced the school's yearbook for various years, with the 1974 edition published as a trade paperback / Parsons School of Design: instructor, Cipe Pineles Burtin; students: Senior Class of Editorial Design / Harper & Row, Publishers / USA, 1974

Lester Beall
1903 (KANSAS CITY, MISSOURI, USA) **- 1969**

With a degree in art history from the University of Chicago, plus painting classes at Chicago's Art Institute, where he also found solace in the library and its collection of European art magazines, Lester Beall began his freelance career in 1927, doing advertising work for clients like the *Chicago Tribune*, Pabst Corporation, and Marshall Field's. In 1935, Beall moved to New York, where he maintained a small office in addition to a home and studio in Wilton, Connecticut, beginning in 1936. One of the commissions that garnered substantial attention for his ability to blend European modernism and Russian constructivism with an American sensibility was his ongoing series of posters, done between 1937 and 1941, for the Rural Electrification Administration. This now-defunct agency of the U.S. Department of Agriculture sought to bring electricity to rural areas, and Beall's simple, iconic red-white-and-blue posters gently explained the solution (arrows running through a faucet) and showed the result (happy children and housewives).

In 1955, after dividing his time over the years between offices in New York and Connecticut, Beall consolidated his operation in Connecticut at Dumbarton Farm, which he had purchased in 1950 and built into a fully operational office. In these years, Beall hired more employees and took on more comprehensive and complex design projects in the burgeoning field of corporate identity, designing not just the logos but detailed manuals outlining their use and regulations for clients like International Paper, Caterpillar Tractor Company, and Martin Marietta. Such manuals are now common practice but were pioneered by designers like Beall, Paul Rand › 159, and firms like Chermayeff & Geismar › 156. Beall's body of work evolved through industries and disciplines until his death in 1969.

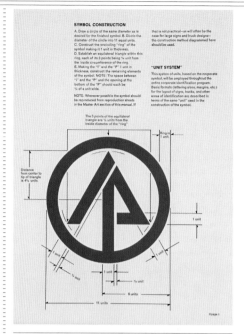

INTERNATIONAL PAPER CORPORATE IDENTITY MANUAL / 1967 / Image: Courtesy of International Paper

CATERPILLAR TRACTOR COMPANY CORPORATE IDENTITY MANUAL / 1967 / Image: Reprinted courtesy of Caterpillar, Inc.

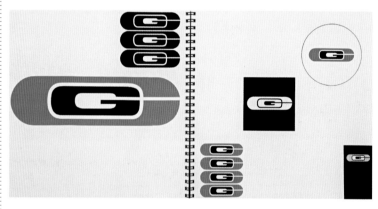

CONNECTICUT GENERAL LIFE INSURANCE CO. CORPORATE IDENTITY MANUAL / 1959

MARTIN MARIETTA CORPORATION CORPORATE IDENTITY MANUAL / 1968

RURAL ELECTRIFICATION ADMINISTRATION POSTERS FOR THE U.S. DEPARTMENT OF AGRICULTURE / 1937–1941 / Images: Courtesy of the Library of Congress, Washington, D.C.

Lester Beall / USA / Images: Courtesy of Lester Beall Collection, Cary Graphic Arts Collection, RIT Libraries

Bradbury Thompson
1911 (TOPEKA, KANSAS, USA) - 1995

While earning his bachelor's degree in economics at Washburn College in Topeka, Kansas, Bradbury Thompson humbly began in the field of editorial design as the editor and designer of the college yearbook. Upon graduation in 1934, Thompson first worked for Capper Publications designing books and magazines; four years later he moved to New York, where he was art director for the printing firm Rogers-Kellogg-Stillson until 1941. In 1938 he became the editor and designer of *Westvaco Inspirations for Printers*, a publication started in 1925 by Westvaco Corporation (formerly West Virginia Pulp and Paper Company, now MeadWestvaco) to showcase the performance of typography, photography, art, and printing techniques on the company's papers. Through 61 issues, until it ceased publication in 1962, Thompson demonstrated not only the aptitudes of the paper but the playfulness and variety graphic design can achieve.

Parallel to *Inspirations*, Thompson maintained an active practice by serving as art director for the Office of War Information's publications division (1942–1945), art director of *Mademoiselle* magazine (1945–1959), and design director of *Art News* and *Art News Annual* (1945–1972). Overall, he designed the format for more than 30 magazines. He was also design consultant for Pitney Bowes and McGraw-Hill Publications and a faculty member at Yale School of Art › 129 beginning in 1956. On a more diminutive scale, Thompson became a member of the U.S. Postal Service Citizens' Stamp Advisory Committee in 1969 and, over the course of his career, designed approximately 100 stamps. Thompson was also curious about typography itself, and in 1950 introduced Alphabet 26, a classic serif typeface in a single case, foregoing the distinction between upper and lowercase. He passed away in 1995 in New York.

Westvaco is much more than a paper company
Westvaco Annual Report 1974
Westvaco is papermaking
Westvaco is agricultural chemicals
Westvaco is consumer products
Westvaco is corrugated shipping containers
Westvaco is envelopes
Westvaco is environmental control chemicals
Westvaco is flexible packaging
Westvaco is food processing chemicals
Westvaco is folding cartons
Westvaco is foreign operations
Westvaco is forest management
Westvaco is housing
Westvaco is industrial processing chemicals
Westvaco is lumber processing
Westvaco is mailers
Westvaco is milk cartons
Westvaco is multiwall bags
Westvaco is point-of-purchase displays
Westvaco is technology licensing
Westvaco is timber sales
Westvaco is water purification chemicals

WESTVACO CORPORATION 1974 ANNUAL REPORT / 1975

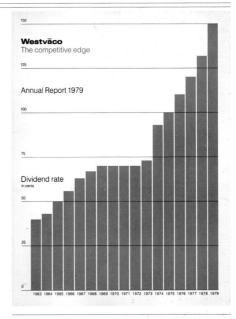

WESTVACO CORPORATION 1979 ANNUAL REPORT / 1980

AMERICA **AND** *USA* **PROPAGANDA BOOKLETS DURING WORLD WAR II** / 1944

Bradbury Thompson / USA

THIS WEEK **MAGAZINE, SPECIAL STORY EDITION FOR THE** *MIAMI NEWS* / October 1964

The Flush-Left, Rag-Right Bible
In 1969, Thompson was commissioned by Field Enterprises, the Chicago media company run by Marshall Field IV, to design a Bible. The project took until 1979, surviving a recession in the early 1970s that halted work until a Washburn College benefactor acquired the interests to the publication. Thompson collaborated with J. Carter Brown, director of the National Gallery of Art, who helped select the accompanying art for each of the 66 books of the bible, and with his Yale colleague, Josef Albers, who designed the frontispieces for each of the three volumes in which the *Washburn College Bible* was published in a limited edition of 400. Typographically, Thompson's bible was quite astute: Instead of the usual justified typesetting, the flush-left, rag-right arrangement was used to highlight the unconventional line breaks, where the reader would normally pause or stop, that were meant to reflect how the text would be spoken.

Erik Nitsche
1908 (LAUSANNE, SWITZERLAND) – 1998

Swiss-born Erik Nitsche began his globetrotting and discipline-crossing career in Cologne, Germany, in 1928, when he joined his professor Fritz Helmut Ehmcke, who was in charge of the design and publicity of *Pressa*, a six-month international exhibition on the modern press. Soon after, around 1930, he headed to Paris, where he worked first for the printing house Draeger Frères and then for Maximilien Vox, who was running Le Service Typographique, a side business of the type foundry Deberny et Peignot.

After graduating from Munich's Kunstgewerbeschule (School of Arts and Crafts)

During his stay in Paris, Nitsche received commissions for numerous illustrations for French and German magazines.

Recognizing the troubled times ahead, Nitsche moved to Los Angeles in 1934, and then relocated to New York in 1936. There he began doing editorial illustrations for magazines like *Harper's Bazaar* › 327 and *Town and Country* and covers for *Fortune* and *Vanity Fair*. In 1938 he was hired as art director for Saks Fifth Avenue › 319, and through the 1940s he did a variety of freelance work as well as a brief stint as art director of *Mademoiselle* magazine and as art director in the New York office of advertising agency Dorland International.

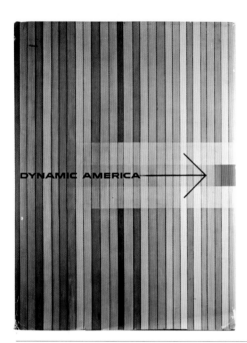

DYNAMIC AMERICA: A HISTORY OF GENERAL DYNAMICS CORPORATION AND ITS PREDECESSOR COMPANIES, Edited by John Niven, Courlandt Canby, Vernon Welsh / Doubleday and General Dynamics / Erik Nitsche / USA, 1960

HAYDN, SYMPHONY NO. 94 IN G MAJOR AND SYMPHONY NO. 101 IN D MAJOR / Decca Records / Erik Nitsche / USA, 1952

LENINGRAD PHILHARMONIC ORCHESTRA, RACHMANINOFF SYMPHONY NO. 2 / Decca Records / Erik Nitsche / USA, 1954

In the early 1950s, now living in Connecticut, Nitsche did posters for movies like *No Way Out* and *All About Eve*, and he designed numerous album covers for Decca Records. At this time he also began his relationship with U.S. defense contractor General Dynamics (GD), first through the Gotham Agency, which had the account and hired him to do some print ads, and later directly, when his work caught the attention of the president and CEO John Jay Hopkins, who vested GD's identity in Nitsche's hands. From 1955 to the early 1960s Nitsche designed a comprehensive identity program—including posters, advertising, annual reports, and more—for GD that hinged on a combination of abstract and figurative imagery with a scientific flair coupled with elegant and simple typography and layouts. An overture

that concluded in the monumental *Dynamic America*, a 420-page book documenting the history of the company. After that, Nitsche ping-ponged between Connecticut and Europe: In the early 1960s he moved to Geneva, Switzerland, where he established Erik Nitsche International, S.A., and designed a number of pictorial books; in the 1970s he returned to Connecticut, where he worked on children's books and other projects; in the early 1980s he left for Munich, Germany, where he designed postage stamps for the West German Ministry of Communications; and in 1996 he returned to Connecticut for medical reasons. He passed away in 1998.

Above and Right GENERAL DYNAMICS NATIONAL ADVERTISING CAMPAIGN AND 1958 ANNUAL REPORT / Erik Nitsche / USA, 1959

FORTUNE MAGAZINE COVER / Erik Nitsche / USA, 1954

Ladislav Sutnar

1897 (PLZEŇ, CZECHOSLOVAKIA) - 1976

Featuring a prolific career that bridges disciplines and removes the boundaries between them, Ladislav Sutnar's life can be told in two chapters: Prague and New York. Sutnar studied at the School of Applied Arts in Prague, Charles University, and the Czech Technical University, learning painting, architecture, and mathematics respectively. Soon after graduation, Sutnar began working on wooden toys, puppets, puppetry sets, costumes, and stage direction, a passion that persisted as he also worked on exhibition design, magazines, books, teaching, porcelain products, and textiles. With several World Fairs in his portfolio, Sutnar was commissioned to design the Czechoslovak National Exhibition at the New York World Fair in 1939—with the onset of war, the exhibition was canceled, and Sutnar was sent to retrieve the materials but, instead, stayed permanently.

While looking for work alongside other exiled designers, Sutnar became art director of Sweet's Catalog Service in 1941, a position he kept for nearly two decades. In 1944, along with architect Knud Löndberg-Holm, Sutnar published *New Patterns in Product Information*. Their ongoing partnership, born at Sweet's, pioneered what is now known as *information design* through many publications. Sutnar also worked for a variety of clients such as *Fortune*, the United Nations, Golden Griffin Books, Knoll, and Bell Telephone Co.—where, although uncredited, he established the convention of delineating area codes with parentheses. In 1961 the show *Visual Design in Action*, a traveling retrospective of his work and a self-funded book, joined both chapters of Sutnar's work, showcasing the prolific career that preceded his years spent as a painter.

CUNO ENGINEERING CORPORATION CATALOG / Ladislav Sutnar / USA, c. 1946

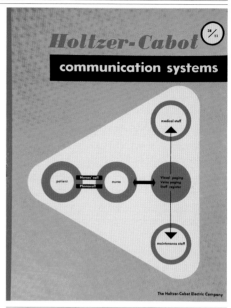

HOLTZER-CABOT ELECTRIC COMPANY CATALOG / Ladislav Sutnar / USA, c. 1944

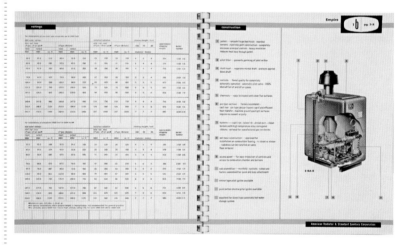

AMERICAN RADIATOR AND STANDARD SANITARY COMPANY CATALOG / Ladislav Sutnar / USA, c. 1950

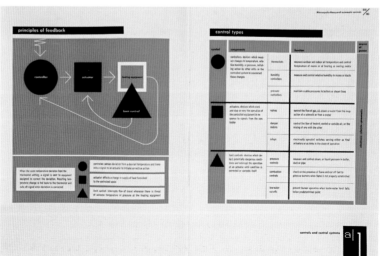

MINNEAPOLIS-HONEYWELL REGULATOR CO. AUTOMATIC CONTROLS CATALOG / Ladislav Sutnar / USA, n. d.

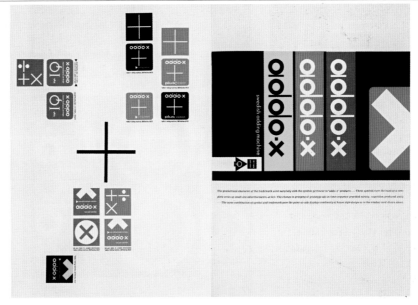

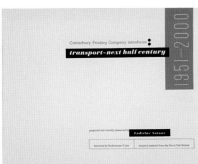

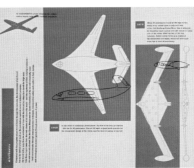

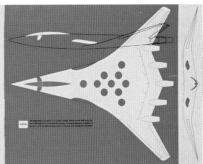

ADVENTURES WITH A LOGOTYPE ADDO-X BUSINESS MACHINES BROCHURE / Ladislav Sutnar / USA, c. 1956–1959

TRANSPORT: NEXT HALF-CENTURY BOOK FOR CANTERBURY PRINTING CO. / Ladislav Sutnar / USA, 1950

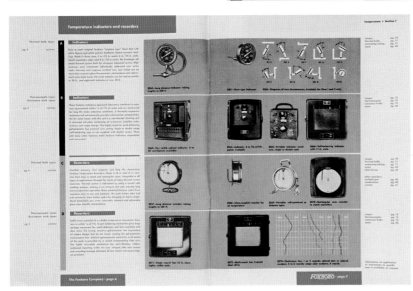

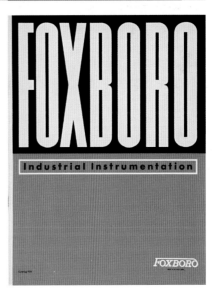

FOXBORO INDUSTRIAL INSTRUMENTA-TION CATALOG / Ladislav Sutnar / USA, 1943

Armin Hofmann
1920 (WINTERTHUR, SWITZERLAND)

After graduating from Zurich's Kunstgewerbeschule (School of Arts and Crafts) in the late 1930s, followed by a lithography apprenticeship in Winterthur and working for a number of studios since 1943, Armin Hoffman moved to Basel in 1946 to establish his own studio and begin his longstanding influence as a faculty member of the Schule für Gestaltung Basel (Basel School of Design). In 1968 he established, with Emil Ruder, the Advanced Class of Graphic Design, where he taught until his retirement in 1986. In 1955 Hofmann taught briefly at the Philadelphia Museum School of Industrial Art and lengthily at Yale School of Art ›129, where he remained a visiting lecturer throughout his career; his teaching methods are well documented in *Graphic Design Manual: Principles and Practice*, published in 1965. As a graphic designer, Hofmann created posters, identities, and advertising for cultural institutions as well as corporations like J.R. Geigy Pharmaceutical Company.

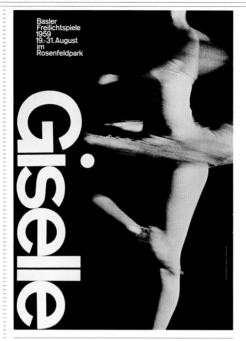

GISELLE **POSTER FOR BASEL THEATRE** / Armin Hoffman / Switzerland, 1959

WILLIAM TELL **POSTER** / Armin Hoffman / Switzerland, 1963

Photos: Courtesy of Museum für Gestaltung Zürich, Poster Collection; Franz Xaver Jaggy

Joseph Müller-Brockmann
1914 (RAPPERSWIL, SWITZERLAND) - 1996

Following studies at both the University of Zurich and the Kunstgewerbeschule (School of Arts and Crafts), Josef Müller-Brockmann apprenticed under designer Walter Diggelmann before establishing his own studio in Zurich in 1936. Over his career he developed numerous projects in different industries, including his famed posters for the Tonhalle Gesellschaft Zürich, the signage system of Zurich's airport, and his appointment as the European design consultant for IBM ›341— all of it in strict adherence to the International Typographic Style. Müller-Brockmann was also an avid educator, teaching at the Kunstgewerbeschule and at the Hochschule für Gestaltung in Ulm, Germany. Along with Richard Paul Lohse, Hans Neuburg, and Carlo L. Vivarelli, he co-founded the journal *Neue Grafik* ›97, which he co-edited for seven years.

BEETHOVEN **POSTER** / Joseph Müller-Brockmann / Switzerland, 1955

DER FILM **EXHIBITION POSTER** / Joseph Müller-Brockmann / Switzerland, 1960

Photos: Courtesy of Museum für Gestaltung Zürich, Poster Collection; Franz Xaver Jaggy

Wim Crouwel
b. 1928 (GRONINGEN, NETHERLANDS)
CURRENTLY GRONINGEN, NETHERLANDS

Wim Crouwel attended both the Academy Minerva, School of Fine Arts and Design in Groningen (1947–1949), and the Institute of Arts and Crafts in Amsterdam (1951–1952). Crouwel established his own firm after graduation and in 1955 established a long-lasting relationship with the Van Abbemuseum, where he created some of his most iconic posters. With working experience as a graphic and exhibit designer, he co-founded Total Design in 1963 with Ben Bos, Friso Kramer, Dick and Paul Schwarz, and Benno Wissing—a multidisciplinary partnership that sought to encompass all aspects of design in a single firm, achieving unity across all fields. In 1964, the director of Van Abbemuseum left to run the Stedelijk Museum in Amsterdam, commissioning posters from Crouwel, who responded with a systematic approach whereby all the work was performed with the same underlying grid ›50. This and other adherences to grid structures earned him the nickname "Gridnik."

Prevalent in Crouwel's work is the use of custom letterforms, a practice that gave way to New Alphabet, a theoretical exercise, done in the late 1960s, of a monospaced type family in various weights and styles, designed solely with 90-degree angles and a 45-degree cut at the joints. Considered unusable by Crouwel, New Alphabet was famously reprised on a Joy Division album cover released in 1988 and designed by Peter Saville ›180. In 1981, Crouwel was the last of the founding partners to leave Total Design as he became a full-time professor at Delft University. He officially retired in 1993, yet he continues to design, fully embracing the technology his Macintosh offers.

RECOMMENDED READING ›390

FERNAND LEGER POSTER FOR VAN ABBEMUSEUM / 1957   HIROSHIMA POSTER FOR VAN ABBEMUSEUM / 1957

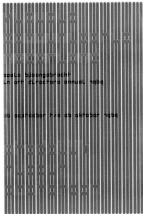

Far Left **VISUELE COMMUNICATIE NEDERLAND** POSTER FOR STEDELIJK MUSEUM AMSTERDAM / 1968

Left **JONGE ENGELSE BEELDHOUWERS** POSTER FOR STEDELIJK MUSEUM AMSTERDAM / 1967

Far Left **EDGAR FERNHOUT** POSTER FOR STEDELIJK MUSEUM AMSTERDAM / 1963

Left **HET NEDERLANDSE AFFICHE 1890-1968** POSTER FOR MUSEUM FODOR AMSTERDAM / 1968

Wim Crouwel / Netherlands

Robert Massin

b. 1925 (LA BOURDINIÈRE, FRANCE)

Robert Massin began his design career in 1948 when he joined one of France's most influential book clubs—which had supplanted traditional publishing houses and the library network after their downfall in World War II—Club français du livre, as editor of *Liens*, its monthly newsletter. There he had the opportunity to design his first book cover and layout, a skill he would soon master and revolutionize. Next he worked as the artistic advisor for another book club, the Club du meilleur livre, from 1952 to 1958, which he helped develop into one of the most prestigious through sophisticated and provocative design and production. Massin was then hired by Gallimard, a French publishing house, where he spent 20 years designing and art directing the covers and layouts of its 10,000 titles.

With Gallimard, Massin published two of his most recognized books: *La Cantatrice Chauve* in 1964 (later published as *The Bald Soprano* in the United States and *The Bald Prima Donna* in the United Kingdom), a play by Eugène Ionesco, in which he manipulated typography as a way to bring the intonation and timing of the play into the flat page; and *La Lettre et l'Image* (*Letter and Image*) in 1970, a book showcasing his vast and eccentric collection of images that reflect the relationship among letters, images, and the cultures they inhabit. In 1979 Massin left Gallimard and engaged with books in a different way: as editor for Gallimard and other publishers; from 1980 to 1982 as associate editor of Atelier Hachette/Massin, an imprint of the publishing giant Hachette; and as a writer, publishing novels and essays. Since 1984, Massin has worked as an independent designer.

LA LETTRE ET L'IMAGE, Massin / First published by Gallimard, later translated to various languages / Massin / France, 1970 (1st ed.)

COVER AND SPREADS FROM *THE BOLD SOPRANO*, Eugène Ionesco / Massin / France, 1965

L'OR: LA MERVEILLEUSE HISTOIRE DU GÉNÉRAL JOHANN AUGUST SUTER, Blaise Cendrars, Club du Meilleur Livre / Massin / France, 1956

LA FOULE FINAL LAYOUT / Grove Press / Massin; lyrics, Édith Piaf; photographic interpretation, Emil Cadoo / USA, 1965

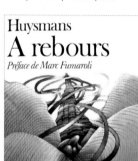

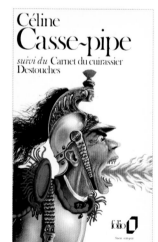

FOLIO SERIES BOOK COVERS / Gallimard / Massin / France, 1972–1974

Robert Brownjohn

b. 1925 (NEWARK, NEW JERSEY, USA) - **1970**

Following a year in Brooklyn's Pratt Institute, Robert Brownjohn left to attend Chicago's Institute of Design in 1944, where the renowned László Moholy-Nagy took him as his protégé, and after his death in 1946, his successor, architect Serge Chermayeff, also embraced Brownjohn as his teaching assistant. It was during this time that Brownjohn's lifelong struggle with heroin and drug addiction began. In 1951, he moved to New York and toiled in both freelance work and the city's nightlife, and by 1956 he began a working collaboration with Ivan Chermayeff (Serge's son) that a year later would become Brownjohn, Chermayeff & Geismar › 156 with the addition of Tom Geismar. First designing letterheads, book covers, and other small projects, their commissions soon became bigger for clients like Pepsi-Cola and Chase Manhattan Bank, but Brownjohn's drug addiction and erratic behavior kept surfacing, and in 1960 he moved to London.

Brownjohn was first employed by J. Walter Thompson and then McCann-Erickson in 1962 as an art director; this wasn't Brownjohn's most prolific period, as his work and ideas went mostly unproduced, but it did establish his reputation as one of the best in London, and he was able to prove it when he designed the iconic titles for the movie *From Russia with Love*, where the credits are projected on a dancer—a feat he topped in the following James Bond installment, *Goldfinger*, where live-action sequences are projected on a gold-hued dancer. With a deeper interest in film, he left advertising and formed a partnership with filmmakers David Cammell and Hugh Hudson in 1965. He continued to work in this field as well as in design, but in 1970 he died of a heart attack at the young age of 44.

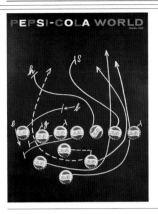

PEPSI-COLA WORLD IN-HOUSE MAGAZINE FOR PEPSI-COLA COMPANY / Brownjohn, Chermayeff & Geismar: Robert Brownjohn / USA, 1958–1961

CHRISTMAS RIBBON HOLIDAY DISPLAY FOR THE PEPSI-COLA BUILDING LOBBY / Brownjohn, Chermayeff & Geismar: Robert Brownjohn / USA, 1958

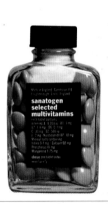

VITAMIN TABLET PACKAGING / Robert Brownjohn / USA, early 1960s

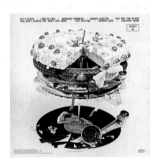

LET IT BLEED, The Rolling Stones / Decca Records / Robert Brownjohn / USA, 1969

Robert Brownjohn designed this letterheading for Michael Cooper of 4 Chelsea Manor Studios Flood Street London SW3 FLAxman 9762

Robert Brownjohn designed this Label for Michael Cooper of 4 Chelsea Manor Studios Flood Street London SW3 FLAxman 9762

MICHAEL COOPER STATIONERY / Robert Brownjohn / USA, 1967

Robert Brownjohn designed this Business Card for Michael Cooper of 4 Chelsea Manor Studios Flood Street London SW3 FLAxman 9762

Chermayeff & Geismar

EST. 1957 (NEW YORK, NEW YORK, USA)

During the 1960s, the practice of corporate identity was firmly established in the United States, and one of the forerunners in the field was Chermayeff & Geismar, a design firm founded in 1957 by Ivan Chermayeff, Tom Geismar, and Robert Brownjohn, who left the partnership in 1960. Chermayeff and Geismar met while they were both at the graduate program of Yale's School of Art › 129 and Architecture. Each pursued a different track—Chermayeff worked for Alvin Lustig › 144 and CBS Records › 300, while Geismar went to the Army's Exhibition Unit, where he designed exhibits and graphics—before coming back together. Initially, their business was comparatively small, designing business cards and letterheads for small clients, but they built up to larger commissions—from Pepsi-Cola in 1958, designing their in-house magazine *Pepsi-Cola World*, and Chase Manhattan Bank in 1960, designing their identity—the result, an abstract icon, was one of the first to forego figurative interpretations or an alphabetic solution.

In the ensuing 50 years, the firm of Chermayeff & Geismar has created more than 100 identity programs, including Mobil, Xerox, PBS, NBC › 344, Univision, Viacom, TimeWarner, the Smithsonian, and *National Geographic*. In addition to their identity output, Chermayeff and Geismar have been prolific in the realm of exhibit design and environmental graphics, creating large-scale projects like the U.S. pavilions in the 1958 and 1970 World Fairs and exhibits for the Ellis Island Immigration Museum, the Statue of Liberty Museum, and the Truman Presidential Library, among others. Posters, corporate literature, signage, and books complement their practice in an unconfined diversity of styles. In 2005, Chermayeff and Geismar separated from their partners—among them Steff Geissbuhler › 157, who had been with the firm for 30 years—and established a smaller studio.

LEXINGTON AVENUE AT 53RD STREET SUBWAY STATION MURALS AND WAYFINDING SYSTEM / architecture, Edward Larrabee Barnes Architects / 1986

UNIVISION LOGO / 1988

ELLIS ISLAND IMMIGRATION MUSEUM / MetaForm, Inc. / 1990

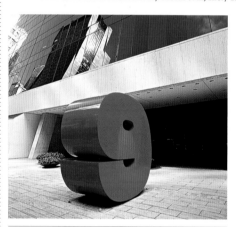

SAKS FIFTH AVENUE HOLIDAY PACKAGING / 1976

B A R N E Y S
N E W Y O R K

9 WEST 57TH STREET / architecture, Skidmore, Owings & Merrill / 1972

BARNEYS NEW YORK LOGO / 1981

Mobil

MOBIL LOGO / 1964

NATIONAL GEOGRAPHIC LOGO / 2001

(PUBLIC BROADCASTING SERVICE) LOGO / 1983

SMITHSONIAN INSTITUTION LOGO / 1997

CHASE MANHATTAN BANK LOGO / 1960

Chermayeff & Geismar / USA

Steff Geissbuhler

b. 1942 (ZOFINGEN, SWITZERLAND)
CURRENTLY NEW YORK, NEW YORK, USA

Equipped with an ability to illustrate and an education from the Basel School of Design ›128 in Switzerland, Steff Geissbuhler has developed a rich portfolio of identities, posters, corporate literature, signage, and environmental graphics that is both freely expressive and formally structured. Upon graduation from Basel in 1964, Geissbuhler first worked at J.R. Geigy Pharmaceutical Company (now Novartis), known for a strong art department headed by Max Schmid. After three years, he moved to the United States to help his Basel classmate, Ken Hiebert, establish a graphic design program at the Philadelphia College of Art (now the University of the Arts); he served there as associate professor until 1973. At the same time he freelanced for Murphy, Levy, Wurman, Architects and Urban Planners, in Philadelphia.

Interested in returning to a full-time practice, Geissbuhler spent a year at Anspach Grossman Portugal in New York before joining Chermayeff & Geismar ›156 in 1974, initially as an associate and, only two years in, as a partner. He spent the next 30 years with the firm. Among his most visible projects were identities for NBC ›344, TimeWarner, Telemundo, and Merck, along with large assignments like signage for the University of Pennsylvania and architectural graphics for the IBM building in New York. These were augmented with a variety of work for cultural and educational institutions around the country. In 2005, Chermayeff and Geismar decided to form a smaller studio, and Geissbuhler established C&G Partners—a name directly derived from Chermayeff & Geismar—with partners Keith Helmetag, Jonathan Alger, and Emanuela Frigerio, founded on the legacy of his previous partners while building their own.

QUESTIONMARK POSTER FOR PUNCT'D EXHIBIT / 2003

NEW YORK IS DANCE POSTER / One of nine posters promoting cultural institutions in New York City /1987

ALVIN AILEY DANCE THEATER 30TH ANNIVERSARY TOUR POSTER AND IDENTITY / 1981

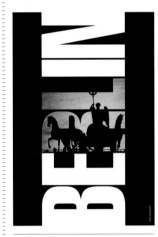

AGI CONGRESS AND EXHIBIT POSTER / 2005

SPORTS ILLUSTRATED AT THE OLYMPICS, A PHOTOGRAPHY EXHIBIT AT THE TIMEWARNER CENTER / 2004

AIGA COMPETITIONS AND EXHIBITIONS POSTER / 2000

TOLEDO MUSEUM OF ART IDENTITY, GRAPHICS, AND ENVIRONMENTAL GRAPHICS / 1999

TIME WARNER AND TIME WARNER CABLE IDENTITY / 1990

C&G Partners; Steff Geissbuhler / USA

Saul Bass
1920 (NEW YORK, NEW YORK, USA) **- 1996**

In a career spanning the 1950s to the 1990s, Saul Bass conquered individual industries—corporate identity, film titling and marketing, packaging, and filmmaking—that are now the realm of specialized agencies with dozens of employees. He attended the vocational Art Students League of New York in 1936 and then Brooklyn College in 1944, working briefly in New York before moving to Los Angeles in 1946, where he worked and freelanced for agencies until 1952, when he established Saul Bass & Associates. His first foray into the movie industry came in 1954 with the advertising image for *Carmen Jones*, a production of Otto Preminger. This was followed by the motif and groundbreaking film titles for Preminger's *Man with the Golden Arm*. Bass continued to work with Preminger as collaborations with Alfred Hitchcock and Stanley Kubrick blossomed in the form not only of posters and film titles but also of the designer's influential input in cinematic sequences.

Bass's interest in filmmaking led him to do short films for companies like Kodak and United Airlines, and Kaiser Aluminum produced *Why Man Creates*, the 1968 documentary that earned Bass an Oscar in that category. Beyond the film industry, Bass was a highly accomplished corporate identity designer, creating iconic logos in every conceivable market, from consumer products to airlines to nonprofits to electronic goods. Some of the biggest identity commissions, including Exxon and AT&T, came after Bass entered a partnership with Herb Yager, who had a seasoned business and marketing acumen, to form Saul Bass/Herb Yager & Associates in 1978. After a respite from film titles in the 1970s and 1980s, Bass worked with Martin Scorsese through the 1990s, creating four more opening sequences, with 1995's *Casino* his last. He passed away in 1996 in Los Angeles.

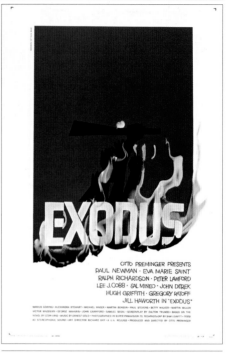

ANATOMY OF A MURDER POSTER / Columbia / 1959   **EXODUS POSTER** / United Artists / 1960

Images: Courtesy of the Academy of Motion Picture Arts and Sciences

CONTINENTAL AIRLINES LOGO / 1965   **UNITED AIRLINES LOGO /** 1965   **THE BELL SYSTEM LOGO REDESIGN /** 1969

DIXIE LOGO / 1969   **QUAKER OATS LOGO** / 1969   **WARNER MUSIC GROUP LOGO** / 1974

GIRL SCOUTS LOGO / 1978   **AT&T LOGO** / 1984   **YWCA LOGO** / 1988

Saul Bass / USA

Paul Rand
1914 (BROOKLYN, NEW YORK, USA) - 1996

Through a career spanning more than 60 years, Paul Rand sustained an inimitable practice that crossed multiple disciplines without sacrificing his commitment to design with the highest quality and care. He was mostly self-taught through a voracious appetite for reading, as art and drawing classes in the early 1930s at Pratt Institute, the Art Students' League, and Parsons School of Design were not necessarily cathartic. Rand made a significant name for himself—first, literally by changing his birth name of Peretz Rosenbaum in 1935—as art director for advertising agency William H. Weintraub & Co., where he worked from 1941 until the firm closed in 1955. Through these years and afterwards, he also created numerous book jackets and magazine covers as freelance assignments as well as designing and illustrating four children's books written by his second wife, Ann Rand.

Best known, perhaps, was Rand's contribution to the growing discipline of corporate identity, and most notable was his work for IBM › 341. He started there in 1956, when Eliot Noyes hired him as design consultant and over the course of three decades Rand oversaw every aspect of IBM's identity, establishing unflinching standards for other designers to implement as well as designing numerous publications and posters himself. Other significant and comprehensive programs were for Westinghouse and Cummins, as well as logos for ABC › 344, Enron, UPS › 342, and Steve Jobs's NeXT. Rand's unwavering pursuit of commitment also applied to his teaching at Yale School of Art › 129, where he was exacting and brutally honest in his critiques—more than 30 years' worth of students can attest to that. He was an avid and authoritative writer, publishing books and dozens of articles over the course of his career. Rand passed away in 1996 in Norwalk, Connecticut.

CUMMINS ENGINE COMPANY, INC. 1973 ANNUAL REPORT / Paul Rand / USA, 1974

IBM TECH III RIBBON PACKAGE / Paul Rand / USA, 1971

WESTINGHOUSE LOGO / Paul Rand / USA, 1960

JOURNAL OF THE AMERICAN INSTITUTE OF GRAPHIC ARTS, NO. 6 / cover design, Paul Rand / USA, 1968 / Image: Courtesy of AdamsMorioka Vault, AIGA

CORONET BRANDY ADVERTISEMENT SHOWCASING THE CORONET BRANDY MAN AND CARBONATED BUBBLES BACKGROUND, DESIGNED IN 1941, THAT IDENTIFIED THE CAMPAIGN / Paul Rand / USA, circa 1945–1948

SPARKLE AND SPIN: A BOOK ABOUT WORDS, By Ann and Paul Rand / Harcourt, Brace & World / USA, 1957

Massimo Vignelli

b. 1931 (MILAN, ITALY)
CURRENTLY NEW YORK, NEW YORK, USA

After studies in architecture in Milan and Venice, Massimo Vignelli was offered a year-long fellowship with Massachusetts-based Towle Silversmiths, a silverware company in 1957. He married Lella Vignelli, with whom he established a lifelong collaborative working relationship as well, and moved to the United States. Vignelli then took a part-time teaching position at the Institute of Design at Chicago's Illinois Institute of Technology (IIT), where he spent two years while also working at the Center for Advanced Research in Design at the Container Corporation of America. In 1960, the Vignellis returned to Milan, where they established the Vignelli Office of Design and Architecture and designed corporate identity projects, packaging, interiors, and furniture.

In January 1965, along with Chicago-based Ralph Eckerstrom, Vignelli co-founded Unimark International, a design firm with headquarters in Chicago and offices in New York, Palo Alto, and Milan. Vignelli headed the Milan office for a short time and then went to New York, planning to stay two years—but the Vignellis never left. In 1971, Vignelli left Unimark and once again established a thriving office, Vignelli Associates, with his wife. From 1980 to 2000, the firm grew exponentially until its founders decided to scale back, slow the pace, and establish a design office in their own home.

The graphic design work produced by Vignelli over five decades consistently abided by strict principles of layout and typography—manifest in devoted adherence to the grid ›50 and a penchant for a select set of classic typefaces—that parlayed into a dominant aesthetic that defined corporate identity, packaging, editorial, and environmental design in the 1960s, 1970s, and 1980s—not to mention a lasting influence well into the first decade of the twenty-first century.

RECOMMENDED READING ›390

NATIONAL PARK SERVICE PUBLICATIONS PROGRAM / 1977

HOUSTON MUSEUM OF FINE ARTS ENVIRONMENTAL GRAPHICS AND SIGNAGE / 1999

BLOOMINGDALE'S LOGO AND PACKAGING / 1972

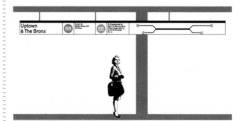

NEW YORK METROPOLITAN TRANSIT AUTHORITY SUBWAY SIGN SYSTEM / 1966

Vignelli Associates / USA

BICENTENNIAL POSTER / 1976

AMERICAN AIRLINES IDENTITY / 1967

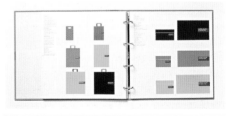

BENETTON CORPORATE IDENTITY / USA and Italy, 1995

Fletcher/ Forbes/Gill

EST. 1962 (LONDON, ENGLAND, UK)

Considering the transatlantic crisscrossing of its three founders, it is serendipity, destiny, or just luck that Alan Fletcher, Colin Forbes, and Bob Gill were able to come together in 1962 to form Fletcher/Forbes/Gill. Starting in 1949, Fletcher first attended Hammersmith School of Art, then transferred to the Central School (where he met Forbes), later enrolled in the Royal College of Art, and, lastly, earned an exchange scholarship to Yale School of Art › 129 in the United States, returning to London in 1959. Working as a freelance designer and illustrator since the early 1950s in New York, Gill moved to London in 1960 to work for advertising agency Charles Hobson—he had been given Fletcher's phone number and called him upon arrival. After graduating from the Central School, Forbes freelanced and then worked for an advertising agency before returning to his alma mater as head of graphic design from 1956 to 1960, when he left to start his own practice. Fletcher rented studio space at his apartment, and they began to collaborate, with Gill joining them as he grew disenchanted in his job.

Fletcher/Forbes/Gill quickly became one of the most sought-after firms in London, as their combined talents offered clients impeccable typography, innovative concepts, clever executions, and, for a small design firm, unparalleled business sense (mostly by Forbes). The firm changed somewhat in 1965 when architect Theo Crosby joined and Gill left; thus began the Crosby/ Fletcher/Forbes era, which saw more complex and ambitious projects for clients like BP, Penguin, Pirelli, and Reuters. At the turn of the decade, two more partners had joined: graphic designer Mervyn Kurlansky and product designer Kenneth Grange. Realizing that changing names constantly wasn't ideal, Fletcher, while reading a witchcraft book, came upon the name of Pentagram › 162—a five-pointed star, one point for each partner—and established the famed firm in 1972.

FLETCHER FORBES GILL LTD. ANNOUNCEMENT BOOK / Alan Fletcher, Colin Forbes, Bob Gill / UK, 1962–1963

 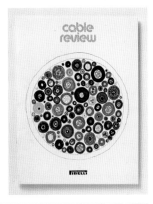 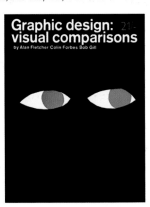

PIRELLI CABLE REVIEW 1 AND 2 / Theo Crosby, Alan Fletcher, Colin Forbes / UK, 1970

GRAPHIC DESIGN: VISUAL COMPARISONS, Alan Fletcher, Colin Forbes, Bob Gill / Studio Books London / Alan Fletcher, Colin Forbes, Bob Gill / UK, 1962–1963

YES / Atlantic Records / Alan Fletcher / UK, 1968–1969

PLASTICS TODAY 23 AND 24 FOR ICI / Colin Forbes / UK, 1969

REUTERS LOGO / Alan Fletcher, Colin Forbes, Bob Gill / UK, 1968

Pentagram

EST. 1972 (LONDON, ENGLAND, UK)
OFFICES AUSTIN, BERLIN, LONDON,
NEW YORK, SAN FRANCISCO

Established in 1972 when Crosby/Fletcher/
Forbes (previously Fletcher/Forbes/Gill ›161), the
partnership of architect Theo Crosby and graphic designers Alan Fletcher and Colin Forbes grew
to include graphic designer Mervyn Kurlansky
and product designer Kenneth Grange, taking
on the black magic-inspired name of Pentagram,
a five-pointed star. This partnership and the
blueprint it established for growth was unique in
several aspects: It was multidisciplinary, allowing
a single firm to offer a broad scope of practices;
it gave each partner an equal salary, equity, and
profit-sharing; it centralized administrative
resources while allowing each partner to operate
in relative independence as active designers
running their own teams and responsible for
their own clients; and it established a precedent
so the accumulated personalities through the
years could compete against large, tiered
corporate agencies and firms. It was Forbes,
for the most part, who was able to establish
this unconventional structure as he took on
the responsibility of setting the parameters
for Pentagram's growth as well as introducing,
and chairing for the next 18 years, the partner
meetings occurring every six months—a task
that grew increasingly complex as partners
around the world joined.

How designers become partners in the firm is
a constant source of discussion in the industry,
but an agreed set of criteria informs the selection process, which was more clearly defined
around 1991, when Forbes decided to delegate
his chairmanship: "A partner must be able
to generate business, a partner must have a
national reputation as an outstanding professional in the chosen discipline, a partner must
be able to control projects and contribute to
the profits of the firm, and a partner must be a
proactive member of the group and care about
Pentagram and the partners." The criteria
emphasize the need for each addition to be
able to perform not just as a designer but as a
businessperson as well—a symbiosis that does

BRITISH GENIUS EXHIBITION FOR CARLTON CLEEVE / Pentagram: Alan Fletcher, Theo Crosby / UK, 1977

POLAROID ADVERTISING CAMPAIGN / Pentagram: John Rushworth / UK, 1988

THE GUARDIAN **NEWSPAPER** / Pentagram: David
Hillman / UK, 1988

PENTAGRAM PAPERS 3: BRUSHES AND BROOMS AND *PENTAGRAM PAPERS 4: FACE TO FACE* / Pentagram: John
McConnell / UK, 1976, 1977

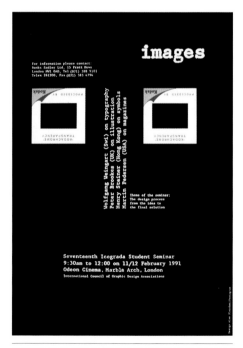

ICOGRADA'S SEVENTEENTH STUDENT SEMINAR POSTER /
Pentagram: Alan Fletcher / UK, 1991

FALSE START FOR 2WICE ARTS FOUNDATION / Pentagram: Abbott Miller; photography, Joachim Ladefoged / USA, 2008

ARIZONA CARDINALS STADIUM ENVIRONMENTAL GRAPHICS / Pentagram: Michael Gericke / USA, 2006 / Photo: Peter Mauss/Esto

DESIGN WITHIN REACH IDENTITY AND COLLATERAL / Pentagram: Kit Hinrichs / USA, 2002–2003 / Photo: Barry Robinson

GREEN WORLD: MERCE CUNNINGHAM FOR 2WICE ARTS FOUNDATION / Pentagram: Abbott Miller; photography, Katherine Wolkoff / USA, 2007

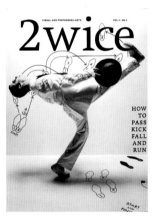

EAT IDENTITY AND PACKAGING / Pentagram: Angus Hyland / UK, 2002 / Photo: Nick Turner

DEUTSCHE KINEMATHEK: MUSEUM FÜR FILM UND FERNSEHEN IDENTITY AND COLLATERAL / Pentagram: Justus Oehler / Germany, 2007 / Photo: Justus Oehler

2WICE 9:2: HOW TO PASS, KICK, FALL, AND RUN FOR 2WICE ARTS FOUNDATION / Pentagram: Abbott Miller; photography, Jens Umbach, Katherine Wolkoff / USA, 2006

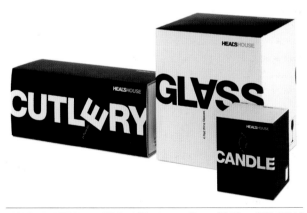

CIRCULAR FOR THE TYPOGRAPHIC CIRCLE / Pentagram: Domenick Lippa / UK, 2007 / Photo: John Ross

HEAL'S IDENTITY AND PACKAGING / Pentagram: Domenick Lippa / UK, 2006 / Photo: John Ross

not always succeed. Across four decades, more than 35 individuals have either been partners or given the opportunity to be through the two-year probationary period, giving the firm a consistent flux as partners join and leave.

Pentagram grew quickly; John McConnell joined in 1974, and then in 1978 Forbes launched a New York office. The firm has since expanded at an organic pace, adding partners not to boost profits or billings but when the right person comes along, and opening locations not to exploit industries or markets but to blend with the partners' original location. Not all additions have proved successful; Peter Saville ›180 and April Greiman ›179, two of the most celebrated designers of the 1980s, did not last more than two years, and a Hong Kong office headed by London-based David Hillman operated just three years.

Consistent throughout Pentagram's history has been a remarkably multidisciplinary practice— first, across disciplines, from corporate identity to packaging, editorial design, posters, and exhibit design; second, across client types, from nonprofit organizations to consumer brands and business-to-business corporations; and, third, across a dizzying number of markets and industries, from fashion to culture and hospitality—all without a specific or implicit adherence to any given style, resulting in an extremely diverse portfolio. In its most recent incarnation, Pentagram's roster comprises mostly third- and fourth-generation partners—San Francisco–based Kit Hinrichs, who joined in 1986, is the longest standing—yet the principles remain the same more than 35 years later.

AMERICAN QUARTER HORSE JOURNAL / Pentagram: DJ Stout / USA, 2001

DAIRY HERD MANAGEMENT MAGAZINE / Pentagram: DJ Stout / USA, 2003

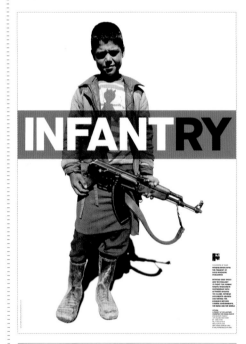

INFANTRY POSTER FOR WITNESS / Pentagram: Harry Pearce / UK, 1994

PANTONE MATCHING SYSTEM / Pentagram: John Rushworth / UK, 2000 / Photo: Nick Turner

ILA NAMING, IDENTITY, AND PACKAGING / Pentagram: John Rushworth / UK, 2006 / Photo: Peter Wood

VISUALIZATION FOR THE *NEW YORK TIMES* MAGAZINE / Pentagram: Lisa Strausfeld / USA, 2006

SCOTCH MALT WHISKEY SOCIETY PACKAGING / Pentagram: Harry Pearce / UK, 2004 / Photo: Richard Foster

GLOBAL CITIES EXHIBITION AT THE TATE MODERN / Pentagram: Angus Hyland, William Russell / UK, 2007

TIME **MAGAZINE REDESIGN** / Pentagram: Luke Hayman, Paula Scher; *Time*: Richard Stengel, Arthur Hochstein / USA, 2007

HARLEY-DAVIDSON OPEN ROAD TOUR EXHIBITION / Pentagram: Abbott Miller / USA, 2002–2003 / Photo: Timothy Hursley

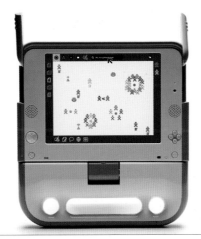

SUGAR INTERFACE DESIGN FOR THE XO LAPTOP FOR ONE LAPTOP PER CHILD FOUNDATION / Pentagram: Lisa Strausfeld / USA, 2007 / Photo: Courtesy of One Laptop per Child Foundation

ONE LAPTOP PER CHILD FOUNDATION IDENTITY / Pentagram: Michael Gericke / USA, 2007

Partners Over the Years, 1972-2008

Key

A Austin	**B** Berlin	**LA** Los Angeles
L London	**NY** New York	**SF** San Francisco
* Passed away		

JOINED	OFFICE	PARTNER	LEFT
1972	L	Theo Crosby*	1994
	L	Alan Fletcher	1991
	L	Colin Forbes	1993
	L	Kenneth Grange	1998
	L	Mervyn Kurlansky	1993
1974	L	John McConnell	2005
1977	L	Ron Herron	1981
1978	L	Howard Brown	1988
	NY	Peter Harrison	1994
1982	L	David Pelham	1986
1986	SF	Kit Hinrichs	–
	SF	Linda Hinrichs	1990
	SF	Neil Shakery	1994
1987	L	Howard Brown	1988
	NY	Etan Manasse*	1990
1988	NY	Woody Pirtle	2005
1989	L	John Rushworth	–
1990	L	Peter Saville	1992
	NY	Michael Bierut	–
1991	L	David Pocknell	1995
	NY	James Biber	–
	NY	Paula Scher	–
	SF	Lowell Williams	2007
1992	L	Daniel Weil	–
1993	NY	Michael Gericke	–
1995	L/B	Justus Oehler	–
1996	SF	Bob Brunner	2007
1998	L	Angus Hyland	–
	L	Lorenzo Apicella	–
1999	NY	Abbott Miller	–
2000	L	Fernando Gutierrez	2006
	A	DJ Stout	–
	LA	April Greiman	2001
2002	NY	Lisa Strausfeld	–
2005	L	William Russell	–
2006	L	Harry Pearce	–
	L	Domenic Lippa	–
	NY	Luke Hayman	–

Otl Aicher

1922 (ULM-SÖFLINGEN, GERMANY) **- 1991**

Not until his early twenties did Otl Aicher make his first foray into the practice of graphic design, creating the posters for a series of gatherings, the Tuesday Lectures, run by an organization he established in his hometown of Ulm at the end of World War II in 1945. The lectures led the way for the Ulmer Volkshochschule, an adult education school and one of Aicher's first clients when he opened his design firm, Büro Aicher, in 1947.

In 1953, with Swiss designer Max Bill, Aicher established the Hochschule für Gestaltung (HfG) in Ulm, a design school for architects and product and graphic designers. In addition to teaching and holding a directorship position from 1962 to 1964, Aicher developed numerous identity projects—including the comprehensive corporate identity for Lufthansa—through the E5 (Entwicklungsgruppe 5), one of the student development teams created at HfG to work with clients outside of academia. The HfG closed in 1968 and Aicher opened Büro Aicher once again, undertaking one of his most prominent projects, the identity, signage, and iconography of the 1972 Summer Olympic Games in Munich ⟩ 357.

In 1972, Aicher and his family purchased a property, already named Rotis, where he built two additional studios and established his residence and office. Over the next two decades, Aicher maintained a healthy practice of identity, collateral, advertising, and poster work for a range of clients, from industrial manufacturers to small towns. Aicher's new abode also served as the name for the four type families—Rotis Grotesk (sans serif), Semigrotesk, Semiantiqua, and Antiqua (serif)—that bridge sans and serif designs. In 1991, tragically, a car struck Aicher as he crossed the highway that divided his property on his lawn mower.

RECOMMENDED READING ⟩ 390

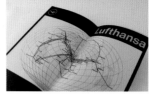

LUFTHANSA SUMMER TIMETABLE / Otl Aicher / Germany, 1968

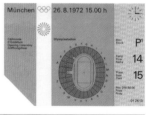

1972 SUMMER OLYMPIC GAMES IN MUNICH MATERIALS / Otl Aicher / Germany, 1966–1972

LIGHT
Rotis Rotis

REGULAR
Rotis Rotis Rotis Rotis

BOLD
Rotis Rotis Rotis Rotis

BLACK
Rotis Rotis

^SANS ^SEMI SANS ^SEMI SERIF ^SERIF

ROTIS TYPE FAMILY / Otl Aicher / Germany, 1988

BRAUN

BRAUN IDENTITY / Otl Aicher / Germany, 1954

Herb Lubalin
1918 (NEW YORK, NEW YORK, USA) - 1981

After graduating from Cooper Union › 129, Herb Lubalin began his career as an art director for Deutsch & Shea Advertising (1941–1942), Fairchild Publications (1942–1943), and Reiss Advertising (1943–1945), followed by 20 years with the advertising firm Sudler & Hennessey, Inc. This trajectory culminated in the establishment of his own firm, Herb Lubalin, Inc., in 1964—a firm that held various names as partnerships with Ernie Smith, Tom Carnase, Roger Ferriter, and Alan Peckolick took place and as international subsidiaries in Paris and London opened.

In retrospect, Lubalin's body of work is not only comprehensive but consistently influential in terms of its exposure within the graphic design profession. As a logo designer, Lubalin injected visual metaphors into typography as well as creating astutely crafted wordmarks that defied traditional letter spacing. Although these are regularly overlooked, Lubalin created a number of cosmetics and sundries package designs. In the editorial realm, he designed and art directed three influential magazines › 322 with provocateur Ralph Ginzburg: *Eros* in 1962, which published only four issues; *Fact:* from 1964 to 1967; and *Avant Garde*, from 1968 to 1971, featuring the namesake geometric sans serif typeface › 374 laden with complex ligatures that was later released through the International Typeface Corporation (ITC) 220. Founded in 1970 by Lubalin with Edward Rondthaler and Aaron Burns, ITC embraced the growing phototypesetting technology and sought to reward typeface designers properly, as piracy was becoming rampantly easy—ITC, of course, carried Lubalin's typefaces. Through ITC, Lubalin edited *U&lc* › 98, a journal of design that served as an endless catalog of their typefaces and was quickly established as a must-have publication in the industry. Herb Lubalin had an uncanny ability to visualize typographic elements in unique solutions that, with his ingenuity, daily tools, and play with emerging technologies, set him apart from his peers.

THE BIBLE LOGO / Herb Lubalin / USA, 1966

AVANT GARDE NO. 6: FIRST ANNIVERSARY ISSUE (ALTERNATE COVER) / Herb Lubalin / USA, January 1969

U&LC MAGAZINE 3, NO. 2 / ITC / USA, July 1976

oh! ah!

OH! LETTERHEAD FOR LI-LIAN OH / Herb Lubalin; lettering, Tom Carnase / USA, 1964
AH! LETTERHEAD FOR ANTHONY HYDE, JR. / Herb Lubalin; lettering, Tom Carnase / USA, 1964

FAMILIES LOGO / Herb Lubalin / USA, 1980

FIRST PLACE LOGO / Herb Lubalin / USA, n.d.

STEELOGRAPH COMPANY LOGO / Herb Lubalin / USA, n. d.

MOTHER AND CHILD PROPOSED MAGAZINE LOGO / Herb Lubalin; lettering, Tom Carnase / USA, 1967

Images: Courtesy of The Herb Lubalin Study Center of Design and Typography at the Cooper Union School of Art

Push Pin Studios
EST. 1954 (NEW YORK, NEW YORK, USA)

While students at The Cooper Union › 131, Seymour Chwast › 171, Milton Glaser › 170, Reynold Ruffins, and Edward Sorel worked after hours as Design Plus, doing a few commissions and silkscreening without much financial success, and, after graduation in 1951, they went their separate ways: Chwast to work for the *New York Times*, Glaser first for *Vogue* and then to study etching in Italy, and Sorel and Ruffins for independent studios. However, Chwast, Sorel, and Ruffins, unfulfilled by their day jobs, began producing a promotional publication, the *Push Pin Almanack* (modeled after the *Farmers' Almanac* with a bevy of illustrated facts, quotes, and even horoscopes), to gain freelance commissions. Back from Italy, Glaser joined them in 1952, and by 1954 they founded Push Pin Studios (Ruffins was not one of the original founders, but joined in 1955).

The *Almanack* was published until 1956; it gave way in 1957 to the *Push Pin Monthly Graphic*, but the *Monthly* was dropped from the title in 1961, when it was evident the publication schedule did not match the name. The *Push Pin Graphic*, showcasing the remarkable and unprecedented stylistic diversity of its members, became a magnet for work and acclaim for Push Pin Studios. Sorel and Ruffins left in 1956 and 1960 respectively, but Push Pin Studios had no problem attracting talent to meet demand: Paul Davis, James McMullan, and Isadore Seltzer were all part of the group throughout the 1960s and contributed to the *Push Pin Graphic* as well. In the early 1970s, Glaser left to start his own studio; Chwast remained in charge (and still is), expanding the pool of illustrators represented through the *Push Pin Graphic*, which continued its run of original content until 1980, through 86 influential issues.

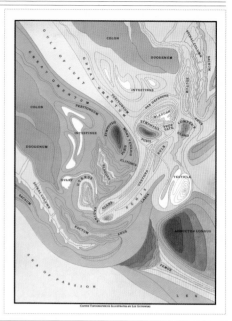

PUSH PIN GRAPHIC **NO. 83:** *COUPLES* / Push Pin Studios / USA, 1980

PUSH PIN GRAPHIC **NO. 52** / This issue consisted of three faux-advertising posters / Push Pin Studios / USA, 1967

PUSH PIN GRAPHIC **NO. 63:** *ALL ABOUT CHICKENS* / The inclusion of a rooster pattern in this issue led to the use of this bird on all subsequent mastheads / Push Pin Studios / USA, 1976

RECOMMENDED READING › 390

PUSH PIN GRAPHIC NO. 53: *CHEW, CHEW, BABY* / Push Pin
Studios / USA, 1967

PUSH PIN GRAPHIC NO. 56: *GOOD & BAD* / Push Pin
Studios / USA, 1971

PUSH PIN GRAPHIC NO. 72: *EXPLORING NEW JERSEY* /
Push Pin Studios / USA, April 1978

PUSH PIN GRAPHIC NO. 81: *OLD BLUE* / Push Pin Studios /
USA, November/December 1979

PUSH PIN GRAPHIC NO. 64: *MOTHERS* / Milton Glaser's final issue / Push Pin Studios / USA, 1976

Milton Glaser

b. 1929 (NEW YORK, NEW YORK, USA)
CURRENTLY NEW YORK, NEW YORK, USA

Milton Glaser—the man behind the iconic I ❤ NY › 344 logo ubiquitous in New York (and innumerable imitators) since 1975—attended the High School of Music and Art and graduated from The Cooper Union › 131 in Manhattan in 1951 before studying under Giorgio Morandi at the Academy of Fine Arts in Bologna, Italy, on a Fulbright scholarship. Shortly after his return, in 1954, Glaser and fellow Cooper Union classmates Seymour Chwast, Reynold Ruffins, and Edward Sorel co-founded Push Pin Studios › 168, where his illustrations and design helped define one of the most influential groups in the profession. Glaser left Push Pin 20 years later.

Cementing his position as a true New Yorker, Glaser co-founded *New York* magazine › 336 with Clay Felker in 1968, art directing it until 1977. Extending his work in the publishing industry, he established WBMG with art director Walter Bernard in 1983; designing over 50 magazines, newspapers, and periodicals until the firm closed in 2003. The majority of his work has, of course, grown from his own design firm, Milton Glaser, Inc., established in 1974, through which he has designed hundreds of posters, identities, publications, packaging, advertising, and interiors for a varied roster of clients—too many and too significant to list in a paragraph. In addition, Glaser contributes to the design community through his considered and evocative writing, soothing and challenging lectures, and his ongoing commitment to education. His weeklong summer courses, where the secrecy of what happens is equal to that of *Fight Club*, sell out year after year after year.

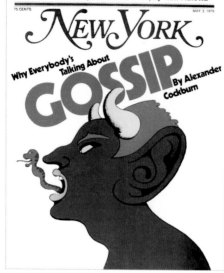

NEW YORK MAGAZINE / Milton Glaser / USA, May 3, 1976

WINDOWS ON THE WORLD IDENTITY AND CHINA / Milton Glaser / USA, 1995

GRAND UNION IDENTITY AND ENVIRONMENTAL DESIGN / Milton Glaser / USA, 1976–1996

THE SCHOOL OF VISUAL ARTS POSTER / art direction, Silas H. Rhodes; design, Milton Glaser; photography, Matthew Klein / USA, 2007

OLIVETTI *VALENTINE* POSTER / Milton Glaser / USA, 1968

Seymour Chwast

b.1931 (BRONX, NEW YORK, USA)
CURRENTLY NEW YORK, NEW YORK, USA

As a member of Abraham Lincoln High School's Art Squad, along with other young prospects like Gene Federico, Alex Steinweiss ›142, and William Taubin, and under the guidance of their teacher Leon Friend, Seymour Chwast got an early taste of life as a commercial artist. Urged by Friend to enter contests, his first published piece came at age 16, in *Seventeen* magazine, art directed by Cipe Pineles ›145. Chwast then attended Cooper Union, where he would meet his future partners, Reynold Ruffins, Edward Sorel, and Milton Glaser ›170, with whom he would set up, still as students, Design Plus, a small design firm cranking a silkscreen printer in a warm New York loft, and later, of course, Push Pin Studios ›168 in 1954—although not through a direct route.

After graduating in 1951, Chwast worked as a junior designer in the promotions department of the *New York Times* and then stumbled through a series of jobs before coming back together with Ruffins and Sorel in 1953 to conceive a regular self-promotion called the *Push Pin Almanack* that showcased their illustration talents. When Glaser returned from studies in Italy he joined them in 1954, establishing Push Pin Studios, serving as the platform from which Chwast delivered his humorous and poignant illustrations. Over the years—as a member of Push Pin Studios, and then as the carrier of the Push Pin name when it was renamed Pushpin Group in 1981—Chwast has designed and illustrated posters, packaging, children's books, and logos, and he continues the tradition of self-publishing with *The Nose*, a 24-page publication "designed to draw attention to relevant social issues as well as trivial ones." Whether socially relevant or trivial, the issues are joyfully illustrated.

NEW YORKER COVER / December 12, 2005

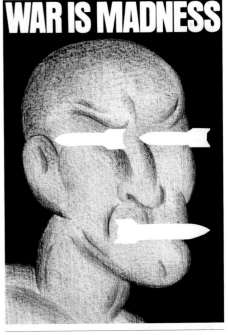

SHOSHIN SOCIETY *WAR IS MADNESS* POSTER / 1986

THE NOSE, NO. 6: EXPLORING THE FOOD WE JUST CAN'T GET ENOUGH OF / 2001

THE NOSE ILLUSTRATION / 2000

FRANKFURTER ALLGEMEINE MAGAZINE COVER ILLUSTRATION / 2000

ARTONE PACKAGING / 1964

END BAD BREATH POSTER / 1968

Seymour Chwast / USA

Sister Mary Corita Kent

FRANCES ELIZABETH KENT

1918 (FORT DODGE, IOWA, USA) - 1986

Raised in Hollywood, Sister Mary Corita Kent entered the Immaculate Heart of Mary Religious Community at the tender age of 18. Sister Corita continued her education by earning a bachelor's degree from the Immaculate Heart College (IHC) and a masters in art history from the University of Southern California.

Her early work can be identified by its use of religious imagery; it was in 1955 that she first introduced words into her work, soon after meeting Charles Eames, whom she considered a source of inspiration. As the work evolved, her use of classical typography shifted to her individual handwriting, and as imagery became an item of the past, popular culture, branding, and the environment were at the heart of her work. A teacher for over 20 years, and the head of the art department of the IHC for four, Sister Corita walked away from Los Angeles and the Order in 1968 and moved to Boston. Having to earn a living, she began designing client-driven work such as book and magazine covers, advertising, greeting cards, logos, and even a U.S. postal stamp—which, with 700 million units sold, is believed to be the most popular stamp to date.

Sister Corita always spoke her mind through her art, something she felt compelled to do as she tackled the Vietnam War, social justice, racism, and poverty, among other important subjects. While her artistic style varied from decade to decade and from public to private work, her experimentation is notable and ahead of her time—especially coming from what is perceived as a conservative environment. While Sister Corita's work is a clear influence on both designers and artists, she has not received the historic recognition that many of her peers have acquired.

RECOMMENDED READING › 390

POWER UP / A series of four serigraphs / Sister Corita / USA, 1965

SOMEDAY IS NOW / Serigraph / Sister Corita, / USA, 1964

PEOPLE LIKE US YES / Serigraph / Sister Corita / USA, 1965

FOR ELEANOR / Serigraph / Sister Corita / USA, 1964

COME ALIVE / Serigraph / Sister Corita, / USA, 1967

IMMACULATE HEART COLLEGE ART DEPARTMENT RULES / stamped out by David Mekelburg / USA, 1968

IMMACULATE HEART COLLEGE CAFETERIA INSTALLATION / Sister Corita and students / USA, c. 1966

Serigraph photography: Joshua White / Images: Reprinted with permission from the Corita Art Center Immaculate Heart Community, Los Angeles

Lou Dorfsman
1918 (NEW YORK, NEW YORK, USA) **- 2008**

First inclined to study bacteriology at New York University but deterred by the high tuition price, Lou Dorfsman was accepted in 1934 into the Cooper Union › 131, which covers its students' tuition, and graduated in 1939. During his education and afterwards he held various design positions; in 1943 he joined the U.S. Army, where a punctured eardrum kept him from active duty. He served as an exhibit designer in the Army until 1946, the year he joined Columbia Broadcasting Company (CBS) under the guidance of William Golden, art director for the organization and designer of the emblematic eye logo › 344. Five years into what would be a 45-year career at CBS, Dorfsman was appointed art director for CBS Radio. Golden managed the growing CBS Television Network until 1959, when he unexpectedly passed away at the age of 48. Dorfsman was assigned as his successor.

Rising to vice president and creative director of the CBS Broadcast group by 1964, Dorfsman was the driving force not only behind the print advertising but of the full spectrum of the identity, from on-air graphics to set design to the interior signage and graphics of the New York headquarters building (designed by Eero Saarinen) to the flabbergasting, 33-foot-wide typographic cafeteria wall › 174. Dorfsman was deeply engaged with the success of the company and its programming as well. When the ratings for anchorman Walter Cronkite dropped, it was his idea that Cronkite appear on the highly rated *Mary Tyler Moore Show*, raising the numbers significantly for both shows; and when CBS was ready to cancel *The Waltons*, Dorfsman devised a print and television ad campaign bluntly aimed at saving the show, which would finish at number one that season. Dorfsman retired from CBS in 1991 and passed away in 2008 in Roslyn, New York.

CBS REPORTS: THE GERMANS /
September 26, 1967

HOW SHARP IS YOUR VISION?,
IN THE *NEW YORK TIMES* /
March 16, 1969

WORTH REPEATING /
November 5, 1964

HA…HA…HA…, IN VARIETY /
March 29, 1961

1945 / **1965**

IN THE PAY OF THE CIA:
AN AMERICAN DILEMMA / 1967

IF YOU'RE APPALLED AT MY
TEXAS, I'M BEWILDERED BY YOUR
ENGLAND / 1967

CBS TELEVISION NETWORK ADVERTISEMENTS / Lou Dorfsman / USA

GASTROTYPOGRAPHICALASSEMBLAGE

In 1965 the Columbia Broadcasting System (CBS) moved into its new headquarters in New York, a 38-story black granite building designed by Eero Saarinen with interiors by Florence Knoll. The signage and wayfinding graphics were designed by Lou Dorfsman › 173, CBS's vice president and creative director, with resolute consistency. The proprietary typefaces created by Freeman Craw, CBS Didot and CBS Sans, were applied to everything from elevator buttons to wall clocks. An exception to this uniformity was made on a 33 × 8-foot wall at one end of the cafeteria. In a CBS Radio interview, Dorfsman recalls discussing the options for the wall with Knoll and CBS president Frank Stanton. Knoll suggested putting up old maps of New York, and when Dorfsman disapproved, Stanton daringly asked, "Okay, wiseguy, what would you do?" Previously, as a birthday gift, Dorfsman had given Stanton a California Job Case—a drawer with dozens of little compartments to sort metal fonts by letter— with samples of metal and wood type. Dorfsman reminded Stanton about it and proposed that a similar idea be deployed on the wall using words

SKETCHES / Herb Lubalin / USA, circa 1965

LOU DORFSMAN EXAMINES THE WALL / USA, 1966

related to food rendered in different typefaces and food objects placed alongside. Stanton approved the idea.

Dorfsman did a rough sketch, commissioned the creation of a single panel, and then enlisted his friend Herb Lubalin ›167, who, along with Tom Carnase, produced a full flat rendering of the wall. More than 1,450 letters were hand-milled in thick pine and slowly assembled on the wall to create a monochromatic type assemblage. The only bursts of color were provided by the food

items strategically peppered on the wall. People who recall the wall have nothing but awe for its impact, which welcomed staff and guests for more than 20 years until the late 1980s, when it was unceremoniously dismantled under new management. Dorfsman arranged for the panels to be taken by designer Nick Fasciano and stored them in his basement, where they remained for another 20 years, slowly deteriorating.

In 2007, *I.D.* magazine ›96 reported on the state of the wall, catching the attention of a new Atlanta

nonprofit organization, The Center for Design Study, headed by Richard R. Anwyl. The Center has become an ambassador for the restoration of the wall, which has gone from Fasciano's basement to his studio, where each letter and food sculpture is being painstakingly stripped, sanded, patched, sealed, and repainted. If someone has a large, empty wall in his or her home, this would make a rather handsome addition.

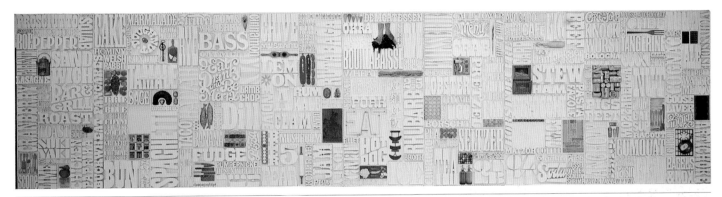

FINISHED WALL / USA, 1966

DIAGRAM OF A CALIFORNIA JOB CASE

Right **DISMANTLED WALL IN THE BASEMENT OF NICK FASCIANO** / USA, 2007

RESTORATION PROCESS OF MORE THAN 1,450 LETTERS AT THE STUDIO OF NICK FASCIANO / USA, 2007

Studio Dumbar
Est. 1977 (ROTTERDAM, NETHERLANDS)

Before establishing Studio Dumbar in 1977, Gert Dumbar attended the Royal Academy of Fine Arts in The Hague and the Royal College of Art in London—he returned in 1985 as visiting professor and headed its graphic design department until 1987—and worked for close to ten years with the Dutch firm Tel Design. Studio Dumbar began with Dumbar and one intern, Michel de Boer, who worked on a freelance basis for the studio after graduation, then became an employee in 1980 and is now creative director. Currently, Studio Dumbar employs around 30 employees and has built a comprehensive branding practice with contributions from strategist Tom Dorresteijn and the opening of Dumbar Branding in Shanghai, China, in 2005. But this is only the most recent manifestation of Studio Dumbar's experience, as it has been designing and developing branding programs for complex institutions like the Dutch Police Force and the Danish Post, among other government and corporate clients, since the early 1980s.

Another aspect of Studio Dumbar is its work for cultural institutions. Dumbar and his staff have created a collection of visually explosive designs—or "free spirit projects," as they call them, where the focus is on "pure, 100% design power." These, over the years, have garnered criticism, mostly as complaints of being too decorative or playful, but, more so, they have attracted positive attention and talent. After Dumbar was invited to lecture at Cranbrook Academy of Art › 130 in 1985, many of its students—like Allen Hori and Martin Venezky—from that point on took internships at his studio, fostering a sense of reciprocal influence. Designers from around the world flock to Studio Dumbar, further contributing to both its uniqueness and its ability to work internationally.

AMSTERDAM SINFONIETTA IDENTITY AND DUTCH ORCHESTRA POSTERS / Studio Dumbar / Netherlands, 2006–2007

HOLLAND DANCE FESTIVAL POSTERS / Studio Dumbar; photography, Lex van Pieterson / Netherlands, 1986, 1989

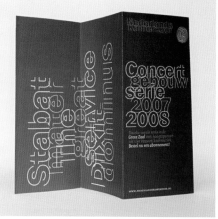

NEDERLANDS KAMERKOOR (NETHERLANDS CHAMBER CHOIR) IDENTITY / Studio Dumbar / Netherlands, 2007–ongoing

DUTCH POLICE FORCE IDENTITY FOR THE MINISTRY OF THE INTERIOR AND THE MINISTRY OF JUSTICE TO THE KINGDOM OF THE NETHERLANDS / Studio Dumbar / Netherlands, 1993 / Photos: Lex van Pieterson

DANISH POST IDENTITY FOR POST DANMARK / Studio Dumbar / Netherlands, 1994 / Photo: Pjotr og Co.

HOLLAND DANCE FESTIVAL POSTERS / Studio Dumbar; photography, Deen van Meer / Netherlands, 1995

omroep voor kunst en cultuur

Champalimaud Foundation

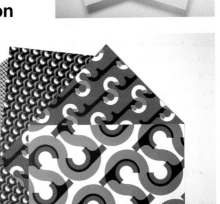

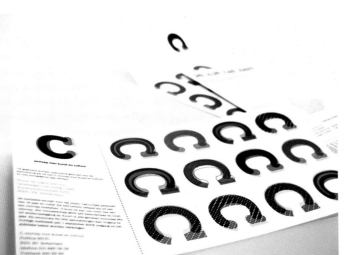

NAMING AND BRANDING OF C, THE DUTCH BROADCASTING ORGANIZATION FOR ART AND CULTURE / Studio Dumbar / Netherlands, 2006–ongoing

THE CHAMPALIMAUD FOUNDATION IDENTITY / Studio Dumbar / Netherlands, 2005–ongoing / Photos: Dieter Schütte

Wolfgang Weingart

b. 1941 (SOUTH OF GERMANY)
CURRENTLY BASEL, SWITZERLAND

After displaying interest and aptitude in painting, Wolfgang Weingart enrolled at Merz Academy in Stuttgart, Germany, in 1958. There he was first exposed to graphic design, typography, and printing methods, and on his spare time, he was able to work with the school's printing press and get a first glimpse of metal type and its potential. Upon graduation in 1960, Weingart began a three-year typesetting apprenticeship at Ruwe Printing in Stuttgart, where he met designer Karl-August Hanke, a former student of Armin Hofmann › 152 at the Basel School of Design › 128 in Switzerland. Hanke encouraged him to forego his apprenticeship and enroll in Basel, an idea his parents rejected. At Ruwe, Weingart learned the trade of typesetting and became enamored of the process.

With a sustained interest in Basel, a year after completing his apprenticeship, he enrolled as an independent student in 1964. Weingart's initial reaction to the teaching method at Basel was negative, regarding it as "an impenetrable, cloister-like fortress," and although he later acknowledged its efficacy, his restlessness grew tiresome to Hofmann and Ruder, who suggested he

commit or leave. With the right decision, his stay at Basel was extended for two more years. In 1968 he became a teacher in the newly established Advanced Class of Graphic Design, where he intended to "build a curriculum in typography that would challenge revered conventions and still respect the traditions and philosophy [of Basel]," an effort Hofmann later called a "model for new typography." Weingart has taught at Basel since then—attracting students around the world and conveying to them a vigorous sense of typographic exploration—and he is now part of the Basel School of Design's Summer Programme.

Over the course of his career, Weingart has maintained a modest practice where his design approaches take shape. For more than 30 years, starting in 1967, he regularly collaborated with Rudolf Hostettler, editor-in-chief of *Typographische Monatsblätter*, a printing trade publication, and produced a string of related covers through the course of a year. He has designed books and catalogs and since 1958 has been regularly commissioned to design posters for cultural and educational institutions. His poster work in the late 1970s and early 1980s allowed him to explore, with the same energy he brought to metal type, the possibilities of layout composition through film; this kinetic, layered work played an influential role in the world of design during the 1980s.

WORLDFORMAT *THE SWISS POSTER, 1900-1984* **FOR BIRKHÄUSER** / Wolfgang Weingart / Switzerland, 1983

WORLDFORMAT *18TH DIDACTA/EURODIDAC* **POSTER FOR THE CONVENTION ON TEACHING AIDS** / Wolfgang Weingart / Switzerland, 1980–1981

UNIVERSITY OF CALIFORNIA AT LOS ANGELES CATALOG / Wolfgang Weingart / Switzerland, 1998

April Greiman
b. 1948 (NEW YORK, NEW YORK, USA)
CURRENTLY LOS ANGELES, CALIFORNIA, USA

April Greiman graduated from the Kansas City Art Institute in 1970, where teachers who had attended the Allgemeine Kunstgewerbeschule in Basel, Switzerland, first introduced her to modernism. Inspired, she pursued her graduate studies under the tutelage of Armin Hofmann › 152 and Wolfgang Weingart › 178 at Basel › 128. While the International Style was the paramount movement at the time, she had the opportunity to experiment alongside Weingart in work, labeled New Wave on its arrival to America, that deviated from the modernist path in a more intuitive and typographically versatile aesthetic. After a short period in New York, Greiman established her studio, Made in Space, in Los Angeles in 1976. From the beginning she defined herself as a generalist, opening herself to opportunities in many fields and across media, including design for the built environment and working with architects to define the identity of buildings.

Starting in 1982, she directed the graphic design department of the California Institute of the Arts › 131. There she had her first serious opportunity to explore the up-and-coming digital tools that would become pivotal in her work—something she opted to explore full-time in 1984, refocusing on her studio and the newly available Macintosh. Two years later, her contribution to the Walker Art Center's *Design Quarterly* › 260 rippled through the design industry as she emblazoned a life-size digital reproduction of her naked body with all sorts of flotsam and jetsam—unlike anything the profession had seen. Since then, her work has continued to marry the exploration of digital tools with her unique sensibilities, generating an oeuvre that maintains these principles, whether the piece is a logo for a restaurant or a 75-foot mural.

CERRITOS CENTER FOR THE PERFORMING ARTS BRAND IDENTITY AND TILE MOTIFS / April Greiman; architecture, Barton Myers / USA, 1993

CHINA CLUB RESTAURANT AND LOUNGE BRAND IDENTITY / April Greiman / USA, 1979–1980 / Photo: Jayme Odgers

ROTO ARCHITECTURE BRAND IDENTITY AND WEBSITE / April Greiman / USA, 1999

19TH AMENDMENT COMMEMORATIVE STAMP FOR WOMEN'S VOTING RIGHTS / April Greiman / USA, 1995

WILSHIRE/VERMONT MIXED-USE METRO STATION PUBLIC MURAL / April Greiman / USA, 2007

Peter Saville

b. 1955 (MANCHESTER, ENGLAND, UK)
CURRENTLY LONDON, ENGLAND, UK

In 1978, shortly before graduating from Manchester Polytechnic, Peter Saville found himself leafing through Herbert Spencer's *Pioneers of Modern Typography*, sharing the work of designers like Jan Tschichold › 140 and Armin Hofmann › 152, instead of his own, with Tony Wilson, who had just started a nightclub called Factory. It earned Saville his first commission for Factory, designing a poster. A year later Wilson and Alan Erasmus put together an album compilation of local bands and, with Saville as art director, founded Factory Records. Saville's output through this label until 1985 was some of his most influential, including his work for Joy Division—renamed New Order after the suicide of their lead singer, Ian Curtis, in 1980—where he had unprecedented freedom. In the mid 1980s, as his interest in the music industry waned, Saville began a meandering trajectory with his studio, established in 1983 as Peter Saville and Associates (PSA) with Brett Wickens.

Although he worked in the fashion world and did album cover assignments through the late 1980s, the business side of PSA suffered, and, at the brink of bankruptcy, Saville became a partner at Pentagram › 162 in 1990. Despite excitement about the potential afforded by the renowned company and championing its structure, Saville, with Wickens at his side, left after the two-year probationary period. In 1993 both moved to Los Angeles to explore a collaboration with Frankfurt Balkind; however, while Wickens thrived and remained in Los Angeles, Saville faltered and quickly returned to London. There, in 1995, in partnership with German advertising agency Meiré and Meiré, Saville established an outpost under the name of The Apartment, a moniker inspired by the live/work pad where Saville operated. Less than three years later, Meiré and Meiré ended the relationship. Saville has continued to work commercially and serves as design consultant for several entities, including Stella McCartney and the city of Manchester.

A FACTORY SAMPLE, various artists / Factory EP / Peter Saville / UK, 1978

FUNKAPOLITAN / Decca Records / design, Peter Saville, Funkapolitan; illustration, Phil Irving; logotype, Geoff Halpin; artwork, Brel Wik / UK, 1982

CONFUSION SINGLE, New Order / Factory / PSA / UK, 1983

MOVEMENT, New Order / Factory / design, Peter Saville, Grafica Industria / UK, 1981

POWER, CORRUPTION, AND LIES, New Order / Factory / PSA / UK, 1983

TALKING LOUD AND CLEAR SINGLE, Orchestral Manoeuvres in the Dark / Virgin / PSA; fabric supplied by Monkwell Fabrics CR 4015 / UK, 1984

THIS IS HARDCORE, Pulp / Island / art direction, Peter Saville, John Currin; design, Howard Wakefield, Paul Hetherington; photography, Horst Diekgerdes; casting, Sascha Behrendt; styling, Camille Bidault-Waddington / UK, 1998

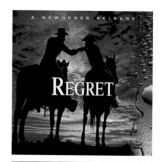

REGRET SINGLE, New Order / London / Pentagram: Peter Saville; image manipulation, Brett Wickens / UK, 1993

Barney Bubbles

1942 (LONDON, ENGLAND, UK) - 1983

After attending Twickenham College of Art in London, Colin Fulcher (Barney Bubbles's birth name) was employed by the Conran Design Group in 1965, working on materials for Terence Conran's swanky Habitat retail stores and exhibitions for D&AD › 249. In 1967 he left his job, changed his name to Barney Bubbles—"[from] the liquid lightshows," explained Julia Thrift in a 1992 article in *Eye*, "using oil and food colouring to create wildly coloured, bubbling backdrops for the psychedelic music of the hippy underground"—and moved into the building occupied by the music company Famepushers. In exchange for space, Bubbles designed any number of requests; this gradually moved him into the underground music scene, first working on magazines like *Friends* (later *Frendz*) and *Oz*, and then on album covers.

In the early 1970s he began his relationship with Hawkwind, a science fiction-inspired psychedelic group (loosely labeled *hippies*), designing their album covers as well as their overall identity, including painting drum kits and amplifiers. In 1976 an acquaintance of Bubbles, Jake Riviera, co-founded Stiff Records with Dave Robinson, representing punk and New Wave artists, and Bubbles became their full-time designer. To the chagrin of both audiences, Bubbles was able to work within two dueling music genres, hippies and punk, and build a body of work that gleefully appropriated past visual tropes from Art Nouveau, Art Deco, constructivism, and artists like Wassily Kandinsky. Despite graphic design history's sparse acknowledgment of Bubbles' contributions, the support of designers he influenced, like Malcolm Garrett and Neville Brody, among other fervent advocates, has now assured his place in the design canon. Bubbles had a troubled life outside of work that ultimately spiraled down to his suicide in 1983.

THIS YEAR'S MODEL, Elvis Costello / Columbia Records / Barney Bubbles / USA, 1978

IMPERIAL BEDROOM, Elvis Costello and the Attractions / Columbia Records / Barney Bubbles / USA, 1982

MUSIC FOR PLEASURE, The Damned / Stiff Records / Barney Bubbles / UK, 1977

IN SEARCH OF SPACE, Hawkwind / United Artists / Barney Bubbles / UK, 1971

SPACE RITUAL, Hawkwind / United Artists / Barney Bubbles / UK, 1973

UNAVAILABLE, Clover / Vertigo / Barney Bubbles / UK, 1977

RECOMMENDED READING › 390

Paula Scher

b. 1948 (WASHINGTON, D.C., USA)
CURRENTLY NEW YORK, NEW YORK, USA

For nearly 40 years, Paula Scher has developed a highly diversified and eclectic body of work. After graduating from the Tyler School of Art in Philadelphia, she joined the advertising and promotion department at CBS Records ›300 in 1972, a position she left in the fall of 1973 to pursue a more creative endeavor at competing label Atlantic Records, where she designed her first album covers. After a year, Scher returned to CBS as art director of the cover department, where she oversaw more than 100 covers a year. Eight years later, she left CBS to work on her own, and in 1984 she co-founded Koppel & Scher with editorial designer and fellow Tyler graduate Terry Koppel. During the six years of their business, she produced identities, packaging, book jackets, and even advertising, including the famous Swatch poster based on previous work by Swiss designer Herbert Matter.

In 1991, after the studio suffered from the recession and Koppel took a position at *Esquire* ›326 magazine, Scher joined Pentagram ›162 as a partner in the New York office. In the years since, she has produced an enviable amount of work across a range of disciplines, from environmental design to book design, and for a diverse group of clients, from nonprofit organizations to multinational conglomerates. Most notable in these dichotomies are identities for the Public Theater ›254 and Citibank ›345, environmental graphics and signage for the New Jersey Performing Arts Center and Bloomberg L.P.'s headquarters. In conjunction with her design practice Scher has taught at the School of Visual Arts ›132 since 1982, been continuously involved with the AIGA ›244, and has written a number of articles on design.

GREAT BEGINNINGS PROMOTION FOR KOPPEL & SCHER / Paula Scher / USA, 1984

***CHANGES ONE* AND *CHANGES TWO* LP COVERS** / Atlantic Records / Paula Scher / USA, 1974

THE METROPOLITAN OPERA IDENTITY AND COLLATERAL / Pentagram: Paula Scher; design, Julia Hoffman / USA, 2006

***TRUST ELVIS* POSTER FOR COLUMBIA RECORDS** / Paula Scher / USA, 1974

BLOOMBERG L.P. CORPORATE HEADQUARTERS ENVIRONMENTAL GRAPHICS / Pentagram: Paula Scher / USA, 2005 / Photo: Peter Mauss/Esto

NEW JERSEY PERFORMING ARTS CENTER LUCENT TECHNOLOGIES CENTER FOR ARTS EDUCATION ENVIRONMENTAL GRAPHICS / Pentagram: Paula Scher / USA, 2001 / Photo: Peter Mauss/Esto

***THE BEST OF JAZZ* POSTER FOR CBS RECORDS** / Paula Scher / USA, 1979

JAZZ AT LINCOLN CENTER IDENTITY AND ENVIRONMENTAL GRAPHICS / Pentagram: Paula Scher / USA, 2004 / Photo: Peter Mauss/Esto

GRAPHIC DESIGN USA: 11, AIGA / Pentagram: Paula Scher / USA, 1990

M&Co.

EST. 1979 (NEW YORK, NEW YORK, USA)

Hungarian-born Tibor Kalman began his career at the Student Book Exchange at New York University (which he attended briefly); he sorted books alphabetically until the day the person responsible for window displays did not show up and Kalman talked his way into designing them. After a short adventure in Cuba, Kalman returned to the bookstore—which later became Barnes & Noble (B&N)—in 1971 as art director for the next eight years, designing shopping bags, ads, and logos. In 1979 he established M&Co. (the M is for his wife, Maira) with two former designers from B&N, Carol Bokuniewicz and Liz Trovato. The impact of M&Co. as a breeding ground for work blending wit, humor, and social consciousness through an approach sinuously shifting between deadpan and expressive wasn't immediate, as it took a few years of doing self-described "ugly" work.

By the mid 1980s, however, with a combination of corporate clients like The Limited and hip, culturally relevant clients like the Talking Heads, and working across disciplines from collateral to product design to film titles, M&Co. attracted public attention, high-profile clients, and talented employees who today run successful firms of their own—Stephen Doyle, Alexander Isley, Emily Oberman, Stefan Sagmeister › 202, and Scott Stowell among them. With lucrative clients, M&Co. was able to express Kalman's concern for social responsibility through holiday promotions: 1990's gift, for example, M&Co. packaged the identical contents of the meals handed out on Christmas Day by the Coalition for the Homeless, along with a $20 bill, and a printed note challenging the recipient to donate it or spend it on a burger. In 1991, M&Co. was tasked with designing Benetton's sociopolitical magazine *Colors* › 331. While this was initially produced at the studio, Kalman closed M&Co. in 1993 and moved to Italy as the full-time magazine editor. Four years later, diagnosed with cancer, he returned to New York and briefly reopened his old firm before passing away in 1999 in Puerto Rico.

INTERVIEW MAGAZINE / Brant Publications / M&Co.: creative troublemaker, Tibor Kalman; design, Kristin Johnson; photography, Michel Comte / USA, November 1990

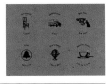

RESTAURANT FLORENT POSTCARDS / M&Co.: Tibor Kalman, Alexander Isley / USA, 1986

THE LIMITED 1986 ANNUAL REPORT / M&Co.: Tibor Kalman, Alexander Brebner; writing, Danny Abelson / USA, 1987

AIGA HUMOR SHOW CALL FOR ENTRIES POSTER / M&Co.: Tibor Kalman, Alexander Isley / USA, 1986

MAKE IT M&CO. ADVERTISEMENT / M&Co.: Tibor Kalman, Carol Bokuniewicz, John Shoptaugh / USA, c. 1979

SECONDHAND WATCH / M&Co.: Tibor Kalman, Scott Stowell / USA, 1991
LULU WATCH / M&Co.: Tibor Kalman, Alexander Isley / USA, 1987
BANG WATCH / M&Co.: Tibor Kalman, Emily Oberman / USA, 1985

SOMETHING WILD FILM TITLES FOR RELIGIOSO PRIMITIVA / M&Co.: Tibor Kalman, Alexander Isley; direction, Jonathan Demme, Caitlin Adams / USA, 1987

STICKY FINGERS FILM CREDITS / M&Co.: Tibor Kalman, Alexander Brebner / USA, 1987

INTERVIEW MAGAZINE / Brant Publications / M&Co.: creative troublemaker, Tibor Kalman; design, Kristin Johnson; photography, Michel Comte / USA, October 1990

Art Chantry

b. 1954 (SEATTLE, WASHINGTON, USA)
CURRENTLY TACOMA, WASHINGTON, USA

The Rocket, a free biweekly newspaper documenting Seattle's music scene, was first published in 1979 as a supplement to the *Seattle Sun* newspaper and, less than a year later, became an independent publication. *The Rocket* was a bastion for Seattle's burgeoning music scene through the 1980s and into the 1990s with the explosion of Grunge, preemptively covering bands like Soundgarden and Nirvana. In 1984 Art Chantry joined as its art director, a position he held on and off until 1993, working with photographers and illustrators to shape the roughed-up style that became associated with Seattle's music scene. Chantry often took freelance assignments as well, working with corporate clients like Nordstrom and Safeco Insurance, fringe organizations like the New City and Empty Space theaters, and cultural institutions like Seattle's Center on Contemporary Art.

Chantry is most admired for his posters. Extracting visual cues from sources as varied as pop art, punk, psychedelia, and comic books and repurposing graphics from a well of existing materials like industrial catalogs, 1940s and 1950s clip art, and found imagery, Chantry's posters are an eclectic collection bound together not by their style but by their process. Working within limited budgets, Chantry puts together his posters by hand cutting and pasting cobbled materials, and uses cheaper and inventive printing processes to produce unique posters. In 2000, Chantry left Seattle, as the city became expensive and the design market he helped create had become too crowded, and moved to St. Louis, Missouri. But in 2006, he returned to Tacoma to attend the School of Visual Concepts—where he had taught for 18 years—to learn the basics of creating graphic design on the computer, a method he had long rejected but, now, the only means for producing his work.

BENT PAGES, Mono Men / Estrus Records / 1995

DRUG MACHINE, Flaming Lips / Sub Pop Records / 1988

ESTRUS RECORDS, *MONO MEN WITH THE MAKERS POSTER* / 1995

LEGS AGAINST ARMS *GIVE PEACE A DANCE* **POSTER** / 1986

Art Chantry / USA

Katherine McCoy

b. 1945 (DECATUR, ILLINOIS, USA)
CURRENTLY BUENA VISTA AND DENVER, COLORADO, USA

An industrial designer from Michigan State University (1967), Katherine McCoy began her career at the Detroit offices of Unimark International, one of the first large corporate identity firms whose modernist philosophy and typographic standards she adopted. McCoy worked at several studios before founding McCoy & McCoy Associates in 1971 with her husband, Michael McCoy. That same year, the duo was asked to co-chair the Cranbrook Academy of Art › 130

design department; they then reinvented the program, guiding students through projects that joined the 2D and 3D departments for more than two decades. Starting with a modernist approach, experimentation and research led the McCoys and their students at Cranbrook to postmodernism and vernacular influences that developed into a unique voice, becoming a polarizing influence in itself during the 1980s and 1990s. McCoy has maintained a close relationship between practice and education, bridging theory, experimentation, and research through her many projects—running a studio, organizing conferences, setting up workshops, teaching, and writing.

RADICAL GRAPHICS/GRAPHIC RADICALS / Chronicle Books / Katherine McCoy; design, Erin Smith, Janice Page / USA, 1999

MCCOY & MCCOY BROCHURE / McCoy & McCoy Associates / USA, 1977

CRANBROOK DESIGN: THE NEW DISCOURSE / Rizzoli International / Katherine McCoy; design assistance, P. Scott Makela, Mary Lou Brous, Allen Hori / USA, 1991

FLUXUS SELECTIONS POSTER FOR CRANBROOK ART MUSEUM / Katherine McCoy / USA, 1989

Ed Fella

b. 1938 (DETROIT, MICHIGAN, USA)
CURRENTLY LOS ANGELES, CALIFORNIA, USA

Ed Fella was first introduced to design at Cass Technical High School in Detroit, where he learned lettering, illustration, and production based on the Bauhaus model. He spent the following 30 years working as a commercial artist in design and advertising and became increasingly interested in more artistic and cultural outlets, which he pursued through personal, off-the-clock projects. He eventually reveled in experimentation in 1985, when he enrolled as a graduate student at Cranbrook Academy of Art › 130 at the age of 47. His typographical compositions and loose interpretations of known styles, such as Art Nouveau, or less known, like the vernacular, appear in the hundreds of after-the-fact posters that he designs and produces himself. A self-titled exit-level designer, Fella continues to teach at CalArts › 131, where he has been since 1987.

ILLUSTRATION FOR THE JAPANESE MAGAZINE *RELAX: 96* / Prismacolor pencil / Ed Fella / USA, 2004

SKETCHBOOK PAGE / Four-color point pen / Ed Fella / USA, 2000

DESIGN MANIFESTO PROJECT FLYER / Offset printing / Ed Fella / USA, 2001

COLLAGE STUDY / Ed Fella / USA, 2005

COMMERCIAL ART ILLUSTRATION STUDIO PROMOTION / Offset printing / Ed Fella / USA, late 1960s

David Carson

b. 1956 (CORPUS CHRISTI, TEXAS, USA)
CURRENTLY CHARLESTON, SOUTH CAROLINA, USA

At the pinnacle of his surfing career, which unofficially began when he was approximately ten years old, David Carson was professionally ranked number eight in the world. Parallel to surfing, Carson graduated in sociology from San Diego State University (SDSU) in 1977 and worked as a high school teacher in Grants Pass, Oregon. In the early 1980s, as he approached the age of 26—an elder by surfing standards—Carson began to discover graphic design, first through a two-week workshop at the University of Arizona in 1980, then by reenrolling in the graphic design program of SDSU, transferring after one month to the Oregon College of Art and then quitting before graduation to take an internship with Surfer Publications. When the magazine he was working for closed, Carson returned to teaching in California, and in 1983 had his first opportunity to design a magazine from start to finish, the 200-page *Transworld Skateboarding*, which he worked on after hours for the next four years. A three-week graphic design workshop in Switzerland in 1983, where Hans-Rudolph Lutz was one of the teachers, further shifted Carson's interest to the industry.

After one year in Boston working on *Musician* magazine, Carson returned to California to help launch a new magazine from Surfer Publications, *Beach Culture*, in 1989. Though it was short-lived, its six issues gave Carson a broad canvas to deploy his exploratory typography—unless a contents page designed using the typeface Hobo is not considered exploratory. With a brief stint as art director of *Surfer*, Carson was given the platform that would launch his career in 1992 when he was brought on as art director of *Ray Gun* ›330, a new magazine aimed at a young demographic and dubbed "the bible of music+style." Over three years and 30 issues, Carson deployed an enthralling number of typographical maneuvers that challenged every single rule imagined, infuriating one part of the design profession and invigorating another. Since 1995, when he established his own design firm, Carson has done work for mainstream brands like Levi's, Lucent, Microsoft, and Pepsi, and has broadened his practice to include identity, motion, advertising, and book design. He also lectures and conducts workshops around the world.

BEACH CULTURE MAGAZINE / David Carson / USA, August/September, October/November 1990

CHICAGO MAGAZINE / art direction, Kerry Robertson; design and photography, David Carson / USA, September 1996

NIKE EUROPEAN ADVERTISING / Reproduced in 12 languages / Wieden+Kennedy (Amsterdam): creative direction, Susan Hoffman; design, David Carson / USA, 1994

BEACH CULTURE MAGAZINE / David Carson / USA, 1991

SIXTEEN STONE, BUSH / Kirtland Records / David Carson / USA, 1994

SALVADOR DALÍ MUSEUM LOGO / David Carson / USA, 2008

FRAGILE, Nine Inch Nails, in-store release date announcement / David Carson / USA, 1999

Susan Kare
b. 1954 (ITHACA, NEW YORK, USA)
CURRENTLY SAN FRANCISCO, CALIFORNIA, USA

With an art major from Mount Holyoke College (1975), and both a masters and a doctoral degree from New York University (1978), Susan Kare arrived in San Francisco to do curatorial work for the Fine Arts Museums of San Francisco. In 1982, a call from high-school friend Andy Hertzfeld, a programmer at Apple Computer, Inc., brought Kare into the design of the graphical user interface for the Macintosh's operating system as she developed the icons and bitmap typefaces. Following Steve Jobs from Apple, Kare became creative director for NeXT, Inc., in 1986, and three years later, she established Susan Kare LLP, further perfecting and adapting her iconography work while delving into typeface, identity, and product design, often collaborating with organizations as diverse as the New York Museum of Modern Art ›121 and Facebook, for whom she designs digital virtual "gifts."

FACEBOOK ICON GIFTS / Susan Kare / USA, 2007

MACINTOSH OPERATING SYSTEM ICONS FOR APPLE COMPUTER / Susan Kare / USA, 1984

CHUMBY INDUSTRIES, INC., IDENTITY AND WEBSITE / Susan Kare / USA, 2007

Margo Chase
b. 1958 (SAN GABRIEL, CALIFORNIA, USA)
CURRENTLY LOS ANGELES, CALIFORNIA, USA

With a degree in biology and two years of medical illustration studies, Margo Chase provides her clients with a detailed and layered sensibility that has become synonymous with her name. Having founded Chase Design Group in 1986, Chase has translated her interest in gothic architecture, medieval manuscripts, technology, and letterforms into a thriving business that encompasses identity, packaging, motion, editorial, exhibition, and interior design. During the late 1990s, Chase created nearly a dozen typefaces for the fledgling digital type foundry [T-26] ›229, some of which were extensions of the wordmarks created for her clients. Perhaps best known for her identity work in the entertainment industry for clients such as Madonna and the popular TV show *Buffy the Vampire Slayer*, Chase's custom typography has evolved over time from manual labor to computer-developed, allowing her more time for other activities, such as competitive aerobatics as a licensed pilot.

BUFFY THE VAMPIRE SLAYER IDENTITY / Margo Chase / USA, 1997

CHARMED IDENTITY / Margo Chase / USA, 1998

BRAM STOKER'S DRACULA IDENTITY / Margo Chase / USA, 1992

CHINESE LAUNDRY IDENTITY, PACKAGING, AND FLEET LIVERY / Margo Chase / USA, 2007

Muriel Cooper
1925 (BROOKLINE, MASSACHUSETTS, USA) – 1994

With a B.A. from Ohio State and a B.F.A. in design and a B.S. in education from Massachusetts College of Art, Muriel Cooper arrived at the Massachusetts Institute of Technology (MIT) in 1952. There she worked in the newly formed Office of Publications until 1958, when she left for Milan on a Fulbright scholarship; on her return, she ran her own design firm. Among her projects in the early 1960s was designing the now iconic logo for MIT Press where, in 1967, she became art director, responsible not just for designing hundreds of book covers but for also running the production of multitude of titles published every year—including seminal titles like Robert Venturi's *Learning from Las Vegas* and Herbert Muschamp's *File Under Architecture*.

In 1974, Cooper segued from MIT Press into teaching at the MIT School of Architecture. There she taught a class called Message and Means in partnership with Ron MacNeil, who had secured and installed two one-color sheet-fed offset presses, immersing the students in a full-cycle learning experience. The class was soon renamed the Visual Language Workshop (VLW) and, in the 1980s, as part of the MIT Media Lab, founded by Nicholas Negroponte in 1985, it evolved from printing to computer programming, interface design, and explorations in three dimensionality as new technologies, hardware, and ideas permeated the workshop and the organization. While Cooper was not a programmer, she understood the potential of not only the computer but also the ability of her students to fully explore this medium in the right learning environment. The efforts of the VLW found a captivated audience in a 1994 presentation by Cooper at the influential TED (Technology, Entertainment, Design) conference. Cooper was deluged with follow-up interest. Unfortunately, she passed away unexpectedly later that year in Boston, Massachusetts.

BEYOND THE MELTING POT, Nathan Glazer, Daniel P. Moynihan / Harvard University Press / 1963

GARDEN CITIES OF TO-MORROW, Ebenezer Howard / MIT Press / 1965

GENERALIZED THERMODYNAMICS, Laszlo Tisza / MIT Press / 1978

THE NEW ARCHITECTURE AND THE BAUHAUS, Walter Gropius / MIT Press / USA, 1965

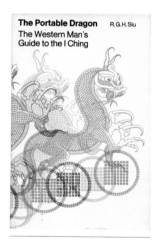

BAUHAUS, Hans Wingler / MIT Press / 1978

THE PORTABLE DRAGON: THE WESTERN MAN'S GUIDE TO THE I CHING, R.G.H. Siu / MIT Press / 1971

A PRIMER OF VISUAL LITERACY, Donis A. Dondis / MIT Press / 1973

THE RESPONSIVE HOUSE, Edited by Edward Allen / MIT Press / 1975

Images: Courtesy of the Morton R. Godine Library, Massachusetts College of Art and Design

Edward R. Tufte

b. 1942 (KANSAS CITY, MISSOURI, USA)
CURRENTLY CHESHIRE, CONNECTICUT, USA

Edward R. Tufte first established an ongoing relationship with educational institutions when he received bachelor's and master's degrees in statistics from Stanford University, a 1968 doctorate in political science from Yale, and finally joined the faculty at Princeton University's Woodrow Wilson School. While Tufte was teaching political economy and data analysis courses, Dean Donald Stokes asked him to take on a statistics course aimed at a group of visiting journalists; the class materials later became the basis of his book *Visual Display of Quantitative Information*. After working closely with statistics pioneer John Tukey on a series of seminars, Tufte relocated to Yale, where in 1982 he completed the manuscript of his first design book. Unsatisfied with his publishing options and determined to work on the design of the book himself—in partnership with designer Howard Gralla—Tufte took out a second mortgage and established the Graphics Press to self-publish his dream book.

With over 30 years in the classroom and 15 of one-day courses taught all over the country, Tufte has educated students, attendees, and readers alike in the art of visual data—from analysis to understanding to its best presentation. Called "the Leonardo da Vinci of data" by the *New York Times*, Tufte brings together many disciplines with design qualities that know no boundaries of time, location, or profession. A strong advocate against the popular and widespread use of PowerPoint as a medium for presenting information, Tufte uses examples from his four self-published books—each taking an average of seven years to complete—to provide followers with visual alternatives. Between his popular courses and writing activities, Tufte also devotes time to fine art and sculpture.

BOOKS BY ED TUFTE / Ed Tufte / USA, 1983–2006

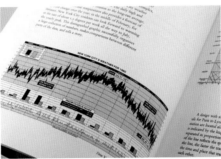
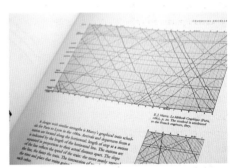

SAMPLE SPREADS FROM VARIOUS BOOKS BY ED TUFTE / Ed Tufte / USA, 1983–2006

Attik

EST. 1986 (HUDDERSFIELD, ENGLAND, UK)
OFFICES LEEDS, NEW YORK, SAN FRANCISCO, LOS ANGELES

In a true story of rags to riches, Simon Needham and James Sommerville, graduates of the Batley School of Art and Design, established their business in Huddersfield in 1986 with a £1,000-grant from the Prince's Trust (an organization that provides money for startup businesses) in the attic of Sommerville's grandmother—yes, hence the name. During a rough patch in the late 1980s, Attik moved their operation to London, and business did pick up—but not necessarily in the industries they were hoping for. So, in 1995 they self-published *Noise*, a noncommercial book peppered with abstract, heavily layered layouts to lure clients in the music and entertainment industries; the *Noise* books (four to date and one in production) became objects of desire among designers. In 1997, William Travis, an Attik employee since 1992, headed to New York to open the first American outpost and with the burgeoning dot-com scene in the West Coast opened a San Francisco office in 1999, the same year Needham started an office in Sydney.

After some rough years following the demise of the dot-com era and the events of September 11, 2001, Attik turned its focus to integrated branding and in 2004 began a relationship with Toyota Motor Corporation, helping them launch the Scion automobile, whose subversive identity package departs from anything the automotive industry had seen or done before. In the same vein, Attik has continued to do work for the thriving and increasingly brand-aware generation of young consumers for companies like Virgin, America Online, and Nike. In 2007, Attik was acquired by global advertising agency Dentsu, giving the firm an even bigger stage on which to work. Needless to say, the £1,000-grant paid off.

SELF-PROMOTION POSTER / Attik / USA, 1990

SCION CAMPAIGN IMAGE / Attik / USA, 2003

A Masters Degree in Attik

In 2003, the first class of students—hailing from the United States, Canada, Singapore, Spain, Ireland, and England—arrived at Huddersfield University to inaugurate the masters program in creative imaging, a joint effort of Attik and the university. The two-year program consists of academic courses coupled with practical assignments on client briefs at Attik's studio with the aim of closing the gap between theory and practice and fostering graduates who can immediately contribute to a design firm or start their own business.

NOISE 3 / Featuring 17 printing techniques as provided by 15 suppliers / Attik / USA, 1997

NOISE 3.5 / Attik / USA, 1997

The Designers Republic

EST. 1986 (SHEFFIELD, ENGLAND, UK)

Originally attracted from London to Sheffield for the music scene in 1979, Ian Anderson studied philosophy at the University of Sheffield and gradually became involved in the music industry. Becoming a manager for the band Person to Person, he designed their flyers and album covers, attracting attention from other bands seeking his services. Anderson first established his firm as ISA-Vision but, as more work came in, he partnered with Nick Phillips and in 1986, on Bastille Day no less, they officially founded The Designers Republic (TDR). Their early work was in the music industry designing album covers, but they catapulted into bigger commissions, despite being in the small market of Sheffield, for global clients like Coca-Cola, Nickelodeon, and Pringles, in a range of disciplines—among other notable forays are all the graphics for *Wip3out*, a videogame for PlayStation.

Parallel to their client work, TDR has actively engendered devotion to its own brand, one defined as much by visual style—a combination of layered colors, iconography, cooptation of cultural symbols, and reinterpretation of Japanese graphics, to point to only a few ingredients— as by a philosophy that challenges consumerism through slogans like "Work, Buy, Consume, Die" and "Buy Nothing, Pay Now." Despite the slogans, TDR launched the Peoples Bureau for Consumer Information, an online retail shop selling posters, T-shirts, and TDR-infused merchandise, eventually opening a store in Tokyo in 2003. TDR has exhibited work around the world, producing posters and banners around a theme and repurposing much of its own work with new meaning. Although consistently led by Anderson, TDR fostered the input of its employees, and many have gone on to establish their own successful firms, including Michael C. Place's Build and Matt Pyke's Universal Everything. In 2009, due to economic stress TDR had to shut down its ongoing operation.

3D-2D–THE DESIGNERS REPUBLIC'S ADVENTURES IN AND OUT OF ARCHITECTURE WITH SADAR VUGA ARHITEKTI AND SPELA MLAKAR / Laurence King / TDR™ SoYo™ North of Nowhere™ vs SVA Ljubljana / The Designers Republic Ltd. / UK, 2000

WINDOWLICKER, Aphex Twin / Warp Records Ltd. / The Designers Republic Ltd. / UK, 1999

"PHO-KU CORPORATION™– WORK. BUY. CONSUME. DIE™" CUSTOMISED TERROR, ARTISTS SPACE NYC SHOW CURATED BY RONALD JONES / USA, 1995; original concept, 1993

DR SISSY™–DR DETH-TOY™ / TDR™ SoYo™ North of Nowhere™ vs The Peoples Bureau for Consumer Information / Shop33 Tokyo, 2004 / DR Sissy™ © 1993 The Designers Republic Ltd.

OPTIMIST THEORY™ LIMITED EDITION M5 GLOBAL PROJECT ALU-BOTTLE "LOVE BEING" FOR THE COCA-COLA COMPANY / The Designers Republic Ltd. / UK, 2004

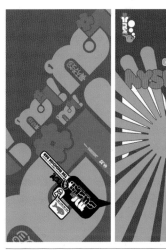

NYSUSHI SUPERFASHIONDISCOCLUB FLYER / Wildstylz Sheffield / UK, 1999

WARP IDENTITY / The Designers Republic Ltd. / UK, 1989–forever

OVAL PROJECT #5 "YEAR ZERO" FOR ISSEY MIYAKE / The Designers Republic Ltd. / Japan, 1999

Chip Kidd

b. 1964 (READING, PENNSYLVANIA, USA)
CURRENTLY NEW YORK, NEW YORK, USA

In a career that started in 1986 after he majored in graphic design from Pennsylvania State University, Chip Kidd has designed, as of mid-2008, nearly 1,000 book covers. The majority of them have been through his first and, so far, only full-time staff position, associate art director at Knopf Publishing Group, an imprint of Random House, Inc, historically noted for its small and celebrated in-house group of designers— including Barbara deWilde, Carol Devine Carson, and Archie Ferguson, along with editor Sonny Mehta—that reinvigorated the practice of book cover design in the mid-1980s. Kidd has also produced covers for HarperCollins, Doubleday, and Scribner, adding to his prodigious output. Media-guzzling books from David Sedaris, Michael Crichton, Dean Koontz, John Updike, and many other remarkable authors have cemented Kidd's popularity and ubiquity.

A voracious fan of comics, their characters, and their memorabilia, Kidd co-authored and designed *Batman Animated* in 1998; published *Batman Collected*, a book showcasing his collection on the subject, in 2001; designed, edited, and provided commentary in 2001's *Peanuts: The Art of Charles M. Schulz*; and is the editor of Pantheon Graphic Novels. Kidd has written two novels—and under fake credits designed their covers—*The Cheese Monkeys* ›108 (Scribner, 2001), which follows the adventures of Happy, an art student at a state university in the 1950s, and its sequel, *The Learners* (Scribner, 2008), which sees Happy, freshly graduated, as an art assistant for an advertising agency in the 1960s. To complement his writing and design, Kidd is the lead vocalist, percussionist, lyricist, and co-songwriter in artbreak.

ALL-STAR SUPERMAN #1, Grant Morrison, Frank Quitely / DC Comics / Chip Kidd / USA, 2005

BUDDHA, VOLUME 4: THE FOREST OF URUVELA, Osamu Tezuka / Vertical / Chip Kidd / USA, 2006

CHIP KIDD: BOOK ONE, Chip Kidd / Rizzoli / Chip Kidd / USA, 2005

THE WIND-UP BIRD CHRONICLE, Haruki Murakami / Knopf Publishing Group, Random House, Inc. / Chip Kidd; photography, Geoff Spear; illustration, Chris Ware / USA, 1997

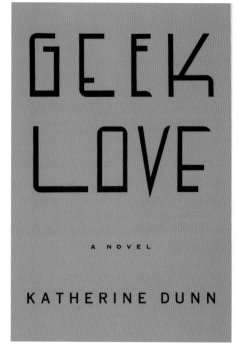

GEEK LOVE, Katherine Dunn/ Knopf Publishing Group, Random House, Inc. / Chip Kidd / USA, 1989

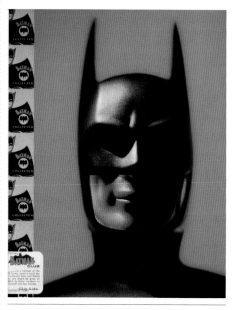

BATMAN COLLECTED, Chip Kidd / Bullfinch | D.C. Comics archives / Chip Kidd; photography, Geoff Spear / USA, 1996

KAFKA ON THE SHORE, Haruki Murakami / Knopf Publishing Group, Random House, Inc. / Chip Kidd; photomontage, Geoff Spear; head sculpture, Eishi Takaoka / USA, 2005

Irma Boom

b. 1960 (LOCHEM, NETHERLANDS)
CURRENTLY AMSTERDAM, NETHERLANDS

Upon graduation from the AKI School of Fine Art in Enschede, the Netherlands, in 1985, Irma Boom worked for the Dutch Government Publishing and Printing Office in The Hague for five years before opening her own design studio in 1991, with book design at the heart of her practice. Working with cultural institutions, publishers, and corporations, Boom's book work is famously unexpected, innovative, and complex; she designs books that use more than 80 spot colors, or are more than 2,000 pages long, or require their own customized paper stock. Boom has been widely recognized for her books, earning the prestigious "Most Beautiful Book in the World" prize at the Leipzig Book Fair for *Sheila Hicks: Weaving as Metaphor*, and the Gutenberg Prize, awarded by the city of Leipzig, Germany to an outstanding designer, in 2001. This was only ten years after starting her practice, making her the youngest designer to receive the prize. Boom is a senior critic at Yale University School of Art › 129 and at the Van Eyck Akademie in Maastricht.

ROYAL DUTCH PTT POSTAGE STAMPS / Irma Boom / Netherlands, 1993

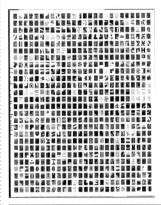

OTTO TREUMANN GRAPHIC DESIGN IN THE NETHERLANDS, Kees Broos, Tom Brandenbarg / 010 Publishers / Irma Boom / Netherlands, 2001

SHEILA HICKS: WEAVING AS METAPHOR, Nina Stritzler-Levine / Yale University Press / Irma Boom / Netherlands, 2006

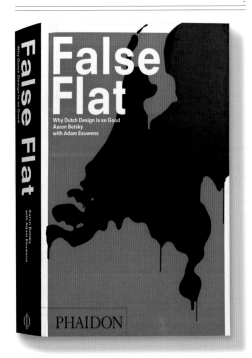

FALSE FLAT: WHY DUTCH DESIGN IS SO GOOD, Aaron Betsky, Adam Eeuwens / Phaidon / Irma Boom / Netherlands, 2004

VSA Partners

EST. 1985 (CHICAGO, ILLINOIS, USA)
OFFICES CHICAGO, NEW YORK, ST. LOUIS, MINNEAPOLIS

After many years of heading a corporate identity firm, Robert Vogele established Communication Design Group, Inc., in 1982, in Chicago's Printers Row. Three years later, emerging talents Ted Stoik and Dana Arnett joined Vogele in a partnership aptly named VSA Partners. With a balance of seasoned experience and youthful eagerness, the small firm started to grow, acquiring clients such as Harley-Davidson—which, 20 years later, is still a main client—and the Chicago Board of Trade, among others. Soon a larger office space was needed to accommodate the larger firm and a new location was scouted across the street, followed by a move to an old auto-dealing shop a decade later. As the firm grew in numbers, so did its reputation for solid work and inventive typography, most notably through annual reports › 294; the 2000 edition for IBM remains a landmark in this discipline.

In the late 1990s, VSA Partners chose to balance their print work with their newly established interactive group, a choice that held the firm afloat through the dot-com bust and allowed them to open additional offices in New York (1998), St. Louis (2003), and Minneapolis (2005). With steady leadership and dedicated teams, VSA Partners has worked across 33 industry sectors that span from boutique clients to Fortune 100 companies. They reinvigorated the Harley-Davidson brand in the 1980s; introduced Cingular's new identity, backed by a $300 million media campaign that showered the nation with the friendly orange jack in 2000; and, most recently, designed the identity—not just once but twice—for the City of Chicago's bid for the 2016 Summer Olympics.

CHICAGO BOARD OF TRADE 1993 ANNUAL REPORT / VSA Partners: art direction and design, Dana Arnett, Curt Schreiber / USA, 1994

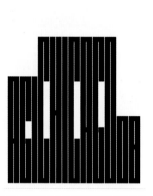

2008 AGI CONGRESS IN CHICAGO / VSA Partners: art direction, Dana Arnett; design, Jackson Cavanaugh / USA, 2008

MOHAWK OPTIONS COLLATERAL / VSA Partners: art direction, Jamie Koval; design, Dan Knuckey / USA, 2004

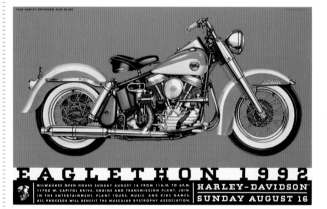

HARLEY-DAVIDSON EAGLETHON POSTER REPORT / VSA Partners: art direction, Dana Arnett, Curt Schreiber; design, Curt Schreiber / USA, 1992

CINGULAR IDENTITY / VSA Partners: art direction, Jamie Koval; design, Dan Knuckey, Ashley Lippard, Thom Wolfe, Greg Sylvester / USA, 2000

CHICAGO 2016
APPLICANT CITY

2016 SUMMER OLYMPIC GAMES CHICAGO, APPLICANT CITY / VSA Partners: art direction, Dana Arnett and Jamie Koval; design, Dan Knuckey, Luke Galambos, Kyle Poff / USA, 2006

Charles S. Anderson

b. 1958 (MINNEAPOLIS, MINNESOTA, USA)
CURRENTLY MINNEAPOLIS, MINNESOTA, USA

From a single city in the United States, Charles S. Anderson has built a remarkable career. He earned a degree in graphic design from the Minneapolis College of Art and Design (MCAD) in 1981 and got his first job at Seitz Graphic Directions with celebrated MCAD teacher Peter Seitz; he spent two years there, followed by two more at Design Center. In 1985 he joined Duffy Design Group, a leading brand and packaging design firm, where he spent four years, eventually becoming partner in 1987 when they became the design arm of Fallon McElligott Advertising. Anderson left in 1989 to establish his own design firm, Charles S. Anderson Design Company (CSA), and began to invigorate modern-day design through the revival of 1930s and 1940s stock commercial clip art and midcentury American kitsch. In the wrong hands these elements might have resulted in dreary nostalgia, but in Anderson's they created a comforting visual language with an edge.

The effects are most evident in the firm's ongoing relationship with paper mill French Paper, which transformed from a lowly competitor when it first approached Duffy Design Group to a late-1990s design industry darling through the exuberant promotions and swatch books created with CSA. While the aesthetic delights designers, CSA has capitalized on this approach with work for national clients like Coca-Cola, Urban Outfitters, and Target. Anderson's passion for American ephemera has turned into a complementary business, CSA Images, that has painstakingly rejuvenated hundreds of clip art images, borders, icons, and word images for digital consumption. And a collection of plastic toys that would make any child hyperventilate has been restored, photographed, and retouched to form a sumptuous collection of images. Anderson remains in Minneapolis.

HALIFAX HEALTH MEDICAL CENTER IDENTITY / art direction, Erik Johnson; design, Erik Johnson, Sheraton Green / USA, 2007

AIGA MINNESOTA DESIGN CAMP POSTER / art direction, Erik Johnson; design, Sheraton Green / USA, 2003

"GO FRENCH" CARD GAME FOR FRENCH PAPER / art direction, Erik Johnson; design, Erik Johnson, Sheraton Green, Jovaney Hollingsworth, Kyle Hames / USA, 2005

MUSCLETONE HEAVYWEIGHT PAPERS "DOUBLE-JOINTED JERRY" PROMOTION FOR FRENCH PAPER / design, Jason Schulte / USA, 1998

NIKE ICONS / art direction and design, Erik Johnson / USA, 1996

BETTY CROCKER LOGO FOR NEWSWEEK / art direction and design, Erik Johnson / USA, 1993

HEAVYWEIGHT PACKAGING PAPERS POSTER FOR FRENCH PAPER / design, Jason Schulte, / USA, 1999

BIRD BATH SOAP FOR POP INK / art direction, Erik Johnson; design, Sheraton Green, Jovaney Hollingsworth / USA, 2006

TURNER CLASSIC MOVIES IDENTITY / One of 50 interchangeable icons / design, Paul Howalt / USA, 1993

All work by Charles S. Anderson Design Company: art direction and design, Charles S. Anderson; additional credits individually noted

Luba Lukova
b. (PLOVDIV, BULGARIA)
CURRENTLY NEW YORK, NEW YORK, USA

Over two decades, Bulgaria-born Luba Lukova has established a strong and opinionated voice through her simple metaphoric illustrations. She worked for a theater in her home country for three years after graduating from the esteemed and demanding Academy of Fine Arts in Sofia Bulgaria in 1986. In 1991 she traveled to the United States to see her work at the Colorado International Invitational Poster Exhibition; planning to spend a few weeks in New York on her way back, she became a permanent New Yorker when she was hired by the *New York Times*'s *Book Review* after dropping off ten slides and a copy of a *Graphis* poster annual that, unbeknownst to her, showcased her work. Working independently Lukova has done illustration and design work across cultural, educational, and social projects, using her unique style of rich, flat colors and economy of line that continually challenges and invites the viewer.

WAR RESISTERS LEAGUE *PEACE* POSTER / 1999

LA MAMA E.T.C., COLUMBIA UNIVERSITY, *THE TAMING OF THE SHREW* POSTER / 1998

AMERICAN FRIENDS SERVICE COMMITTEE *CENSORSHIP* POSTER / 2003

INTERNATIONAL ANTI-POVERTY LAW CENTER *SUDAN* POSTER / 1998

SOCIAL JUSTICE 2008, Luba Lukova / Clay & Gold / 2008

Louise Fili

b. 1951 (ORANGE, NEW JERSEY, USA)
CURRENTLY NEW YORK, NEW YORK, USA

Born to Italian immigrants, Louise Fili's first trip to Italy as a 16-year-old unleashed her fascination with packaging and photography as she collected pasta packaging, wrappers, and labels—something she continues to do as she scours flea markets across the world and photographs signs and typographic façades. After graduating from Skidmore College, Fili worked briefly for Alfred A. Knopf books in 1975 and then worked for Herb Lubalin › 167 from 1976 to 1978. She then joined Pantheon Books as art director, where she designed more than 2,000 book covers—among them *The Lover* › 291— in just over a decade. In 1989 she established Louise Fili Ltd., where she sought to diversify her work; her passion for cooking and her love for design blended as she delved into restaurant identity work and food packaging. Fili has a unique ability to reinterpret historical influences into modern-day products, her editorial work, and the books she has authored.

SFIDA WINE LABELS FOR MATT BROTHERS / 2000

MERMAID INN RESTAURANT IDENTITY / 2004

CALIFORNIA GRAPE SEED OIL PACKAGING FOR WILLIAMS-SONOMA / 1999

THE PINK DOOR RESTAURANT IDENTITY / 1999

SFOGLIA RESTAURANT IDENTITY / 2006

TIFFANY & CO. IDENTITY / 2007

LATE JULY ORGANIC CRACKERS PACKAGING / 2005

MARGARITA MIX PACKAGING FOR EL PASO CHILE COMPANY / 1999

LE MONDE RESTAURANT IDENTITY / 1998

BELLA CUCINA PACKAGING / 1999–2002

Modern Dog

EST. 1987 (SEATTLE, WASHINGTON, USA)

Lacking job offers after graduating from Western Washington University and a move to Seattle, Robynne Raye and Michael Strassburger established Modern Dog in 1987 with little intention of turning it into a formal business. However, for more than 20 years Modern Dog has thrived, developing numerous posters for the music and theater industries as well as advertising, packaging, and products for a diverse clientele. Its early years were a precedent for the owners' current approach and business model, even if they wouldn't call it that.

Working with low budgets and, by extension, low pay, Modern Dog did poster work for fringe theaters, acting as each project's photographers, illustrators, letterers, and production artists, expressing the do-it-yourself extemporaneous attitude and aesthetic that permeates much of their work. To supplement their poster assignments, Raye procured ski manufacturer K2 as a client in 1989, designing advertisements for them in the beginning. The relationship has blossomed over ten years as K2 has became one of the leading snowboarding brands.

Since 1998, Modern Dog has been working with Blue Q, a purveyor of eclectic products—soaps, coin purses, air fresheners—for whom they develop products like magnets, breath sprays, and chewing gum, taking in a low design fee upfront but reaping the benefits in royalties. All the while, Raye and Strassburger continue to produce quick-witted posters, including a miscellany of self-promotional posters announcing their lectures around the country, some of which disappear from walls minutes after they've been hung. Both of them teach at Cornish College of the Arts in Seattle—and, yes, they both own dogs.

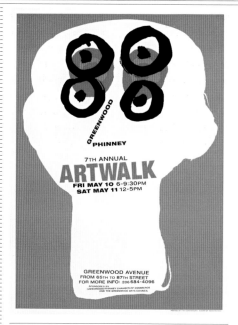

GREENWOOD ARTS COUNCIL ARTWALK POSTER / Modern Dog: design, Robynne Raye / USA, 2002

K2 SNOWBOARDS PRODUCT BROCHURE / Modern Dog / USA, 1995

BLUE Q CAT BUTT MAGNETS / Modern Dog / USA, 2001

OLIVE DOG PRODUCT PACKAGING / Modern Dog / USA, 2007

HEARTBREAK HOUSE SEATTLE REPERTORY THEATRE POSTER / Modern Dog: design, Vittorio Costarella / USA, 1993

AMPHETAZINE COVERS / Modern Dog / USA, 1991–2001

BLONDIE POSTER FOR HOUSE OF BLUES / Modern Dog: design, Michael Strassburger / USA, 2004

Aesthetic Apparatus
EST. 2002 (MINNEAPOLIS, MINNESOTA, USA)

Dan Ibarra and Michael Byzewski met in 1998 while working at Planet Propaganda in Madison, Wisconsin. The friendship soon blossomed as a shared love for printmaking and music led to homemade limited-edition concert posters. As their work gained public notice, the duo gained courage, and Aesthetic Apparatus was established in 2002, part of a new generation of gig-poster designers; their poster work has been a constant area of attraction. The use of abrupt juxtapositions, found imagery, and interesting typography identifies much of their work, as does the craft; they personally silkscreen posters in the studio—typically sold online, or at concerts, nicely supplementing their income and maintaining a steady ink flow. Aesthetic Apparatus has developed a unique and morphing style they aptly apply to diverse projects spanning identity, packaging, illustration, editorial work, and even their popular YouTube videos—including one where they scream gleefully, pointing at their process instead of speaking.

Left to Right **THE SWELL SEASON** POSTER FOR AEG LIVE / 2008

CAKE POSTER / 2006

FIRST AVENUE POSTER / 2005

WE ARE SCIENTISTS POSTER / 2006

Aesthetic Apparatus / USA

Small Stakes
EST. 2003 (OAKLAND, CALIFORNIA, USA)

After donating his design abilities to the Ramp—the basement of a church that served as a venue for music performances in Berkeley, California—in 2003 Jason Munn established Small Stakes, naming the studio after a song by Spoon about taking chances. Munn's poster work for local independent bands began to get noticed—first using found art and later maturing into his own illustration. As the design, production, and infrastructure of his posters grew, so did his popularity. His illustratively and typographically simple and playful designs, often presented in soft-spoken flat colors, led to an array of commissions from clients such as Chronicle Books, Patagonia, and Capitol Records. Thus, the little Stake that could has expanded into new areas of design such as clothing, bags, CD packaging, and editorial illustrations.

Left to Right **DANIEL JOHNSON** CONCERT POSTER / 2007

SFMOMA COLLEGE NIGHT WITH NOISE POP POSTER / 2006

THE BOOKS CONCERT POSTER / 2006

TREASURE ISLAND MUSIC FESTIVAL POSTER / 2007

The Small Stakes / USA

Rick Valicenti

b. 1951 (PITTSBURGH, PENNSYLVANIA, USA)
CURRENTLY CHICAGO, ILLINOIS, USA

Upon receiving his BFA from Ohio's Bowling Green State University in 1973, employment prospects for Rick Valicenti were scarce. Not willing to go unemployed, he worked for a steel mill, hard hat and all. He developed an interest in photography and enrolled in the University of Iowa, earning MA and MFA degrees in photography in 1975. Valicenti then moved to Chicago, where he found commercial photography uninspiring. Intrigued with graphic design, he managed to find employment as a paste-up production artist until 1978, when he started working for Bruce Beck, who had been running a reputable design firm. When Beck retired, Valicenti started his own business, R. Valicenti Design, in 1981, which initially did editorial and corporate collateral work. It was in 1988 that two of Valicenti's most enduring clients, Gilbert Paper and the Lyric Opera of Chicago, first sought his services and provided canvases for him to develop his unique style of design, photography, lettering, illustration, and messaging.

In 1989, Valicenti reinvented his firm as Thirst. He became more selective in his clients and collaborators, and in 1995, looking for a better balance between life and work, he moved the office to Barrington, a Chicago suburb. Through the 1990s and into the 2000s, Valicenti and Thirst—as it is continually shaped by its employees and their unique strengths and interests—blossomed into an inimitable amalgam of client and self-initiated work. Valicenti has also displayed an entrepreneurial bent, initiating business like the type foundry Thirstype (now Village › 233), the interactive spin-off 3st2, and the digital imaging studio Real Eyes. In 2007, Valicenti relocated Thirst to Chicago.

365: AIGA YEAR IN DESIGN 29 /
3ST: design and illustration,
Rick Valicenti, John Pobojewski /
USA, 2007

GILBERT PAPER *PRINT THIS MOMENT* **POSTER INSERT FOR** *WIRED* **MAGAZINE** / 3ST: Rick Valicenti, William Valicenti / USA, 1994

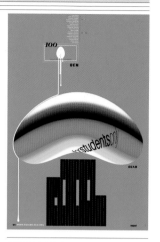

CHICAGO STUDENT DESIGN CONFERENCE 2008 POSTER FOR ALLIANCE GRAPHIQUE INTERNATIONALE / 3ST: Rick Valicenti; typography, Rick Valicenti, Dana Arnett; illustration, Rick Valicenti, Matt Daly / USA, 2008

"SO FIVE MINUTES AGO" EDITORIAL ILLUSTRATION FOR *I4DESIGN* **MAGAZINE** / 3ST: Rick Valicenti; 3D illustration, Rick Valicenti, Matt Daly / USA, 2008

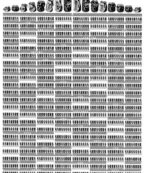

INTELLIGENT DESIGN: THE RED AND BLUE STATE OF MIND / The book of Genesis was converted to binary code and reproduced using Pepsi One cans as the 1s and Coke Zero cans as the 0s / 3ST: Rick Valicenti; illustration, Rick Valicenti, Gina Garza; typography, Rick Valicenti, John Pobojewski; programming, John Pobojewski, Robb Irrgang / USA, 2005

What's in a Name?

In 1988, while reviewing layouts for a Philippe Starck catalog through fax, Starck referred to the third item in a series not as "3rd" but rather as "3st," which Valicenti coopted for his own purposes. He now uses both spellings, Thirst and 3st.

Bruce Mau

b. 1959 (SUDBURY, ONTARIO, CANADA)
CURRENTLY TORONTO, ONTARIO, CANADA

Bruce Mau left the Ontario College of Art and Design in Toronto before graduating, choosing instead to join the firm Fifty Fingers in 1980. Two years later he worked at Pentagram › 162, London, immersed in a multidisciplinary environment that would become a personal trait upon his return to Toronto, where he co-founded the firm Public Good and Communications. In 1985, Bruce Mau Design opened its doors. The firm has allowed Mau to work across many disciplines, including branding, identity, editorial, product development, and environmental design—often partnering with architects on projects such as the Walt Disney Concert Hall in Los Angeles (with Frank Gehry) and the book *S, M, L, XL* › 283 (with Rem Koolhaas). Mau's own 600-plus-page book, *Life Style*, published in 2000 and produced in eight different fabric covers, reflects the multidisciplinary background, client roster, and way of thinking that identifies him— providing insightful information and visual cues to past projects and beyond.

In 2003 Mau established The Institute Without Boundaries, a postgraduate studio-based program with the School of Design at George Brown College in Toronto, where a select group of students collaborates for a year with a public project in mind. *Massive Change*, a study "not about the world of design, but about the design of the world" through 11 economies—urban, movement, energy, information, image, market, material, military, manufacturing, living, wealth, and politics—resulted in a book and traveling show that exposed the first year of findings and conclusions. The second project, *World House*, is centered on future housing, where sustainability, ecological balance, and universality play key roles.

RECOMMENDED READING › 390

ART GALLERY OF ONTARIO IDENTITY / Bruce Mau Design / Canada, 2008

INTERACTIVECORP HEADQUARTERS / Bruce Mau Design / Canada, 2007

¡GUATEAMALA! IDENTITY FOR THE FUNDACIÓN PROYECTO DE VIDA / Bruce Mau Design / Canada, 2004

MASSIVE CHANGE EXHIBITION / Bruce Mau Design / Canada, 2004–2006

In 1998, Bruce Mau developed an incomplete 43-point manifesto, based on his experiences, that is applied to every project:

Allow events to change you / Forget about good / Good is a known quantity / Process is more important than outcome / Love your experiments / Joy is the engine of growth / Go deep / Capture accidents / Study / Drift / Begin anywhere / Everyone is a leader / Growth happens / Harvest ideas / Keep moving / Slow down / Don't be cool / Ask stupid questions / Collaborate / _____ / Stay up late / Work the metaphor / Be careful to take risks / Repeat yourself / Make your own tools / Stand on someone's shoulders / Avoid software / Don't clean your desk / Don't enter awards competitions / Read only left-hand pages / Make new words / Think with your mind / Organization = Liberty / Don't borrow money / Listen carefully / Take field trips / Make mistakes faster / Imitate / Scat / Break it, stretch it, bend it, crush it, crack it, fold it / Explore the other edge / Coffee breaks, cab rides, green rooms / Avoid fields / Laugh / Remember / Power to the people

Stefan Sagmeister

b. 1962 (BREGENZ, AUSTRIA)
CURRENTLY NEW YORK, NEW YORK, USA

Stefan Sagmeister was on his way to become an engineer when his involvement with *Alphorn*, a left-wing magazine in Bregenz, Austria, altered his course—he moved to Vienna and was accepted at the University of Applied Arts on his second attempt. In 1987, with a Fulbright scholarship, Sagmeister continued his studies at the Pratt Institute in New York. Three years later he completed his military obligations in community service and worked as a graphic designer in Vienna before joining the Leo Burnett advertising agency in Hong Kong in 1991. Back in New York, Sagmeister worked at M&Co. › 183, a dream of his, for six months before Tibor Kalman announced he was closing the studio.

This led to Sagmeister, Inc., established in 1993, which began with family and friends as clients and produced projects that soon opened the way into the music, fashion, and editorial industries. One designer and one intern often aid Sagmeister, maintaining a small and manageable studio that allows him to attend to the detail and experimentation he craves. The year 2000 was quiet for the design community. Sagmeister took the year off, feeling repetitive and somewhat stale in his work, to rethink, reevaluate, and refocus. Upon reopening his firm in 2001 he published *Sagmeister: Made You Look*, where he compiled his good and bad projects to date. He continues to impress and inspire through his work, lectures, and his ongoing typographic musings, titled *Things I Have Learned So Far*.

ZUMTOBEL AG ANNUAL REPORT / Sagmeister, Inc.: art direction, Stefan Sagmeister; design, Stefan Sagmeister, Matthias Ernstberger; photography, Bela Borsodi; prototype, Joe Stone / USA, 2002

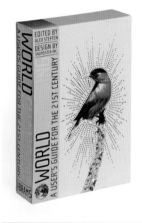

WORLDCHANGING: A USER'S GUIDE FOR THE 21ST CENTURY, Alex Steffen / Abrams / Stefan Sagmeister, Inc.: art direction, Stefan Sagmeister; design, Matthias Ernstberger, Roy Rub / USA, 2006

AIGA NEW ORLEANS POSTER / Sagmeister, Inc.: illustration, Stefan Sagmeister, Peggy Chuang, Kazumi Matsumoto, Raphael Rüdisser; photography, Bela Borsodi; paint box, Dalton Portella / USA, 1997

BRIDGES TO BABYLON, Rolling Stones / Virgin Records / Sagmeister, Inc.: art direction, Stefan Sagmeister; design, Stefan Sagmeister, Hjalti Karlsson; photography, Max Vadukul; illustration, Kevin Murphy, Gerard Howland, Alan Ayers / USA, 1997

HUGO BOSS PRIZE CATALOG COVER FOR THE GUGGENHEIM MUSEUM / Sagmeister, Inc.: art direction, Stefan Sagmeister; design, Sarah Noellenheidt, Matthias Ernstberger; production, Lara Fieldbinder, Melissa Secundino / USA, 2004

ANNI KUAN DESIGN FASHION BROCHURE / Sagmeister, Inc.: design, Stefan Sagmeister, Hjalti Karlsson; photography, Tom Schierlitz; illustration, Martin Woodtli / USA, 1999

Michael Bierut

b. 1957 (CLEVELAND, OHIO, USA)
CURRENTLY NEW YORK, NEW YORK, USA

Unlike the many designers who stumble on the profession or are not intrigued by it until the late teenage years, Michael Bierut's determination to become a graphic designer started when he was 15 years old as he stumbled on *Aim for a Job in Graphic Design/Art*, a 1968 book by Columbia Records › 300 art director S. Neil Fujita, in his school library. Two books later—*Graphic Design Manual* by Armin Hoffman and *Graphic Design* by Milton Glaser › 170—Bierut was hooked. With a degree from the University of Cincinnati's College of Design, Architecture, Art, and Planning and an internship with Chris Pullman at the Boston public television station WGBH, Bierut's first job in 1980 was with one of the most prominent designers of the time, Massimo Vignelli › 160.

After ten years and a rise to vice president of design at Vignelli Associates, Bierut joined Pentagram › 162 in 1990 as a partner in the New York office and has since become one of the firm's most visible personalities. He does high-profile work for organizations like Harley-Davidson, the New York Jets, Saks Fifth Avenue › 319, United Airlines, and for cultural and educational institutions like Brooklyn Academy of Music, Museum of Arts and Design, and Yale School of Architecture. He has been involved with the profession as president of the New York chapter of the AIGA › 244 (1988–1990) and then as president of the national organization (1998–2001). He is most recently and popularly one of the founders of the blog Design Observer › 113, where his endless array of topics and endless display of knowledge have earned him a devout following. His interest in all things graphic design is so legendary that an alternative to this book could have been an audio book where Bierut recites everything he knows.

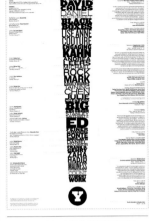

YALE SCHOOL OF ARCHITECTURE LECTURES, EXHIBITIONS, SYMPOSIA SPRING 2004 POSTER / Pentagram: Michael Bierut / USA, 2004

MUSEUM OF SEX / Pentagram: Michael Bierut; design, Brett Traylor / USA, 2002

100 YEARS OF HARLEY-DAVIDSON / Pentagram: Michael Bierut; design, Elizabeth Ellis / USA, 2002

UNITED AIRLINES BRAND IDENTITY AND LIVERY / Pentagram: Michael Bierut, Daniel Weil; design, Brett Traylor, David Gibbs / USA, 2003–2004

TED BRAND IDENTITY / Pentagram: Michael Bierut, Daniel Weil; design, Brett Traylor, David Gibbs / USA, 2003–2004

THE LIBRARY INITIATIVE / Pentagram: Michael Bierut; design, Rion Byrd; illustration, top Lynn Pauley, bottom Peter Arkle; architecture, Richard Lewis / USA, 2001 / Photo: Peter Mauss/ Esto, Kevin Chu/KCJP

THE NEW YORK TIMES BUILDING ENVIRONMENTAL GRAPHICS / Pentagram: Michael Bierut / USA, 2007

Brian Collins

b. 1961 (LEXINGTON, MASSACHUSETTS, USA)
CURRENTLY NEW YORK, NEW YORK, USA

Brian Collins's unparalleled level of energy and restlessness continuously shapes his professional path. After attending Parsons School of Design and Massachusetts College of Art and running a couple of independent studios in Boston, spending time in London in between, Collins joined Duffy Design Group in 1990. His third studio followed, in Minneapolis, before joining Foote Cone & Belding/San Francisco to work on Levi Strauss & Co., MTV › 352, and Amazon.com in 1995. Three years later Collins moved to New York City and began his tenure with Ogilvy & Mather's in-house design team, the Brand Integration Group (BIG) › 205, where his passion and dedication translated into well-known clients, worldwide projects, and a long list of recognitions and awards. The first designer to participate in the World Economic Forum in Davos, Switzerland, in 2005, Collins was named Peak Performer in Design by *Fast Company*; a year before, the Massachusetts College of Art and Design named him Distinguished Alumnus.

More recently, Collins has divided his efforts by working on public good projects, such as the annual forum "Designism: Design for Social Change," held at the Art Directors Club › 245 in New York City, teaching in the graduate program in design at the School of Visual Arts › 132, and his newly founded firm COLLINS:, which he established upon leaving BIG in 2007. His latest projects include the Alliance for Climate Protection "we" campaign and the CNN Grill at the 2008 Democratic and Republican National Conventions. A constant traveler, Collins can also be found speaking at many design and business conferences, where he continually motivates and inspires attendees professionally and personally.

BP HELIOS HOUSE / creative direction, Brian Collins; design, Chuck Rudy, Mark Aver, Christian Cervantes, Jung Ha, David Harlan, Allbriton Robbins, Noah Venezia; architecture, Office DA: Monica Ponce de Leon, Nader Tehrani; JohnstonMarkLee / USA, 2007

KODAK IDENTITY PROGRAM / creative direction, Brian Collins; design, Allen Hori, Weston Bingham, Christian Cervantes, Peter Kaplan / USA, 2005–2006

ALLIANCE FOR CLIMATE PROTECTION "WE" CAMPAIGN / COLLINS:: Brian Collins, John Moon, Mickey Pangilinan; The Martin Agency: Ty Harper, Raymond McKinney, Sean Riley, Mike Hughes; Village Type & Design: Chester Jenkins / USA, 2008

HERSHEY'S TIME SQUARE STORE / Ogilvy & Mather: creative direction, Brian Collins; design, Weston Bingham, Edward Chiquitucto, Roman Luba / USA, 2003

THE ECOLOGY OF DESIGN / design, Brian Collins, Sarah Nelson; project participants, R.O. Blechman, Paul Davis, Joe Duffy, Vivienne Flesher, Brad Holland, Edward Sorel, Gary Panter, Helene Silverman, Paul Rand, Mark Wald, Sharon Werner / USA, 1996

COCA-COLA GLOBAL IDENTITY / creative direction, Brian Collins; design, Richard Bates, Barry Deck, Mark Aver, Christian Cervantes, Arden de Brun, Apirat Infahsaeng, Tracy Jenkins, Peter Kaplan, Ali Madad, Charles Watlington / USA, 2006

THE OFFICE OF NATIONAL DRUG CONTROL POLICY CAMPAIGN "WHAT'S YOUR ANTI-DRUG?" / Ogilvy & Mather: creative direction, Brian Collins, Charles Hall; design, Patrik Bolocek / USA, 2000

BIG
**BRAND INTEGRATION GROUP,
OGILVY & MATHER WORLDWIDE
EST. 1996** (NEW YORK, NEW YORK, USA)

Ogilvy & Mather's in-house Brand Integration Group, better known as BIG, was founded in 1996 by then chief creative officer Rick Boyko. The group was tasked with finding new ways to connect brands and consumers. Two years later, the fresh stewardship of Brian Collins › 204 led the firm to eradicate the dividing lines between advertising and design, as Collins set out to establish a firm that functioned more like a lab that retained the energetic, experimental nature of graduate school than an office—providing multiple seating areas in which to converse, large chalk-friendly walls on which to sketch and have fun—while working on mainstream projects. The high energy of the firm was palpable to visitors and newcomers as they walked down red-lined halls peppered with seven-foot boards showcasing every iteration and idea across all projects.

BIG distinguishes itself by an unconventional experience-driven approach to client needs: In 2002, a Hershey › 309 billboard assignment became a 12-story chocolate factory in New York's Times Square; three years later, Dove's international traveling photography exhibit, *Campaign for Real Beauty*, became a unique and memorable advertising campaign; in 2005, New York City was covered by the city's bid for the 2012 Summer Olympic Games › 206; and 2007 brought to life BP's Helios House, the first environmentally certified gas station, among many other projects. In 2007 Collins departed and Richard Bates assumed leadership, continuing the tradition to challenge expectations. Over the years, BIG has been exceptional in attracting talented and seasoned designers like Barry Deck, Rebeca Méndez, and Allen Hori, as well as a younger generation that included Luke Hayman, now partner at Pentagram; Alan Dye, now with Apple; and Bobby C. Martin Jr., now with Nokia.

BRAND INTEGRATION GROUP IDENTITY / BIG: Brian Collins, Alan Dye / USA, 2003

BRILL'S CONTENT MAGAZINE **REDESIGN** / BIG: Brian Collins, Luke Hayman / USA, 1999

DOVE'S "REAL BEAUTY" EXHIBITION LAUNCHING ITS NORTH AMERICAN CAMPAIGN / BIG: Brian Collins, David Israel, Leigh Okies, Satian Pengsathapon / USA, 2005

SPRITE'S GLOBAL DESIGN PROGRAM / BIG: Brian Collins, Weston Bingham, Iwona Waluk, Jason Ring / USA, 2005

COCA-COLA HOLIDAY CAN DESIGN / BIG: Brian Collins, Hee Chun, Barry Deck / USA, 2005

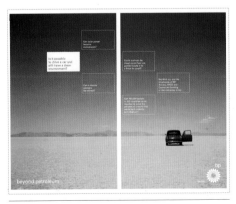

BP "BEYOND PETROLEUM" CAMPAIGN LAUNCH / BIG: Brian Collins, Michael Kaye, Rebeca Méndez, David Fowler / USA, 2000

TRIBECA FILM FESTIVAL IDENTITY / BIG: Brian Collins, David Israel, Nathalie Hennequin / USA, 2004

Wolff Olins

EST. 1965 (LONDON, ENGLAND, UK)
OFFICES LONDON, NEW YORK, TOKYO

Since its founding in 1965 in Camden Town, London, Wolff Olins has been developing corporate and brand identity work that defies established conventions. This is not gratuitous praise but rather an objective assessment of their record. As an abridged library of examples: In 1971, they employed a hummingbird to identify Bovis Construction, a tropical bird native neither to the United Kingdom nor the construction industry; in 2003, they used the tagline "We are Macmillan. Cancer Support" to function as the logo for Macmillan Cancer Support; and, of course, they created the publicly conflicting and allegedly seizure-inducing logo for the 2012 Summer Olympic Games › 359 in London.

In its 40-plus years, Wolff Olins has morphed and adapted its business and creative structure while maintaining the equity of its founding partners, Michael Wolff and Wally Olins. Wolff left in 1983 to join Addison. Olins, now chairman of the brand consultancy Saffron, left in 2001, having gradually stepped back from running the business since 1997, when a management buyout team headed by Brian Boylan, a member of Wolff Olins since the late 1960s and now the chairman, took over. The firm started growing in the early 1990s, opening offices in Madrid and Barcelona (1991–2007), New York (1998–present), San Francisco (2001–2006), and Tokyo (2001–present through advertising agency Hakuhodo), and was purchased by Omnicom in 2001. In 2007, the New York and London offices became the sole hubs of Wolff Olins, with an active interchange of employees between them. The firm's current creative lead and executive creative director is Patrick Cox, who spent from 1987 to 1995 with Wolff Olins and came back in 2002 to extend the tradition of work that challenges branding and identity dictums.

TATE IDENTITY / **Wolff Olins** / UK, 2000

MACMILLAN CANCER SUPPORT BRAND REINVENTION / **Wolff Olins** / UK, 2006

NEW MUSEUM IDENTITY / **Wolff Olins** / USA, 2007

ORANGE IDENTITY / Wolff Olins / UK, 1994

NEW YORK CITY IDENTITY / Wolff Olins / USA, 2007

Cato Partners

EST. 1971 (SYDNEY, AUSTRALIA)
OFFICES AUSTRALIA, NEW ZEALAND, SPAIN,
MEXICO, DUBAI, INDONESIA, SINGAPORE

Before establishing his own firm, Ken Cato graduated from the Royal Melbourne Institute of Technology in 1966 and worked in a variety of environments, including a direct mail house, a design studio, and briefly in advertising, until 1970, when he co-founded Cato Hibberd Design in Australia with Terry Hibberd. From this modest beginning, Cato's rising trajectory has seen its share of partners and iterations. In the mid-1970s it became Cato Hibberd Hornblow Hawksbury Design; Hornblow and Hawksbury left in the late 1970s, leaving Cato and Hibberd as partners until 1982, when Hibberd retired. The business then became Ken Cato Design Company, followed by just Cato Design and, in 2003, Cato Purnell Partners. This list is not meant to confuse but rather to point out the collaborative and enterprising attitude that has defined the firm, now a global network of offices with nearly 100 employees across Australia, New Zealand, Spain, Mexico, Dubai, Indonesia, and Singapore.

Each office operates under the Cato Partners umbrella but runs independently and is often defined by local partnerships, like Cato Saca Partners in Mexico and Consulus Cato Partners in Singapore. Through its international scope, Cato Partners has worked on a remarkable number of global brands, producing identity work, environmental graphics, and packaging that resembles the work of a boutique design firm rather than that of a design conglomerate. As head of one of the most visible firms in Australia, Cato has played a significant role in bringing attention to the design community there, most notably by conceiving the first AGIdeas, the student conference hosted by the Alliance Graphique Internationale (AGI) › 247, in 1991, when their congress was held in Australia; he was also president of AGI from 1997 to 2000.

MELBOURNE SPORTS AND AQUATIC CENTRE IDENTITY AND SIGNAGE / 1996

BENQ PACKAGING AND VISUAL LANGUAGE / Taiwan, 2008

SEVEN NETWORK EXTERNAL SIGNAGE / 2000

AGIDEAS 2008 INTERNATIONAL DESIGN WEEK PROGRAM / 2008

world central
DUBAI

DUBAI WORLD CENTRAL IDENTITY /
Each individual city is represented by a symbol expressive of its type of activity / 2006

Cato Partners / Australia (except for BenQ)

Michael Johnson

b. 1964 (DERBYSHIRE, ENGLAND, UK)
CURRENTLY LONDON, ENGLAND, UK

For Michael Johnson, establishing his own design firm, johnson banks, at the age of 28 in 1992 was the culmination of eight years, eight employment positions, two firings, and residence in four major cities across the world. After graduating from college, Johnson spent two years with Wolff Olins › 206 in the mid-1980s, where he was pegged as a "suit that could draw" and was unable to find his place as either a designer or consultant. He then went to work for several studios in Sydney and Melbourne, punctuated by six months in Tokyo; he came back to London to work at Sedley Place and made a final, three-year stop at Smith & Milton, where he at last found and developed his own design voice.

With modest beginnings in print design and two employees, johnson banks grew into a full-fledged design firm with six or seven full-time employees working on significantly large and comprehensive identity projects for cultural institutions and government agencies. The firm now services clients in Paris, Tokyo, and the United States.

Representative of Johnson's design aesthetic and a process that eschews typical solutions and favors ideas are two of his postage designs for the Royal Mail. The "Fruit 'n' Veg" stamp set, issued in 2003, features straightforward images of fruits and vegetables but is accompanied by 76 stickers with which people can customize their stamps, à la Mr. Potato Head. In 2007, Johnson designed a set to commemorate the Beatles, using the band's album cover artwork and employing a challenging diecut that follows the jumbled shape of what are meant to be piles of Beatles albums. Johnson has been actively involved with the Design and Art Direction (D&AD) › 249 group, including a year serving as one of the organization's youngest presidents in its history.

BRITISH FILM INSTITUTE (BFI) IDENTITY AND BRANDING / johnson banks: Michael Johnson, Pali Palavathanan / UK, 2006

PLEASURE BEACH, BLACKPOOL, THEME PARK REBRANDING / johnson banks: Michael Johnson, Kath Tudball, Julia Woollams / UK, 2005

THE BEATLES POSTAL STAMPS COMMEMORATING THE FIFTIETH ANNIVERSARY OF LENNON AND MCCARTNEY HAVING MET / johnson banks: Michael Johnson / UK, 2007

THINK LONDON LOGO / johnson banks: Michael Johnson, Julia Woollams / UK, 2004

FRUIT 'N' VEG POSTAL STAMPS / johnson banks: Michael Johnson, Andrew Ross, Sarah Fullerton / UK, 2003

"SEND A LETTER" FROM THE JOHNSON BANKS POST OFFICE, INAUGURATED AT THE V&A MUSEUM / johnson banks: Michael Johnson, Kath Tudball, Julia Woollams / UK, 2005

MOUSE AWARDS LOGO AND AWARD / johnson banks: Michael Johnson, Kath Tudball / UK, 2008

RECOMMENDED READING › 390

Vince Frost

b. 1964 (BRIGHTON, ENGLAND, UK)
CURRENTLY SYDNEY, AUSTRALIA

Initially working as a freelancer after graduating from West Sussex College of Design, Vince Frost was hired by the London office of Pentagram › 162 in 1989, and after a short three years he was promoted, becoming the youngest associate partner (the highest position other than partner) to date at 27 years old. In 1994 Frost set out on his own as Frost Design, beginning a slew of magazine projects with *Big Magazine* and *Saturday Magazine* for *The Independent* newspaper. In addition, he moved to Tokyo to serve as art director for the 1998 launch of *Vogue* in Japan, only to step back from the position after eight months as the publication struggled. He also collaborated with editor Dan Crowe to launch the literary magazine *Zembla*, which further developed Frost's proficiency in editorial design.

In 2003, at the kind behest of his Australian wife, who wanted to be in her home country, Frost found the right professional opportunity by entering into a partnership with Garry Emery, an established Australian designer, and together they formed emeryfrost, with offices in Melbourne and Sydney. The partnership led to many significant projects and collaborations, but by the end of 2005 the designers went their separate ways, with Frost keeping his office in Sydney; he also kept an outpost in London, as he had maintained clients there, including *Zembla*, which eventually folded in 2005. Frost Design now comprises approximately 30 employees, and its client and project roster is numerous, diverse, and eclectic, thanks in part to the firm's refreshing openness to the potential in any given project, whether it's the identity for music label Mushroom Records, an album cover for the Spice Girls, or the annual report for a company called Supercheap Auto.

SYD_AN_CEY COMPANY

SYDNEY DANCE COMPANY IDENTITY / Frost Design: Vince Frost / Australia, 2005

D&AD *AMPERSAND* **MAGAZINE** / Frost Design: Vince Frost / Australia, 2006

ZEMBLA **MAGAZINE** / Frost Design: Vince Frost / Australia, 2003

POL OXYGEN STRETCH **MAGAZINE** / Frost Design: Vince Frost / Australia, 2006

BIG **MAGAZINE** / Frost Design: Vince Frost / Australia, 2005

Daniel Eatock

b. 1975 (BOLTON, ENGLAND, UK)
CURRENTLY LONDON, ENGLAND, UK

After studying communication design at Ravensbourne College in London, Daniel Eatock earned an MA from the Royal College of Art › 135 in 1998 and secured a coveted position overseas in the Walker Art Center's › 354 design department fellowship program. There he met Sam Solhaug, an architect working in the exhibit group, with whom he collaborated—first at the Walker's carpentry shop, and later, when Eatock had returned to London and Solhaug visited in 2000 for a few weeks, at Pentagram's › 162 own carpentry shop—on a plywood table prototype to show at the Milan Furniture Fair. They dubbed their informal collaboration Foundation 33; it soon became a formal business when their table's promotion representative introduced them to Katie Hayes, marketing manager for Britain's Channel 4, who gave them the opportunity to pitch the identity for the original production of the reality show *Big Brother*. That pitch is the now globally iconic eye that mutates in an endless number of visual styles.

With Foundation 33 growing, in 2004 it was approached by startup advertising agency Boymeetsgirl and became its design wing, but the relationship lasted just a year. In 2005 Eatock went independent and established Eatock, Ltd. Since then, he has maintained a practice that balances commissioned work with an incessant flow of creative exercises and ideas meticulously catalogued on his ever-growing website, built using his own custom web application, Indexhibit™, devised with Jeffery Vaska. Unlike other designers' websites, which are usually fully polished and edited, Eatock's serves as a rough repository not just of projects but of loose and unfinished ideas as well as collaborative, user-contributed collections; for no particular reason, there are at least four videos of Eatock dancing to the tune of car alarms.

***PANTONE PEN PRINT* SERIES** / A complete set of Letraset TRIA Pantone markers, arranged by color, was placed under a stack of 500 sheets for a month; the series is determined by the number of pages printed, where the sheet farthest from the ink received the first number, which also corresponds to the individual price of each print / Daniel Eatock / UK, 2006

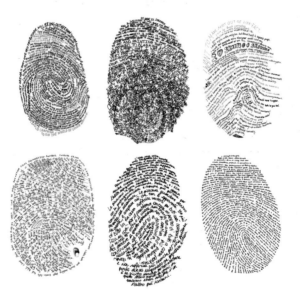

AS A CLASS ASSIGNMENT AT RAVENSBOURNE COLLEGE, students were asked to create a typographic self-portrait. Richard Holley, one of Eatock's fellow students, wrote a short text about himself and placed it within the contours of his fingerprint in his own handwriting. Many years later, Eatock, inspired by this solution, created an ongoing invitation on his website for people to create their own "Holley Portrait" / Daniel Eatock, various / UK, 2007–ongoing

PROPOSED LOGO FOR THE SUMMER OLYMPIC GAMES 2012 / Combining the Olympic Rings and the RAF Roundel popular in the 1960s / Daniel Eatock / UK, 2007

BIG BROTHER 7 IDENTITY / Daniel Eatock / UK, 2006

DEPFORD THRIFT MARKET DISCARDED OBJECT REDESIGN FOR THE DEPTFORD DESIGN CHALLENGE / Daniel Eatock / UK, 2007

RECOMMENDED READING › 390

ITC Dynadis

REPRESENTATIVES
Of Letterforms

214
Origins

Selecting the mid-fifteenth century—when Johannes Gutenberg successfully printed his 42-line Bible using a textura blackletter typeface cast in metal—as a starting point for the story of the evolution and development of typeface design, highlighting its most significant practitioners, events, and technological advancements, the overview in the following six pages spans more than six hundred years. Each century could easily merit its own book, so the purpose of the overview is merely to help establish the key developments and sources of reference that laid the foundation for typeface design and designers in the latter half of the twentieth century, when metal typesetting ceded its stronghold in the production of printed materials to phototype-setting, which gave way to the digital revolution.

A note on the artwork in this section: All illustra-tions are one-color interpretations of the original design and are not exact replicas.

221
Post-1984

The ripples caused by the 1984 introduction of the Macintosh computer—and the advances it made in the reproduction and rasterization of typography—were not felt immediately. Its technology was relatively primitive, but by the beginning of the 1990s Apple and other software developers further developed the tools to design, produce, and distribute digital typefaces that would have designers and entrepreneurs looking fully forward. The public embrace of the Internet as a mode of distribution and marketing in the late 1990s and early 2000s dramatically expedited the growth and impact of the typeface design industry.

(1447 - 1528)
Erhard Ratdolt
GERMANY, ITALY

/ Moved from Germany to Venice in 1475, where he established a printing business

/ Designed and printed perhaps the first recorded type specimen sheet in 1486, showcasing his black letter, Roman and Greek typeface designs

1440s - 1450s / GERMANY

Johannes Gutenberg › 288 innovates the method for creating metal-cast type: A steel punch, containing the master shape of a letter, is stamped in a softer brass matrix, creating a "positive" that is then placed in a mold / SHOWN Nineteenth Century engraving illustrating (from left to right) the punch, matrix and type mold created by Gutenberg

(1480 - 1561)
Claude Garamond
FRANCE

/ Was one of the first punch cutters to work independently and sell his fonts to printers

/ His first Roman appeared in 1530 in *Paraphrasis in Elegantiarum Libros Laurentii Vallae* by Erasmus

(1420 - 1480)
Nicolas Jenson
FRANCE, GERMANY, ITALY

/ Sent to Mainz in 1458 by Charles VII of France to learn about the improvements in printing and movable type

/ Established in Venice in the late 1460s as a printer and publisher

/ Created some of the first Roman serifs of the Renaissance, moving away from Black Letter and segueing from calligraphic writing

/ The tilted crossbar in the lowercase "e" is a signature style of Jenson's Romans, which have also come to be known as Venetian serifs

1494 / ITALY

Aldus Manutius established the Aldine Press in Venice, becoming one of the most important publishers and printers of the Renaissance / SHOWN Dolphin and anchor colophon of the Aldine Press

(1450 - 1518)
Francesco Griffo da Bologna
ITALY

/ Worked with printer Aldus Manutius in Venice

/ Designed typeface for Pietro Bembo's *De Aetna*—in 1929, Stanley Morison based the Bembo typeface on this book

/ Created the first italic typeface in 1499

Adobe Jenson
Robert Slimbach
ADOBE / 1996 / USA

Stempel Garamond
D. Stempel AG (Foundry)
LINOTYPE / 1925 / GERMANY

1555 / NETHERLANDS

Christophe Plantin establishes the Plantin Press in Antwerp

(1513 - 1589)

Robert Granjon
FRANCE, NETHERLANDS, ITALY

/ Worked as punch cutter, printer and designer in various cities across Europe

/ Designed Civilité, a black letter script in the late 1550s that was broadly used in France

(1580 - 1658)

Jean Jannon
FRANCE

/ Worked in the printing office of the Calvinist Academy in Sedan since 1610

/ Derived from the typefaces of Claude Garamond, Jannon created a Roman and italic typeface in 1621 for his own use—because of its similarity however, Jannon's typefaces were initially mistaken as Garamonds

(1692 - 1766)

William Caslon I
UK

/ First British type designer and punch cutter to lead a successful enterprise

/ Designed Hebrew and Arabic alphabets before his first Romans in the early 1720s

/ His work was also popular in the United States

(1712 - 1768)

Pierre-Simon Fournier
FRANCE

/ Prolific type designer and punch cutter through his own foundry

/ Was one of the first to design and package typefaces together as a type family › 63

/ In a 1738 type specimen Fournier presented his fonts based on a 12-point measuring system he had devised a year earlier

(1706 - 1775)

John Baskerville
UK

/ Established a printing business and type foundry in 1750

/ With John Handy as his punch cutter, Baskerville designed various original Romans

/ As a printer, he experimented with custom inks, producing rich blacks, and with paper, achieving highly glossy surfaces

/ Married his mistress and former housekeeper, Sarah Eaves, in 1764—Zuzana Licko's revival of his work is named after her › 381

1743 / NETHERLANDS

The printing house Joh. Enschedé en Zonen acquires the type foundry of Hendrik Wetstein

(1764 - 1836)

Firmin Didot
FRANCE

/ Representative of the third generation of the Didot family, with roots in printing and publishing as far back as the mid eighteenth century

/ Designed the first Modern Roman in 1784, with thin serifs and high contrast in its strokes—all contemporary Didot typefaces are based on his work

(1740 - 1813)

Giambattista Bodoni
ITALY

/ Was director of the Stamperia Reale, the official press of Ferdinand, Duke of Parma for 45 years

/ Taking cues from Baskerville's Romans with high contrast and Didot's flat serifs, Bodoni designed his own Modern typeface in the late 1790s

/ After his death in 1813, his widow Paola Margherita finished Bodoni's *Manuale Tipografico*, an exemplary, exhaustive type specimen of Bodoni's collection and own designs

Gilles Le Corre
GLC / 2008 / France

Frantisek Storm
STORM / 1997 / CZECH REPUBLIC

George William Jones
LINOTYPE / 1930 / UK

W CASLON JUNR LETTERFOUNDER

TWO LINES ENGLISH OPEN

1816 / UK

William Caslon IV, through his family's Caslon Foundry, offers the first commercial sans serif, named Two Lines English Egyptian / SHOWN Detail of 1816 Caslon Foundry type specimen

1817 / UK

The first slab serif typeface, named Antique, appears in a type specimen published by Vincent Figgins

1827 / USA

Darius Wells invents a lateral router that, in combination with a pantograph machine, makes the mass-production of wood type possible.

1837 / GERMANY

Johann Christian Bauer establishes the Bauer Foundry—it closes in 1972

1859 / USA

William Hamilton Page establishes William Page & Company, producing carefully cut wood types and luscious type specimens—as it grew into one of the biggest wood type manufacturers it was purchased by the Hamilton Company in 1891

1880 / USA

Edward J. Hamilton founds the Hamilton Company in Two Rivers, Wisconsin it becomes the largest producer of wood type

1884 / USA

Linn Boyd Benton invents a pantograph machine that engraves steel punches, eliminating the task of the punch cutter

1885 / SPAIN

Jacob de Neufville establishes the Fundición Tipográfica Neufville, later acting as the Spanish branch of the Bauer Foundry

1886 / USA

Ottmar Mergenthaler invents the first typesetting machine, the Linotype

1887 / USA

Tolbert Lanston invents the Monotype typesetting machine

1890, 1896 / UK, USA, GERMANY

Mergenthaler establishes Mergenthaler Linotype Company in Brooklyn, New York and Mergenthaler Linotype & Machinery, Ltd. in Manchester, England in 1890; followed by Mergenthaler Casting Machines in Berlin in 1896 (later known as Linotype GmbH)

1887, 1897 / USA, UK

Lanston establishes the Lanston Monotype Machine Company in Washington D.C. in 1887 and the Lanston Monotype Corporation, Ltd. in London, England in 1897—they later become independent entities

(1834 - 1896)

William Morris
USA

/ Morris established the Kelmscott Press in 1891, employing his own presses, paper and typefaces

/ He designed two typefaces: Golden Type, a Venetian serif, influenced by the work of Nicolas Jenson; and a black letter in two sizes, Troy (18 point) and Chaucer (12 point)

1892 / USA

Headed by Linn Boyd Benton the American Type Founders is born from the merger of twenty-three independent type foundries, becoming the largest foundry in the United States—it closes in 1993

(1872 - 1948)

Morris Fuller Benton
USA

/ Began working in 1896 at the American Type Founders (ATF), the company established by his father, Linn Boyd Benton, in 1892

/ Designed more than 200 typefaces, including a number of extensions of existing typefaces to create comprehensive type families like Cheltenham (1902)

/ Some of the diverse typefaces he designed include Franklin Gothic (1904), Engravers Old English (1907), Hobo (1910), Broadway (1928), and Bank Gothic (1930)

/ Retired from ATF in 1937

RELATED TYPEFACES

P22 Morris Troy

P22 Morris Golden

Richard Kegler
P22 / 2001 / USA

BANK GOTHIC

Morris Fuller Benton
ATF / 1930 / USA

American Type Founders publishes two comprehensive and luscious catalogs, the 1300-page *American Specimen Book of Type Styles* (SHOWN) in 1912 and the 1148-page *Specimen Book and Catalog* in 1923

1912, 1923 / USA

1925 / HUNGARY

Edmund Uher develops one of the first phototypesetting machines, dubbed the Uhertype

1926 / UK

Writing under the pseudonym of Paul Beaujon, Beatrice Warde demonstrates in *The Fleuron* journal that some typefaces attributed to Claude Garamond are the work of Jean Jannon

(1889 – 1967)

Stanley Morison

UK

/ Co-founded the Fleuron Society in 1922 with Francis Meynell, Holbrook Jackson, Bernard Newdigate and Oliver Simon—through it he published and edited *The Fleuron*, a journal of typography

/ Joined Monotype Corporation in 1923 as its typography consultant, where he oversaw the revival of a significant number of typefaces

/ In 1931, was commissioned by *The Times* to create a new typeface for the newspaper, leading to the contentious design of Times New Roman › 385

1936 / USA

Edward Rondthaler and Harold Horman—who in 1928 began developing the Rutherford Photo-Letter Composing Machine—establish Photo-Lettering, Inc., in New York, popularizing phototypesetting and offering hundreds of typefaces / SHOWN *Alphabet Thesaurus Nine Thousand* catalog cover, 1960

(1865 – 1947)

Frederic W. Goudy

USA

/ One of the most prolific and versatile type designers; created more than 100 typefaces ranging from sans serifs to black letters

/ Designed most notoriously Copperplate Gothic (1901), Goudy Old Style (1916), and Goudy Text (1928)

/ Among his students at the Frank Holme School of Illustration were W. A. Dwiggins and Oswald Bruce Cooper

(1879 – 1940)

Oswald Bruce Cooper

USA

/ Established Bertsch & Cooper, a lettering studio, with business partner Fred Bertsch in 1904

/ Designed the Cooper type family for the Barnhart Brothers & Spindler (BB&S) foundry from 1918 to 1924, including the popular weights of Cooper Black and its italic counterpart › 388

Goudy Heavyface

Frederic W. Goudy

MONOTYPE / 1925 / USA

Cooper Old Style

Oswald Bruce Cooper

BB&S / 1918 / USA

(1885 - 1972)

Lucian Bernhard
USA

/ Before moving to the United States in 1922 was an accomplished poster designer in Germany, introducing the Sachplakat ("Object Poster") style

/ His first typeface, Bernhard Antiqua, was released by the Flinsch Foundry in Frankfurt in 1913

/ Starting in 1928 collaborated with American Type Founders on numerous typefaces, including the popular Bernhard Gothic (1929)

(1880 - 1956)

W. A. Dwiggins
USA

/ After a long career as a commercial artist, letterer and book designer, began designing typefaces in the late 1920s for Mergenthaler Linotype

/ Released five commercial typefaces—Metroblack (1927), Electra (1935), Caledonia (1939), Eldorado (1953), and Falcon (1961)—and generated dozens of incomplete initial designs that were catalogued by Mergenthaler Linotype

(1872 - 1944)

Edward Johnston
UK

/ Designed one of the first Modern Chancery italics, with punch cutter Edward Prince, for the Harry Kessler's Cranach Press in the early 1900s

/ In 1906 published one of the most significant books on calligraphy, *Writing & Illuminating & Lettering*

/ Was one of the founding editors in 1913 of *The Imprint*, a short-lived but influential journal

/ Commissioned by Frank Pick, publicity officer for the London Underground, Johnston designed Johnston Sans in 1916

(1882 - 1940)

Eric Gill
UK

/ Was a prolific sculptor, engraver, and letter-cutter in addition to typeface designer

/ His first typeface, Perpetua, a serif, was commissioned by Stanley Morison in 1925

/ Based on Johnston Sans, he created Gill Sans for the Monotype Corporation in 1927

1878 - 1956

Paul Renner
GERMANY

/ Designer, educator, and writer best known for his geometric sans serif, Futura, released in 1928

1955 / UK

Beatrice Warde pens the often quoted essay, "The Crystal Goblet, or Printing Should be Invisible" / SHOWN *The Crystal Goblet: Sixteen Essays on Typography* title page, The Sylvan Press, 1955

1957 / FRANCE

Charles Peignot founds the Association Typographique Internationale (ATypI), and remains its president for 16 years

1972 / SPAIN

When the Frankfurt, Germany based Bauer Foundry closed in 1972 Fundición Tipográfica Neufville acquired its materials and changed its name to Fundición Tipográfica Bauer

---

RELATED TYPEFACES

Metroblack
W.A. Dwiggins
LINOTYPE / 1927 / USA

ITC Johnston
Richard Dawson, Dave Farey
ITC / 1999 / USA

(b. 1927)
Ed Benguiat
USA

/ After working for *Esquire* magazine and running his own studio, Benguiat joined Photo-Lettering Inc. in 1962 becoming head of its publishing department and designing literally hundreds of display typefaces

/ Was part of the rise of the International Typeface Corporation › 220 in 1970 and helped Herb Lubalin launch its marketing publication, *U&lc* › 98

/ Credited with more than 600 typefaces, among them ITC Souvenir (1970), ITC Tiffany (1974), and ITC Bauhaus (1975)

(b. 1928)
Adrian Frutiger
FRANCE

/ Joined Deberny & Peignot in 1952 after moving to Paris from Zurich

/ Beyond Univers › 372, designed a number of broadly used typefaces, among them Serifa (1967), Frutiger (1975), and Avenir (1988)

(b. 1918)
Hermann Zapf
GERMANY

/ Through Rudolf Koch's *Das Schreiben als Kunstfertigkeit* ("The Art of Writing") and Edward Johnston's *Writing & Illuminating & Lettering* Zapf taught himself calligraphy and lettering

/ Designed his first typeface, a Fraktur black letter called Gilgengart, for D. Stempel AG type foundry and Linotype GmbH in 1938

/ Served in the Cartographic Unit of the German army during World War II

/ For D. Stempel AG, Zapf designed Palatino (1950) and Optima (1952)

/ Working with David Siegel, he designed Zapfino in 1998 for Linotype, a script typeface with various alternates for each character—five years later, with Akira Kobayashi, Linotype released Zapfino Extra to take advantage of OpenType

/ Zapf has been one of the few type designers to produce designs in metal, phototypesetting, and computer

(1910 - 1983)
Roger Excoffon
FRANCE

/ Parallel to a successful graphic design practice, Roger Excoffon designed some of the most adventurous typefaces of the 1950s through the small Marseilles foundry, Fonderie Olive

/ Banco (1951), Mistral (1953), Choc (1955), and Calypso (1958) are remarkable in both their playfulness and their production as metal fonts, since this kind of display typefaces would be more common until 20 years later through phototypesetting

/ Excoffon's most comprehensive type family was Antique Olive, released in different weights and widths between 1962 and 1966

1985 / USA

Jim von Ehr and Kevin Crowder found Altsys and release FONTastic, a bitmap font editor—a year later they release Fontographer, the first Bézier point editor compatible with PostScript

1993 / RUSSIA, USA

Based in St. Petersburg, Yuri Yarmola heads the development of FontLab 2.0, a powerful font editing software, released in the United States by Pyrus North America Ltd

BANCO

Roger Excoffon
FONDERIE OLIVE / 1951 / FRANCE

ITC Benguiat

Ed Benguiat
ITC / 1977 / USA

Optima

Hermann Zapf
D. STEMPEL AG / 1952 / GERMANY

ITC

EST. 1970 (NEW YORK, NEW YORK, USA)

After centuries of metal typesetting, phototypesetting became the prevailing method of developing, distributing, and reproducing typefaces in the 1970s. Cementing the viability and popularity of the process was the International Typeface Corporation (ITC), founded in 1970 by designers Herb Lubalin › 167 and Aaron Burns—partners in Lubalin, Burns & Co.—and Ed Rondthaler, owner of Photo-Lettering, Inc., a photocomposition and typesetting firm established in 1936 that built a library of more than 7,000 typefaces and was one of the most successful vendors of display type for advertising agencies. ITC also triggered a change in the way typefaces were distributed and how designers were remunerated: With metal typesetting, manufacturers like Linotype and Monotype provided the equipment necessary to produce type and in conjunction sold proprietary typefaces designed to work on

their machines; ITC, on the other hand, provided the source material to reproduce their typefaces on any phototypesetting machine and paid designers a royalty based on the amount of orders of their designs. Unfortunately, the wide availability of the material increased the risk for piracy.

ITC built a significantly large library of typefaces with contributions from designers like Ed Benguiat, Tom Carnase, and Tony DiSpigna, among others, offering an optimistic selection of display typefaces that were heavily and attractively marketed by ITC through its popular *U&lc* (*Upper & lowercase*) › 98 publication, which showcased the library while providing unique and engaging content to the growing list of subscribers. In the 1990s, after acquisition by the holding company Esselte in 1986, ITC adapted to the digital design and distribution of typefaces by establishing an e-commerce site that changed its old method to sell directly to end-users. In 1999, Esselte closed ITC and sold the library and name to Agfa Monotype Imaging.

1986

1988

1989

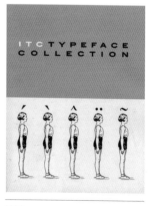

1998

1999

Matthew Carter

b. 1937 (LONDON, ENGLAND, UK)
CURRENTLY CAMBRIDGE, MASSACHUSETTS, USA

With experience in metal type, photo-type, and digital type, Matthew Carter has excelled in designing an array of typefaces in the various technologies; his classical, experimental, functional, and decorative typefaces and type families have influenced designers around the world for over 40 years. After a yearlong punch-cutting internship at the printing house Ensechedé in Haarlem, Netherlands, Carter freelanced for six years in London, first as a typemaker and later as a type designer. In 1965 he moved to New York as house designer for Mergenthaler Linotype, where he spent the next six years. Back in London in 1971, Carter continued freelancing for Linotype, producing several typefaces, including the technologically creative Bell Centennial › 382.

Recognizing the potential in the sale of type, Carter and three colleagues from Linotype, Mike Parker, Cherie Cone, and Rob Friedman, established Bitstream, a digital type foundry, in 1981 in Cambridge, Massachusetts. With the proliferation of personal computers and desktop publishing, the company enjoyed great success during the 1980s—but with the growth of the company, financial and administrative duties left Carter with little time to design. In 1991, alongside Cone, he co-founded Carter & Cone Type, Inc., where he has designed some of his most lauded typefaces, including the now ubiquitous Verdana for Microsoft, the malleable type family for the Walker Art Center › 354, and a sophisticated proprietary serif for Yale University. Aside from crafting his own work, Carter is affably committed to helping others through official type critiques as well as unofficial ones; he is stopped in the halls of the many conferences he attends to offer his views to anyone who asks politely.

Big Caslon Roman
ABCDEFGHIJKLMN
OPQRSTQUVWXYZ&
ÆŒ&abcdefghijklmnop
qrstuvwxyzfiflßæœctst

Big Caslon Italic & Swash
ABCDEFGHIJKLMNOP
QRSTQUVWXYZ&ÆŒ
&ABCDEFGJKMN
PQRTYkvwz.abcdefghijklm
nopqrstuvwxyzfiflßæœctspst

BIG CASLON / 2000

ITC Galliard Roman
ABCDEFGHIJKLMNOPQRSTUVWXYZ&ÆŒ
abcdefghijklmnopqrstuvwxyzæœfffifjflffiffllß &
1234567890$¢£€¥ƒ 1234567890 ...
$¢1234567890,.-/$¢1234567890,.- ¹²³⁴⁵⁶⁷⁸⁹⁰ (abdehilmnorstv)

ITC GALLIARD SMALL CAPS
ABCDEFGHIJKLMNOPQRSTUVWXYZ&ÆŒÇÐŁŠŽÞQ

ITC Galliard Italic
ABCDEFGHIJKLMNOPQRSTUVWXYZ&ÆŒ
abcdefghijklmnopqrstuvwxyzæœfffifjflflffiffllfrßij
1234567890$¢£€¥ƒ 1234567890 ...
$¢1234567890,.-/$¢1234567890,.- (abdehilmnorstv)

Galliard was designed as a four-weight family for Mergenthaler Linotype in 1971. Three years later it was acquired by the International Typeface Corporation and re-released as ITC Galliard. The Carter & Cone digitization of the regular weight of Roman and Italic, done in 1992, includes the flourished final letters and other peculiars that were part of the original photocomposition fonts.

ITC GALLIARD / ITC / 2000

Yale Design Roman & *Italic*
ABCDEFGHIJKLMNOPQRSTUVWXYZ&
1234567890 abcdefghijklmnopqrstuvwxyzæœfifl
ABCDEFGHIJKLMNOPQRSTUVWXYZ&
1234567890 abcdefghijklmnopqrstuvwxyzæœfifl

Yale Admin Roman & *Italic*
ABCDEFGHIJKLMNOPQRSTUVWXYZ&
1234567890 abcdefghijklmnopqrstuvwxyzæœ
ABCDEFGHIJKLMNOPQRSTUVWXYZ&
1234567890 abcdefghijklmnopqrstuvwxyzæœ

YALE SMALL CAPS
ABCDEFGHIJKLMNOPQRSTUVWXYZ&
1234567890

Yale Street (for campus signs)
ABCDEFGHIJKLMNOPQRSTUVWXYZ&
1234567890 1234567890
abcdefghijklmnopqrstuvwxyzæœfifl

YALE / 2004

Big Figgins Roman
ABCDEFGHIJKLMN
OPQRSTUVWXYZ&
abcdefghijklmnopqrstu
vwxyz 1234567890

Big Figgins Italic
ABCDEFGHIJKLM
NOPQRSTUVWXYZ
&abcdefghijklmnopqrs
tuvwxyz 1234567890

BIG FIGGINS / Originally named
Elephant (1992) / 1998

MANTINIA · MCMXCIII
CAPS ᴬᴬBᴮCᶜDᴰEꟳFᶠGᴳHᴴ
AND IᴵJᴶKᴷLᴸMᴹNᴺOᴼPQQ
SUPERIOR Rᴿ SᔆSᵀTᵁUᵛV
CAPS WᵂXˣYʸ&ꟴZꟴꟀꟁ ÆÅŒ
FIGURES 1234567890
SMALL·CAPS acehiorstuwyz
LIGATURES ꜪVꜾCTꜲHꜲUPꜲIA
ꜴꜲCTUꜲTWTYMꜲPꜲMDꜲMBꜲE
ALTERNATIVES T&YꜲRꜲQQ
TALL·CAPITALS ITLY
INTERPOINTS ◆ ◆ ·

MANTINIA / 1993

Miller Display Roman
¶ABCDEFGHIJKLMNOPQRS
TUVWXYZ&ÆŒ&ÁÀÄÂÅÇÉ
ÈËÊÍÌÏÎÑÓÒÖÔÕØŚÚÙÛÜÝŸŽ
ÐŁPABCDEFGHIJKLMNOPQRSTU
VWXYZ&ÆŒ&ÁÀÄÂÅÇÉÈÊÍÌÏÎÑ
óòöôõøśúùûüÿžðłþ^ꟶabcdefg
hijklmnopqrstuvwxyzæœfffifjflffi
ffllßáàäâãçéèêíìïîñóòöôõøśúù
üÿžðłþµ1234567890½⅓¼¾½12345
67890ᵃᵉ@$¢£¥ƒ€x%‰·§*†‡*
©℗™.,:;-!¿?"""''""○〔〕◇/‖◇\\
»—─…,·_#÷=×¬<>`´ ˜¨¯˙˝

MILLER DISPLAY / 1997

Shelley Volante
ABCDEFG
HIJKLMN
OPQRSTU
VWXYZ
&
abcdefghijklmnopqrs
stuvvwxyz
1972

SHELLEY SCRIPT / 1972

Verdana
Latin ABCDEFGHIJKLMNO
PQRSTUVWXYZ&abcdefghi
jklmnopqrstuvwxyzæœfifl
1234567890$¢£¥@%#+
Greek ΑΒΓΔΕΖΗΘΙΚΛΜΝΞ
ΟΠΡΣΤΥΦΧΨΩαβγδεζηθικλ
μνξοπρςστυφχψω
Cyrillic АБВГДЕЖЗИЙКЛМ
НОПРСТУФХЦЧШЩЪЫЬЭ
ЮЯабвгдежзийклмнопрст

VERDANA / 1994

Matthew Carter / USA

 RECOMMENDED READING › 390

The Font Bureau, Inc.

EST. 1989 (BOSTON, MASSACHUSETTS, USA)

Uniting two complementary professional backgrounds, publication designer Roger Black and type designer David Berlow founded The Font Bureau, Inc., in 1989. Drawing letters by hand early in his career at the New York office of Linotype in 1978, Berlow's interest in and knack for digital typography grew when he joined Boston-based Bitstream › 221 in 1981 and adapted to the technologies of Adobe Postscript and, later, Apple's competing TrueType in the late 1980s. Also taking advantage of the Macintosh was Black, a seasoned art director of magazines like *Rolling Stone* › 328, *New York* › 336, and *Newsweek*. He started his own business focusing on the design of newspapers and magazines in 1989, the same year he and Berlow establish Font Bureau. With Black embarking on numerous publication designs and Font Bureau creating proprietary type families, the foundry's output has ballooned to more than 1,500 typefaces today, and more and more publications turn to them for workhorse typefaces that have their own flair.

On the retail side, Font Bureau boasts an extensive and well-rounded collection of typefaces and type families from traditional serifs to dingbats; proprietary work is added to the growing list upon expiration of its exclusivity.

SLOOP / Inspired by the calligraphic work of Raphael Boguslav / Richard Lipton / USA, 1994–2002

QUIOSCO / Which allows for compactness without compromising legibility / Cyrus Highsmith / USA, 2006

MILLER / Matthew Carter / USA, 1997–2000

MODERNO FB / Evolving for various clients starting with *Esquire Gentleman* and ending with *Montreal Gazette* / David Berlow / USA, 1994–2008

GIZA / Based on Vincent Figgins's 1845 specimen / David Berlow / USA, 1994

FB TITLING GOTHIC / Ideal for newspaper titling due to its nearly 50 styles / David Berlow / USA, 2005

POYNTER / Designed to work from four-point to display sizes / Tobias Frere-Jones, David Berlow / USA, 1997–2000

Adobe Fonts

EST. 1984 (MOUNTAIN VIEW, CALIFORNIA, USA)

Since 1982, Adobe Systems has had a stronghold on the handling and processing of computer-based typography. They started with the revolutionary PostScript language, which, in the broadest of definitions, allowed for smooth and curvaceous printing; this was enhanced by Adobe Type Manager (ATM) in 1989, which rendered on-screen typography smooth as well. ATM Deluxe was introduced in 1997 as a font management system. During the late 1990s, in a joint effort with Microsoft, Adobe introduced the OpenType format, which allows for infinite flexibility. And, of course, dozens of type families are bundled with every Adobe application, putting hundreds of Adobe typefaces in the hands of designers over the years.

At the outset, Adobe's library consisted of existing typefaces culled from the ITC and Linotype libraries under the direction of Sumner Stone, who was director of typography from 1984 to 1991. In 1989 Adobe began creating its own typefaces under the label Adobe Originals, with Robert Slimbach and Carol Twombly leading the effort. Early designs were revivals of Garamond and Caslon and, soon after, new designs included Trajan › 368, Lithos, and Chaparral by Twombly and Minion, Utopia and Poetica by Slimbach, and the joint effort on the now ubiquitous Myriad, designed in collaboration with Fred Brady and Christopher Slye and quickly becoming part of the designer lexicon. With the introduction of OpenType and its implementation in the company's popular Creative Suite › 317 applications, Adobe has ported all of its typefaces to this format with expanded glyph sets and support for multiple languages, further entwining itself with the general design and application of typography.

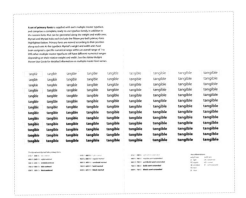

MYRIAD SPECIMEN BOOK / Fred Brady; art direction, Laurie Szujewska; design, Margery Cantor, James Young; typeface design, Robert Slimbach, Carol Twombly / 1992

TRAJAN SPECIMEN BOOK / Fred Brady; art direction and design, Laurie Szujewska; typeface design, Carol Twombly / 1993

TEKTON SPECIMEN BOOK / Fred Brady; art direction, Laurie Szujewska; typography direction, Sumner Stone; design, Min Wang; typeface design, David Siegel / 1990

OPEN TYPE: ADOBE TYPE LIBRARY TYPE GUIDE / 2000

ADOBE TYPE MANAGER DELUXE 4.1 / 1999

ADOBE WEBTYPE 1.0 / 1997

OPEN TYPE BROCHURE / 2002

Adobe Systems Incorporated / USA

Emigre Fonts

EST. 1986 (BERKELEY, CALIFORNIA, USA)

The third issue, in 1985, of Rudy VanderLans' *Emigre* › 100 magazine was completely typeset with the coarse bitmap typefaces designed by his wife, Zuzana Licko 225, who was literally breaking ground on the emerging technology of digital design and development of typefaces through the Macintosh. As the magazine gained prominence and Emigre Fonts was established in 1986, designers began using their typefaces, and because most designers were not yet working on the computer, Licko would typeset the requested text in the computer, print it, reduce it with a Photostat camera, and mail the art for final compositing to the designer. It was only later, into the late 1980s and early 1990s, that Emigre distributed its fonts through floppy disks. In 1994 Tim Starback, the jack-of-all-trades staff member of Emigre, helped launch Now Serving, an online bulletin board that allowed users to purchase and download fonts—the first instance of what is now universal practice.

While Licko has developed a large library, with nearly 30 type families to her credit—including the immensely popular Mrs. Eaves › 381—Emigre Fonts has benefited from a vast array of designers who have contributed to the evolution of typeface experimentation that define the foundry. Early typefaces came from Jeffery Keedy (Keedy Sans, 1989), P. Scott Makela (Dead History, 1990), and Barry Deck (Template Gothic › 382, 1990); interestingly, none of them were typeface designers. Emigre continues to encourage illustrators like Mark Andresen and letterers like Ed Fella › 185 to apply their aesthetics to the alphabet. In addition, the foundry attracted typeface designers like Jonathan Barnbrook, Conor Mangat, Claudio Piccinini, and Christian Schwartz › 231. Through the lifespan of *Emigre*, the typefaces from its foundry were continually on display and played as significant a role as the content.

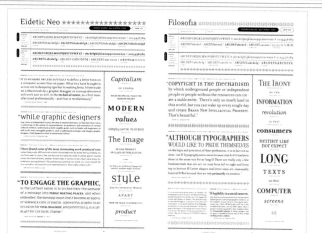

EMIGRE ADVERTISING / Emigre:
Rudy VanderLans / USA

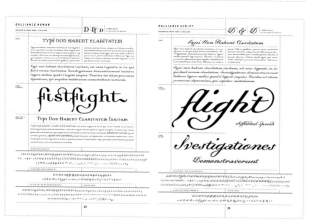

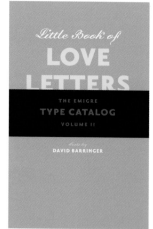

EMIGRE CATALOGS / Emigre: Rudy VanderLans / USA

Zuzana Licko

b. 1961 (BRATISLAVA, CZECHOSLOVAKIA)
CURRENTLY BERKELEY, CALIFORNIA, USA

With a degree in graphic communications from the University of California at Berkeley, no formal training in typeface design, and a nearly blank slate in the realm of digitally produced and designed typefaces, and without preconceptions or the hindrance of the rules of the trade, Czechoslovakia-born Zuzana Licko broke ground in the creation of uniquely designed coarse bitmap fonts parallel to the introduction of the Macintosh in 1984 and the publication of *Emigre* › 100, edited by her husband, Rudy VanderLans. Within the printing and screen resolution limitations, Licko developed remarkably innovative designs like Emigre, Emperor, Oakland, and Universal (now bundled and remastered as Lo-Res › 383) that gradually paved the way—especially as type development and rendering technology improved—for smooth and more traditional designs like Citizen, Triplex, Matrix, and Senator, which are all descendants and interpretations of her first designs.

In the early 1990s Licko's typeface designs became less constrained by technology and, at the same time, exploited the malleability and scalability it allowed with designs like Narly, which used a basic skeleton that could be rendered in multiple ways, and Variex, a type family consisting of increasingly thicker strokes hinged at the center as determined by the computer. While it would probably have been easier to self-impose and maintain a status quo of experimental designs, Licko ventured into designing text typefaces that were revivals and modern interpretations of two classic designs, Baskerville and Bodoni, with Mrs. Eaves › 381 and Filosofia as the respective results in 1996, the former being the most commercially successful typeface in the Emigre Fonts library. With sans serifs like Solex and Tarzana, blackletters like Totally Gothic and Totally Glyphic, and the swirling Hypnopeadia patterns, Licko's nearly 30 type families represent a daringly diverse output.

MATRIX / 2007

HYPNOPAEDIA ILLUSTRATIONS / 1997

SOLEX / 2000

COLD WATER CANYON
Indigenous Shrubs *of* Santa Monica
chromolithography
PRESIDENT
sliding aluminum doors
MINUTE
Bakersfield, *California*
ENVIRONMENTALLY SOUND RECYCLED PAPER
Antecedents
JUAN BAUTISTA *de* ANZA

FILOSOFIA / 1996

TARZANA ADVERTISING AND SKETCH / 1998

FAIRPLEX / 2002

Emigre: Zuzana Licko / USA

Erik Spiekermann

b.1947 (STADTHAGEN, GERMANY)
CURRENTLY BERLIN, GERMANY AND SAN FRANCISCO, CALIFORNIA, USA

Born in 1947, the German typographer, designer, writer, and font impresario showed his entrepreneurial gifts early by running a basement printing press to fund his studies at Berlin's Free University. After seven years consulting in London upon his graduation, he returned to Berlin in 1979 to establish MetaDesign—later expanding to San Francisco (1992) and London (1995) to form the largest independent design firm at the time. In 2001, Erik left MetaDesign and partnered with Susanna Dulkinys of San Francisco to form United Designers Network, renamed SpiekermannPartners in 2007, with offices in Berlin, London, and San Francisco. He travels a lot.

As if running multinational design firms were not enough, Spiekermann established FontShop International ›227, a mail-order font distributor, along with partner (and then wife) Joan Spiekermann in 1989. Then, in 1990, the Spiekermanns partnered with Neville Brody to launch FontFont, a library of unique typefaces, including Erik's own FF Meta ›376, a widely used sans serif. Other typefaces by Erik include ITC Officina, FF Info, and FF Unit, complemented by a range of proprietary fonts for a variety of clients including Nokia, Bosch, and Deutsche Bahn. Erik's *Stop Stealing Sheep and Find Out How Type Works*, first published in 1993, is required reading for every designer.

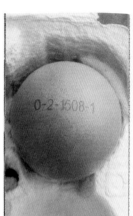

STOP STEALING SHEEP AND FIND OUT HOW TYPE WORKS, Erik Spiekermann, E.M Ginger / Adobe Press / USA, 1993 (1st ed.), 2003 (2nd ed.)

ITC OFFICINA / Erik Spiekermann / Germany, 1990

FF META AND META SERIF / Erik Spiekermann (FF Meta Serif, Christian Schwartz, Kris Sowersby) / Germany, 1991, 2007

DB Sans stands for *Sans Serif* typefaces.

Condensed are the *narrower* cuts, while **Compressed** explains *itself*.

DB Head is the version for **big headlines** and **short** messages.

The *Antiqua typefaces* are DB **Serif** & DB **News**.

DB TYPE / Commissioned by Deutsche Bahn / Erik Spiekermann, Christian Schwartz / Germany, 2005

FontShop International
EST. 1989 (BERLIN, GERMANY)

Founded in 1989 by Joan Spiekermann and Erik Spiekermann ›226 (then husband and wife), FontShop International (FSI) was the first mail-order distributor of digital fonts. Since its launch, a handful of independent FontShops around the world license the premise from FSI. Although one of their main objectives was to nurture and grow the FontFont foundry—established in 1990 by the Spiekermanns along with Neville Brody—FontShop retails fonts from more than 50 other foundries around the world. In addition, FSI provides a range of publications for designers: In 1991, FontShop published the first edition of *FontBook*, a massive sampler and reference guide of digital typefaces; in 2001, it began publishing *Font*, a print publication on typography and design; and from 1990 to 2000, it published the experimental *FUSE* magazine and accompanying fonts, sponsoring the namesake conferences in 1995 and 1998.

FONTSHOP LOGO / FontShop International / USA, 1990

FUSE / FontShop International and Neville Brody / UK, 1990–2000 / Photo: Stephen Coles

FONT 006 / FontShop International: design, Conor Mangat; editing, Amos Klausner, Stephen Coles / USA, 2007 / Photo: Stephen Coles

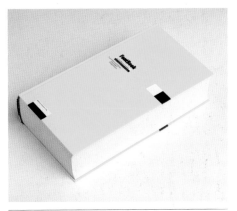

FONTBOOK / FontShop International / USA, 2006 (4th ed.)

FONTBOOK / Weathered from its intense use by Pentagram partner Michael Bierut and his team over the course of a decade / USA, 1998

House Industries

EST. 1993 (WILMINGTON, DELAWARE, USA)

Andy Cruz and Rich Roat, who had started a design firm, Brand Design Co., earlier that year, also established House Industries in 1993. With little work and the fresh instigation of a third member, Allen Mercer, they decided they needed a product to sell, not a service. Based on existing lettering projects and original designs by Mercer, House Industries produced its first mailer announcing the release of ten typefaces. This first batch, and others produced through 1997, were display faces designed with almost every imaginable visual quirk—scribbly, squiggly, jaggedy, blobby—and delivered via floppy disks the three partners painstakingly put together everyday. This immersion relationship with their typefaces' packaging later evolved into a defining trait as future releases, cohesively bundled into themed collections, were distributed in highly elaborate and expensively produced kits.

Inside the marketable appeal of these packages are carefully constructed typefaces specific to a time or culture (sometimes *sub*culture) that House Industries revitalized through collaborations or by mining their vast archive of source material, which ranges from the lettering of artists like Ed "Big Daddy" Roth and Chris Cooper to revivals of Ed Benguiat's work, 1950s bowling alleys, 1960s horror movies, the modernist architecture of Richard Neutra, and more. As House Industries has grown—with the addition of lettering master Ken Barber in 1996, technological wizard Tal Leming in 2001 (he left in 2005), and collaborations with Christian Schwartz ‹ 231—so has their library and its versatility, with popular sans serifs like Neutraface and Chalet as well as innovative OpenType families like Studio Lettering and Ed Benguiat Fonts. House Industries also develops original merchandise ranging from modest T-shirts to funky pillows to an ambitious reproduction of Richard Neutra's Boomerang chair.

HOUSE33 STORE SIGN AT 33 MARSHALL STREET, LONDON / House Industries / UK, 2004 / Photo: Mark Lebon

SCRAWL FONT COLLECTION MAILER / House Industries / USA, 1995 / Photo: Carlos Alejandro

CUSTOM PAPERS GROUP SWATCHBOOKS / House Industries / USA, 1996 / Photo: Carlos Alejandro

Bigfoot, the Loch Ness Monster, and René Albert Chalet

In the promotional materials for Chalet released in 2000, House Industries paid high praise to René Albert Chalet, the forgotten Swiss modernist designer responsible for these typefaces. Industry heavyweights like Michael Bierut, Jonathan Hoefler, Matthew Carter, and Erik Spiekermann contributed testimonials deploring Chalet's lack of recognition and commending the importance of his work. Soon after, the industry tried to catch up with history and recognize this man. Unfortunately, he never existed. Ken Barber concocted this fictional character and fleshed out his story with biographical bits from (real) designers like W.A. Dwiggins, Adrian Frutiger, and Jan Tschichold. Despite the hoax being revealed, it's not rare to find a blog author recounting Chalet's history today.

STREET VAN PACKAGING / House Industries / USA, 1996 / Photo: Carlos Alejandro

BIG DADDY ROTH PARTY AT HOUSE INDUSTRIES POSTER / House Industries / USA, 1997

NEUTRA BOOMERANG CHAIR COMPLEMENTING THE RELEASE OF NEUTRAFACE / House Industries / USA, 2002 / Photo: Carlos Alejandro

[T-26]
EST. 1994 (CHICAGO, ILLINOIS, USA)

Launched by Chicago-based Segura, Inc., in 1994, the digital type foundry [T-26] was representative of the significant shift the type industry was experiencing: a multitude of designers who could now create typefaces without the training or experience of their predecessors. This is not to say they were not talented, but suddenly *anyone* could be a type designer. [T-26] sought to license and distribute typefaces from startup designers or students—even including the work of traditional print designers like Michael Strassburger, Greg Samata, Paul Sahre, Margo Chase › 187, and (future) *Helvetica* › 373 director Gary Hustwit. The [T-26] library amassed a wide range of display typefaces with grunge, techno, retro, organic, and myriad other uncategorizable aesthetics that were all supported by the foundry's own. Fonts were delivered in burlap bags, new designs were promoted in hefty newsprint catalogs, and trade magazine ads made the typefaces covetable.

[T-26] CATALOGS AND TYPE SPECIMENS / USA

P22 Type Foundry
EST. 1994 (BUFFALO, NEW YORK, USA)

What began as a thesis project by Richard Kegler on Marcel Duchamp that, in part, included digitizing the artist's handwriting, turned into the first official typeface of P22. Established in 1994 by Kegler and his wife, Carima El-Behairy, the foundry has since—working with museums and estates—revived the handwriting of Paul Cézanne, Paul Gauguin, and Leonardo da Vinci, as well as typefaces from specific art periods like Art Deco, Art Nouveau, Arts and Crafts, Futurism, and Pop Art. Its goods are sold in museum gift shops, often accompanied by promotional items like mugs, coasters, or playing cards. A recent collaboration with the London Transport Museum yielded the elegant Underground Pro Set, based on the designs of Edward Johnston. The P22 Type Foundry holds the collections of the Lanston Type Company, Rimmer Type Foundry, and the Sherwood Type Collection, and it serves as the umbrella for International House of Fonts, started in 2001, which licenses original type designs.

ASSORTED TYPE COLLECTION PACKAGING / P22: Richard Kegler / USA, 1995–1998

CONSTRUCTIVIST PACKAGING AND PROMOTIONAL MUG / P22: Richard Kegler / USA, 1995

MATADOR / P22: Arthur Baker / USA, 2007

CÉZANNE / Commissioned by the Philadelphia Museum of Art / P22: Michael Want, James Grieshaber / USA, 1996–2005

TERRACOTTA / Based on the early designs of Frank Lloyd Wright / P22: Christina Torre / USA, 2001

WOODCUT FONT AND ORNAMENTS / P22: Richard Kegler / USA, 2004

Hoefler & Frere-Jones

EST. 1989 (NEW YORK, NEW YORK, USA)

In 2004, typeface designers Jonathan Hoefler and Tobias Frere-Jones entered a formal partnership and established the New York–based Hoefler & Frere-Jones foundry, but their inevitable typographic symbiosis was already decades in the making. In an almost fairy-tale fashion, both designers were born in 1970, six days apart; they both developed a precocious taste for type in their teenage years and had designed typefaces before turning 20; and they bid each other out for rare type specimens later on. Hoefler, a self-taught designer, started his career working with editorial designer Roger Black, who established Font Bureau › 222 with David Berlow in 1989, giving Hoefler early exposure to the field and his first typeface commissions. Hoefler established the Hoefler Type Foundry that same year. Frere-Jones graduated from Rhode Island School of Design › 134 in 1992 and joined Font Bureau, where he spent seven years and designed widely popular typefaces like Interstate, based on the signage of the U.S. Federal Highway Administration. In 1999 he joined Hoefler, and five years later they established their partnership.

Hoefler & Frere-Jones is continually commissioned by organizations and design firms to develop custom type families to establish unique typographic languages for publication and branding purposes. Luckily for the rest of the profession, many become retail fonts after the exclusivity contracts run out—magazines like *Sports Illustrated*, *GQ*, and *Martha Stewart Living* › 335 have yielded Champion (later Knockout › 379), Gotham › 378, and Archer respectively. As aficionados of type history and owners of an enviable library of historical reference material, Hoefler and Frere-Jones are firmly rooted in tradition, yet their work is consistently contemporary in its execution and performance and supported by exhaustive research and development.

Hoefler & Frere-Jones / USA

Clockwise **TYPEFACE SAMPLING** / 2006

VERLAG / 1996–2005

CHRONICLE / 2002–2007

NUMBERS COLLECTION / 1998–2007

Christian Schwartz

b. 1977 (CONCORD, NEW HAMPSHIRE, USA)
CURRENTLY NEW YORK, NEW YORK, USA

FontHaus released Christian Schwartz's first typeface, Flywheel, in 1992 when he was only 14 years old. A design graduate from Carnegie Mellon University, Schwartz briefly worked at MetaDesign in Berlin and Font Bureau › 222 in Boston, Massachusetts, before venturing forth as a freelance type designer in 2001. Thriving on collaborative work, Schwartz then partnered with Roger Black to create type families for the *Houston Chronicle* (2003) and with Paul Barnes for *The Guardian* (2005), as well as his previous boss, Erik Spiekermann › 226, on corporate faces for Bosch (2004) and Deutsche Bahn (2005). While working on these proprietary type families, Schwartz also worked independently on typefaces he released through FontFont, Village › 233, Emigre › 224, and House Industries › 228. In 2006 he established Schwartzco, Inc., a studio and foundry, where his reputation for speed and attention to detail continue to thrive in his personal work and evolving partnerships.

WEALTHY SOCIALITE
Bohemian Neighbor
Brick
VERY UNUSUAL ARCHITECTURE
$9,532/month is almost worth it for the location
Cocktail Hour
TONIC SPILLED ALL OVER THE SOFABED

FARNHAM / 2003

protégez l'enfant
tanzfest
8–18 OCTOBRE
der film

GRAPHIK / Commissioned by Robert Priest and Grace Lee at Condé Nast *Portfolio* and Meirion Pritchard at *Wallpaper** / 2007–2008

JOB CUTS ANNOUNCED
Westminster
Sea Levels Rising
Paradise
BRING ON THE SPRING
Modernism

GUARDIAN EGYPTIAN / Commissioned by Mark Porter at *The Guardian* / design, Paul Barnes / 2004–2005

¡Las Cabezas Grandes!
Believer
AMAZING COINCIDENCES ON VERMONT AVE.
MAINTENANCE
Estimado Sr. Patata
Mañana

LOS FELIZ / Emigre / 2001

Christian Schwartz / USA

Joshua Darden

b. 1979 (NORTHRIDGE, CALIFORNIA, USA)
CURRENTLY NEW YORK, NEW YORK, USA

At the age of 13, in 1993, Joshua Darden established his first design firm, ScanJam, along with Tim Glaser, and, by age 15, Darden had published his first typeface, Diva. After designing a number of typefaces for GarageFonts, Darden joined the Hoefler & Frere-Jones › 230 type foundry in 2000 (first as a freelancer and then as a full-time employee), and then established his own Brooklyn-based foundry, Darden Studio, in 2004, which focuses on the design of custom typefaces while its retail library wins wide acclaim. With more than 120 styles—in Big, Display, Micro, Sans, and Text iterations—Darden's Freight family, released in 2005, is his most comprehensive and successful project yet. Omnes, a round sans serif originally designed as a custom typeface for a national retail chain, comes in nine weights from the delicate Hairline to the bullying Black, all with highly finessed italics. Corundum Text, a revival of Pierre-Simon Fournier's work, was a winning entry in the competitive TDC2 2007 annual.

GEM
DRIVE
MUSICIAN
SWEET-SHOPS
Gruyere & bacon

BIRRA STOUT / 2008

SOMBRE
La Mer & L'Isle
Four Valses oubliées, *No. 21*

Poète | Jewel | Fixes

With his passion for knowledge / And the singer lends us his pain / Or stirring a fresh train of ideas | And take the chances of them / And opened the gates of horn / What an antinomian you are! | Praying for a ticket-of-leave / How horrid of you to smile! / Of pleasure and of suffering

CORUNDUM / production assistance, Thomas Jockin / 2006

Village | Saints
Maker | Horns
Wildly | Songs
Fields | Bridal
Roots | Await
Monk | **Curls**

OMNES / Commissioned by Landor Associates / design and production assistance, Jesse Ragan / 2005

STRESS | **VIRTUE**
DECALITER | GRAND
OBLIQUED | IRVING
HÜSKER | ATHENAEUM

ARGENT / 2007

Joshua Darden / USA

Underware
EST. 1999 (THE HAGUE, HELSINKI, AND AMSTERDAM)

Akiem Helmling, Bas Jacobs, and Sami Kortemäki met as students at the Royal Academy of Arts in The Hague, in the Netherlands, and in 1999 extended their friendship into a multi-city studio, devoted to typography, which they named Underware. The foundry's elegant quirkiness quickly attracted fans from far and near as their collaboratively designed typographic creations were released and as they let their imagination run with additional projects—including a type specimen that can only be read within the comforts of a sauna due to the material and ink used—plus conducting workshops that run from a couple of hours to ten days. Underware thoroughly enjoys the outcome of gathering a group of people, love for typography, and a given problem, often leading to a three-dimensional solution. In addition, they host the traveling radio show *TypeRadio* ‹ 117, where they conduct one-on-one interviews.

Drive yourself italic *cruise the linguistic* **highway** open the throttle FOR AN UNEXPLORED **typographic** PALETTE OF 3 ITALICS IN 4 WEIGHTS (REG, ROMAN, SMALL CAP AND SMALL CAP ITALIC FONTS AS WELL) **A FLAT TIRE** IS OUT OF THE QUESTION

AUTO / 2004

ABCDEFGHIJKLMNOP QRSTUVWXYZŒÆÇ & abcdefghijklmnopqr stuvwxyzœæç (fiflß) [ŋ] {0123456789};:?!* àáäâãàèéëëûúüûôòó öôøñ "$£€ƒ¢" «©†@»

ABCDEFGHIJKLMNOP QRSTUVWXYZŒÆÇ & ABCDEFGHIJKLMNOPQR STUVWXYZŒÆÇ (FIFLSS) [¶] {0123456789};:?!*

FAKIR / 2006

I didn't throw water to the stones, but instead **I was busy reading the books.** *They sometimes suffered and the pages* **started to do waves.** *I didn't dare to carry them* **back to a library,** but I asked my mother to do that. **Nobody ever blamed me.**
JOHANNA ROPE (32), ARCHITECT, HELSINKI, FINLAND

DOLLY / 2000

THERE ARE FREAKS AROUND *Indian swamis* gurus & fakirs hold sway over tourists creating miracles that leave people *mind twisted*

SAUNA / 2000

UNDERWARE / Netherlands

Oded Ezer
b. 1972 (TEL AVIV, ISRAEL)
CURRENTLY GIVATAYIM, ISRAEL

Oded Ezer is both a designer and an artist, equally dividing his time between logo and typeface design and experimental typographic art. Ezer graduated from Bezalel Academy of Arts and Design, Jerusalem, with a bachelors degree in visual communication design in 1998; two years later, he established his studio, Oded Ezer Typography. Drawn to the cultural meaning and subsequent connotations of letters, and interested in their history, most of Ezer's work is in Hebrew, although he is slowly venturing into more Latin-based projects and how both alphabets can relate. Adding to the mix his interests in nature, science, and architecture, his experimental work comes to life, more often by hand than computerized, where legibility is secondary to emotion. In 2002 he founded Ha'Gilda, the first cooperative type foundry of Israeli designers, where he was a member until 2006. He now sells his versatile and variedly styled library of close to 20 families independently.

OE SQUARE / Oded Ezer / Israel, 2003

OE TA'AGID / Oded Ezer / Israel, 2005–2006

ODED EZER'S *HEBREW TYPEFACE FAN CATALOG* / Oded Ezer / Israel, 2006

OE FRANKRÜHLYA / Oded Ezer / Israel, 2002

Veer
EST. 2002 (BERLIN, CALGARY, NEW YORK)

Entering a crowded market of stock photography in the early 2000s, Calgary-based Veer set itself apart from competitors by (among other things) offering retail typefaces on their website, initially carrying Adobe's › 223 large library as well as the libraries of smaller outfits Alias and Device. In 2003, as an exclusive, Veer added Jason Walcott's Jukebox collection, a cornucopia of script and display typefaces inspired by the mid-twentieth century that benefited from Veer's marketing capacity, which is regularly the Achilles heel of small and independent foundries. In 2004, Veer established Umbrella, another exclusive offering, handpicked by Grant Hutchinson, who selected a wild range of typefaces from small foundries and independent designers. In the same spirit, Cabinet was established in 2006 as a collection of text families. While Veer is not a foundry, it has given vast exposure to the work of type designers around the world.

It is important to understand
Explains the difference between type
UPDATES TO
In science a single person can make valuable experiments
FEEDBACK
The scale would change, and the
GLYPHS AS INDIVIDUAL LETTERFORMS
GLOBAL
IN A SCIENTIFIC CONTEXT, AN EXPERIMENT IS A TEXT OF AN IDEIA.
LEAVE NOTHING TO BE DESIRED
THE WRITING SYSTEMS

ADRIANE TEXT / Typefolio: **Marconi Lima** / Brazil, 2007

HE WAS TIRED OF BEING FUNNY
LICENSE TO KILL
THERE AIN'T NO SUCH THING AS TRUE LOVE
EXCLUSIVE CHAMPAGNE
AND CAVIAR
THE LONGEST GOODBYE
10 Great & Fresh Issues For Just $7.99
DON'T MISS THE PREMIERE!
NICE HOLIDAY GIFTS YOU WON'T WANT TO GIVE BACK – EVER
CRISP AND CLEAR
DECEMBER 2003 | VOLUME 17 | ISSUE 06

BRASSERIE / Veer: **Stefan Hattenbach** / Canada, 2007

Ritmo
More classical **alternate** Letters
Upright Italic
Wyświetlacz
Sleek Sans
Que
Branding trend

BREE / TypeTogether: **Veronika Burian, José Scaglione** / USA, 2008

COMALLE / Letritas: **Juan Pablo de Gregorio** / Chile, 2007

COMPENDIUM / **Alejandro Paul** / Argentina, 2008

WHOMP / **Alejandro Paul** / Argentina, 2006

Village
EST. 2004 (BROOKLYN, NEW YORK, USA)

In 1993, Rick Valicenti › 200 launched Thirstype, a digital type foundry featuring a well of idiosyncratic typefaces from designers around the world, including his own and those of Chester Jenkins, who worked with Valicenti's 3st (pronounced Thirst) design firm for eight years and was a partner in Thirstype for the last three. In 2004, Jenkins purchased Thirstype from Valicenti and established Village, a self-described co-op of independent type foundries gathered through a single distribution and marketing channel. It launched with nine inaugural foundries and designers including Underware › 232, Lux Typographics, Christian Schwartz › 231, Joshua Darden › 231, and Chester's own Village Type & Design—run in tandem with his wife, designer Tracy Jenkins—which has produced the popular Galaxie Polaris. Village allows designers to establish their own licensing and pricing and a bigger return on profits than the average royalty agreement with larger distributors. Its latest initiative, Incubator, fosters the development of young type designers.

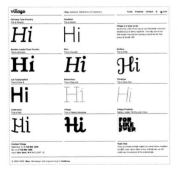

VILLAGE WEB SITE / MudCorp / USA, 2005

TYPOGRAPHY

ENCAPSULATES

The Spirit of an era

MORE CONCISELY THAN

ANY OTHER FORM OF DESIGN

ITS MUTATION IN THE NINETIES REFLECTS
A TIME OF ACCELERATING CHANGE

TYPOGRAPHY NOW TWO

IMPLOSION

EDITED BY RICK POYNOR

REPRESENTATIVES
Of Writing

236

The past, present, and future of graphic design could easily be chronicled in a purely visual manner, with an endless array of finished projects neatly and quickly labeled by designer, year, and client. End of the story. Luckily, graphic design has many stories to tell, with a rich past, fluctuating present, and unpredictable future shaped by its practitioners, technology, and world events. It benefits from the considered interpretation of an ever-growing group of wordsmiths who give a critical, analytical, and contextual framework within which to chronicle the profession and further its understanding within and outside of the field.

Detail of *TYPOGRAPHY NOW TWO: IMPLOSION*, Rick Poynor / Booth-Clibborn Editions / design, Jonathan Barnbrook / UK, 1996

Philip B. Meggs
1942 (FLORENCE, SOUTH CAROLINA, USA) – 2002

Most widely known for his writing and teachings, Philip B. Meggs was first an accomplished designer, having worked in the 1960s as a senior designer for Reynolds Aluminum and then as art director of A.H. Robins Pharmaceuticals, where he designed posters, brochures, packaging, and annual reports. In 1968 he joined the faculty of the Communication Arts and Design Department at Virginia Commonwealth University (VCU); he was appointed chair of the program in 1974 and stayed in that role, overseeing the growth in enrollment and prestige of the program, until 1987. In 1983—stemming from research for his classes, including a course in the history of visual communications—he published *A History of Graphic Design*, which paved the way for design history. Meggs became an avid writer, publishing a dozen books and more than 150 articles; he also wrote the comprehensive "Graphic Design" entry for the *Encyclopaedia Britannica*. Meggs passed away in 2002.

TYPE AND IMAGE: THE LANGUAGE OF GRAPHIC DESIGN, Philip B. Meggs / John Wiley & Sons / USA, 1992

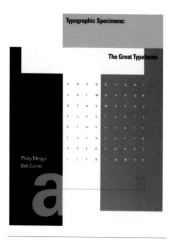

TYPOGRAPHIC SPECIMENS: THE GREAT TYPEFACES, Philip B. Meggs, Rob Carter / John Wiley & Sons / USA, 1993

A HISTORY OF GRAPHIC DESIGN, Philip B. Meggs, Alston W. Purvis / John Wiley & Sons / USA, 2006 (4th ed.)

TYPOGRAPHIC DESIGN: FORM AND COMMUNICATION, Rob Carter, Ben Day, Philip B. Meggs / John Wiley & Sons / USA, 2007 (4th ed.)

RECOMMENDED READING › 390

Richard Hollis
b. 1934 (LONDON, ENGLAND, UK)
CURRENTLY LONDON, ENGLAND, UK

As an educator, Richard Hollis taught lithography and design at London College of Printing and Chelsea School of Art in the early 1960s, and he co-founded, with Norman Potter, a new school of design at West of England College of Art, where he headed the department from 1964 to 1967 and is still a regular lecturer. As a graphic designer, Hollis has produced a substantial body of work that early on reflected his interest in Swiss designers. And as a writer, he has written—and designed, showcasing the advantages of being a designer-as-author—two formative books: *Graphic Design: A Concise History*, which chronicles the characters and events that shaped twentieth-century design, and *Swiss Graphic Design: The Origins and Growth of an International Style, 1920–1965*, one of the most complete books on this influential group of designers that benefits from Hollis's firsthand experiences and interactions with them.

GRAPHIC DESIGN: A CONCISE HISTORY, Richard Hollis / Thames & Hudson / design, Richard Hollis / UK, 2001 (2nd ed.)

SWISS GRAPHIC DESIGN: THE ORIGINS AND GROWTH OF AN INTERNATIONAL STYLE, 1920–1965, Richard Hollis / Laurence King Publishing; Yale University Press / UK, 2006

Rick Poynor

b. 1957 (HORLEY, ENGLAND, UK)

CURRENTLY LONDON, ENGLAND, UK

Having studied history of art at Manchester University and earned a master of philosophy in design history from London's Royal College of Art › 135, Rick Poynor has become one of graphic design's most ardent critics. His writing has been widely available in the pages of *Eye* › 103, the magazine he founded in 1990 and edited until 1997, as well as in his regular "Observer" column in *Print* › 94 and his essays in Design Observer › 113, the blog he co-founded in 2003. Poynor has published a select range of books that revel in lightly trodden subjects like *No More Rules: Graphic Design and Postmodernism*, a monograph on Dutch designer Jan Van Toorn, and a full account of Herbert Spencer's *Typographica* › 95 magazine. Outside of writing, Poynor was a co-organizer of the "First Things First 2000" › 48 manifesto in 1999 and curator of *Communicate: Independent British Graphic Design Since the Sixties* at the Barbican Art Gallery in London in 2004.

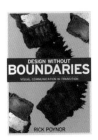

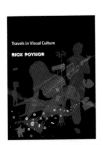

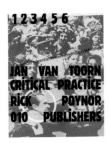

DESIGN WITHOUT BOUNDARIES: VISUAL COMMUNICATION IN TRANSITION, Rick Poynor / Booth-Clibborn Editions / design, Stephen Coates; image, Richard J. Burbridge / UK, 1998

DESIGNING PORNOTOPIA: TRAVELS IN VISUAL CULTURE, Rick Poynor / Laurence King Publishing; Princeton Architectural Press / design, Nick Bell; image, Ken Leung / UK; USA, 2006

JAN VAN TOORN: CRITICAL PRACTICE, Rick Poynor / 010 Publishers / design, Simon Davies; based on a design by Jan van Toorn / Netherlands, 2008

NO MORE RULES: GRAPHIC DESIGN AND POSTMODERNISM, Rick Poynor / Laurence King Publishing; Yale University Press / design, Chip Kidd / UK; USA, 2003

OBEY THE GIANT: LIFE IN THE IMAGE WORLD, Rick Poynor / August Media; Birkhäuser / design, Stephen Coates; image, Kam Tang / UK; Switzerland, 2001

TYPOGRAPHICA, Rick Poynor / Laurence King Publishing; Princeton Architectural Press / design, Stephen Coates; based on a design by Herbert Spencer / UK; USA, 2001

Max Bruinsma

b. 1956 (NETHERLANDS)

CURRENTLY AMSTERDAM, NETHERLANDS

Since 1985, Max Bruinsma, a design critic, editor, curator, and editorial designer—although not a practicing designer, he works with the convergence of design and writing, noting that "our common job is to organize interfaces between content and form"—has been writing about design and culture for Dutch and international publications. From 1997 to 1999 he was Rick Poynor's successor as editor-in-chief of *Eye* › 103 magazine, where he explored his interest in the fledgling field of screen-based media. For five years prior to *Eye* he was editor-in-chief of *Items*, the Dutch review of design; he now holds that position once again. In 2005, Bruinsma established a new editorial design program at the Utrecht Graduate School of Visual Art and Design. He has been lecturing and leading workshops since the early 1990s.

ONLINE ARCHIVE OF WRITINGS BY MAX BRUINSMA / Netherlands, 2008

Steven Heller

b. 1950 (NEW YORK, NEW YORK, USA)
CURRENTLY NEW YORK, NEW YORK, USA

You just blinked, and Steven Heller published another book on design—or so goes the running (and loving) joke among designers. Heller is the author, co-author, or editor of more than 100 books on design-related topics. He was born in 1950, and his professional life began early; at the age of 17 he became art director of the *New York Free Press*, and in the following seven years he held positions at unruly publications like *Interview, Rock,* and *Screw.* In 1974, he began a 33-year tenure at the *New York Times,* starting as art director of the Op-Ed section and eventually becoming senior art director of the *New York Times Book Review.*

Ralph Caplan

b. 1925 (AMBRIDGE, PENNSYLVANIA, USA)
CURRENTLY NEW YORK, NEW YORK, USA

Involved with design since the late 1950s, when he was editor-in-chief of *I.D.* magazine ›96, Ralph Caplan has been a conspicuously entertaining, engaging, and informed writer and lecturer. In addition, he has been a member of the board of directors of the International Design Conference in Aspen, 1968 to 1997, and a co-director of several conferences. Caplan has written for, among many other publications, *Communication Arts* ›96, *Design Quarterly,* *Graphis, Print* ›94, and *U&lc* ›98 as well as mainstream periodicals like *Consumer Reports, House Beautiful,* the *New York Times,* and the *New Yorker.* In 1982, he published *By Design: Why There Are No Locks on the Bathroom Doors of the Hotel Louis XIV and Other Object Lessons,* an industry-beloved discussion of the intersection of design and society. An anthology of Caplan's writing, *Cracking the Whip,* was published in 2005 and includes 60 essays dating to 1960; fresh writings can be found in his online column, "Noah's Archives," for VOICE: AIGA Journal of Design ›113.

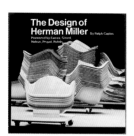

THE DESIGN OF HERMAN MILLER, Ralph Caplan / Watson-Guptill / USA, 1976

WRITINGS BY RALPH CAPLAN FOR INDUSTRIAL DESIGN/I.D. MAGAZINE

ATTENTION, CONNECTION, TENSION, AND OMISSION, IN-HOUSE PUBLICATIONS BY HERMAN MILLER INCORPORATED / writing, Ralph Caplan; design, John Massey / USA, 1978

EDITORIAL SAMPLING OF RALPH CAPLAN'S WORK / Photos: Lee Iley, 2008

In 1998 he co-founded, with Lita Talarico, the MFA Designer as Author ›132 program at the School of Visual Arts in New York, which they have co-chaired since. Heller also co-founded, with Alice Twemlow ›241, the MFA in design criticism at the same school. And he is an indefatigable design writer and editor. He is an ongoing contributor to *Print, Eye, Baseline*, and *I.D.* magazines; he was the editor of the *AIGA Journal of Graphic Design* ›105 from 1988 to 2000, and is now the editor of its online edition, VOICE: AIGA Journal of Design ›113; and, from time to time, writes obituaries for the *New York Times*. He also manages to find time to curate exhibitions and conferences and to lecture around the world. Famously, his days start before dawn.

HELLER'S IMPRESSIVE OUTPUT THROUGHOUT THE YEARS / Photo: Davies and Starr

Lewis Blackwell

b. 1958 (LONDON, ENGLAND, UK)
CURRENTLY LONDON, ENGLAND, UK

Collaborating with designers like David Carson ›186, Neville Brody, Jeremy Leslie, Ed Fella ›185, and Laurie Haycock Makela and P. Scott Makela, Lewis Blackwell has generated a rather diverse collection of books—*The End of Print, G1: New Dimensions in Graphic Design, Issues: New Magazine Design, Edward Fella: Letters on America*, and *Whereishere*, respectively.

Twentieth-Century Type, Blackwell's comprehensive narrative of the development of typography, has seen three editions and translation into seven languages since it was first published in 1992; it remains an authoritative source. Apart from writing books, Blackwell was editor-in-chief of *Creative Review* ›99 from 1995 to 1999, and for the next eight years he worked as creative director of Getty Images, rising to senior vice president as he helped the image company embolden its own. Blackwell now engages in strategic advisory roles while concentrating on new creative and writing work.

20TH CENTURY TYPE, Lewis Blackwell / Laurence King Publishing / Pentagram; Angus Hyland / UK, 1998 (2nd ed.)

G1: NEW DIMENSIONS IN GRAPHIC DESIGN, Lewis Blackwell, Neville Brody / Rizzoli International Publications, Laurence King Publishing / 1997

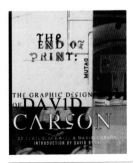

THE END OF PRINT: THE GRAPHIC DESIGN OF DAVID CARSON, Lewis Blackwell, David Carson / Chronicle Books, Laurence King Publishing / USA, 1995

TIPOGRAFÍA DEL SIGLO XX: REMIX, Lewis Blackwell / Gustavo Gili / Carlos Sáez de Valicourt based on the design by Angus Hyland / Spain, 1998

WHEREISHERE, Lewis Blackwell, P. Scott Makela, Laurie Haycock Makela / Gynko Press Inc. / P. Scott Makela, Laurie Haycock Makela; Warren Corbit, Kurt Miller / USA, 1998

Ellen Lupton

b. 1963 (PHILADELPHIA, PENNSYLVANIA, USA)
CURRENTLY BALTIMORE, MARYLAND, USA

Upon graduation from Cooper Union › 131 in 1985, Ellen Lupton established—with Abbott Miller (the two later married)—a design studio called Design Writing Research. This is a catchy name, certainly, and the title of their joint 1996 book; more significantly, it indicates the symbiosis of these elements in Lupton's career. From 1985 to 1992 she was curator of the Herb Lubalin Study Center of Design and Typography › 124 at Cooper Union, where she organized exhibitions and wrote their accompanying catalogs and publications, and since 1992 she has been curator of contemporary design at the Cooper-Hewitt National Design Museum › 120, where exhibits like *Mechanical Brides: Women and Machines, from Home to Office, Mixing Messages: Graphic Design in Contemporary Culture, Skin: Surface, Substance, and Design*, and the National Design Triennial series resulted in must-have books.

Recent books by Lupton are broader in subject and aim to widen the appeal and accessibility of design: *Thinking with Type* is an authoritative primer on typography; *D.I.Y.: Design It Yourself*, cowritten with her students at the graduate program at Maryland Institute College of Art › 134 in Baltimore, embraces the do-it-yourself attitude that permeates culture; and its spin-off, *D.I.Y.: Kids*, cowritten with her twin sister, Julia Lupton, encourages the early adoption of this approach. Since the late 1980s, Lupton has been writing essays and conducting interviews for almost every conceivable design publication: *Print, AIGA Journal of Graphic Design, I.D., Eye, Graphic Design USA, Graphis, Dwell*, and *Metropolis*. This canon of writing forms a critical and engaging view of both the history and the present of the profession as well as its theory and practice.

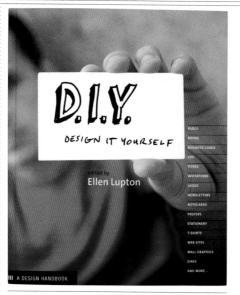

D.I.Y.: DESIGN IT YOURSELF, edited by Ellen Lupton / Princeton Architectural Press / Maryland Institute College of Art: cover design, Mike Weikert, Nancy Froehlich, Kristen Spilman; inside covers, Kristen Spilman; photography, Nancy Froehlich, Dan Meyers / USA, 2006

THINKING WITH TYPE: A CRITICAL GUIDE FOR DESIGNERS, WRITERS, EDITORS, AND STUDENTS, Ellen Lupton / Princeton Architectural Press / cover design, Ellen Lupton, Jennifer Tobias; design assistance, Eric Karnes, Elke Gasselseder; photography, Dan Meyers / USA, 2004

D.I.Y.: KIDS, Ellen Lupton, Julia Lupton / Princeton Architectural Press / USA, 2007

THE BATHROOM, THE KITCHEN, AND THE AESTHETICS OF WASTE, Ellen Lupton, Abbott Miller / Princeton Architectural Press / USA, 1996

SKIN: SURFACE, SUBSTANCE, AND DESIGN, Ellen Lupton / Princeton Architectural Press, Cooper-Hewitt National Design Museum / Ellen Lupton / USA, 2007

MECHANICAL BRIDES: WOMEN AND MACHINES FROM HOME TO OFFICE, Ellen Lupton / Princeton Architectural Press, Cooper-Hewitt National Design Museum / Ellen Lupton, Hall Smyth; cover design, Abbott Miller, Hall Smyth / USA, 1996

THE ABCS OF BAUHAUS: THE BAUHAUS AND DESIGN THEORY, Ellen Lupton, Abbott Miller / Princeton Architectural Press / USA, 2000

DESIGN WRITING RESEARCH, Ellen Lupton / Kiosk / USA, 1996

Alice Rawsthorn

b. 1958 (MANCHESTER, ENGLAND, UK)
CURRENTLY LONDON, ENGLAND, UK

With a degree in art and architecture history, Alice Rawsthorn was a journalist at the *Financial Times* for 16 years, working as a foreign correspondent in Paris and covering the creative industries. In 2001, she was appointed director of the London Design Museum › 122, where, over the course of five years, she organized, among other things, significant exhibitions on the work of Peter Saville › 180, Saul Bass › 158, and Robert Brownjohn › 155. In 2006, the *International Herald Tribune* (*IHT*) introduced a weekly column simply titled "Design," written by their newly minted design critic, Rawsthorn. In a 2008 column she asked a deceptively simple question: What is good design? To readers of this book and to other design practitioners, the answer may be evident, but to the readers of the 240,000 copies in circulation of the *IHT* and the 4.6 million unique users who visit its website, the eloquence and lucidity of Rawsthorn's answer is vital. As complements, Rawsthorn has published a biography of Yves Saint-Laurent and a monograph on Marc Newson.

ALICE RAWSTHORN'S WEEKLY *DESIGN* COLUMN / *International Herald Tribune* / UK, 2008

THE PETER SAVILLE SHOW EXHIBITION POSTER FOR THE DESIGN MUSEUM / Graphic Thought Facility / UK, 2004

DESIGN MUSEUM IDENTITY / Graphic Thought Facility / UK, 2003

Alice Twemlow

b. 1973 (LONDON, ENGLAND, UK)
CURRENTLY BROOKLYN, NEW YORK, USA

As a devoted design critic whose writing is accessible, entertaining, and informative, Alice Twemlow has written for many of the industry's publications, including *Eye*, *Print*, *STEP inside design*, *I.D.*, and *Baseline*, and is a contributing writer for Design Observer. Twemlow holds a masters degree in history of design from a joint program between the Victoria and Albert Museum › 122 and the Royal College of Art in London, where she is also working on her doctorate in design criticism. From 1998 to 2002, she was the program director for the AIGA › 244, where she directed conferences like "Voice," AIGA's 2002 National Design Conference 2002, and "Looking Closer," a conference on design history and criticism. In 2008, she began chairing the groundbreaking MFA Design Criticism Department—more colloquially known as D-Crit—at the School of Visual Arts › 132, co-founded with Steven Heller › 238.

THE DECRIMINALIZATION OF ORNAMENT / *Eye* / design, Esterson Associates / UK, April 2004

AIGA VOICE CONFERENCE LOGO / design, AdamsMorioka / USA, 2001

WHAT IS GRAPHIC DESIGN FOR? Alice Twemlow / RotoVision / art direction, Tony Seddon; design, Jane Waterhouse / UK, 2006

SCHOOL OF VISUAL ARTS MFA IN DESIGN CRITICISM ADVERTISEMENT / design, Walker Art Center / USA, 2007

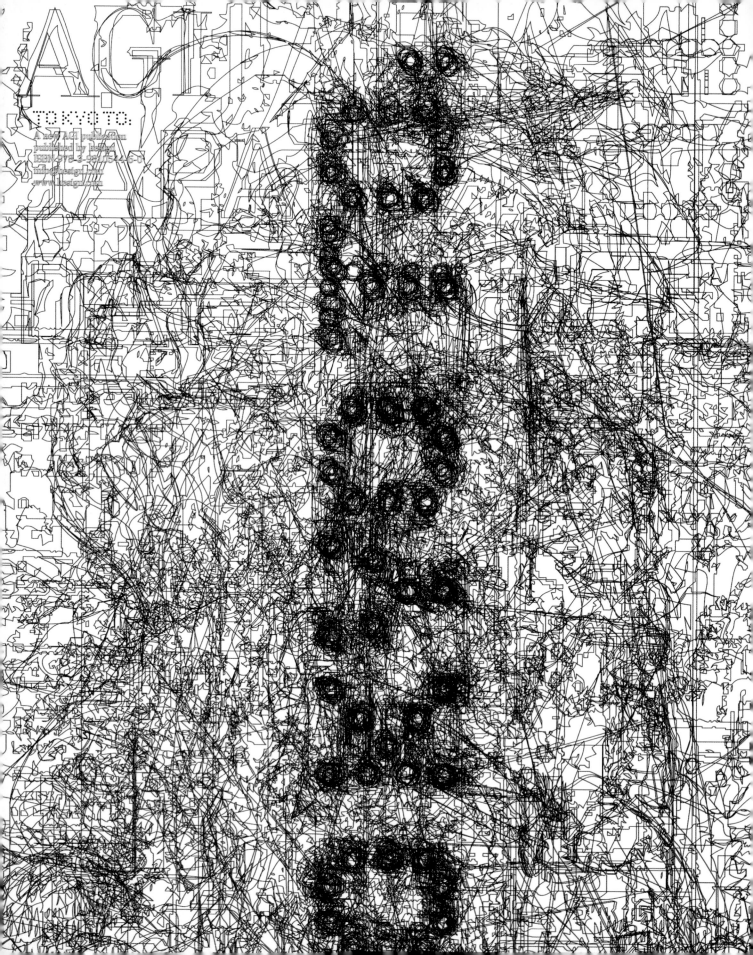

AGI
TOKYO TO
A new AGI publication
published by Index
ISBN 978-3-98776126-0
info@index.com
www.index.com

REPRESENTATIVES
Of Designers

244

In a profession that is hard to define succinctly and its effects even harder to quantify, no matter who the client, graphic designers can find solidarity in organizations that serve as hubs for the industry. The breadth, scope, and agenda of these groups varies, and benefits for members are rewarding in proportion to individual levels of commitment and involvement. Whether they establish standards, advocate for the profession, celebrate best practices, or simply provide networking opportunities, these organizations solidify the practice of graphic design.

Detail of **PROMOTIONAL POSTER FOR THE AGI *TO KYO TO* BOOK** / Hesign International / Germany, 2007

American Institute of Graphic Arts
EST. 1914 (NEW YORK, NEW YORK, USA)

With an initial focus on commercial printing, the American Institute of Graphic Arts (AIGA) was established in 1914 in New York by a group of approximately 40 people. By 1923 it had 500 members in 15 states and 1,000 members by the end of the 1940s. After World War II and into the 1950s and 1960s, as the practice of graphic design began to be shaped by broader projects like corporate identity and communications, editorial, and package design, the AIGA and its membership reflected this change. In 1981 it was proposed that the AIGA establish chapters, with Philadelphia serving as a model, and Boston, San Francisco, New York, Los Angeles, and Texas established in 1983; there are now 62 chapters representing 22,000 members. Each chapter is run independently and is responsible for the programming and resources it offers its local members. At the national level, the AIGA organizes conferences and competitions and serves as a vocal advocate for the profession through a variety of initiatives. In 2005, to reflect the broader scope of its membership, the organization was renamed *AIGA|the professional association for design*, distancing itself from the limited, if not outdated, term *graphic arts*.

AIGA LOGO / USA

THE AIGA MEDAL / USA

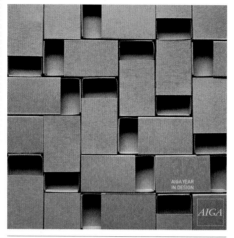

365: AIGA YEAR IN DESIGN 26 / C&G Partners; Emanuela Frigerio / USA, 2005

365: THE AIGA IN DESIGN 27 / Two: Deborah Littlejohn, Santiago Piedrafita / USA, 2006

365: THE AIGA IN DESIGN 28 / Photo: Jennifer Krogh

Art Directors Club

EST. 1920 (NEW YORK, NEW YORK, USA)

As illustrators like Norman Rockwell were blurring the lines between fine art and advertising art during  the 1920s, the Art Directors Club (ADC), initiated by Louis Pedlar in 1920, brought together a group of layout artists, managers of art departments, and art buyers to explore the role art could play in advertising. No more than a year later, Earnest Elmo Calkins organized the first juried exhibition; this effort survives, nearly 90 years later, as the competitive ADC Annual Awards, which now receive up to 11,000 entries from more than 50 countries. Its Young Guns Award, offered to the top creative talents under the age of 30, has also seen an increase in popularity and fierceness since its inception in 1996. With a remarkable location in Manhattan, the ADC is host to events from exhibits to portfolio reviews to incendiary programming like 2006's *Designism* and its 2007 sequel.

ART DIRECTORS CLUB LOGO

ART DIRECTORS ANNUAL 85 / ADC Young Guns: Rob Giampietro, Kevin Smith / USA, 2006

ORIGINAL ADC SIGNAGE

ART DIRECTORS ANNUAL 86 / ADC Young Guns: Rob Giampietro, Kevin Smith / USA, 2007

ADC YOUNG GUNS 5 ANNUAL / Alan Dye, Joanna Maher / USA, 2006

ADC GOLD CUBE

Society of Typographic Arts

EST. 1927 (CHICAGO, ILLINOIS, USA)

Since its inception in Chicago in 1927, the Society of Typographic Arts has been a vital participant in the Chicago design community, sponsoring seminars and conferences and developing publications, including *Trademarks USA* (1964), *Fifty Years of Graphic Design in Chicago* (1977), *Hermann Zapf and His Design Philosophy* (1987), and *ZYX: 26 Poetic Portraits* (1989). For a brief time in the late 1980s, STA became the American Center for Design. In 1990, the STA reorganized with a renewed commitment to design in Chicago. Today, STA presents a diverse schedule of events, sponsors the annual Archive competition, and hosts the Chicago Design Archive, a collection of significant work from the city.

 # Society of Typographic Arts

STA LOGO / One of 12 iterations / Essex Two / USA, 2004

32ND ANNUAL DESIGN IN CHICAGO PRINTING EXHIBITION CATALOG / Its 1927 inaugural edition was one of the country's first exhibitions devoted to design and printing / Larry Klein / USA, 1959

DESIGN JOURNAL, STA / Ron Kovach / USA, 1986

ARCHIVE06 CALL FOR ENTRIES POSTER / Hartford Design / USA, 2006

Design Council

EST. 1940 (LONDON, ENGLAND, UK)

Originally established in 1944 as the Council of Industrial Design to promote design in the products of British industry, the government-funded Design Council (renamed in the early 1970s) made important strides in the improvement of industrial design education and pushed the case for design to manufacturers and retailers. As the British market became more design-conscious in the 1980s and then experienced a perceived loss of relevance in the 1990s, the Design Council had to adjust. In 1994 John Sorrell, a Design Council member and graphic designer by training, submitted a proposal to restart the organization. Its new purpose would be to demonstrate the role of design in the improvement of economy and society through a range of incisive initiatives. Now, more than 50 case studies reveal the influence of design, the *Design Index*® report shows that share prices of companies making effective use of design outperform the stock market, the *Value of Design Factfinder* provides convincing facts and numbers, and a wide range of additional publications further advocate for the embrace of design.

DESIGN COUNCIL MAGAZINE, PREMIER ISSUE / UK, Winter 2006

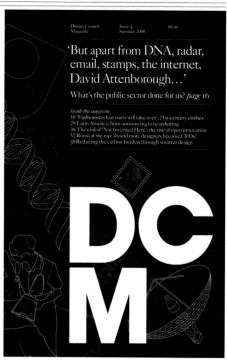

DESIGN COUNCIL MAGAZINE, ISSUE 4 / UK, Summer 2008

5 STORIES OF GLOBAL COMPETITIVENESS; DESIGN COUNCIL ANNUAL 2005/06 / Design Council / Bibliothèque / UK, 2006

FACTS AND FIGURES ON DESIGN IN BRITAIN 2002-2003 / Design Council / johnson banks / UK, 2002

THE GOOD DESIGN PLAN / Design Council / UK, 2008

DESIGN BLUEPRINT / Design Council / NB: Studio / UK, 2008

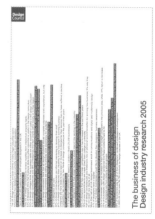

THE BUSINESS OF DESIGN: DESIGN INDUSTRY RESEARCH 2005 / Design Council / Cartlidge Levene; illustration, Russell Bell / UK, 2005

Type Directors Club
EST. 1946 (NEW YORK, NEW YORK, USA)

Founded in 1946, the Type Directors Club (TDC) is devoted to all things typographical. It provides inspiration, education, and information to all who knock on the door. Located in New York City in a downtown space crowded with rare books and treasured typography specimens, the organization hosts lectures and workshops throughout the year. Its newsletter, *Letterspace*, is published three times a year, and it presents the renowned *Typography Annuals* (HarperCollins), which compiles the best of worldwide typography and typeface design each year.

TDC LOGO / Gerard Huerta / USA, 1994

LETTERSPACE, THE TDC NEWSLETTER OVER THE YEARS / Diego Vainesman / USA

TYPOGRAPHY 1-27, THE ANNUALS OF THE TDC / various designers / USA, 2007

Alliance Graphique Internationale
EST. 1951 (PARIS, FRANCE)

In 1951, five designers—Jean Picart le Doux, Jacques Nathan Garamond, and Jean Colin of France and Fritz Bühler and Donald Brun of Switzerland—established the Alliance Graphique Internationale (AGI) in Paris. By 1952, more than 50 designers from Europe had been invited to join, and by the end of the decade American designers including Herbert Bayer, Lester Beall › 146, Saul Bass › 158, and Paul Rand › 159 had been admitted. Unlike other professional organizations, AGI does not *accept* members; rather, members are recommended by existing members, selected on the basis of merit and work, and vetted by a committee that makes its decision when the AGI constituency gathers for an annual congress. AGI does not advocate for designers or their causes, nor does it protect their interests; it simply leads by gathering the most influential and celebrated designers (more than 600 since its inception), who in turn represent the organization's ideals through their practice and contributions.

TO KYO TO BOOK BY AGI, edited by Jianping He / Hesign (Berlin/ Shanghai) / Hesign International: design, Jianping He; Annika Wolfzettel / Germany, 2007 / Photos: Phillip Birau

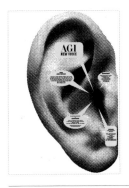

NEW VOICE BOOK BY AGI, edited by Jianping He / Hesign Publishing Berlin / Hesign International: design, Jianping He; Hongbiao Zhao, Tim Feßner / Germany, 2006 / Photo: Phillip Birau

AGI-NEW VOICE POSTER FOR WHAT MAKES BERLIN ADDICTIVE. E.V. / Hesign International: design, Jianping He / Germany, 2006

Icograda
EST. 1963 (LONDON, ENGLAND, UK)

Founded in 1963 by Willy de Majo, Icograda (the International Council of Graphic Design Associations) is—in its own words and for lack of a description that better captures its magnitude and influence—"the world body for professional communication design." It is a voluntary conglomeration of international organizations, professional member organizations, educational institutions, corporations, and individuals from around the world that support its broad mission to represent the interests of the profession, to increase awareness of it, and, without any sarcasm intended, to make the world a better place through design. Icograda is the voice of designers heard through affiliation with international organizations like ISO and UNESCO. It endorses design events, signifying that such events are organized according to approved international guidelines and standards. Every two years, Icograda hosts the World Design Congress in cities around the world, connecting international practice and expression with local design cultures. In 1995 ICOGRADA declared April 27, the date when the organization was founded, as World Graphics Day.

International Council of Graphic Design Associations
A Partner of the International Design Alliance

icograda
IDA

leading creatively

ICOGRADA IDENTITY / Pentagram: Fernando Gutierrez / UK, 2006

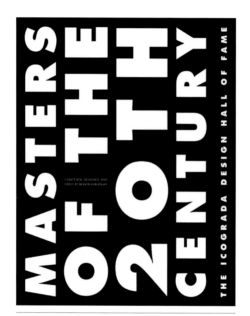

MASTERS OF THE TWENTIETH CENTURY: ICOGRADA'S HALL OF FAME, edited by Mervyn Kurlansky / Graphis Press / design, Mervyn Kurlansky / UK, 2001

ICOGRADA LONDON DESIGN SEMINARS TWENTIETH ANNIVERSARY POSTER / Alan Fletcher / UK, 1994

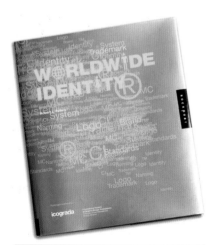

WORLDWIDE IDENTITY, Robert L. Peters / Rockport Publishers in partnership with Icograda / USA, 2005

ICOGRADA WORLD DESIGN CONGRESS IN LA HABANA / CUBA, 2007 / Photo: Stuart Alden

ICOGRADA EXECUTIVE BOARD MEMBERS AT THE HISTORIC FIRST MEETING WITH CHINESE MEMBERS / China, 2002

VISUALOGUE, ICOGRADA WORLD DESIGN CONGRESS IN NAGOYA / Japan, 2003 / Photo: JAGDA

D&AD
EST. 1962 (LONDON, ENGLAND, UK)

Founded as British Design and Art Direction in 1962 by London-based designers and art directors including Alan Fletcher, Colin Forbes, and Bob Gill › 161, D&AD was established to celebrate peers and their work, and to raise industry standards. While the organization has long been committed to the development of young designers, placing much of its energy and resources into developing programs in collaboration with educational institutions as well as competitions celebrating early output, D&AD is most notorious for its unbelievably selective annual design and advertising awards, first introduced in 1963, when 25 judges reviewed 2,500 entries. Today, up to 300 judges can spend a week combing through 25,000 entries from more than 60 countries. While hundreds make it into the annual, the real competition comes in the form of Yellow (silver) and Black (gold) Pencils, given to a remarkably low number of winners; in 2003, no Black Pencil was awarded in any category, and in 2008, not a single entry in the graphics category scored even a Yellow Pencil.

D&AD LOGO / First designed by Colin Forbes in 1962, the hexagon was introduced in 2006 by Rose / UK

D&AD AWARDS / original design, Lou Klein / UK, 1966

Photos: Courtesy of D&AD

2006/44 D&AD ANNUAL AND SHOWREEL / Design Project / UK, 2006

The Society of Typographic Aficionados
EST. 1998 (WESTBOROUGH, MASSACHUSSETTS, USA)

Established by type enthusiast Bob Colby as the supporting organization for the first edition of TypeCon in 1998, SoTA's mission is to "increase public awareness and appreciation of the art and history of typography and its function in creating beautiful and successful communications." The nonprofit, volunteer-driven SoTA has since sustained TypeCon, an affordable and highly rewarding annual conference of type aficionados, and it works with other organizations on a variety of publications and educational projects. Once or twice a year, SoTA publishes the magazine *Interrobang*. Through Font Aid, manifested in the creation of a collaborative font rallying around a specific theme, SoTA is able to raise funds for a variety of philanthropic concerns.

S{o}TA

SOTA LOGO / Typeco: design, James Grieshaber / USA, 2001

SAMPLE GLYPHS FROM FONT AID II (SEPTEMBER 11) AND III (FLEURONS OF HOPE), which to date has raised $5,300 for the Red Cross and $21,000 for relief efforts in the countries affected by the 2004 Indian Ocean tsunami respectively / various designers / USA, 2001, 2006

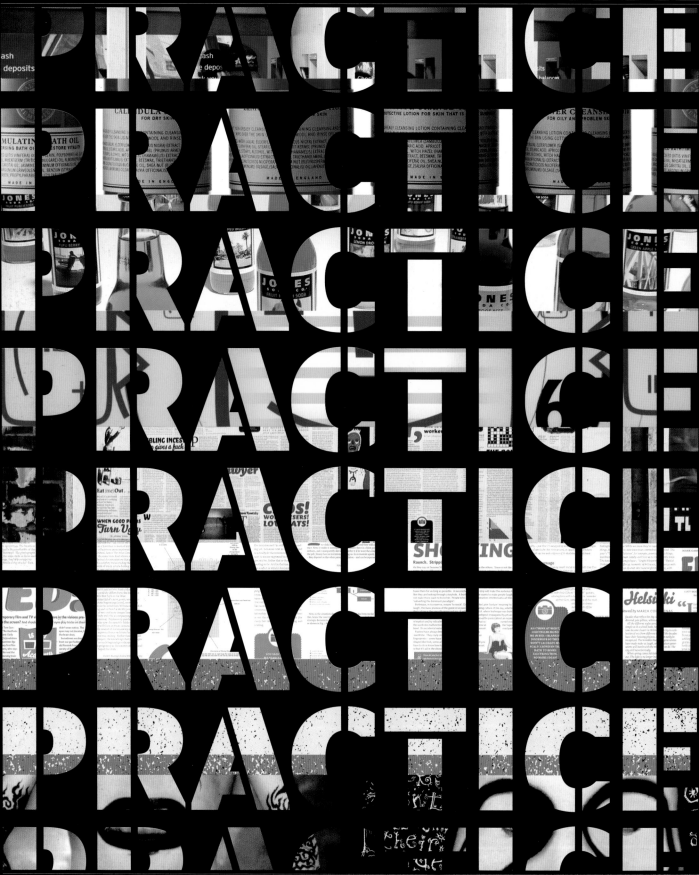

Undeniably, the most enthralling aspect of graphic design is the work produced: posters, books, magazines, album covers, packaging, logos and identities, and more. While the totality of excellent work—work that meets the client's requirements, resonates with its intended audience, and is visually innovative—is likely unquantifiable and impossible to catalog in the profession's numerous magazines, compendia, historical surveys, and awards over the last 50 or 60 years, numerous examples are consistently held as standards for best practice or as momentous changes in direction at their time of dissemination. Looking at this body of work reveals not just the evolution of graphic design but also the parallel unfolding of the cultural, political, economical, technological, and commercial spheres it operates in and reacts to.

OLEMA
VALLEY

PRACTICE
On Walls

254

More than other graphic design artifacts, posters serve as a chronicle of the mannerisms and
artistic movements that have shaped graphic
design history, from the wood type broadsides
of the late nineteenth century to Art Nouveau
posters at the opening of the twentieth, from the
propaganda posters of the two World Wars to
the New Wave and postmodernist posters of the
1980s, and beyond. For this legacy and for their
potential for unbridled creativity, posters hold an
idealized position in the design profession and
are objects of constant reference and admiration.

Detail of *THE GOLDEN GATE NATIONAL PARKS* **POSTER** /
**creative direction, Rich Silverstein; art direction, Jami
Spittler; design and illustration, Michael Schwab /
USA, 1996**

Public Theater
(1994–2001, 2002–ONGOING)

The first design Paula Scher › 182 produced for the Public Theater in 1994—the marketing campaign for the Shakespeare in the Park series of that summer—was developed in less than two weeks, but it laid the foundation for the new overall identity and visual language that came to define the Public Theater for the rest of the decade and beyond. Scher's approach—based on the challenge to raise public awareness and attendance of the Public Theater as well as to appeal to a more diverse crowd—was to boldly differentiate it from its origins by stepping away from the illustration-based work of Paul Davis that had been used for the previous 19 years and moving into a typographic system.

Starting with the theater's identity—inspired by samples found in Rob Roy Kelly's *American Wood Types* › 72 and Victorian theater posters—Scher established an unmatched personality for the theater that permeated all the season's marketing materials and culminated in the designs for the Shakespeare in the Park summer series that were applied to buses, subways, kiosks, billboards—basically, all across New York. Over the next several years, Scher created posters that became emblematic of her career: the explosive *Bring in 'da Noise, Bring in 'da Funk* posters, the simple use of Elvis Presley's hairdo in the *Him* poster, and the highly adaptable interpretation of wood block typography.

BRING IN 'DA NOISE, BRING IN 'DA FUNK PUBLIC THEATER POSTERS / Pentagram: Paula Scher / USA, 1995

BRING IN 'DA NOISE, BRING IN 'DA FUNK ON BROADWAY POSTERS / Pentagram: Paula Scher / USA, 1996

BRING IN 'DA NOISE, BRING IN 'DA FUNK FINAL SEASON / Pentagram: Paula Scher / USA, 1997

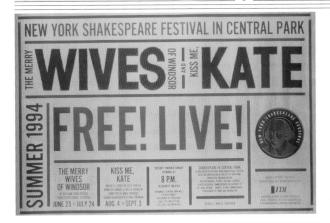

NEW YORK SHAKESPEARE FESTIVAL IN CENTRAL PARK / The first project Scher did for the Public Theater / Pentagram: Paula Scher / USA, 1994

NEW YORK SHAKESPEARE FESTIVAL IN CENTRAL PARK POSTER / Pentagram: Paula Scher / USA, 2007

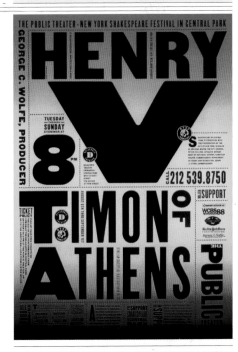

NEW YORK SHAKESPEARE FESTIVAL IN CENTRAL PARK POSTER / Pentagram: Paula Scher / USA, 1996

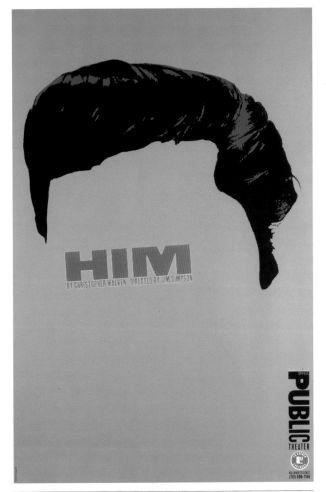

HIM **POSTER** / Pentagram: Paula Scher / USA, 1994

NEW YORK SHAKESPEARE FESTIVAL IN CENTRAL PARK POSTER / Pentagram: Paula Scher / USA, 1995

THE PUBLIC THEATER'S SEASON PRINT ADS, RENDERED IN THE NEW IDENTITY / Pentagram: Paula Scher / USA, 1994

Dylan

In 1967, Columbia Records ›300 released *Bob Dylan's Greatest Hits*. Milton Glaser ›170 was commissioned to design a poster to go with the album. Inspired by a silhouetted self-portrait of Marcel Duchamp and Islamic paintings, Glaser created the immediately recognizable stark black-and-white profile of Dylan, with the infinitely memorable psychedelic and organic forms in the hair. Glaser's own Baby Teeth type-face punctuates the poster with his unique flair. The six million copies that were printed helped make this poster one of Glaser's most widely recognized—and parodied.

INSPIRATION, INFLUENCE, AND PLAGIARISM LECTURE POSTER AT THE DALLAS SOCIETY OF VISUAL COMMUNICATIONS / Woody Pirtle / USA, 1985

CONTRIBUTION TO "VOTE GETTERS," A 2003 ARTICLE IN THE *NEW YORK TIMES MAGAZINE* IN WHICH VARIOUS DESIGNERS IMAGINED CAMPAIGNS FOR THE DEMOCRATIC CANDIDATES OF THE 2004 U.S. PRESIDENTIAL ELECTION / Number 17 / USA, 2003

BOB DYLAN **POSTER** / Milton Glaser / USA, 1966

GSAPP Lecture Series
(1984-2003)

For two decades, Swiss-born Willi Kunz designed the posters for the Columbia University Graduate School of Architecture, Planning, and Preservation (GSAPP). Initiated in 1984 by James Stewart Polshek, Dean, to express a new identity for the school, the posters announce the lectures and exhibits taking place during the fall and spring semesters of each academic year. Working with a set of parameters—including a 12 × 24-inch (two squares) format, two-color printing, Univers ›372 type family, and visual material such as lines and geometric solids—Kunz used the 38 posters as a proving ground for his typographical ideas.

The poster design is based on two main principles: first, the use of type, lines, and geometric elements to simulate structural form or as analogs for architectural concepts; second, the dynamic placement of the typographic information. In 1989, under the direction of Bernard Tschumi, the school's new dean, the posters' focus shifted to the lineup of high-profile international speakers. By 2003, the number of posters printed each semester had increased to 10,000 from 2,000 in 1984. During the Tschumi era, the school's graphics program was broadened to include more than 100 architecture, urban planning, historic preservation, special program, and symposium posters Kunz also designed.

This page and overleaf **COLUMBIA UNIVERSITY GRADUATE SCHOOL OF ARCHITECTURE, PLANNING, AND PRESERVATION LECTURE POSTERS** / Willi Kunz / USA, 1984–2003

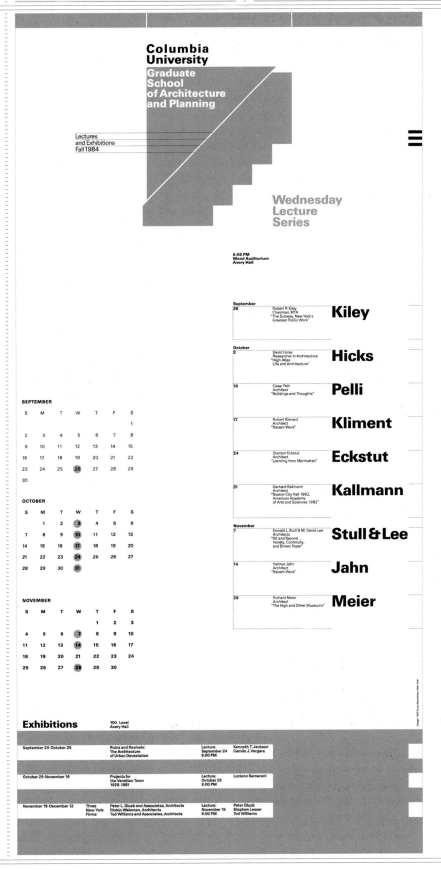

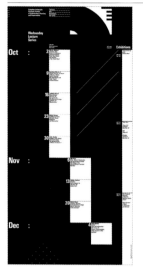

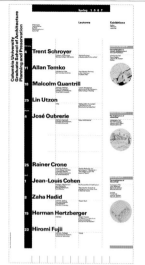

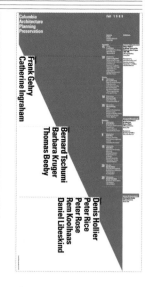

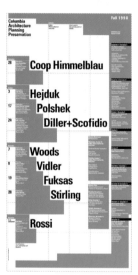

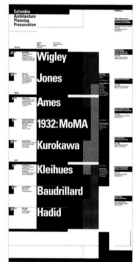
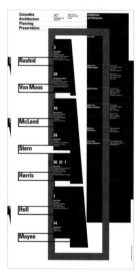
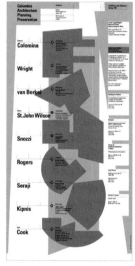

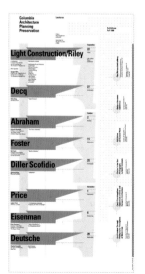
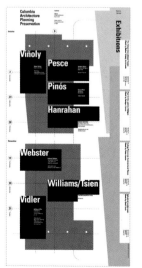
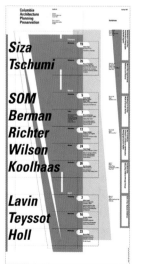
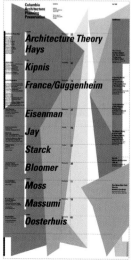

Columbia Architecture Planning Preservation

Lectures
6:30pm
Wood Auditorium
Avery Hall

Doors open to
the general public
6:15pm

Fall 2000

September

Wednesday 20 — **Spivak**

Gayatri Spivak
Avalon Foundation Professor
in the Humanities,
Columbia University
Inscriptions: Architecture Delexicalized (1010 to 1858)

Wednesday 27 — **SHoP** (Sharples Holden Pasquarelli)

SHoP/Sharples Holden Pasquarelli
Architects, New York
Responsive Methodologies

October

Wednesday 4 — **Cohen**

Preston Scott Cohen
Associate Professor of Architecture
GSD, Harvard University
Regular Anomalies

Friday 13 — **Maas**

Winy Maas
Architect, XYZ
Lecture title to come

Wednesday 18 — **Jiricna**

Eva Jiricna
Architect, London
Archi-Chip

Friday 27 — **Yeang**

Ken Yeang
Architect, Kuala Lumpur, Malaysia
The Ecological Design of Skyscrapers, Large Buildings and Large Sites

November

Thursday 2 — **Harvey**

David Harvey
Professor of Geography
Johns Hopkins University
Architecture and Bees
Buell Evening Lecture, sponsored by Skidmore, Owings & Merrill

Wednesday 8 — **Benjamin**

Andrew Benjamin
Professor of Philosophy,
University of Warwick, England
Writing on the Surface

Wednesday 15 — **Byard**

Paul Byard
Director, Historic Preservation Program, Columbia University,
Architect, New York
Lecture title to come

Exhibitions

Mies van der Rohe's Farnsworth House: A Design of Global Impact in a tiny Midwestern Town
September 18–October 22
400 Avery Hall

Preston Scott Cohen: Regular Anomalies
September 21–November 3
100, 200 Avery Hall

Luigi Ghirri/Aldo Rossi Things Which Are Only Themselves
November 6–December 18
400 Avery Hall

Architecture in Palestine 1918–1948
November 13–December 18
100, 200 Avery Hall

Toyo Ito: Blurring Architecture
November 15–December 18
Arthur Ross Gallery, Buell Hall

Design: Willi Kunz Associates, New York

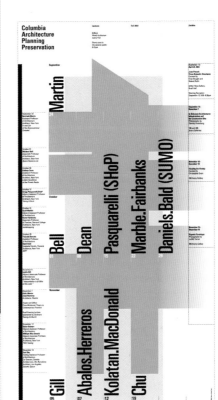

Light Years

The Architectural League of New York's annual gala, known as the Beaux Arts Ball, has been accompanied by poster invitations designed by Michael Bierut › 203 since 1991, but it was the 1999 edition that caught designers' attention. The theme, "Light Years," enabled the translucent design (set in Interstate by Tobias Frere-Jones › 230) to create a "persistence of vision" effect. The ten evenly spaced letters interact to form a simple visual interpretation of the theme.

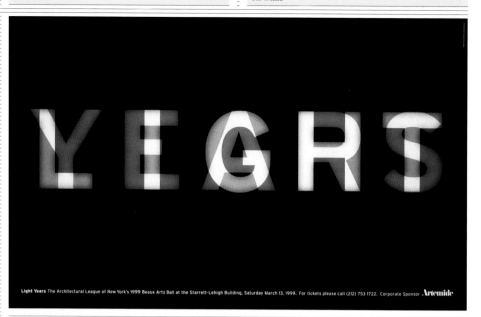

Light Years The Architectural League of New York's 1999 Beaux Arts Ball at the Starrett-Lehigh Building, Saturday March 13, 1999. For tickets please call (212) 753 1722. Corporate Sponsor *Artemide*

ARCHITECTURAL LEAGUE OF NEW YORK *LIGHT YEARS* POSTER / Pentagram: Michael Bierut; design, Nicole Trice / USA, 1999

The Spiritual Double

The subject of issue no. 133 of the Walker Art Center's › 345 *Design Quarterly* (1986) was April Greiman › 179, which she was invited to design herself. As Greiman recalls, almost a year passed between the invitation and the final product—six months alone in deciding what to do with the opportunity. Opting out of the typical 32-page format of the magazine, Greiman created a single 6 × 2-foot poster that showed her naked, in actual size, overlayed with smaller images, a timeline, questions, and quotes—even a second portrait added at the last minute showing her new hairdo. Greiman explored and stretched the incoming technology of the Macintosh as far as she could: working with a Macvision video digitizer, spending months compositing on MacDraw, and printing out the result on a LaserWriter, the first laser printer compatible with Macintosh. In its excessive imagery, layering, and information, this poster represents an antithesis to design's dedication to minimizing visual clutter and signaled a transition into the effervescent design that later characterized postmodernism.

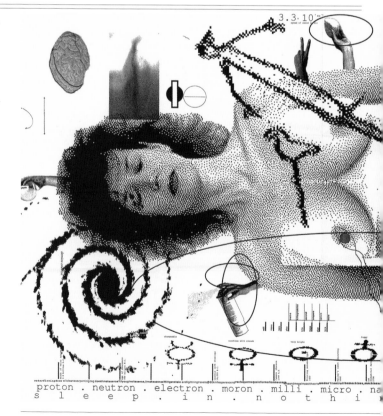

DESIGN QUARTERLY NO. 133 FOR THE WALKER ART CENTER / April Greiman / USA, 1986

King Kong and Godzilla

In commemoration of the fortieth anniversary of the atomic bombing of Hiroshima, designers were asked to develop posters as part of a traveling exhibition, *Images for Survival*, a gift to the Museum of Modern Art in Hiroshima. Encouraging reconciliation between the United States and Japan, Steff Geissbuhler ›157 interpreted these two giants as Godzilla and King Kong, hand in hand, walking into the sunset, which is optimistically rendered as Japan's flag.

PEACE **POSTER** / Steff Geissbuhler / USA, 1985

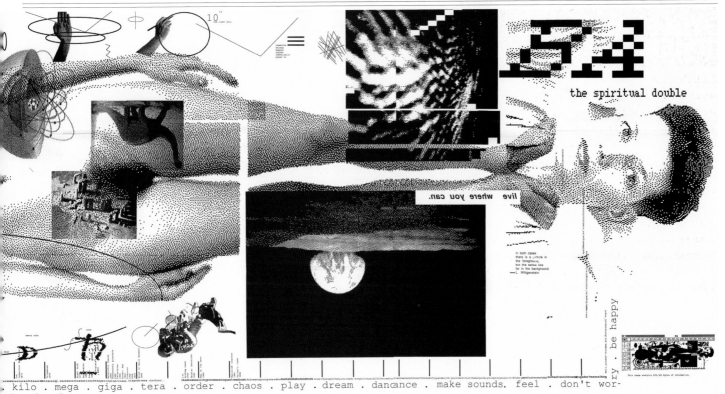

Chicago: The Musical

As a revival of the 1975 Broadway production and a precedent for the 2002 movie, *Chicago: The Musical* is the longest-running musical revival, with more than 4,500 performances in New York and 15,000 worldwide since its opening in November 1996. With stark, minimalist set and costume design, Drew Hodges, founder and creative director of SpotCo, an advertising agency specializing in the entertainment industry, devised a campaign that showcased and dramatized this minimalist aesthetic while selling the idea of a sexy, tantalizing, energetic show through black-and-white photography—shot by fashion photographer Max Vadukul—in spliced layouts, punctuated by the now instantly recognizable *Chicago* logo, which was built from samples found in Rob Roy Kelly's *American Wood Types* › 72.

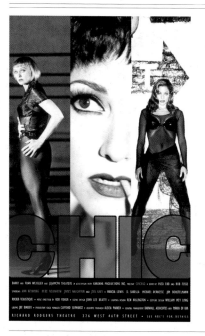

CHICAGO: THE MUSICAL BRANDING / SpotCo: art direction, Drew Hodges, Vinny Sainato; design, Jay Cooper; photography, Max Vadukul, Len Prince, Richie Fahey; producer, Mark Rheault / USA, 1997–2008

OBEY
(1989-Present)

Appearing in a spontaneous and combustive manner, stickers featuring the photocopied face of the enormous (now deceased) wrestler Andre the Giant, accompanied by the tagline "Andre the Giant Has a Posse" plus his stature and weight, appeared nationwide during the early 1990s. The first batch of stickers was created by Shepard Fairey, then a student at Rhode Island School of Design ›134; he was demonstrating to a skateboarder colleague how to do paper-cut stencils, happened upon an image of the wrestler in the newspaper, and adopted it as the mascot for their group of skateboarders. Their freshly printed stickers from Kinko's spread all over the world and blossomed into a globally recognizable image and language.

In 1993, Titan Sports, Inc. (now World Wrestling Entertainment, Inc.), threatened to pursue legal action against Fairey for using Andre the Giant's name and image, which they owned, sparking Fairey to create the stylized version of the wrestler's face paired with the mandate "OBEY"—a trademark Fairey now owns. Using this new icon, Fairey and countless cohorts have pasted "OBEY" posters around the world. It has served as the foundation for dozens of derivatives Fairey built on its dramatic aesthetic—to the chagrin of critics, by appropriating historical imagery from Russian, Chinese, European, and American activist artists. "OBEY," like many of the iconic brands it's meant to mock and defy, has become one of the most recognizable icons of recent time.

ANDRE THE GIANT HAS A POSSE STICKER / USA / **Photo: Kylie Johnson**

OBEY POSTER ON A DUMPSTER / Canada / **Photo: Tanja Niggendijker**

OBEY POSTER ON A JUNKYARD WALL / USA / **Photo: Jeanne Lopez**

Set the Twilight Reeling

Set the Twilight Reeling is an acutely personal album by Lou Reed, something Stefan Sagmeister › 202 was able to convey through the design by meshing lyrics and artist. The artist's distress is readily apparent in the close-up portrait overlaid with hand-drawn lettering, not unlike scribbling doodles or a brooding mind. Here, the lyrics take center stage while the record information recedes into the background.

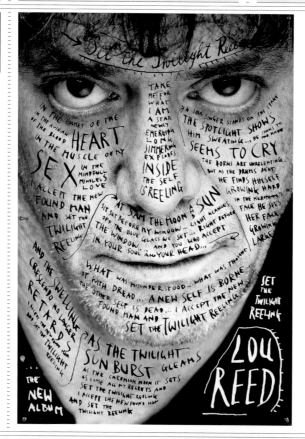

SET THE TWILIGHT REELING POSTER FOR WARNER BROS. MUSIC, INC. / Sagmeister, Inc.: art direction, Stefan Sagmeister; photography, Timothy Greenfield Sanders / USA, 1996

AIGA Detroit

After eight hours of tedious work by Martin Woodtli, the intern at the time, and incremental pain as sustained by Stefan Sagmeister › 202, an iconic poster was carved into design history. While the use of the poster in itself was of a small scale—to announce a lecture for the Detroit chapter of AIGA and Cranbrook Academy of Art › 130—its impact quickly extended through the design community. The audacity of its designer, the poster's sexuality, and its personal stand all added fuel to its shock value.

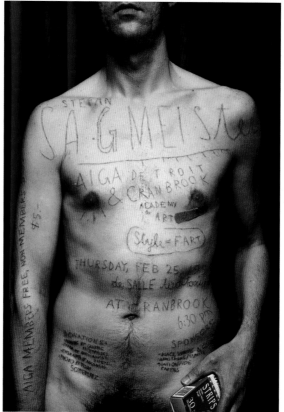

AIGA DETROIT POSTER / Sagmeister, Inc.: art direction, Stefan Sagmeister; photography, Tom Schierlitz; skin etching, Martin Woodtli / USA, 1999

Apartheid/ Racisme

For more than 40 years, South Africa suffered under the racial segregation of the National Party's apartheid system, which made discrimination against nonwhites legal. In 1986, the Rencontre Nationale contre l'Apartheid (National Gathering Against Apartheid) was formed in France to support the abolition of apartheid and mobilize the public to take action—and the group used the power of the poster to communicate the message. Pierre Bernard, one of the founders of Grapus—a collective founded with François Miehe and Gérard Paris-Clavel that focused on creating socially conscious work, including a remarkable collection of streetbound posters—designed a strikingly resonant poster for the cause. Drawn with a black Pentel pen and ink in the familiar structure of a didactic map, the image, which at first glance looks like a skull, is meant to portray Africa as a human face missing its chin because of cancer, which Bernard likens to apartheid. The filled-in counterspaces of the words are not just a stylistic mannerism; rather, they are filled with the missing "flesh" of the face, of Africa.

APARTHEID/RACISME **POSTER** / **Pierre Bernard** / **France, 1986**

Racism

In August 1991, the Crown Heights neighborhood in Brooklyn, New York, was rattled by four days of riots between its Jewish and African-American residents, ignited by a car accident in which Yosef Lifsh struck a young Guyanese boy. Two years later, during the race for New York City mayor, Rudolph Giuliani used the riots as a key issue against his competitor, Mayor David Dinkins, questioning his management, or lack thereof, of the situation. The news was awash again in this polemic, the term racism thoroughly aired in the media and designer James Victore took notice. This poster was his response, hoping to instill gravitas back into the word. On February 26, 1993, while on press at Ambassador Arts, Inc., for this poster, Victore heard the news of the World Trade Center bombing and immediately heard the police and fire truck sirens blaring down Eleventh avenue. The poster was put up in Brooklyn soon after, giving it an enhanced timeliness.

RACISM **POSTER** / **James Victore** / **USA, 1993**

PUBLIC SERVICE AIDS POSTER PROMOTING THE USE OF CONDOMS / Art Chantry /
USA, 1997

THURSDAY POETRY READINGS POSTER FOR BIBLIO'S IN NEW YORK / Alexander
Gelman / USA, 1995

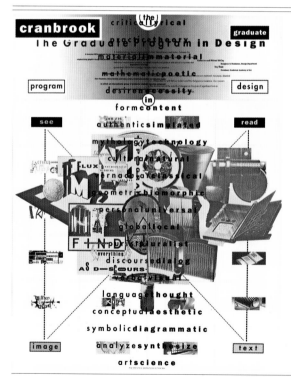

CRANBROOK DESIGN POSTER / Where McCoy layers student projects with a
communications theory diagram and a listing of polemic oppositions / Katherine
McCoy / USA, 1989

KNOLL *HOT SEAT* POSTER / This poster served a dual purpose—as an invitation for a
special chili cook-off and to introduce a new seating collection by Bill Stephens for
Knoll / Woody Pirtle / USA, 1982

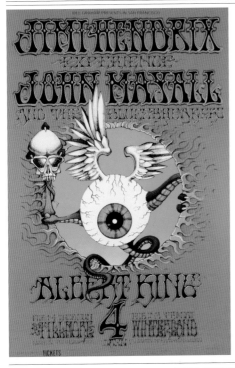

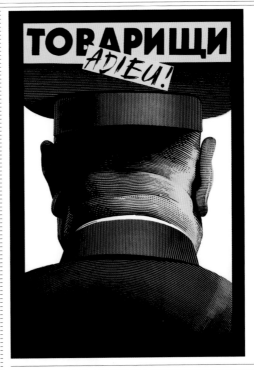

FOR A JIMI HENDRIX, JOHN MAYALL, AND ALBERT KING SHOW, GRIFFIN'S PSYCHEDELIC TRADEMARKS—THE SUNGLASS-WEARING SKULL AND THE EYEBALL—GAIN CENTER STAGE / Richard Griffin / USA, 1968

COMRADES, IT'S OVER! POSTER FOR THE HUNGARIAN DEMOCRATIC FORUM, AS THE COUNTRY EMBRACED DEMOCRACY / A year later, the poster was translated into Russian / Istvan Orosz / Hungary, 1989

MEXICAN MUSEUM TWENTIETH ANNIVERSARY POSTER FOR BACCHUS PRESS / Jennifer Morla, Craig Bailey / USA, 1995

WITH THE GROWING ATTRACTION OF ALL THINGS ATHLETIC, THE EXHIBITION *SPORTDE-SIGN* AT THE MUSEUM FÜR GESTALTUNG ZÜRICH DELVES INTO THE SOCIAL, *CULTURAL,* AND TECHNICAL ASPECTS OF THE EAGER AMATEUR AND THE PROFESSIONAL ARENAS / Martin Woodtli / Switzerland, 2004

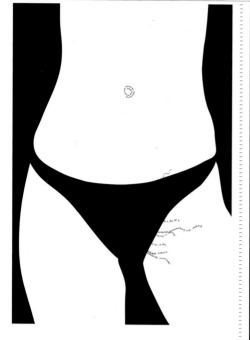

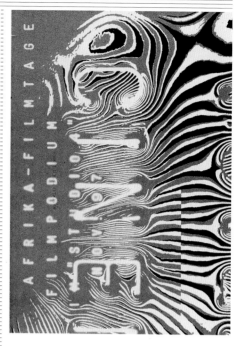

CLOTHING COLLECTION POSTER FOR LABORATORY FOR SOCIAL AND AESTHETIC DEVELOPMENT / Fons Hickmann / Germany, 2002

CIUDAD JUÁREZ: 300 WOMEN KILLED, 500 WOMEN MISSING POSTER / Alejandro Magallanes / Mexico, 1997

THE CINEMAFRICA FILM FESTIVAL PROMOTES FILMS MADE BY AFRICANS IN ORDER TO BRING AWARENESS TO THE CURRENT REALITY OF THE CONTINENT / Ralph Schraivogel / Sweden, 2007

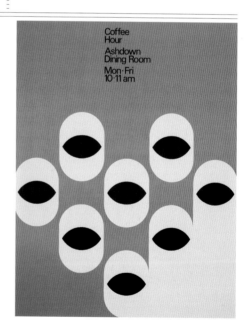

SOUNDING: PAUL EARLS, COMPOSER, FELLOW, CENTER FOR ADVANCED VISUAL STUDIES POSTER / Printed black on metallic paper, the reproduction shows the actual item's imperfections and glare

ART AND ENVIRONMENT: THREE FORUMS SPONSORED BY THE CENTER FOR ADVANCED VISUAL STUDIES POSTER, Kresge Little Theatre

COFFEE HOUR POSTER

Massachusetts Institute of Technology event posters / MIT Office of Design Services: design director, Jacqueline Casey / USA, 1972

JOHNNY CASH SHOW POSTER / Hatch Show Print: Jim Sherraden / USA, 1967

FUCKING A, A CONTEMPORARY TAKE ON THE SCARLET LETTER, POSTER / Pentagram: Paula Scher / USA, 2002

BIC BIROS ADVERTISING POSTER / Ruedi Külling / Switzerland, 1970

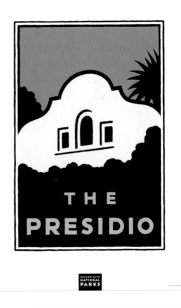

THE GOLDEN GATE NATIONAL PARKS POSTER SERIES / creative direction, Rich Silverstein; art direction, Jami Spittler; design and illustration, Michael Schwab / USA, 1996

SUBWAY MAPS

Subway maps present a tough design problem: devising the simplest and most accessible design representation of a complex system. In addition, the maps must convey a multitude of functions, from connections to the physical location of stations, and be understood by thousands of commuters every day. Luckily, Harry Beck (né Henry C. Beck), an engineering draftsman employed with the London Transport, solved this problem more than 70 years ago, and his solution is the foundation for many of today's subway maps.

In 1908, Frank Pick was appointed publicity officer for the London Underground › 346, and in the following two decades he drastically improved the system's uncoordinated presentation, communication, advertising, and signage. He commissioned some of the era's most influential artists, like Man Ray, to create artwork for the Underground's advertising, and calligrapher Edward Johnston to develop a unifying typeface in 1916. The resulting Johnston Sans typeface was used throughout the system and advertising and, of course, became part of the visual landscape of London, still visible today.

Johnston also redesigned the famed roundel logo for the Underground in 1918.

In 1933, the London Underground was merged with other underground railway companies, tramways, and bus companies, forming the London Passenger Transport Board (known as the London Transport), and Pick was appointed its managing director. With an increasingly complex underground service, Pick commissioned Beck to design a map. Beck solved the problem by ignoring the geography above ground and focusing instead on

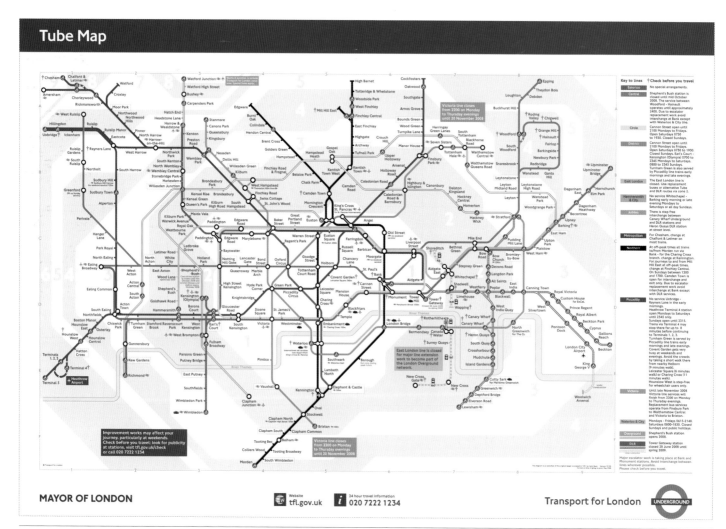

LONDON UNDERGROUND MAP / Harry C. Beck / UK, 1933 / **Version shown: 2008**

establishing the relationship between stations; the only sense of place or scale included was an abstraction of the River Thames. Set solely in 90- and 45-degree angles, the map depicted the different lines by assigning each one color, and the stations were clearly marked by small nibs protruding from the lines. As the city and underground system has evolved, so too has the map, but the original design is still in use.

Almost 40 years later, in 1970, on the other side of the Atlantic, Massimo Vignelli › 160 was working on a comprehensive signage system for New York's subway through the Metropolitan Transit Authority. Vignelli, with Unimark International at the time, redesigned the existing subway

map, designed by George Salomon in 1959. Like Beck's, Vignelli's map used strictly 90- and 45-degree lines, color-coded lines, and a geographical abstraction of the city above the subway—Central Park, for example, was rendered as a square, instead of the 3-to-1 ratio it actually is. Unlike Beck's map, Vignelli's did not last long in its service to commuters, mostly due to its liberties with the geography, and it was replaced in 1979 by an anatomically correct map, still in use today.

As part of a five-year relationship with the Transportation Authority of Berlin (BVG), Erik Spiekermann › 226, with MetaDesign in 1992, designed a thorough corporate identity and

signage project that unified every aspect of the transportation system, from subway to light rail to buses, including the design of all related maps. While the other maps required slightly different approaches, the subway map was a new interpretation of Beck's design, utilizing the same design principles and foregoing geographical accuracy, without complaints from government or commuters. From these examples, it may be possible to conclude that Europeans have a more acute understanding of spatial relationships than New Yorkers do.

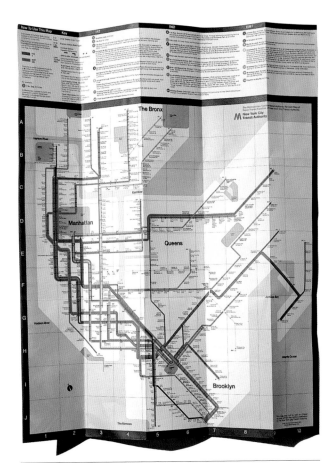

NEW YORK CITY SUBWAY MAP / **Unimark International: Massimo Vignelli** / **USA, 1970**

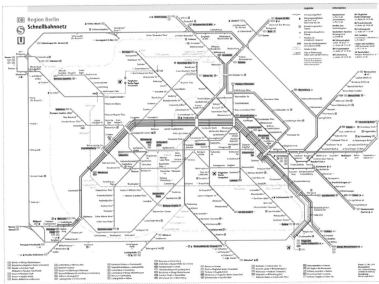

BERLIN SUBWAY MAP / **MetaDesign: Erik Spiekermann** / **Germany, 1992**

Uncomplicated products for a clean and happy pet

Mrs. MEYER'S
CLEAN DAY

AROMATHERAPEUTIC Pet Products contain all natural essential oils which provide a special singular fragrance for your four-legged friends.

Herbs **CLARY SAGE** and **CHAMOMILE** are soothing and **CALMING** for your dear pet and have

CLARY SAGE CHAMOMILE SCENT

a distinctively **WARM** and **HERBAL** fragrance. & very **GENTLE & NICE** for you and your pet.

OATMEAL PET SHAMPOO

DIRECTIONS: Sparky may not like getting a bath, but sometimes he needs one! Wet him down and lather him up, then rinse well. Oatmeal extract is gentle and soothing, while Vitamin E helps promote a shiny coat. Isn't that nice?

16 FLUID OUNCES 473 ML

Mrs. MEYER'S
CLEAN DAY

AROMATHERAPEUTIC Pet Products
a natural essential oils provide a sp
ce for your four-legged frien

CLARY SAGE
CHAMOMILE
soothing and
ing for your
pet, has

CLARY SAGE CHAMOMILE SCENT

WAR HERB
fragra
GENTLE & NICE
you and

FRESHENING SPRAY

8 FLUID OUNCES 236 ML

Uncomplicated products for a clean and happy pet

Mrs. MEYER'S
CLEAN DAY

AROMATHERAPEUTIC Pet Products
All natural essential oils provide a special fragrance for your four-legged friends.

CLARY SAGE CHAMOMILE, soothing, and **CALMING** for your dear pet, has a

CLARY SAGE CHAMOMILE SCENT

distinctive **WARM & HERBAL** fragrance, so **GENTLE & NICE** for you and your pet.

ODOR REMOVING CARPET CLEANER

DIRECTIONS: Spray Spot's spot, but don't saturate. Let it set 1-2 minutes. Blot gently (don't rub!). Rinse area with a wet cloth or sponge when stain is removed. Really tough stains might need multiple treatments.

22 FLUID OUNCES 649 ML

PRACTICE
On Shelves

274
Books

From simple paperbacks to sturdy hardcovers to opulent coffee-table specimens, books remain one of the most consistent sources for rich visual, tactile, and intellectual experiences— and one of the most pleasurable challenges for graphic designers, whether the job is a book jacket or a cover-to-cover design. As miniature posters, book covers have long fascinated designers for their challenge to create something not only memorable and gripping but also able to serve as a visual megaphone in service of the content, giving the viewer an immediate sense of the entire book. And the prospect of designing an internal structure to deliver text and imagery across hundreds of pages through considerate pacing, is even more pleasurable when the daunting task of composing all the material takes its final form.

298
Music

Perhaps this is not a universal experience, but the majority of graphic designers will merrily admit that the album covers that accompanied their youth had something to do with their desire or inclination to design, and although not all of them have album covers to their credit, the zeal to give visual form to ideas was most likely bred in lengthy listening sessions. It's fair to acknowledge that album covers do not exert the same influence they once did as the work has transitioned—both in size and social context— from 12-inch LPs to 5-inch jewel cases browsed through in music stores among fellow listeners to 72-dpi digital images online browsed through solo in a computer. So it is with a slight sense of nostalgia that the profession constantly remembers the individual designers or in-house groups at different labels that gave shape to the cultural force music can be.

A note on the artwork in this section: While it would be ideal to show the artwork as it was originally released, specifically for LPs, acquiring such work is sometimes prohibitive. In these cases, the CD version of the work, which may be slightly different, is shown.

306
Consumer Goods

With literally dozens of choices for every type of product, be it a rudimentary necessity or a luxurious indulgence, and sometimes with only vaguely varying degrees of quality separating them, the manner in which these products are presented and packaged becomes increasingly important as the defining differentiator; this phenomenon affords graphic designers the opportunity to influence consumers at the critical point-of-purchase. The physical attributes of a product—its shape, its label, the box or bag it comes in—can be as important as the product itself in building a bond with the consumer and catapulting it into being the first or only choice among the competition.

MRS. MEYER'S CLEAN DAY IDENTITY AND PACKAGING FOR CLEAN & COMPANY LLC / Werner Design Werks, Inc.: design, Sharon Werner, Sarah Nelson / USA, 2001

Penguin Books

First published in 1935 under the helm of British publisher The Bodley Head, its managing director, Allen Lane, began Penguin Books as a way to provide affordable, good-quality paperbacks of fiction and nonfiction reprints. With ten titles in its original offering, the paperbacks launched with the deceptively simple and now iconic covers designed by 21-year-old Edward Young: three horizontal bars—the top and bottom color-coded (orange for fiction, green for crime, dark blue for biography)—sandwiching a white bar—one bar holding the Penguin Books cartouche, the next one the title and author, set in Gill Sans › 370, and the last one the habitat for its logo › 346, a penguin, also designed by Young. With its initial success, Penguin Books became independent in 1936, and by 1937 the company had sold three million paperbacks—marking only the beginning of a torrent of titles under numerous collections and imprints that generated a voluminous number of infinitely varied and memorable book covers diverging from the original.

Penguin Books' covers have evolved with the appointment of different creative leaders. Most significant was Jan Tschichold's › 140 post–World War II reign from 1947 to 1949, when he was brought in to coalesce the

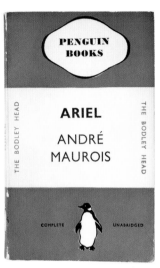

Clockwise

WITHOUT MY CLOAK, Kate O'Brien / UK, 1949

ARIEL, André Maurois / UK, 1935

EXPLOSIVES, John Read / UK, 1942

SAILING, Peter Heaton / UK, 1949

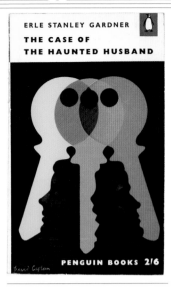

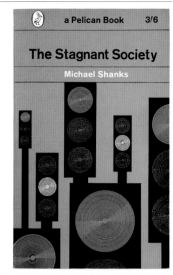

THE GREAT ESCAPE, Paul Brickhill /
illustration, Abram Games / UK, 1957

THE CASE OF THE HAUNTED HUSBAND,
Erle Stanley Gardner / illustration,
David Caplan / UK, 1957

FLAMES IN THE SKY, Pierre Clostermann /
illustration, Abram Games / UK, 1958

THE STAGNANT SOCIETY, Michael
Shanks / Germano Facetti / UK, 1964

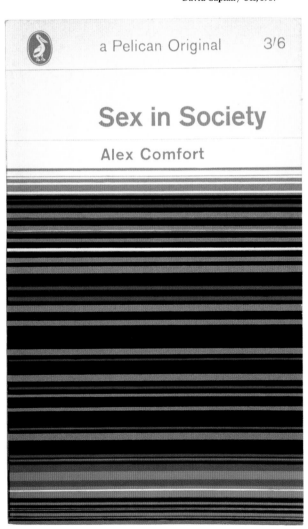

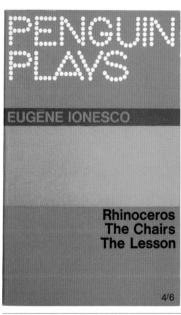

MAN AND SUPERMAN, George Bernard Shaw /
Denise York / UK, 1965

RHINOCEROS, THE CHAIRS, THE LESSON,
Eugène Ionesco / Denise York / UK, 1967

SEX IN SOCIETY, Alex Comfort /
Jock Kinneir / UK, 1964

growing library and its diminishing print and production standards. Tschichold overhauled every aspect of the paperbacks, from the cover to the inside text to the logo, and through the *Penguin Composition Rules* document he ensured that printers and typesetters abided by the new standards. Others have taken the covers in different directions, sometimes literally. Hans Schmoller, who took over Tschichold, oversaw the implementation of a vertical cover grid in 1951. In 1957, Schmoller invited Abram Games to design a range of full-color covers with a new layout. In 1961, art director Germano Facetti, with a new cover grid by Romek Barber, redesigned the crime and classics series and made wider use of commissioned photography and illustrations. Alan Aldridge, put in charge of fiction covers in 1965, took an eclectic approach that veered completely away from previous consistency and treated each cover separately—although his science fiction covers were unified by a black background, purple typography, and his own wild illustrations.

Aldridge left in 1967. After a year without a fiction art director, Penguin Books hired David Pelham, who brought a versatile layer of consistency—chiefly the logo on either top corner of the book and standard designs for the spines and back covers—that then allowed interpretations for the cover

TERMINAL BEACH, J.G. Ballard / illustration, David Pelham / UK, 1974

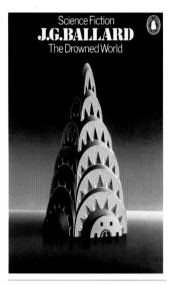

DROWNED WORLD, J.G. Ballard / illustration, David Pelham / UK, 1976

THE MERCHANT OF VENICE, William Shakespeare / illustration, Paul Hogarth / UK, 1980

PERICLES, William Shakespeare / illustration, Paul Hogarth / UK, 1986

FRANKENSTEIN, Mary Shelley / Pentagram: Angus Hyland; photography, SMK Foto / UK, 2003

LATER ROMAN EMPIRE, Ammianus Marcellinus, selected and edited by Walter Hamilton / Pentagram: Angus Hyland; photography, Art Archive / Dagli Orti / UK, 2004

MEDITATIONS, Marcus Aurelius, translated by Maxwell Staniforth / Phil Baines / UK, 2004

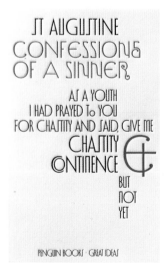

CONFESSIONS OF A SINNER, St. Augustine, translated by R.S. Pine-Coffin / Catherine Dixon / UK, 2004

art and typography. Although certain authors were given a specific design that carried over several titles, the consistency that had distinguished Penguin Books slowly disappeared into the 1980s and 1990s.

As a twenty-first-century publisher, Penguin Books competes in an increasingly design-conscious market populated by covers of outstanding quality, and its fiction and nonfiction covers, under the direction of Jim Stoddart, now run a wide gamut defined by the marketing and creative needs of each title, and many different designers are hired for the individual jobs. Special collections like the Modern Classics in 2000 by freelance designer Jamie Keenan, the Penguin Classics in 2003 by Pentagram's ›162 Angus Hyland, and the deliciously tactile Great Ideas in 2004 by David Pearson briefly evince Penguin's original approach, but with its massive reach and a concern with design since the beginning, Penguin Books is a constant and influential public mirror of the growth and evolution of the disciplines and practice of printing, design, art direction, photography, illustration, and book publishing itself.

THE INNER LIFE, Thomas Kempis / Penguin: David Pearson / UK, 2004

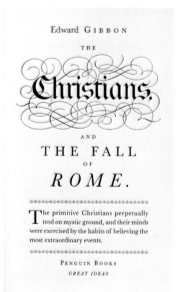

THE CHRISTIANS AND THE FALL OF ROME, Edward Gibbon / Phil Baines / UK, 2004

CIVILIZATIONS AND ITS DISCONTENTS, Sigmund Freud / Penguin: David Pearson / UK, 2004

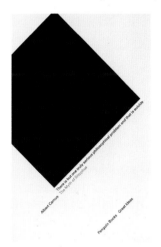

THE SYMPOSIUM, Plato / Penguin: David Pearson / UK, 2005

THE MYTH OF SISYPHUS, Albert Camus / Penguin: David Pearson / UK, 2005

THE WORK OF ART IN THE AGE OF MECHANICAL REPRODUCTION, Walter Benjamin / Penguin: David Pearson / UK, 2008

BOOKS V. CIGARETTES, George Orwell / Penguin: David Pearson / UK, 2008

New Directions

Established in 1936 by 22-year-old James Laughlin, New Directions became a haven for poets and writers—like Tennessee Williams, Ezra Pound, and William Carlos Williams—who fell outside the mainstream of literature, as Laughlin printed what other publishers wouldn't. Covers for some of New Directions' earliest work, including annual anthologies of recent writing and poems, were simple and, in contrast to its successors, relatively unattractive, with centered arrangements of serif typography. "A writer friend had told me," recalls Laughlin in his (self-described) auto-bug-offery, *The Way It Wasn't*, "that I ought to investigate a young chap who was doing 'queer things' with type." The young chap was Alvin Lustig › 144, and their first meeting in the late 1930s developed into a 15-year relationship that yielded some of the most iconic and pioneering book covers of the time.

From his first cover for Laughlin—a concoction of metal pieces from his type cases for Henry Miller's *The Wisdom of the Heart* in 1941—Lustig was able to develop, especially as he delved into the New Classics series around 1945, a visual language that, rather than relying on literal translations or representations, was driven by abstract symbols and interpretations of the writers' texts rendered through striking color combinations (typically limited to two or three) and paired rather dexterously with either handlettering or typography. Covers for the Modern Reader series, 1946 to 1955, were similar in philosophy but starkly contrasting in their execution: dramatic, symbolic photography in black and white complemented by more restrained typography. Lustig continued to work on New Directions covers through his blindness, brought on by diabetes, until his death in 1955.

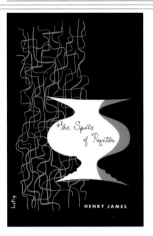

THE SPOILS OF POYNTON, Henry James / New Directions, New Classics / 1943

THREE TALES, Gustave Flaubert / New Directions, New Classics / 1944

EXILES, James Joyce / New Directions, New Classics / 1946

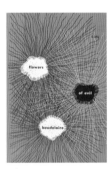

FLOWERS OF EVIL, Charles Baudelaire / New Directions, New Classics / 1946

THE WANDERER, Alain Fournier / New Directions, New Classics / 1946

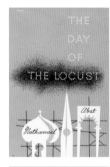

THE DAY OF THE LOCUST, Nathanael West / New Directions, New Classics / 1950

LIGHT IN AUGUST, William Faulkner / New Directions, Modern Reader / 1946

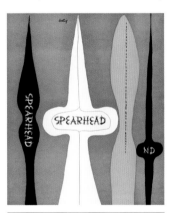

SPEARHEAD / New Directions / 1947

3 TRAGEDIES, Federico García Lorca / New Directions, Modern Reader / 1948

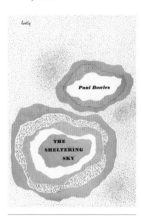

THE SHELTERING SKY, Paul Bowles / New Directions / 1948

Alvin Lustig / USA

Zone Books

When Bruce Mau › 201 started his firm, Bruce Mau Design (BMD), in Toronto in 1985, one of his first projects was designing *Zone 1|2: The Contemporary City*, the inaugural double issue of the independent publisher Urzone, established that same year. This was the beginning of a relationship that thrived on the cerebral combination of the books' topics and their design. With the success of *Zone 1|2*, Urzone initiated an ambitious publishing program, and over the next 15 years BMD designed every single book, now a collection of more than 50 titles, as well as Zone Books' catalogs and marketing materials—allowing Zone, as noted in Mau's *Life Style*, to "explore certain terrain that would not have been accessible in the higgledy-piggledy production hierarchies of conventional publishing."

Updating Jan Tschichold's *Penguin Composition Rules*, BMD developed a set of conceptual design strategies that characterized many of the books. The "image weave," for the Zone Readers series, featured two images that could be seen simultaneously; the "Zone morph" drew 380 interpolations of the word *Zone* in different typefaces for the running heads; the "constant tonal length," considers the full body of text as a long piece of string that fluctuates when a single part changes. In isolation, these may seem farfetched conceits, but in the context of the body of work they form a uniquely designed set of books. BMD also went to great lengths in designing the physicality of the books, creating unique paper stocks or formulating the perfect ink, like "Zone Black," which had enough density to print richly on uncoated paper. By engaging in a lengthy and committed relationship, Zone Books and BMD were able to form a fluctuating identity hinged on the liaison between content and form.

ASSORTED *ZONE* COVERS / Zone Books / Bruce Mau Design / Canada

MATTER AND MEMORY, Henri Bergson; Translated by N.M. Paul and W.S. Palmer / Zone Books / Bruce Mau Design / Canada, 1991

ZONE 6: INCORPORATIONS, edited by Jonathan Crary and Sanford Kwinter / Zone Books / Bruce Mau Design / Canada, 1992

ACCURSED SHARE, VOLUME 1: CONSUMPTION, Georges Bataille; translation, Robert Hurley / Zone Books / Bruce Mau Design / Canada, 1991

SAMPLES OF THE ZONE MORPH, AN INTERPOLATION OF TYPEFACES LIKE BODONI, DIN, AND FUTURA THAT RESULTED IN 380 NEW TYPOGRAPHIC TREATMENTS, ONE FOR EACH PAGE OF *ZONE 6: INCORPORATIONS* / Bruce Mau Design / Canada, 1992

ZONE 1|2: THE CONTEMPORARY CITY, edited by Michel Feher and Sanford Kwinter / Zone Books / Bruce Mau Design / Canada, 1985

McSweeney's

In 1998, Dave Eggers published the first issue of the literary journal *McSweeney's Quarterly Concern* as a collection of magazine-rejected work, and in both its endearing design naiveté and forgivable technical scarcity it established a visual aesthetic that contrasted brightly with the visual excess of the web-driven tail end of the 1990s. The first issues were designed by Eggers himself—an accomplished writer, as attested to by his acclaimed *A Heartbreaking Work of Staggering Genius*, but not nearly an equally celebrated graphic designer—who chose Garamond 3 as the publication's default typeface, later to become its signature typeface. McSweeney's website, launched in 1999, boldly stated on its "About Us" page, "Design: Nothing will be designed"; as in the *Quarterly*, the prickly content and writing steered the design and commanded all the attention.

Between 2000 and 2001 the *Quarterly*, now with support by freelance designer Elizabeth Kairys, began a steep and lauded climb in production values. First it was loose booklets in a box; then, alternate dustjackets, rubber bands, foil stamping on cloth spines, faux-leather covers, and numerous folds, pockets, and flaps turned these books into objects worth keeping. In 2002, Eli Horowitz joined Eggers as managing editor—and second designer-without-formal-training—of McSweeney's, which was now publishing, along with the *Quarterly*, books and a new magazine, *The Believer*. The slowly growing library of books, by authors like David Byrne, Michael Chabon, and Nick Hornby, have received the same treatment as the *Quarterly* and have been lusciously produced and designed despite—or perhaps because of—Eggers's and Horowitz's blissful ignorance of the rules and principles of graphic design.

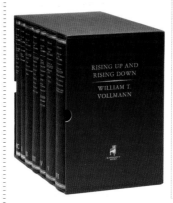

RISING UP AND RISING DOWN, William T. Vollmann / McSweeney's: design, Dave Eggers / USA, 2003

MCSWEENEY'S ISSUE 3 / McSweeney's: design, Dave Eggers / USA, 1999

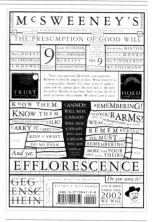

MCSWEENEY'S ISSUE 9 / McSweeney's: design, Dave Eggers / USA, 2002

ALL KNOWN METAL BANDS, Dan Nelson / McSweeney's: design, Alvaro Villanueva, Dan Nelson, Eli Horowitz, Autumn Wharton / USA, 2008

MCSWEENEY'S ISSUE 27 / Cover art for the stories-booklet portion / McSweeney's: artist, Scott Teplin / USA, 2008

MCSWEENEY'S ISSUE 17 / McSweeney's: design, Dave Eggers, Brian McMullen (Pantalaine and Yeti Researcher portions) / USA, 2005

MAPS AND LEGENDS, Michael Chabon / McSweeney's: design, Dave Eggers, Eli Horowitz, Jordan Crane; cover and jacket illustration, Jordan Crane / USA, 2008

THE PEOPLE OF PAPER, Salvador Plascencia / McSweeney's: design, Salvador Plascencia, Eli Horowitz, Rachell Sumpter; cover illustration, Rachell Sumpter / USA, 2005

Photos: Joseph McDonald

Pocket Canons

Conceived by Matthew Darby and published by Scottish publishing house Canongate Books in 1997, the Pocket Canons presented 12 (of the 66) books from the King James Bible in a significantly contemporary approach. Each book, sold separately in pocket book form, featured an introduction by popular figures from the world of contemporary culture, from writer Will Self to musician Nick Cave—igniting controversy that atheists and Buddhists, not Christians, were penning them. The Pocket Canons were packaged, by biblical standards, unconventionally as well.

Designed by Angus Hyland from Pentagram's ›162 London office as if they were covers for modern works of fiction, each book uses a single, stark black-and-white photograph culled from existing stock photography that

alludes to its content: a nuclear explosion, the equivalent of a modern-day Armageddon, for Revelation; a reflective body of water for Genesis; a winding road for Exodus; and, perhaps too obvious not to, a whale, for Jonah. The title of each book is set in lowercase neon-orange Univers ›372, further modernizing the centuries-old texts, now available for 1 sterling pound (US$1.70 at the time) each. The series was successful, triggering a second print run in Britain (totaling 900,000 copies in circulation) and more than a dozen other countries purchasing rights to translate and distribute. In 1999, Canongate Books released a second series with 12 more books—including an introduction from the rock band U2's singer, Bono—also designed by Pentagram. And in 2005 they released *Revelations: Personal Responses to the Books of the Bible*, an anthology of all the introductions—it was not designed by Pentagram.

THE POCKET CANONS BOOK DESIGN FOR CANONGATE BOOKS / Pentagram: Angus Hyland / UK, 1997–1999 / **Photo: Nick Turner**

The Medium Is the Massage

Canadian writer, scholar, critic, media theorist (and myriad other nouns) Marshall McLuhan had a remarkable facility to construct small bursts of words and sentences, often referred to as *McLuhanisms*, like "The future of the book is the blurb," or "Art is whatever you can get away with," and in 1964, in the pages of *Understanding Media: The Extensions of Man*, he coined the expression "The medium is the message." He posited that the medium—everything from television to railways to light bulbs—regardless and independent of the content it is meant to deliver has its own messages and is as much responsible for changes in human affairs as its content. In 1967, the famous McLuhanism was meant to be the title for *The Medium Is the Massage: An Inventory of Effects*, except that a typesetter error rendered "Message" as "Massage"—an error McLuhan was rather pleased with and approved to publish.

The Medium Is the Massage is not a book by McLuhan but rather a collection of excerpts from his writings and statements, selected and organized by graphic designer Quentin Fiore and author, editor, and book packager Jerome Agel. Through extreme crops of photography, changes in typographic scale, and repetition of elements, Fiore, who had worked as a lettering artist for Lester Beall › 146 and then established his own design practice, introduced a highly kinetic structure that, perhaps oxymoronically, was rigorously executed through a simple grid and the consistent deployment of Akzidenz Grotesk › 369. Seventeen publishers turned down the opportunity to publish *The Medium Is the Massage* before Bantam Books published it as a paperback. The initial run of 35,000 was quickly followed by two equal runs, and the book eventually sold close to a million copies worldwide.

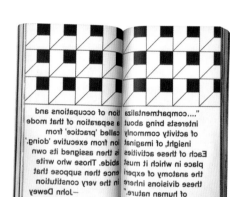

THE MEDIUM IS THE MASSAGE: AN INVENTORY OF EFFECTS, Marshall McLuhan, Quentin Fiore / Bantam Books / USA, 1967

S, M, L, XL

In theory, *S, M, L, XL* was 264 pages designed and finished in 265 days, but in practice, the collaboration of Dutch architect Rem Koolhaas and designer Bruce Mau ›201 engorged to 1,344 pages and finished in 1,185 days (five years). Released in 1995 as a monograph of Koolhaas and the work of his firm, Office for Metropolitan Architecture (OMA), *S, M, L, XL* went well beyond the expectations and traditions of an architect's monograph. Chiefly, the book doesn't revolve around the 30-plus houses, buildings, and urbanism projects selected but instead is a windmill of discordantly harmonious text and images, with projects organized not by sector, discipline, or chronological order but by size: from small (houses and villas) to extra-large (urban planning).

S, M, L, XL is also unusual in that, despite being a monograph on Koolhaas, its designer is given as much credit as its subject, both literally and figuratively: Other than Koolhaas's name being printed in color, Mau's name is given equal billing, and the book is associated as much with its delivery as with its content. Clad in a selection of relatively austere typefaces—Times New Roman ›385, Bell Gothic, and Monotype Grotesque—the book presents Koolhaas's projects, thoughts, worldviews, and much, *much* more through a comprehensive barrage of distinctly arranged images that range from project drawings to a picture of an eyeball being sliced, all in deadpan layouts. As a connecting thread through the book, an alternative dictionary runs on the left edge of nearly every left-handed page with terms like *Babel*, *confidence*, and *iffy*. *S, M, L, XL* reflects not just the title of the book but also the experience of discovering the smallest details embedded in this extra-large book.

This massive book is a novel about architecture. Conceived by Rem Koolhaas—author of *Delirious New York*—and Bruce Mau—designer of Zone—as a free-fall in the space of the typographic imagination, the book's title, *Small, Medium, Large, Extra-Large*, is also its framework: projects and essays are arranged according to scale. The book combines essays, manifestoes, diaries, fairy tales, travelogues, a book-within-the-book on the contemporary city, with work produced by Koolhaas's Office for Metropolitan Architecture over the past twenty years. This accumulation of words and images illuminates the condition of architecture today—its splendors and miseries—exploring and revealing the corrosive impact of politics, context, the economy, globalization—the world.

MONACELLI PRESS

Small, Medium, Large, Extra-Large
Office for Metropolitan Architecture
Rem Koolhaas with Bruce Mau

S,M,L,XL

O.M.A.
Rem Koolhaas
with **Bruce Mau**

MONACELLI PRESS

S, M, L, XL, Rem Koolhaas, Bruce Mau / Monacelli Press / Bruce Mau Design / Canada, 1995

SHV Think Book 1996-1896

In 1896, a group of eight Dutch trading families founded the Steenkolen Handels-Vereeniging (SHV, or Coal Trade Association) and soon established itself as the leading trader in German coal in Western Europe. During the twentieth century, SHV diversified into oil, transportation, and even consumer retail with the introduction of Makro, a chain of self-service wholesale stores in 1968, now with 33 stores in Europe; today, SHV is one of the largest private trading groups in the world. To commemorate the organization's centenary, its president, Paul Fentener van Vlissingen—who inherited a large shareholding in the company from his father, Frits Fentener van Vlissingen II, whose own father had been one of the founding members—commissioned Dutch book designer Irma Boom ›193, five years in advance, to create a commemorative book.

The brief was completely open-ended and the budget was not necessarily a concern, as van Vlissingen simply asked for something "unusual," musing that whatever it cost, it would certainly be cheaper than opening a new Makro store. Working closely with van Vlissingen and historian Johan Pijnappel, Boom delved into a five-year process. Three and a half of those years were spent on research, unearthing materials from the archives of SHV across Europe; these came together in 2,136 pages weighing nearly 8 pounds and measuring more than 4 inches thick, requiring a steel sheet on the spine to ensure its structure. Organized in reverse chronological order, the book has no page numbers or index. The viewer is coaxed into loosely exploring the book, a seemingly endless juxtaposition of archival imagery and text. The book is a winner of the "Most Beautiful Book in the World" prize awarded at the Leipzig Book Fair.

SHV THINK BOOK 1996-1896 / Irma Boom / Netherlands, 1996

Fackel Wörterbuch: Redensarten

From 1899 to 1936, Karl Kraus, an Austrian writer and journalist, self-published, edited, and authored *Die Fackel* ("The Torch"), a journal he used to launch scathing criticisms of Austrian society, making sure no political leader, artist, or author went unnoticed. Kraus was also highly concerned with language and the implications of every choice or mistake made in its use. Through *Die Fackel*, he regularly attacked other writers for their grammatical shortcomings. In 1999, the Austrian Academy of Sciences published *Fackel Wörterbuch: Redensarten* (Torch Dictionary: Idioms), a selection of 144 entries across 1,056 pages culled from the 37 issues of *Die Fackel*, which totaled more than 30,000 pages. The dictionary's full title, for the record, is *Wörterbuch der Redensarten zu der von Karl Kraus 1899 bis 1936 herausgegebenen Zeitschrift 'Die Fackel.'*

Working with Evelyn Breiteneder and Hanno Biber, literary scientists at the Academy, Los Angeles-based designer and educator Anne Burdick began a two-year collaborative process to structure and design the linguistically and visually complex dictionary. At its most basic, the book is divided in three vertical sections; the middle section carries the bulk of the content, including direct reproductions from *Die Fackel*, and the left and right columns are divided by "documentation texts" that quantify and categorize and "interpretive texts" for editorial commentary. At its most detailed, each entry requires the careful design of nine textual functions, and the essays at the beginning and ending of the book use a complex system of reference and quotation that prompted Burdick to invent a "multilevel system of punctuation." Not being a book designer per se, Burdick was rather surprised when the book won the "Most Beautiful Book in the World" prize at the Leipzig Book Fair after the editors had submitted it.

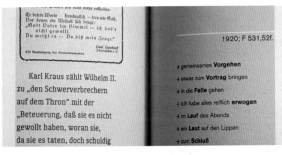

Exploded Entry / Artikel-Schema

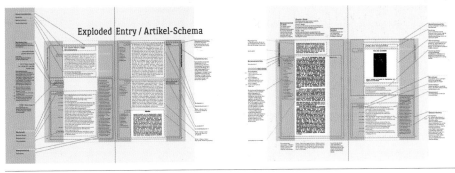

WÖRTERBUCH DER REDENSARTEN ZU DER VON KARL KRAUS 1899 BIS 1936 HERAUSGEGEBENEN ZEITSCHRIFT 'DIE FACKEL,' Karl Kraus, Die Fackel / Österreichischen Akademie der Wissenschaften / design, Anne Burdick; typography consultant, Jens Gelhaar; photography, Susan L. Burdick / USA, 1999

VAS: An Opera in Flatland

Flatland, a satire of the social tropes of Victorian England published in 1884 by prolific author and clergyman Edwin Abbott, is narrated by Square, who talks about his two-dimensional world and describes meeting a sphere from the third dimension, among other story lines. *Flatland* has remained an influential book in literary and mathematical circles, serving as inspiration and reference for numerous authors, among them Steve Tomasula. In 1995, as an extension of another book he was writing, Tomasula began developing *VAS: An Opera in Flatland*, an exploration of genetic engineering and its influence on the body. Taking the characters from *Flatland*, Tomasula tells the story of Square, his wife, Circle, and their daughter, Oval, as the patriarch considers a vasectomy. The book has a kinetic, layered design by Stephen Farrell—who, coincidentally, had earlier written and rendered an essay informed by *Flatland*.

Tomasula and Farrell had worked together in a similar fashion at the literary magazine *Private Arts* and then at *Emigre* › 100. Around 1999, Farrell began giving *VAS* its unconventionally arresting look. The book uses only three spot colors: blood, matched from Farrell's own blood; flesh, based on Crayola's discontinued "flesh" color; and black. The text relies on three type families—Clarendon › 375, Univers › 372, and Cholla—to carry the story's dominant voices, with a number of accent typefaces peppered throughout. Imagery was drawn from various sources: books on evolutionary biology, anthropology, and eugenics, genetics supply catalogs, doll catalogs, and plastic surgery and egg donor websites. Despite its unconventional content, *VAS* found a championing publisher in Barrytown | Station Hill Press, Inc. with additional distribution from Winterhouse Editions. Its first hardcover, published in 2002, sold out promptly. The University of Chicago Press handled the softcover edition, now in its second printing.

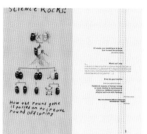

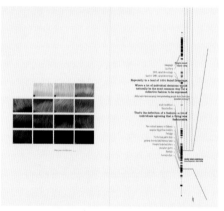
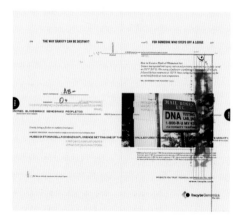
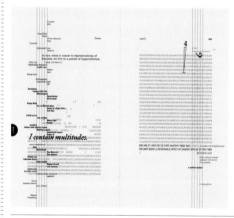
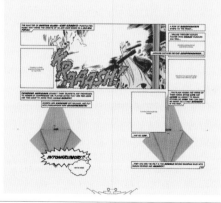

VAS: AN OPERA IN FLATLAND, Steve Tomasula, Stephen Farrell / Barrytown | Station Hill Press, Inc. / art and design, Stephen Farrell / USA, 2002

America (The Book)

As a spinoff from the popular comedy news program *The Daily Show with Jon Stewart*, Warner Books released *America (The Book): A Citizen's Guide to Democracy Inaction*—written by Jon Stewart and the show's motley crew of writers and "correspondents"—a comically ravaging assessment of the United States and its political process in 1994, satirizing everything Americans presumably learned in high school. Shaped and imagined just like a high school textbook, *America (The Book)* was designed by Paula Scher › 182 and her team, Julia Hoffmann and Keith Daigle, at Pentagram's › 162 New York office. The writers, already at work for close to a year, began working with Pentagram with only nine months left in their schedule.

Working collaboratively with them, Scher, Hoffmann, and Daigle developed a visual language and structure that allowed visual manifestations of the text-based jokes, designing charts, timelines, graphs, quizzes, faux documents, and anything else that would elicit a laugh at the expense of America. The book wasn't without challenges, the least of which may have been the more than 50 potential covers presented. The cover eventually selected featured a bald eagle, but as it is legally impossible to photograph these birds (an endangered species), a very (*very*) steep price was paid for a day of shooting a golden eagle. With some patience and wrangling, the photograph was taken with both Stewart and the eagle—a rope holding the eagle was removed in Photoshop. For the infamous graphic showing naked Supreme Court justices, Pentagram turned to a nudist colony in Vermont to supply appropriate poses. The latter joke earned the book a ban from Wal-Mart. But other than that, it was a runaway success, with 2.5 million copies printed by 2005; it spent 49 weeks on the *New York Times* bestseller list, and the subsequent "Teacher's Edition" featured corrections by a "real-life bearded college professor."

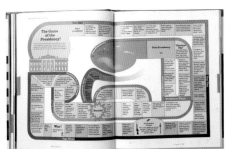

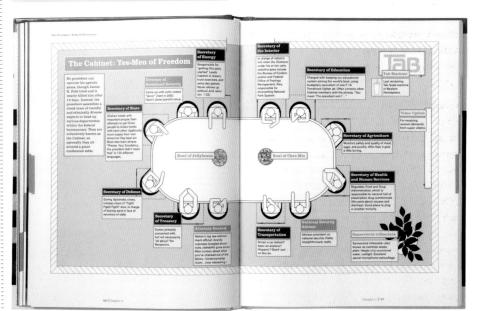

THE DAILY SHOW WITH JON STEWART PRESENTS AMERICA (THE BOOK): A CITIZEN'S GUIDE TO DEMOCRACY INACTION, Jon Stewart and the writers of The Daily Show / Warner Books / Pentagram: Paula Scher; design, Julia Hoffman, Keith Daigle / USA, 2004

FORTY-TWO-LINE BIBLE

Trained as a goldsmith and later developing skills as a gem cutter and metalworker, Johannes Gutenberg was not responsible for the invention of movable type—in one form or another, it had been developed in China centuries before—but for concocting numerous innovations that made it a viable method of production. First was the method for creating metal-cast type: A steel punch, containing the master shape of a letter, is stamped in a softer brass matrix, creating a "positive" that is then placed in a mold (a key aspect of Gutenberg's invention) and filled with a metal alloy (Gutenberg's proprietary formula) to create the type. Then were Gutenberg's improvements on the printing press, derived from wine and cheese presses, which resulted in improved speed and precision. Furthering these advances was not affordable, and Gutenberg

BIBLIA LATINA, 42 LINES FOL. 131V–132R / Photo: **Courtesy of The Pierpont Morgan Library, New York PML 13**

borrowed a substantial amount of money from Johann Fust, a wealthy Mainz merchant and financier who accepted Gutenberg's equipment as collateral. A second loan from Fust was meant to finance the production of a Bible per Gutenberg's aspirations.

Around 1452, Gutenberg began the printing of the forty-two-line Bible. First with two and then four presses, the 1,282 pages were typeset in a textura blackletter; spaces for ornamental initial caps were left blank, to be filled in later by hand. It is estimated that 210 copies were produced. In 1455, for undefined reasons, Fust sued Gutenberg, and when he failed to appear in court, Fust seized all equipment and work—reaping the benefits of the sale of the momentous forty-two-line Bible. Gutenberg continued printing, producing a Catholicon (religious dictionary) for Johannes Balbus in 1460. As far as historic status goes, good guys do finish first—Gutenberg's name is synonymous with printing, Fust's not as much.

Ulysses

In 1918, *The Little Review*, an American literary publication, began publishing installments of Irish writer James Joyce's *Ulysses*; in 1920, it was tried under obscenity charges and ordered to cease publication. *Ulysses* was banned in the United States until 1933, when Random House was able to lift the ban and publish the first American edition in 1934. The book is considered a foremost example of modernist literature, and the Random House covers, especially the first edition, by Ernst Reichl, and the 1949 edition, by E. McKnight Kauffer, also serve as examples of modernism. It was in this simple, typographic-driven vein—in particular McKnight's use of the oversized *U*—that the editor and art director of Random House's Vintage books asked Carin Goldberg to create a book cover for a 1986 reprint. Goldberg's eventual solution paid homage to a 1928 Paul Renner poster for a Zurich exhibition of work from the Bavarian Trade Schools.

During the 1980s, designers like Peter Saville ›180 and Barney Bubbles ›181 in the United Kingdom and Charles S. Anderson ›195, Paula Scher ›182, and Goldberg in the United States began mining historical resources in their work, and as questions about appropriation arose during the height of postmodernism, work like Goldberg's *Ulysses* cover came under fire as being abusive of history. "One symptom of this tendency," wrote Tibor Kalman ›183, Abbott Miller, and Karrie Jacobs in "Good History/Bad History," a 1991 article for *Print* ›94, "has been the production of graphic design in which style is a detachable attribute, a veneer rather than an expression of content. This is nowhere clearer than in the so-called historicist and eclectic work which has strip-mined the history of design for ready-made style." Goldberg doesn't dwell on the debate. "I moved on," she quipped in a 2007 interview for *STEP* ›102, "the day after I handed in the comp."

BAVARIAN TRADE SCHOOLS EXHIBITION POSTER / Paul Renner / Germany, 1928

ULYSSES, James Joyce / Random House / Carin Goldberg / USA, 1986

The Lover

"At the age of fifteen," wrote Marguerite Duras in 1984's *The Lover*, "I had the face of pleasure, and yet I had no knowledge of pleasure. There was no mistaking that face." Duras's memoir chronicling her affair as a 15-year-old girl with a Chinese businessman nearly twice her age in 1930s colonial Indochina begins with reflections on her facial features and their transformation over time—a state of flux elegantly captured in the author's photograph that graces the cover designed by Louise Fili ⟩ 197, then art director at Pantheon. The photograph of Duras, taken at the time of her affair, is vignetted, isolating the face from all context and directly engaging the reader.

As in many of her covers, Fili's *Lover* interpolated an historical aesthetic, in this case 1930s Art Deco, with her unconventional instinct to revive found letterforms from the printed ephemera and packaging she collects from flea markets around the world. For *The Lover*, she worked with letterer and designer Craig De Camps to create the red, elongated letters with their barely present shadows. In contrast to other book covers of the time, Fili's simple three-color cover was subtly loud.

THE LOVER, Marguerite Duras / Pantheon / Louise Fili / USA, 1983

EVERYTHING IS ILLUMINATED, Jonathan Safran Foer / Perennial, an imprint of HarperCollins / Jonathan Gray / USA, 2002

THE DRUID KING, Norman Spinrad / Knopf Publishing Group, Random House / Doyle Partners: Stephen Doyle / USA, 2003

DREAMER, Charles Johnson / Scribner / Pentagram: Angus Hyland / UK, 1999

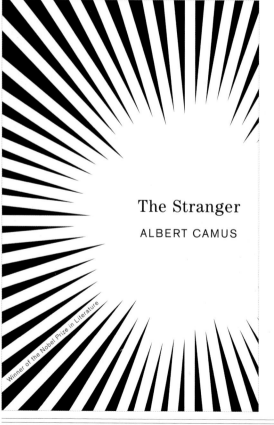

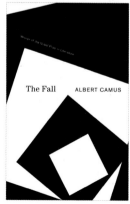

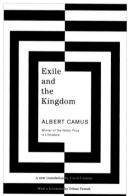

ALBERT CAMUS SERIES / Vintage / art direction, John Gall; design, Helen Yentus / 1989, 1991, 1991, 1991, 2007

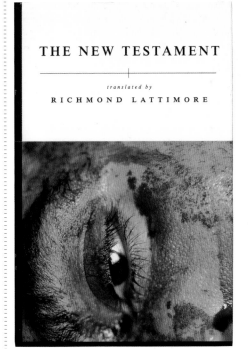

DARKNESS AT NOON, Arthur Koestler / Scribner / Paul Sahre / USA, 2006

JURASSIC PARK, Michael Crichton / Knopf Publishing Group, Random House / Chip Kidd / USA, 1990

THE NEW TESTAMENT, translated by Richmond Lattimore / North Point Press / Chip Kidd; photography, Andres Serrano / USA, 1996

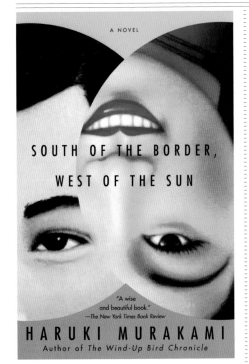

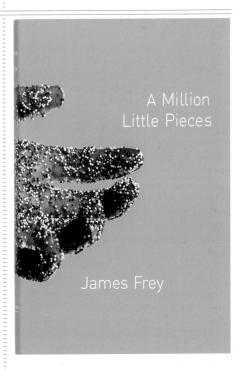

SOUTH OF THE BORDER, WEST OF THE SUN, Haruki Murakami / Vintage / John Gall / USA, 2000

MAO: L'UOMO, IL RIVOLUZIONARIO, IL TIRANNO, Philip Short / Rizzoli / Mucca Design: art direction, Andrea Brown / Italy, 2006

A MILLION LITTLE PIECES, James Frey / Anchor / Rodrigo Corral / USA, 2003

ANNUAL REPORTS

Formed in 1934 as an agency of the U.S. federal government, the Securities and Exchange Commission (SEC) is responsible for overseeing the stock market and preventing corporate malfeasance in stock sales and financial reporting to shareholders. As part of the Securities Exchange Act of 1934, all publicly traded corporations became required to submit quarterly and annual reports detailing their finances. Little did the

SEC know that 50 and 60 years later, annual reports would be one of the most lucrative and creative categories of project for the graphic design profession.

For the first 10 or 12 years, centered arrangements and margin-to-margin typography were the norm in four- or eight-page documents. By the early and mid-1940s, corporations saw

the potential of the annual report as a public relations vehicle to communicate not just with their shareholders and the government but with employees, prospective investors, and the media. At first it was the cover of the annual report that received most of the attention, but steadily, as print and type production became more affordable and accessible, corporations developed the inside with more care to showcase their

 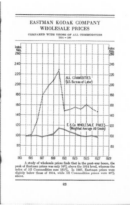 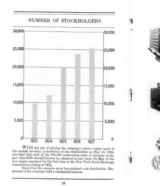 

EASTMAN KODAK COMPANY 1927 ANNUAL REPORT / USA, 1926

TIME WARNER, INC., 1989 ANNUAL REPORT / Frankfurt Gips Balkind, NY/LA: cover photography, Scott Morgan / USA, 1990

TUPPERWARE CORPORATION 2001 ANNUAL REPORT / SamataMason / USA, 2002

story through photographs, diagrams, and rich narrative stories.

By the mid-1950s, annual reports were attracting talented graphic designers who began to orchestrate the story, design, and production of these documents. A notable early contribution was by Erik Nitsche › 148, who was in charge of the identity of General Dynamics, which he extended from advertising to annual reports, presenting a cohesive design for the company. In the 1960s and 1970s, esteemed designers like Saul Bass › 158

and Lester Beall › 146 included annual reports in their multidisciplinary practices. Paul Rand › 159 created reports that adhered to bigger identity programs for IBM and Cummins, and in-house design executives like Lou Dorfsman › 173 at CBS and John Massey at Container Corporation of America executed consummate documents. The practice kept growing through the late 1970s and 1980s, with design firms like Arnold Saks and Jonson Pedersen Hinrichs & Shakery taking on multiple annual reports every year. Even Push Pin Studios › 168 was in on the action.

Up to that point, annual reports were handsomely produced and designed, but they followed relatively conventional norms by presenting text and image in a clear, professional manner. In 1989 Warner Communications, Inc., and Time, Inc., merged to form one of the largest media and entertainment companies in the world, and its groundbreaking annual report served to signal a new kind of company. Designed by Frankfurt Gips Balkind, the report was a restlessly kinetic display of information that presented expressive bursts of text, facts, and imagery in condensed

 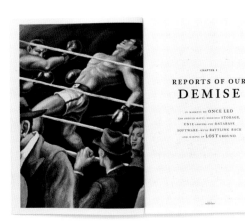 

IBM 2000 ANNUAL REPORT / VSA Partners: art direction, Curt Schreiber, Jeff Walker; design, Greg Sylvester, Scott Hickman / USA, 2001

bundles for quick consumption. Printed in black and yellow, green, orange, and pink fluorescent colors, the report did not just speak to its shareholders and the media, it screamed. The *New York Times* even covered the report to mixed peer reviews, with Alan Siegel claiming it "trivializes an important and valuable company," while Stephen Doyle complained that "[the] report is sometimes so confusing, it might as well have been printed in a foreign language." Frankfurt Gips Balkind's work set the stage for a new breed of graphically emotional annual report.

As the 1990s wore on, a few firms surfaced as the leaders in this discipline, creating dozens of annual reports every year and dominating awards shows: Cahan & Associates, VSA Partners › 194, and SamataMason, along with smaller firms or solo designers like Tolleson Design, Thirst › 200, and Jennifer Sterling. The concept, execution, and production of their work were consistently impressive and turned the annual report into a creative venture that required engaging storytelling, confident pacing,

imaginative photography and illustration, flawless typography, and ingenious information graphics. By the end of the century, annual reports for corporations and nonprofit organizations were some of the most coveted and celebrated projects. This near-obsession has lent itself to mockery. Virtual Telemetrix, a fictitious corporation created by designer John Bielenberg, issued an annual report in 1993 and 1997 with faux text, imagery, and diagrams poking fun at both designers and clients. In 2001, for the

FOR GOURMETS ONLY **2001 PODRAVKA ANNUAL REPORT** / Bruketa&ŽinićOM: creative direction, Davor Bruketa, Nikola Zinic / Croatia, 2002

BON APPETIT **2002 PODRAVKA ANNUAL REPORT** / Bruketa&ŽinićOM: creative direction, Davor Bruketa, Nikola Zinic / Croatia, 2003

SECRETS OF GOOD CUISINE **2003 PODRAVKA ANNUAL REPORT** / Bruketa&ŽinićOM: creative direction, Davor Bruketa, Nikola Zinic; art direction and design, Maja Bagic; photography, Marin Topic / Croatia, 2004

FEED ME **2004 PODRAVKA ANNUAL REPORT** / Bruketa&ŽinićOM: creative direction, Davor Bruketa, Nikola Zinic; photography, Marin Topic, Domagoj Kunic / Croatia, 2005

EXCERPT OF THE ETERNAL DEBATE ABOUT THE HEART **2005 PODRAVKA ANNUAL REPORT** / Bruketa&ŽinićOM: creative direction and writing, Davor Bruketa, Nikola Zinic; art direction and design, Imelda Ramovic, Mirel Hadzijusufovic; photography, Domagoj Kunic / Croatia, 2006

WELL DONE **2006 PODRAVKA ANNUAL REPORT** / Bruketa&ŽinićOM: creative direction and writing, Davor Bruketa, Nikola Zinic; art direction and design, Imelda Ramovic, Mirel Hadzijusufovic / typography, Nikola Djurek; illustration, Nikola Wolf ; photography, Domagoj Kunic / Croatia, 2007

forty-fifth Mead Show Annual—the now defunct premiere competition for annual reports—VSA Partners designed a pocket-sized compendium that featured the winners as well as humorous tips for the industry, presented in bundles of 45, as in "45 Ways to Say Change," "45 Ways to Photograph an Executive," and "45 Things You Forgot in Order to Win This Award."

Back in 1987, the SEC had already allowed for smaller reports to be filed, and starting in 1993 it required that Form 10-K, the nuts and bolts of the financial information, be submitted electronically, leaving the adorned printed annual report as a kind of optional luxury for corporations. As budgets tightened after 2001, some corporations took their annual report online, attempting to bring the same kind of design emphasis to the medium or simply posting a PDF document on their website. Attractive printed annual reports are still being created, but without the same fervor and volume of the 1990s, and design firms that counted on the income of annual report season have diversified into other disciplines. As 2008 comes to an economically dismal close, with most corporations having little to no good news to share, the annual report might soon return to its roots as a dull, obligatory document.

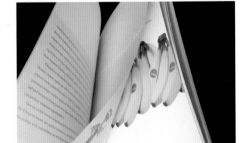

SWISS ARMY BRANDS, INC. 2001 ANNUAL REPORT / SamataMason / USA, 2002

CHIQUITA BRANDS INTERNATIONAL, INC. 2001 ANNUAL REPORT / SamataMason / USA, 2002

After baking the pages are filled with recipes

Blue Note Records

Brought together by German immigrant Alfred Lion, pianists Albert Ammons and Meade Lux Lewis recorded the first Blue Note Records album in January 1939. Later that year, Lion's childhood friend Francis Wolff, a photographer, arrived in New York from Germany and joined Lion in his spare time to evolve Blue Note through their mutual passion for jazz. Through the 1940s—with a two-year interruption starting in 1941, when Lion was drafted into the U.S. Army—Blue Note increased its library and embraced the changing sounds of jazz, working with artists like Thelonious Monk, Fats Navarro, and Bud Powell. One of their first album cover designers was saxophonist Gil Melle, who also recorded under Blue Note. In the late 1940s and early 1950s, two other designers contributed to the label: Paul Bacon, who later became a prolific book cover designer; and John Hermansader, whose simple and bold use of photography and typography preceded the iconic covers produced between 1956 and 1967 by Reid Miles.

Arriving in New York from Los Angeles, Miles was hired by Hermansader as his assistant, giving him the opportunity to woo Lion and Wolff with his work for Blue Note. Following a brief position at *Esquire* ›326 magazine, Miles was hired as the designer for Blue Note in 1956. Combining the soulful black and white photographs Wolff took during recording sessions, depicting the artists in their true element, with impeccably simple yet infinitely varied typographic treatments and lone bursts of color, Miles established the singularly distinctive look of Blue Note. Interestingly, Miles much preferred classical music over jazz, often giving away the album copies he received from Blue Note. Miles designed approximately 500 covers until 1967 when, two years after Liberty Records purchased Blue Note, he and Lion left. Wolff stayed at the label until his death in 1971.

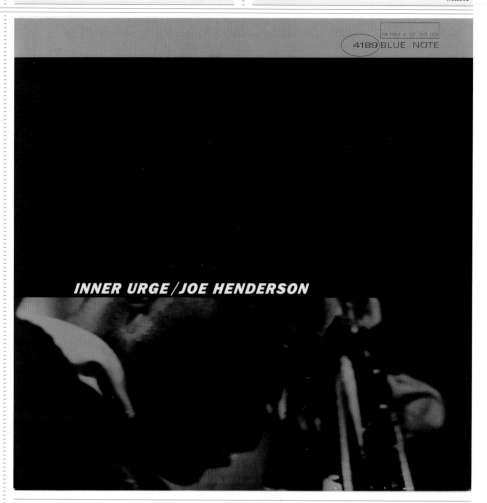

INNER URGE, Joe Henderson / 1964

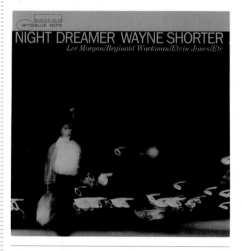

NIGHT DREAMER, Wayne Shorter / 1964

SOUL STATION, Hank Mobley / 1960

Blue Note Records / design, Reid Miles; photography, Francis Wolff (except for *Out to Lunch!*) / USA

OUT TO LUNCH!, Eric Dolphy / photography, Reid Miles / 1964

IT MIGHT AS WELL BE SPRING, Ike Quebec / 1961

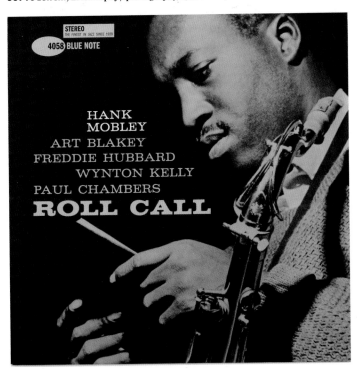

ROLL CALL, Hank Mobley / 1960

BLUE TRAIN, John Coltrane / 1957

Columbia Records

Established in 1888, Columbia Records went through several ownership changes and became a blip in the library of the American Record Corporation (ARC) by 1934. However, in 1938 Columbia Records was reestablished when Columbia Broadcasting System (CBS) purchased ARC. Through the next four decades, it produced an astounding number of memorable and influential album covers through the stewardship of its famous art directors, designers, and freelance illustrators and photographers. The initial responsibility fell on Alex Steinweiss › 142—who, unofficially, invented the album cover by using artwork and typography together for the previously stale pasteboard folders for 78 rpm records. Steinweiss remained at Columbia Records until 1944, when he joined the U.S. Navy, but he continued designing for them independently until the early 1950s. Meanwhile, staff member (and eventual renowned illustrator) Jim Flora took his position, but, weary of the office's dynamics, left in 1950, leaving an inspiring trail of his artwork in numerous album covers.

In 1954, S. Neil Fujita, previously at advertising agency N.W. Ayer & Son, was appointed art director. While many of his album covers featured his own illustrations, he introduced bolder and more dramatic photography and typography. Taking one year off to run his own studio in 1957—Roy Kuhlman unceremoniously filled in—Fujita left in 1960. Having worked for Alexey Brodovitch › 143 at *Harper's Bazaar* › 327, Bob Cato was the next art director in 1959. His social flair played well across the art department, sales and marketing, and even with musicians and artists like Andy Warhol, Robert Rauschenberg, and R. Crumb. In 1960 Cato hired John Berg, and the two worked together until Cato's departure in 1968. With Berg at the helm and Columbia Records enjoying increasing success throughout the 1970s, the label's creative department became a magnet for talented designers—among them Paula Scher › 182, Carin Goldberg, and Henrietta Condak—and was a commanding bastion of album cover design until the mid 1980s. At that point, Columbia Records lost steam; it was purchased by Sony in 1988.

CHICAGO V / In more than a dozen covers for Chicago, John Berg kept the size and position of the logo consistent, rendering it differently each time / design, John Berg; illustration, Nicholas Fasciano / 1969

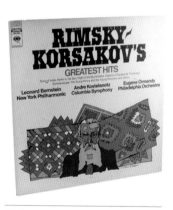

RIMSKY-KORSAKOV'S GREATEST HITS / illustration, Milton Glaser / 1971

SCARLATTI: SIX SONATAS; VILLA-LOBOS: FIVE PRELUDES, John Williams / design, Paula Scher; cover art, courtesy of the Victoria and Albert Museum / 1972

RAMSEY LEWIS' NEWLY RECORDED, ALL-TIME, NON-STOP GOLDEN HITS / design, John Berg, Karen Lee Grant; illustration, James Grashow / 1973

MAHLER: SYMPHONY NO. 1, New York Philharmonic / design, John Berg, Hiroshi Morishima, Richard Mantel; illustration, James McMullan / 1973

ON STAGE, Loggins and Messina / 1974

SUITE FOR FLUTE AND JAZZ PIANO, Jean-Pierre Rampal / design, John Berg, Andy Engel; illustration, Roger Huyssen / 1975

LAND OF THE MIDNIGHT SUN, Al Di Meola / design, Paula Scher; photography, Jerry Abromowitz / 1976

GREATEST HITS OF 1720, Philharmonia Virtuosi of New York / design, Robert Biro; illustration, Laszlo Kubinyi / 1977

4AD

As employees of Beggars Banquet—an independent record label formed in 1977 from a series of new and used record stores in London opened in 1974—Ivo Watts-Russell and Peter Kent launched Axis, a subsidiary label, in 1979. An identically named label forced them to change their name, and they settled on 4AD. By the end of their first year, with seminal bands like Modern English and Bauhaus, 4AD released nearly 20 records, and Kent left to establish another label, while Watts-Russell remained in charge.

1981 marked the beginning of a long collaboration between 4AD and Vaughan Oliver, who began his career almost gnawingly. Drawn to the idea of designing record covers, he enrolled in Newcastle Polytechnic in 1976 for graphic design but focused on illustration while avoiding typography and graphic design altogether; not until he was working at packaging firm Michael Peters & Partners (MP&P), where he was obligated to use it, did he discover the potential of typography as something he could subvert through his own approach.

Oliver knew Watts-Russell through their shared interest in music and frequent meetings at clubs. He began working on a freelance basis with 4AD while still at MP&P, eventually becoming a full-time employee in 1983. He was responsible for the majority of the firm's album covers through the late 1980s, establishing the mysterious and uncommon visual language the label, designer, and bands like the Pixies and the Cocteau Twins became known for. Working in collaboration with photographer Nigel Grierson, the firm's work was credited as Envelope 23 until 1988, when Grierson left and Oliver adopted the name V23 working collaboratively with designer Chris Bigg. In 1998 they established a formal partnership when they left the 4AD offices, allowing them to work on other projects while still taking commissions from 4AD, which also began working with other designers—but it was that early, practically unadulterated output by Envelope23 and V23 that gave 4AD much of its luster and appeal.

DOOLITTLE, Pixies / 4AD / v23: art direction and design, Vaughan Oliver; photography, Simon Larbalestier / UK, 1989

BOSSANOVA, Pixies / 4AD / v23: art direction and design, Vaughan Oliver; design assistance, Chris Bigg; photography, Simon Larbalestier; globe, Pirate Design / UK, 1990

COME ON PILGRIM, Pixies / 4AD / v23: art direction and design, Vaughan Oliver; photography, Simon Larbalestier / UK, 1987

TREASURE, Cocteau Twins / 4AD / 23 Envelope / UK, 1984

FILIGREE AND SHADOW, This Mortal Coil / 4AD / 23 Envelope; photography, Nigel Grierson / UK, 1986

Hipgnosis

Doing book covers for Penguin Books › 274 in the late 1960s under the moniker of Consciousness Incorporated, Storm Thorgerson and Aubrey Powell, whose early circle of friends included Pink Floyd's Syd Barrett and Roger Waters, established Hipgnosis in 1968 to accommodate the commission to design Pink Floyd's second album, *A Saucerful of Secrets*; the relationship lasted for more than two decades and nearly a dozen album covers. At first, the Hipgnosis facilities consisted of Powell's bathroom as a darkroom, but the firm soon established a studio in London, and in 1974, musician and photographer Peter Christopher joined as an assistant, later becoming a partner. Both Thorgerson and Powell studied film and had no formal concept of design—at least not in the typical sense of typographic and layout knowledge—and their proficiency in photography wasn't immediate, so their album covers were invariably driven by the narrative of a single image concocted in their imagination...and what an imagination.

With today's digital technology, it's easy to forget that the surreal compositions of Hipgnosis actually existed to be photographed—for example, the 120 inflatable red balls lined up in the Moroccan desert for *Elegy* or the 40-foot-long inflatable pig hoisted over Battersea Power Station for *Animals*. Other covers were exceptional works of retouching and paste-up, bringing to life some of the most unexpected concepts, and many illustrators and lettering artists—notable among these was George Hardie—further contributed to the diversity of Hipgnosis's covers. The group separated in 1983, but the visual legacy they left was probably as important as the cultural imprint left by the musicians they collaborated with: Peter Gabriel, Genesis, Pink Floyd, Led Zeppelin, and Black Sabbath.

ANIMALS, Pink Floyd / Columbia Records / sleeve design, Roger Waters; organized by Storm Thorgerson, Aubrey Powell; graphics, Nick Mason; photography, Aubrey Powell, Peter Christopherson, Howard Bartrop, Nic Tucker, Bob Ellis, Bob Brimson, Colin Jones; inflatable pig, E.R.G. / USA, 1977

PETER GABRIEL | 1 / Charisma Records / Hipgnosis / UK, 1977

HOUSE OF THE HOLY, Led Zeppelin / Atlantic Recording Corporation / Hipgnosis / UK, 1973

PETER GABRIEL | 3 / Charisma Records / Hipgnosis / UK, 1980 (Note: this is a reissue; the design differs from the original)

TECHNICAL ECSTASY, Black Sabbath / Vertigo Records / Hipgnosis / UK, 1976

ELEGY, The Nice / Charisma Records / Hipgnosis / UK, 1971

Sun Ra

Born on the South Side of Chicago in the early 1950s, Sun Ra—birth name Herman Poole Blount, legal name Le Sony'r Ra—was a complex jazz artist with an incongruous mythology. He claimed to be from another planet and lived by a philosophy described as "an unexpected hybrid of space-age science fiction and ancient Egyptian cosmo religious trappings" in a 1989 press kit from A&M Records, one of the many labels that distributed his recordings. With friend and fellow mystic follower Alton Abraham as manager, he established El Saturn Records in 1955, one of the first independent artist-owned labels in the industry. Ra performed with a growing, fluctuating cadre of musicians (as many as 30) known as the Arkestra, with everyone draped in outlandish robes, headgear, and footwear. Lest this sound like a circus, be assured their contribution to jazz is highly regarded.

The eccentricity of Ra and his Arkestra permeated the design and production methods of their album covers, mostly because either Ra or some other member of the Arkestra regularly drew the artwork. Space-age and otherworldly themes and Egyptian iconography were regular visual tropes of the group, as were hero portraits of Ra taking over the full cover. The albums were rarely mass produced; quite the contrary, they were often hand-printed in the recording studio through silkscreen or by producing metal plates, inking them by hand, and printing cover by cover; in some cases an Arkestra member would simply draw the cover, which would exist as a one-off edition. As Ra and his Arkestra swayed across New York and Philadelphia, performing everywhere from the Egyptian pyramids to *Saturday Night Live*, they produced hundreds of small-run album covers that were, indeed, out of this world.

NOTHING IS..., Sun Ra / ESP-Disk / design, Raphael Boguslav, Howard Bernstein, Baby Jerry; cover photography, Thomas Hunter / USA, 1970

LANQUIDITY, Sun Ra / Philly Jazz, Inc. / photography, Charles Shabacon / USA, 1978

THE MAGIC CITY, Sun Ra and His Solar Arkestra / Saturn Records / art direction, Rothacker Advertising & Design; cover art, William White / USA, 1966

JAZZ IN SILHOUETTE, Sun Ra and His Arkestra / Saturn Records / art direction, Spencer Drate and Judith Salavetz; disc graphics, Marcolina Design / USA, 1958

ATLANTIS, Sun Ra and His Astro Infinity Arkestra / Saturn Records / art direction, Rothacker Advertising & Design / USA, 1969

SUPER-SONIC JAZZ, Sun Ra and His Arkestra / "About the cover: With your mind's eye you are invited to see other scenes of the space age by focusing your eyes on the cover and your mind on the music. The scenes are from the space void." / Saturn Records / USA, 1957

STICKY FINGERS, Rolling Stones / Columbia Records / cover concept, Andy Warhol; design, Craigbrauninc. / USA, 1971

GOD SAVE THE QUEEN SINGLE, Sex Pistols / Virgin Records / Jamie Ried / UK, 1977

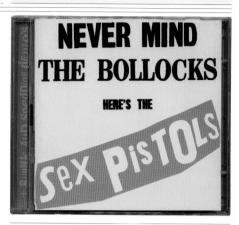

NEVER MIND THE BOLLOCKS, HERE'S THE SEX PISTOLS / Virgin Records / Jamie Ried / UK, 1977

NEVERMIND, Nirvana / Geffen Records / art direction and design, Robert Fisher; cover photo, Kirk Weddle / USA, 1991

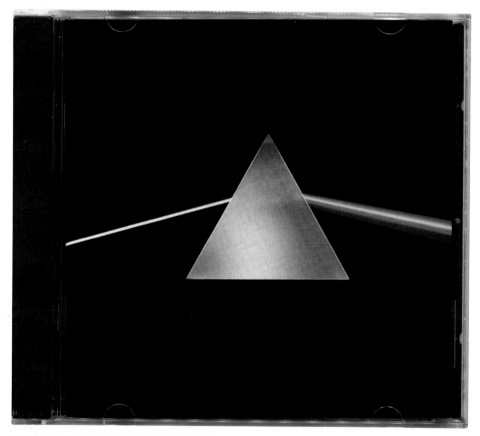

DARK SIDE OF THE MOON, Pink Floyd / Harvest Records / Hipgnosis: Nicholas Thirkell Associates; George Hardie / UK, 1973

LOOK INTO THE EYEBALL, David Byrne / Virgin Records / Doyle Partners: photography, Stephen Doyle / USA, 2001

THE INFORMATION, Beck / The booklet comes with a selection of stickers so the cover can be customized / Interscope Records / Big Actice, Mat Maitland, Gerard Saint; Beck / USA, 2006

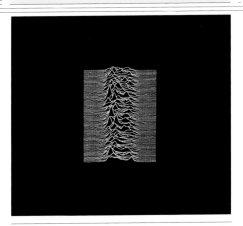

UNKNOWN PLEASURES, Joy Division / Factory Records / art direction, Peter Saville; design, Saville Parris Wakefield; photography, Kevin Cummins / UK, 1979

X&Y, Coldplay / EMI Records Ltd. / art direction and design, Tappin Gofton; photography, Kevin Westenberg, Tom Sheehan, Coldplay / USA, 2005

BLUE MONDAY single, New Order / Factory / design, Peter Saville, Brett Wickens / UK, 1983

SGT. PEPPER'S LONELY HEARTS CLUB BAND, Beatles/ EMI Records Ltd. / art direction, Robert Fraser; design, Peter Blake, Jann Haworth; photography, Michael Cooper / UK, 1967

This is a RECORD COVER. This writing is the DESIGN upon the record cover. The DESIGN is to help SELL the record. We hope to draw your attention to it and encourage you to pick it up. When you have done that maybe you'll be persuaded to listen to the music - in this case XTC's Go 2 album. Then we want you to BUY it. The idea being that the more of you that buy this record the more money Virgin Records, the manager Ian Reid and XTC themselves will make. To the aforementioned this is known as PLEASURE. A good cover DESIGN is one that attracts more buyers and gives more pleasure. This writing is trying to pull you in much like an eye-catching picture. It is designed to get you to READ IT. This is called luring the VICTIM, and you are the VICTIM. But if you have a free mind you should STOP READING NOW! because all we are attempting to do is to get you to read on. Yet this is a DOUBLE BIND because if you indeed stop you'll be doing what we tell you, and if you read on you'll be doing what we've wanted all along. And the more you read on the more you're falling for this simple device of telling you exactly how a good commercial design works. They're TRICKS and this is the worst TRICK of all since it's describing the TRICK whilst trying to TRICK you, and if you've read this far then you're TRICKED but you wouldn't have known this unless you'd read this far. At least we're telling you directly instead of seducing you with a beautiful or haunting visual that may never tell you. We're letting you know that you ought to buy this record because in essence it's a PRODUCT and PRODUCTS are to be consumed and you are a consumer and this is a good PRODUCT. We could have written the band's name in special lettering so that it stood out and you'd see it before you'd read any of this writing and possibly have bought it anyway. What we are really suggesting is that you are FOOLISH to buy or not buy an album merely as a consequence of the design on its cover. This is a con because if you agree then you'll probably like this writing - which is the cover design - and hence the album inside. But we've just warned you against that. The con is a con. A good cover design could be considered as one that gets you to buy the record, but that never actually happens to YOU because YOU know it's just a design for the cover. And this is the RECORD COVER.

GO2, XTC / Virgin Records / Hipgnosis / UK, 1978

Altoids

Smith & Co. was a confectionery business started in London by William Smith in 1780, and one of its first products was Altoids, a lozenge intended to remedy indigestion, not bad breath. Altoids were marketed through pharmacies by Smith & Co., along with other products like Benoids and Zenoids, through the 1920s, and in the 1930s as a diet pill or food supplement. During World War II, the confectioner had a contract to ship Altoids to the armed forces. It is not clear when Altoids came to the United States. Some sources say it was as early as 1918 and others as late as 1980, but what *is* certain is that Altoids have enjoyed considerable popularity in America. Part of its early appeal was the metal tin, introduced in the 1920s to replace little cardboard boxes that tended to spill or crush the chalky mints. Altoids gained traction in the mid- to late 1990s with a comically relentless and sometimes abrasive advertising campaign by Leo Burnett, but what has separated Altoids from its minty competitors is its distinctive tin packaging, which invokes Old World nostalgia while warning the public of their "curious" strength.

Tiffany & Co.

"Charles Lewis Tiffany has one thing in stock that you cannot buy of him for as much money as you may offer," a 1906 *New York Sun* article has been paraphrased as stating. "He will only give it to you. And that is one of his boxes." The founder of Tiffany & Co. understood how to control his brand from the beginning. The article further explains how no robin's-egg blue box or bag bearing the company's name could leave the store without "an article which has been sold by them and for which they are responsible." The Tiffany blue box has come to mean many things beyond the jewelry it encases: luxury, romance, and expectation. The box and the blue—designated Pantone 1837, based on the year it was founded, not Pantone's color spectrum and numbering—have remained consistent all these years, and in 2003, Pentagram's ›162 Paula Scher added a level of consistency and luxury by redrawing the wordmark and having it foil-stamped instead of printed on the boxes, which are now wrapped, inside and out, with a custom made paper with a luxurious matte finish. Hearts around the world flutter.

TIFFANY & CO. IDENTITY AND PACKAGING / Pentagram: Paula Scher / USA, 2003 / **Photos: Nick Turner**

Absolut

Absolut rent bränvin, Swedish for "absolute pure vodka" was a spirit created by Lars Olsson Smith in 1879 in the small village of Åhus, Sweden. In 1917, Vin & Sprit (V&S), a national monopoly for the production, import, export, and wholesale trade of alcoholic beverages, took over, and in the 1970s looked to export the product to the United States. V&S hired advertisers Lars Börje Carlsson and Gunnar Broman to create a bottle design and advertising. Among many options they gathered for presentation was a medicine bottle with a short neck and rounded shoulders. In the late 1970s, Broman and representatives from V&S traveled to the United States, the latter to find a distributor and the former to secure a partnership with the prestigious advertising agency N.W. Ayer & Son in New York. Broman succeeded and proceeded to design the clear bottle with the name and legend printed directly on it—an anomaly in the spirit consumer category. After many rejections, distribution was secured with Carillon Importers, who hired ad agency TBWA to promote the product. Despite consumer research showing the name to be presumptuous and the bottle to be ugly and hard to read, TBWA centered its advertising campaign on it to create the now legendary ad series, with artists like Keith Haring, Ed Ruscha, and Andy Warhol.

ABSOLUT VODKA / Gunnar Broman, Lars Borje Carlsson / Sweden, 1979

ABSOLUT FAMILY / Sweden, 1986–2008

RECOMMENDED READING › 390

Lucky Strike

Since its introduction in 1871 as chewing tobacco sold in green metal tins by the R.A. Patterson Tobacco Company, Lucky Strike has used a red circle with its name spelled in black, broken in two lines. Purchased by the American Tobacco Company (ATC) in 1905, by the 1930s Lucky Strike developed its original design into a green-dyed pack with simplified typography in the red circle, now with gold, white, and black concentric circles around it, creating the iconic bull's-eye. Looking to attract a female consumer base, ATC commissioned Raymond Lowey, a successful industrial and identity designer, to improve the pack—it is told that ATC's president, George Washington Hill, bet him $50,000 to improve sales. Lowey removed the green color, simplified the logo, and placed it on the front and back of the pack. The new design launched in 1942, and Lowey won the bet. More than 60 years later, the pack remains nearly unchanged.

RECOMMENDED READING › 390

Coca-Cola

On May 1886 at Jacob's Pharmacy in Atlanta, Georgia, pharmacist Dr. John S. Pemberton made Coca-Cola by combining carbonated water with a syrup of his own invention. Through the end of the nineteenth century and the beginning of the twentieth, Coca-Cola was consumed only at soda fountains, where a tender mixed the beverage on demand and served it in a glass. Joseph A. Biedenharn, a soda fountain owner in Vicksburg, Mississippi, was one of the first to offer Coca-Cola in a bottle around 1894, but it was Benjamin F. Thomas and Joseph B. Whitehead of Chattanooga, Tennessee, who arranged a contract to bottle it exclusively on a large scale starting in 1899. For the next 15 years, Coca-Cola was packaged in a straight-sided bottle with an embossed logo and a diamond-shaped label. Facing product imitation, Coca-Cola sought to differentiate itself through a unique bottle, calling for a design that "even if broken," as the design brief stated, "a person could tell at a glance what it was." Alexander Samuelson and Earl R. Dean of the Root Glass Company in Terre Haute, Indiana, developed the hobble skirt-shaped, pale-green tinted bottle in 1916. The bottle has since undergone evolutions—its latest incarnation, a smooth aluminum bottle designed by Turner Duckworth in 2007, is being tested for broad distribution—but it remains one of the most recognized designs in the world.

RECOMMENDED READING › 390

COCA-COLA PACKAGING FOR COCA-COLA CLASSIC, COCA-COLA ZERO, AND DIET COKE / Turner Duckworth / USA, 2006–2007

COCA-COLA CLASSIC, 8-OZ GLASS BOTTLE / USA, 1916

Campbell's Tomato Soup

After a few years of operation under different names, the Joseph Campbell Preserve Co. was established in 1891, specializing first in canning produce and, later, soup. The first tomato soup label was created in 1895 with elaborate lettering and an illustration of two men carrying a red beefsteak tomato against a white background. In 1897, condensed soup was introduced with the same design, now on a split horizontal background of blue and orange. The first red and white label debuted in 1898, after the company's treasurer attended a Cornell University football game, admired their red and white uniforms, and suggested those colors for the label. At the 1899 National Export Exposition in Philadelphia, the soup was awarded a gold medallion for excellence, and an image of the medallion was placed on the label. This was replaced with the medallion won at the 1900 International Exposition in Paris, which remains on the label to this day. The design was streamlined in 1942 by removing the address from the bottom and a pair of torches to the side. Aside from minor improvements over the years, the tomato soup label looks nearly as it did more than 60 years ago.

CAMPBELL'S TOMATO SOUP LABEL / USA, 1978–1998, 2001

Hershey's Chocolate Bar

As a school dropout at the age of 13 and an apprentice confectioner, Milton S. Hershey was an improbable entrepreneur, but by 1900 he had sold his first caramel business for a reported $1 million and started a new venture to develop affordable chocolate. The result was the five-cent Hershey's Chocolate Bar. Setting up a factory in 1903 in Derry Church, Pennsylvania, to mass-produce his chocolate, Hershey created an unprecedented town structure, including a transit system, school, stores, community center, and even its own post office, to support his employees. The town was renamed Hershey in 1906.

The success of the chocolate bar was instant, and the ritual of peeling off the silver foil surrounding it had tongues salivating for close to a century. Packaged in a glossy yet silky wrapper, the design was first introduced on a white background, switching to the signature dark maroon color in 1902. Until 1911, the lettering was an adorned serif; in 1912 a blocky sans serif was introduced that boldly evolved over the years. In 2003, the silver foil and paper wrapper were replaced by a single plastic wrapper like that used by the rest of the market—an understandable change that limits material waste, but a big blow to nostalgia.

RECOMMENDED READING › 390

Toblerone

With the Matterhorn as the backdrop for the city of Bern, Switzerland—and, as one version goes, as the inspiration for the chocolate bar's triangular shape and peaks—Theodor Tobler and Emil Baumann introduced Toblerone in 1908. Over the years, the triangular packaging has remained constant, although the typography has evolved and icons have come and gone. First was the eagle, which in 1920 was replaced by a bear—the heraldic symbol of Bern—only to return in 1930 grasping a *T* in its claws. From 1969 onward, an abstract Matterhorn with the word *Tobler* on it served as the logo until 2000, when brand consultancy SiebertHead introduced a streamlined redesign with a new logo depicting the Matterhorn in a simple drawing and the silhouette of a bear barely but playfully discernable on its surface. Curious? Look for it below.

Fossil

Tom Kartsotis, a Dallas-based entrepreneur, began importing watches in different design styles from the Far East in 1984, based on advice from his brother, Kosta, and selling them to department stores and boutiques; one of his most popular styles was a range of retro watches. In 1986 they began designing and manufacturing their own watches; the first line was named Fossil, after their affectionate nickname for their own father. Tim Hale, who had been doing freelance work for Tom, joined Fossil as its art director in 1987, and Kosta joined in 1988, as the company enjoyed rapid success. The latter, on a trip to Europe, returned with a tin pencil box, noting how well their watches fit into it. The first Fossil watches in a tin were on shelves in 1989.

Building from the retro premise of the product, Hale established a highly mutable system for the design of the tins that joyfully references American ephemera from the 1940s and 1950s: Matchbooks, consumer packaging, sports trading cards, lifestyle magazines, travel brochures, and hotel soap wrappers all serve as continuous inspiration for Hale and his team of graphic designers, who take visual cues from the source material and reinterpret in the tins. Not just mimicking styles, the designers try to incorporate the techniques and materials from that era and then digitize it. The result on the shelves—in department stores and Fossil's more than 100 retail stores—is a distinctive and immediately identifiable package that is consistently refreshed; the company introduces new designs four or five times a year. Two decades and 1,000 tin designs later, Hale and his team are far from losing their well of inspiration as the 1970s and 1980s become the new retro.

FOSSIL TINS / USA, © 2002 Fossil Design

Dr. Bronner's Magic Soaps

The descendant of three generations of German soapmakers, Emmanuel Heilbronner immigrated to the United States in 1929 at the age of 21, working with various soap companies in the East before establishing himself in the 1930s in Milwaukee and dropping the first syllable from his last name. In the 1940s, now a self-titled doctor, Bronner began to draft and persistently share a plan for world peace in "Spaceship Earth" through unity of religion. In 1945 Dr. Bronner was arrested for speaking without a permit at the University of Chicago and institutionalized in the Elgin State Insane asylum. He escaped six months later and fled to Los Angeles. There, in his small apartment, he began mixing soap with a broom handle, which he sold while expounding on his theories at the Pershing Square public park. When he noticed people bought his soap but did not bother to listen to him talk, he started writing his philosophy on the labels.

In the late 1960s, Dr. Bronner's Magic Soaps gained popularity with the hippie culture because of its all-natural ingredients, durability, and its equal effectiveness in cleaning groovy locks of hair, bell-bottom jeans, and Volkswagen vans. Packaged extremely simply in brown plastic bottles with one-color labels—the text on Dr. Bronner's products became evolving soliloquies on its founder's philosophy, referred to as "The Moral ABC." The labels of the 32-ounce soap package each carry as many as 3,000 words expressing Dr. Bronner's thinking, which references everything from Mao Tse-tung to Albert Einstein, Joseph Stalin, and Halley's Comet. Dr. Bronner passed away in 1997, but his sons maintain his legacy and are overseeing their increased popularity. The Bronners have declined purchase offers, and while sale may still be a possibility, the labels will be safe: A provision in the company's charter states they must remain the same.

MAGIC SOAPS / Cosmic Egg / USA

Jones Soda

After years as a professional skier and instructor, Peter van Stolk established Urban Juice and Soda Company (UJS) in Vancouver, Canada, in 1987 to distribute niche beverages like AriZona teas, Just Pik't Juices, and West End Soda. He later began bottling a root beer manufactured by Thomas Kemper Brewing Co. in Seattle. In 1994, van Stolk concentrated on developing his own beverages, introducing the bottled water Wazu in 1995 and the carbonated flavor drink Jones Soda in 1996. With the motto "Run with the little guy..." and no marketing budget, van Stolk promoted Jones Soda by placing coolers in strategic spots catering to his 18- to 24-year-old demographic: skate parks, tattoo parlors, and clothing stores. Through word of mouth and by exuding an authenticity that large beverages can only dream of, Jones Soda quickly became a cult favorite among the younger generation.

Rather than spending upwards of a quarter-million dollars for a custom bottle mold, van Stolk opted for stock components, combining a clear bottle with a simple screw cap that allow the energetic colors of eccentric flavors like Blue Bubble Gum, Chocolate Fudge, and Fufu Berry to show through. Designed by Vancouver- and Chicago-based SamataMason, the Jones Soda bottles are deceptively simple. The labels display the name unobtrusively inside a white or black background that frames a photograph—the key to Jones Soda's ability to make a connection with its customers. The first 35 labels were images by Vancouver-based photographer Victor John Penner, but after that, Jones Soda turned to user-generated content long before mainstream products did. Jones Soda customers submit photos online (more than 875,000 so far). Winners are picked in-house and stamped on each subsequent batch of bottles, and at myjones.com, anyone can order a 12-pack with their own photographs.

JONES SODA PACKAGING FOR URBAN JUICE & SODA / SamataMason: design, Dave Mason, Victor John Penner, Pamela Lee / USA, 1994–1995 / Photos: Victor John Penner

Tazo

A master tea maker, Steve Smith founded the Stash Tea Company in 1972 in Portland, Oregon, and oversaw its growth and popularity as one of the most successful tea companies in the United States until he left in 1994. With vast experience in the tea industry, he realized the marketing of tea was anything but exciting, so he set out to create a new kind of tea company with innovative blends and an engaging story. With partner Steve Lee, also a founder of Stash Tea, Smith imagined a brand that would revolve around the theme of "Marco Polo meets Merlin the Magician with some *Raiders of the Lost Ark* sprinkled in for good measure." Working with Portland locals Steve Sandoz of Wieden + Kennedy and Steve Sandstrom of Sandstrom Partners, they decided to create a brand-new mythology and history around the tea. Sandoz came up with the name Tazo, devoid of meaning so they could imbue it with their own—although later, when Smith had his tea leaves read by a Roma (gypsy), he learned it means "river of life" in her language, Romany.

Sandoz continued to develop the language for Tazo, mixing fact with fiction and giving it an eccentric and ancient voice, sometimes going so far as to translate his copy to another language and then back into English. The design by Sandstrom followed in the same vein, with typography that looked as if it had been lifted from ancient, if not alien, inscriptions or manuscripts. Yet, despite its ancient grounding, Tazo feels decidedly contemporary and has a strong presence on the shelf. Tazo was purchased by Starbucks in 1999, giving it a wider exposure, and even though the packaging has gradually played down the tea's lore, Tazo still manages to tell an engaging story in a monotonous category.

TAZO TEA PACKAGING / Sandstrom Partners: creative direction, Steve Sandstrom / USA, 1994–ongoing

Target Halloween

With design mavens like Michael Graves, Isaac Mizrahi, and Cynthia Rowley creating design-conscious wares at affordable prices, the large retailer Target has been a consumer favorite since the late 1990s, when Graves's elegant and friendly line of housewares (including a toaster worth hugging) premiered in 1999. In 2005 it introduced its "Design for All" campaign—"Great design. Every day. For everyone."—further establishing it as a fashionable shopping destination.

For all of its success in creating affordable design alternatives and introducing innovations like the ClearRx ▸ 318 prescription bottle, one of Target's most advanced design solutions may be for one of its most elementary challenges: Halloween. Prior to 2001, Target adorned its stores in typical Halloween regalia, peppering pumpkins, ghosts, and bats throughout. These were proper efforts to set the mood for the holiday, but they were not memorable. Right before the 2000 Halloween season, Target commissioned Werner Design Werks (WDW) in St. Paul, Minnesota, to create an identity for 2001. Target did not have a specific design brief for Sharon Werner and Sarah Nelson of WDW, but they did require a system that dozens of manufacturers, vendors, and partners could implement on their own. Werner and Nelson created a family of characters—witch, ghost, vampire, Frankenstein, and spider, among others—with a cohesive

TARGET CORPORATION HALLOWEEN CAMPAIGN / Werner Design Werks, Inc.: design and illustration, Sharon Werner, Sarah Nelson / USA, 2001

illustration style as well as a range of patterns, borders, and frames. They created two style guides, one for "hardlines" (plates, glasses, etc.) and one for "softlines" (pajamas, T-shirts, wrappers, etc.), and handed them to Target in December 2000. By Halloween 2001, Target and its vendors had generated an unimaginable amount of products and decorations based on the style guides and even created a television commercial, which was a first for Target's Halloween efforts.

The success of the WDW identity and style guide was followed in 2003 by Minneapolis-based Charles S. Anderson Design (CSA) › 195. They created a set of ghoulish characters, borders, and patterns that were

translated into candy wrappers and three-dimensional applications, and they also introduced a new decorative element for the stores: five-foot-high vacuum-formed, vintage-inspired masks that hang from the ceilings. Some graphic designers patiently waited for Target to put out the masks for trash collection to snatch one up.

Other notable contributions have been by the San Francisco-based firm Office, led by former CSA designer Jason Schulte, and New York-based Parham Santana in 2006, who added diversity by relating Halloween to the Latin Day of the Dead and referenced the cut-paper technique used to decorate small, rural towns and their plazas. Halloween for All.

TARGET CORPORATION HALLOWEEN CAMPAIGN / Target: creative direction, Eric Erickson; art direction, Ron Anderson / Charles S. Anderson Design Company: art direction, Charles S. Anderson; design, Charles S. Anderson, Todd Piper-Hauswirth, Erik Johnson, Kyle Hames, Sheraton Green, Jovaney Hollingsworth / USA, 2003

Martha Stewart Everyday

Around 1995, the discount chain Kmart closed more than 200 stores, nearly faced bankruptcy, and suffered dismal revenues. Among other comeback strategies was the initiative to expand brand-name and private-label lines, one of them Martha Stewart, who had become associated with Kmart in 1987. Under the moniker Martha Stewart Everyday (MSE), in 1997 Kmart established a line of products spanning utensils, bedding, tableware, and glassware, for dining, outdoor living, the kitchen, and the bath—products for the everyday. Since its inception and for the next five years, Stephen Doyle of Doyle Partners led a team that designed the identity and full range of packaging for MSE.

Doyle was contracted by Kmart but worked in close collaboration with the creative in-house group at Martha Stewart Living Omnimedia (MSLO)—including his wife and MSLO chief creative officer Gael Towey and with Stewart herself—especially as they oversaw the photography of the products to extend the brand aesthetic they had successfully established in their flagship magazine › 335. Doyle brought a sense of accessibility and playfulness to mass-market retailing that had seldom been present on shelves prior to MSE. Through a vibrant color palette punctuating pure white backgrounds that permeated both the products and the packaging, MSE became a flexible yet cohesive product line that was easily identifiable and approachable, as most items were packaged so they could be touched. The packages were also peppered with information, recipes, and charts of related products, extending the brand promise of Martha Stewart: inspiration and information.

MARTHA STEWART EVERYDAY PRODUCTS FOR KMART / Doyle Partners: creative direction, Stephen Doyle; design, Rosemarie Turk, Lisa Yee, Vivian Ghazarian, Ariel Apte / USA, 1997–2000

Adobe CS1, CS2

After establishing itself as an intrinsic ingredient to the mid-1980s desktop revolution with the development of the PostScript language adopted by Apple Computer, Adobe Systems entered the consumer software market in 1987 with Adobe Illustrator version 1-88, followed by Adobe PhotoShop version 1 in 1988. Over the next 20 years, these two programs became the de facto applications for designers worldwide—Macromedia Freehand fanatics excluded—as each version became more refined, powerful, and accessible. While features changed, the visual identity—from packaging to the startup screen and application icon for the desktop—remained constant through the twentieth century. Illustrator was represented by Sandro Botticelli's *The Birth of Venus*, while PhotoShop was identified by a floating eye, often accompanied by a camera lens. These visual cues became as ubiquitous as their software.

By 2002, Illustrator and PhotoShop had reached versions 10 and 7 respectively, and InDesign version 1.5, had begun to gain traction. Looking to present a unified front, Adobe developed the Creative Suite (CS), bringing all of its applications under the same version number, standardizing the user interface with an integrated design. Introduced in 2003, the software received major improvements, and so did the design. Gone were Venus and the eye. San Francisco-based MetaDesign, lead by creative director Brett Wickens and design director Conor Mangat, created a new identity around the theme of nature as a "metaphor for the creative process, reflecting precision, beauty, and aspiration." Imagery within silhouettes against a white background provided the zest that declared CS a whole new set of software. Adobe CS2 followed in 2005, and MetaDesign provided a handsome evolution of its original design, taking the elements of each application—flower for Illustrator, feather for PhotoShop, butterfly for InDesign, and stars for GoLive—and exposing, literally, their inner beauty. Nick Veasey, the famed British photographer-cum-radiographer, create the ghostly X-ray images. Like the software, the design was a worthy upgrade.

ADOBE CS1 PACKAGING / MetaDesign: creative direction, Brett Wickens; design, Brett Wickens, Conor Mangat, Kihwan Oh; photography, Brett Wickens, Stephen Underwood / USA, 2003

ADOBE CS2 PACKAGING / MetaDesign: creative direction, Brett Wickens; design, Brett Wickens, Hui-Ling Chen; radiography, Nick Veasey / USA, 2004

Target ClearRx

When Deborah Adler was a student in the School of Visual Arts Designer as Author MFA program › 132, her 2002 thesis project—a reaction to her grandmother accidentally taking her grandfather's pills—laid the blueprint for Target's innovative ClearRX prescription bottle and redesigned communication system, launched in 2005. Through a partnership with Target and collaboration with Milton Glaser › 170, Deborah managed to address a half-century-old problem. The new amber-colored prescription bottle sits firmly on its cap. Each family member is assigned a band color that identifies his or her bottles. Labels clearly show the medication name on top, followed by dosage instructions, doctor information, and refill options, while the back features clear warning icons. A card with additional patient information is tucked behind the back label. To sweeten Deborah's contribution to thousands of users, Target offers cherry or grape flavoring.

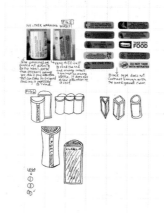

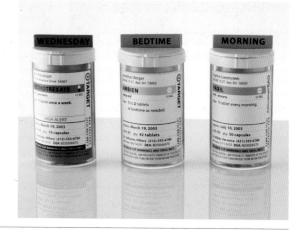

SAFERX THESIS PROJECT FOR THE SCHOOL OF VISUAL ARTS DESIGNER AS AUTHOR MFA / Deborah Adler / USA, 2002

PATIENT INFO CARD

Target A Guest

Rx: 6666057-1375

date filled: 03/17/06

drug disp: METFORMIN 500MG

description: THIS MEDICINE IS A(N) FILM-COATED WHITE OVAL-SHAPED TABLET IMPRINTED WITH 93 ON ONE SIDE AND 48 ON THE OTHER SIDE. ADD INFO: WHITE TO OFF-WHITE

directions: Take one tablet by mouth twice daily with meals

⊙ **TARGET PHARMACY**
900 Nicollet Mall
Minneapolis, MN 55403
(877)798-2743

METFORMIN 500MG

Common Uses:
This medicine is used to lower blood sugar in diabetic patients. It may take 1 month to see the full effect.

If you miss a dose of this medicine:
Take a missed dose as soon as possible. If it is almost time for the next dose, skip the missed dose and return to your regular schedule. Do not take a double dose or extra doses. Do not change dose or stop medicine. Talk with healthcare provider.

Target A Guest

AMOXICILLIN 500MG

Capsule   Generic for: Amoxil

Take one capsule by mouth three times daily for 10 days

qty: 30

refills: No

Dr. C Wilson

disp: 03/17/06   TST

mfr: NDC: 00781-2613-05

(877)798-2743 Rx 6666056-1375

⊙ **TARGET PHARMACY**
900 Nicollet Mall
Minneapolis, MN 55403

PATIENT INFO CARD

TARGET CORPORATION CLEARRX PACKAGE / Deborah Adler; industrial design, Klaus Rosburg / USA, 2005

Saks Fifth Avenue

Since its inception in the early 1900s and the opening of its flagship store on Manhattan's Fifth Avenue in 1924, Saks Fifth Avenue has stood for high-end quality, elegance, and fashion. Throughout its history, many designers and typographers, including Frederic W. Goudy, Alexey Brodovitch › 143, Erik Nitsche › 148, Tom Carnase, and Massimo Vignelli › 160, have been involved in Saks's advertising and design, yet an iconic identity or cultural marker like Tiffany & Co.'s › 306 blue or Burberry's check pattern have eluded it. In 2004, Saks commissioned Pentagram › 162 partner Michael Bierut › 203 to design a new logo and overarching identity that could be applied to their numerous packaging needs, from shopping bags to boxes of various sizes. Going through the logo history of Saks, Bierut noted that it has often employed script lettering, and a 1973 version lettered by Tom Carnase caught his attention.

Bierut worked with type and logo designer Joe Finocchiaro to update Carnase's logo with more slender lines. He then placed the new white lettering within a black square, cropping off its edges, and proceeded to slice it into 64 smaller squares that could be configured in, literally, hundreds of millions of configurations. The logo itself remains intact and appears throughout the identity, but the endless combinations of little black and white squares are giddily applied to every conceivable packaging surface. The result is an extremely mutable identity that remains consistent in its color and texture. Now consumers proudly flaunt their purchases in iconic Saks Fifth Avenue shopping bags.

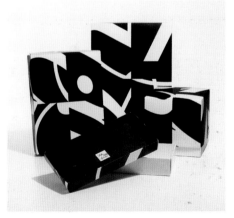

SAKS FIFTH AVENUE IDENTITY AND BRANDING APPLICATIONS / Pentagram: Michael Bierut / USA, 2006–2007 / **Photos: Courtesy of Saks Fifth Avenue / Street Photo: Elizabeth Bierut**

PRACTICE
On Newsstands

322

A well-designed magazine is a unique amalgam of disciplines: The cover must have a recognizable logotype; the photography and illustration, from cover to cover, must be ingeniously and creatively art directed; the typography must be at once rigid and structured in the body copy as well as evocative and playful in the headlines, almost as if typesetting a novel and designing a poster on the same page; the pacing must allow the reader to jump back and forth and navigate to their favorite destinations; and it must balance the design of the front and back of the book with the editorial features by creating a consistent yet flexible feel throughout. The evolution of the magazine could probably be documented through the epidemic growth of cover lines, and while these bursts of text on the cover may represent the decline of mainstream editorial design, various designers and publishers have managed to create engaging publications within the industry's standards and expectations for their time.

Detail of **PLAYBOY 21, NO. 1** / art direction, Art Paul; photography, Dwight Hooker / USA, January 1974

Eros, Fact:, Avant Garde

Through an influential partnership between Ralph Ginzburg and Herb Lubalin › 167, three distinct magazines were published in the 1960s: *Eros, Fact:,* and *Avant Garde.* Ginzburg, who had worked as an editor at *Esquire* › 326 and had also published several books, began working with Lubalin in 1962 to design his first quarterly magazine, *Eros,* named after the Greek god of love and desire, and devoted to eroticism, love, and sex through history, politics, art, and literature. Lubalin was given free reign in the design, and with a variety of display typefaces driven by the content, tasteful photography, and bold layouts, *Eros* published four issues, as the fifth installment never made it past the production table. While no expense seems to have been spared in the hardbound 96-page magazine, its legal woes led to its demise as the original promotional letter seeking charter subscribers, received by millions of individuals, made its way into court. After years of legal proceedings, the wording of the letter, not the magazine itself, was ruled obscene, and Ginzburg was sentenced to three years in prison.

Ginzburg and Lubalin partnered a second time in a political journal named *Fact:* that, as its name implies, sought to set the record straight and expose hidden truths. First published in 1964, *Fact:*'s design approach was directly related to budgetary constraints; they often commissioned a single illustrator for all of the articles in one issue for a flat fee. With the use of limited colors and bold headlines, often set in serif typefaces, a minimalist elegance was accomplished that stood apart from the competing publications of the time. In its first year, Ginzburg was sued for defamation by then Republican presidential candidate Barry Goldwater, a conflict he lost after several years. Ginzburg's financial payout forced him to cease publication of *Fact:,* but his determination was not entirely dampened.

EROS MAGAZINE NO. 2 / Herb Lubalin; photography, Donald Snyder / USA, Summer 1962

EROS MAGAZINE NO. 3 / Herb Lubalin; photography, Bert Stern / USA, Autumn 1962

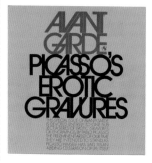

AVANT GARDE #8: PICASSO'S EROTIC GRAVURES / Herb Lubalin / USA, September 1969

AVANT GARDE PROTOTYPE ISSUE / Herb Lubalin / USA, 1974

Images: Courtesy of The Herb Lubalin Study Center of Design and Typography at the Cooper Union School of Art

Avant Garde, launched in 1968, was a magazine that also challenged the social status quo, although less abrasively than its predecessors, by including essays, reportage, and fiction covering politics, art, and culture. Lubalin established a highly geometric structure in the publication, most readily noted in the masthead, lettered by Tom Carnase, where perfect circles, straight lines, multiple ligatures, and minimal kerning space were a custom precedent for the subsequently developed typeface ▸ 374. After 16 issues, *Avant Garde*'s final issue was published as Ginzburg began serving a reduced sentence of eight months in prison. Although a revival was attempted upon his release, Ginzburg's financial situation was not equal to the task.

FACT: / Herb Lubalin / USA, July/August 1964

FACT: / Herb Lubalin / USA, January/February 1965

AVANT GARDE #3: REVALUATION OF THE DOLLAR / Herb Lubalin; cover dollar illustrations, Tom Carnase / USA, May 1968

ANDY'S GIRLS SPREAD FROM AVANT GARDE #3 / Herb Lubalin / USA, May 1968

BELLES LETTRES: A PHOTO ALPHABET SPREAD FROM AVANT GARDE #14 / Herb Lubalin; Ed Van Der Elsken, Anna Beeke / USA, Summer 1971

Playboy

After graduating from the University of Illinois, Hugh Hefner held various jobs in publishing companies before working for *Esquire* › 326, then considered one of the most sexually charged publications for men, in part because of Alberto Vargas's pin-up girls. In 1953, while employed at *Children's Activities* magazine, Hefner began assembling a new kind of magazine for men, one defined by an elusive lifestyle of both cultural and material sophistication and riches that also celebrated sex as an everyday occurrence and not the taboo it was considered; the title was *Stag Party*. Working with cartoonist Arv Miller, who created the layouts and a stag mascot, Hefner's initial dummy was unsatisfying; it was Art Paul, a Chicago designer and illustrator educated at László Moholy-Nagy's Institute of Design, who lay the foundation for the next 30 years.

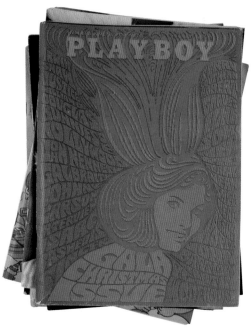

PLAYBOY **MAGAZINE** / art direction, Arthur Paul / USA, 1967 and 1974

One of Paul's first objections was the name. Given, in addition, a threat from a hunting magazine named *Stag*, Hefner selected *Playboy* as the title and a bunny as its mascot. Miller's stag was kept, his head replaced. The now famous icon of the bunny profile, drawn by Paul, made its debut in the third issue, and from that moment on it became Paul's visual quiz for *Playboy*'s readers: Find the bunny in the sophisticated, witty, and conceptual covers of the 1960s and 1970s—a far cry from today's blunt displays of cleavage. Inside, Paul complemented the erudite articles and interviews with a simple yet frolicsome layout that allowed for typographic play and the integration of illustrations from some of the most respected fine artists and commercial illustrators of the time. Whether people purchased *Playboy* for the articles or the nudes, for 30 years their favored content was always beautifully presented.

Esquire

With no publication for men comparable to *Vogue* or *Harper's Bazaar* ›327, in 1933 publisher David A. Smart and editor Arnold Gingrich launched *Esquire*, a magazine combining fiction, sports, humor, poetry, fashion, and other elements of a lush lifestyle targeted at men. Publishing the work of writers like Ernest Hemingway and F. Scott Fitzgerald gave *Esquire* a proper reputation, but the pin-up girls drawn by Alberto Vargas and George Petty drew the wrong kind of attention when the Postmaster General attempted to revoke its second-class mailing privileges for its "obscene" content, culminating in the Supreme Court ruling in favor of *Esquire* in 1946. Over the years, especially in the roaring 1960s, the magazine gained notoriety for its journalism and content, fiercely embodied by the covers created by advertising giant George Lois.

Esquire's art direction is richly storied, with many notable figures appearing in its masthead, including Paul Rand ›159 in the mid 1930s, Henry Wolf in the 1950s, Sam Antupit in the 1960s, Milton Glaser ›170 in the 1970s, and Roger Black in the 1990s, but it's the covers of Lois that are most deeply embedded in American visual culture. After leaving ad agency Doyle Dane Bernbach, he established Papert Koenig Lois in 1960 and took his first commission from *Esquire* in 1962—where, boldly (or foolishly), he showed a picture of Lloyd Patterson (well, someone posing as him) defeated at the hands of Sonny Liston...before the *fight* had occurred. Through poignant and visionary images (regularly photographed by Carl Fischer) and cover lines usually reserved for print ads, Lois's covers for the next ten years arguably helped *Esquire* climb out of economic and editorial troubles. More important, they reflected a tempestuous era ripe for visual commentary.

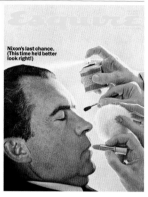

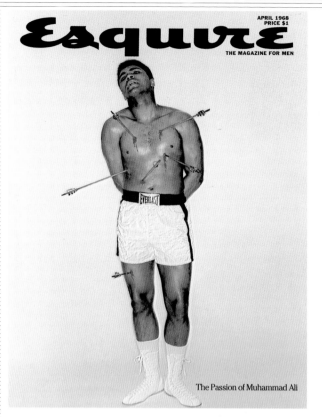

The Passion of Muhammad Ali

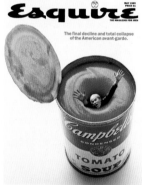

ESQUIRE MAGAZINE / George Lois; photography, Carl Fischer / USA, 1965–1969

Harper's Bazaar

Harper and Brothers, a growing print and publishing house, established *Harper's Bazaar* in 1867 as an early vehicle for Victorian fashion. It was purchased in 1912 by William Randolph Hearst, and it is a property of Hearst Corporation to this day. While *Harper's Bazaar* has long been an arbiter of fashion and has remained relevant through its content, it has also served as an exemplar of editorial design on more than one occasion. The first was in the 1930s, when newly appointed editor-in-chief Carmel Snow began to assemble a team to help revolutionize the notion of magazine design and photography. The team included Martin Munkacsi, who freed fashion shoots from the studio and into the world, and Alexey Brodovitch › 143, who freed the page to take pleasure in white space and the finely tuned pacing of text and image.

Brodovitch commissioned European artists like Man Ray, Salvador Dali, and A.M. Cassandre and fostered the work of American photographers like Lisette Model, Diane Arbus, and Richard Avedon, who spent 20 years as a staff photographer until 1965. Upon Brodovitch's departure in 1958, Henry Wolf assumed the role of art director and infused the magazine with his own acuity and typographic sensibilities. His tenure ended in 1961 and was followed by the collaborative art direction of Ruth Ansel and Bea Feitler. Another significant editorial and creative gust came when Liz Tilberis became editor-in-chief in 1992, appointing Fabien Baron—reeling from successful turns at Italian *Vogue* and Andy Warhol's *Interview*—as the creative director. With a fresh cut of the magazine's Didot type family by Hoefler & Frere-Jones › 230, Baron introduced an assertive balance of sculptured typography and vibrant photography to create an assertive publication. Tilberis passed away in 1999, and Baron left that same year.

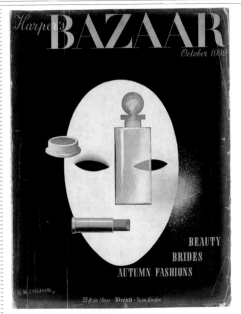

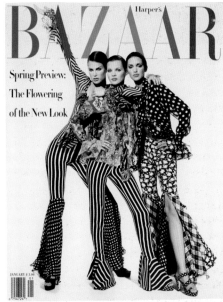

Rolling Stone

In 1967, amid the social, political, and cultural upheaval of the time and the accompanying surge of the underground press, music critic Ralph J. Gleason and 21-year-old rock-and-roll aficionado Jann S. Wenner launched *Rolling Stone*, a publication with music as its journalistic epicenter. *Rolling Stone* deftly established itself as an influential publication for a new generation not just of readers but of writers like Hunter S. Thompson and Cameron Crowe and photographers like Annie Leibovitz, and it fostered the contributions of numerous art directors. Initially art directed by John Williams for one year, then Robert Kingsbury until 1974, two distinctive elements were the logo, drawn by psychedelic poster designer Rick Griffith, and the Oxford (or Scotch) Rule, a double thick-and-thin-stroke border, perhaps the simplest visual device but a defining one for *Rolling Stone*.

Following Mike Salisbury and Tony Lane, Roger Black introduced a more cohesive system in 1976, hiring lettering artist Jim Parkinson to redesign the logo and create a sturdy serif type family based on Griffith's work, giving the magazine a distinctive look and feel. Black left in 1978 and, through the 1980s, *Rolling Stone* gradually veered away from this design, ending in layouts dominated by sans serif typography. In 1987, Fred Woodward, who had gingerly risen as art director in other magazines, joined, and for the next 14 years he infused the layouts with unbridled typographic play that gave feature stories their own unique flavor, while a four-part type family, code-named The Proteus Project, designed by Hoefler & Frere-Jones ‹230›, brought some consistency, aided by the reintroduction of the Oxford Rule. With fellow art director Gail Anderson, *Rolling Stone* offered some the most venturesome double-page spreads of the 1990s.

AXL ROSE LOST YEARS, *Rolling Stone* magazine / art direction, Fred Woodward; design, Fred Woodward, Gail Anderson; illustration, Alex Ostroy / USA, May 11, 2000

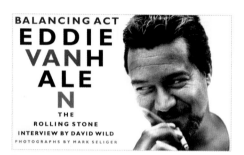

BALANCING ACT: EDDIE VAN HALEN, *Rolling Stone* magazine / art direction, Fred Woodward; design, Geraldine Hessler; photography, Mark Seliger / USA, April 6, 1955

MAN OF THE YEAR: DAVID LETTERMAN, *Rolling Stone* magazine / art direction, Fred Woodward; design, Fred Woodward, Geraldine Hessler; illustration, David Cowles / USA, January 12, 1995

CHRIS ROCK STAR, *Rolling Stone* magazine / art direction, Fred Woodward; design, Fred Woodward, Gail Anderson; photography, Mark Seliger / USA, October 2, 1997

LADY SOUL, *Rolling Stone* magazine / art direction, Fred Woodward; design, Siung Tjia; photography, Mark Seliger / USA, February 18, 1999

DMX REIGNS AS THE DARK PRINCE OF HIP-HOP, *Rolling Stone* magazine / art direction, Fred Woodward; photography; Albert Watson / USA, April 13, 2000

Spy

For more than two years, before its first issue hit newsstands in October 1986, *Spy* magazine was an impalpable alternative to the New York publishing industry, inhabited by magazines like *New York* › 336, the *New Yorker*, and the *Village Voice*, in the minds of Kurt Andersen and E. Graydon Carter, then architecture critic for *Time* and writer for *Life*, respectively, and spurred by the business savvy of Tom Phillips, an investment banker. This alternative was perhaps best described in a preemptive direct mail piece calling for subscribers: "*Spy* is the funny, fearless, fast-paced magazine for smart New Yorkers.... *Spy* is polished and satirical, sophisticated yet mischievous, well-dressed but slightly ill-mannered, literate, urbane—and just a little dangerous."

Spy launched an onslaught on the social, economical, political, and cultural layers of the city and its most public figures through a mix of irreverence, snark, and even meanness, presented through a design brimming with typography, charts, graphs, dingbats, and floating heads. In retrospect, Donald Trump and white space suffered most in the hands of *Spy*. The prototype and early issues were designed by Drenttel Doyle Partners, and in 1987 Alexander Isley, previously employed at M&Co. › 183, became art director, taking *Spy* into an even more nuanced and mannered visual direction that reveled in satirical diagrams and infographics while maximizing the ridiculing impact of less than stellar black and white photography. Isley left less than two years later and was succeeded by B. W. Honeycutt. *Spy* consistently struggled to secure advertisers, finally breaking even three years in, only to be met by a recession; it was sold in 1991 and eventually folded in 1998. Today, the design and journalistic voice of *Spy* are apparent, and missed, in all media.

Drenttel Doyle Partners: art direction, Stephen Doyle / October 1986

Art direction and design, Alexander Isley; photography, Deborah Feingold / April 1989

Art direction and design, Alexander Isley / March 1987

Art direction and design, Alexander Isley / April 1988

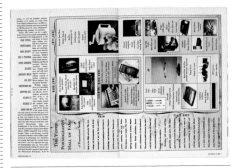

Art direction, Alexander Isley / December 1987

Welcome to Rat City!

Art direction and design, Alexander Isley; photography, Neil Selkirk / May 1988

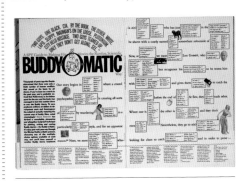

Art direction, B.W. Honeycutt / February 1993

SPY MAGAZINE / USA

Ray Gun

Looking to start a new kind of publication hinging on style and attitude that would cover the changing face of music in the throes of grunge and other evolving musical styles not covered by MTV › 352, *Rolling Stone* › 328, or *Spin*, Marvin Scott Jarrett, who had previously run *Creem* magazine, turned to David Carson › 186, based on his work at the short-lived *Beach Culture*, to be the inaugural art director. While still working at *Surfer* magazine, Carson put together the first issue at night and on weekends, and in 1992 *Ray Gun* was launched—epitomizing Carson's rule-bending design approach and giving his style a relatively mainstream audience. Unlike typical relationships between editor and art director, Carson and Jarrett worked in different cities, rarely if ever discussing the design direction of the content other than the covers. Jarrett granted Carson unlimited freedom, and the results ignited pyrotechnics of praise and scorn from the music, publishing, and design industries—and engendered endless imitation.

At the core of Carson's technique was the vigorous dismantling of typography; he distorted letterforms, separated words, squeezed paragraphs, and disfigured layouts—sometimes for the benefit of a story, other times not. At their most commendable, *Ray Gun*'s pages were kinetic and engaging, and at their most disruptive, a story would be rendered in Zapf Dingbats. Perhaps lost in the midst of Carson's designs was his role as art director; aptly commissioning work from energetic new photographers, illustrators, and type designers, generously crediting their contributions in the magazine. GarageFonts, a digital type foundry, was established in 1993 to distribute and nurture the typefaces used in *Ray Gun*. Carson and Jarrett ended their collaboration in 1995 after 30 issues. The magazine pursued different design directions with various art directors before it folded in 2000.

RAY GUN **MAGAZINE** / **David Carson** / **USA, 1992–1995**

Colors

Three individuals played a major role in the creation of *Colors* magazine: Luciano Benetton, founder of the Italian clothing company Benetton; photographer Oliviero Toscani, in charge of Benetton's advertising; and designer Tibor Kalman ›183. In 1991, Toscani approached Kalman about developing a multicultural magazine, sponsored solely by Benetton, that would appeal to the somewhat dissatisfied and politicized younger generation—a platform both men relished. Available throughout the world in five different bilingual versions (French/English, Spanish/English, etc.), the magazine found its global approach when it adopted thematic issues, beginning with Race in the fourth issue. Two years into the project, Kalman closed his New York studio, M&Co., and moved to Rome to devote his full energy to *Colors*.

Kalman directed a unique magazine whose lack of decorative elements and visual devices and limited use of sans-serif typefaces allowed the photography and content to speak more loudly than the design; the content managed to both enthrall and enrage, often shocking people into starting a conversation, which is just what *Colors* set out to do. In 1995 Kalman completed his final issue, number 13, as a wordless publication inspired by Charles and Ray Eames's film *Power of Ten*. After his departure, Fernando Gutierrez, who had worked with Kalman on his last issue, took charge of the magazine, redesigning it to follow a more journalistic and in-depth approach. As the magazine progressed, Benetton's communication research center, Fabrica, in Treviso, Italy, took over the magazine. In 2004 Number 17, the design firm of Emily Oberman (who designed the original *Colors* logo while employed at M&Co.) and Bonnie Siegler, designed the magazine alongside then editor Kurt Andersen for a brief period. *Colors* is currently again under the supervision of Fabrica.

COLORS NO. 1 / M&Co.: design, Emily Oberman; cover photography, Oliviero Toscani / 1991

COLORS NO. 2 / M&Co.: design, Gary Koepke; cover photography, Associated Press / Spring 1992

COLORS NO. 3 / M&Co.: design, Paul Ritter; cover photography, Steve McCurry / Fall 1992

COLORS NO. 6: *ECOLOGY* / M&Co.: design, Scott Stowell; cover photography, Marcus Muzi / March 1994

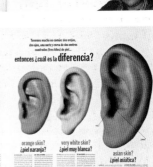

Above and Right **COLORS** NO. 4: *RACE* / M&Co.: design, Paul Ritter; cover photography, Oliviero Toscani / Spring, 1993

COLORS MAGAZINE / Editor in Chief, Tibor Kalman / USA, Italy, 1991–1995

The Face

Focusing on the changing face of fashion at the outset of the decade, editor and publisher Nick Logan launched *The Face* in 1980 with a minimal budget, a limitation that perhaps gave it its edge. *The Face* quickly became a popular style manual of low-budget street culture and fashion that eventually, like other subversive fads, was coopted by commercialism and advertising—a snag also faced by its art director, Neville Brody. His tenure began in 1981, after two years of working for independent record labels. At first, the design felt almost tentative, using commercial typefaces in relatively simple layouts. Slowly, *The Face* morphed into a kinetic playground for typographic exploration and the graphic flotsam and jetsam it left in its path.

By 1984, Brody had instituted a highly expressive design and other magazines had begun mimicking the style of *The Face*. Brody introduced the first custom typeface with issue number 50, establishing a daringly unique aesthetic. In the subsequent 25-plus issues, new typefaces would appear as soon as the reader had become familiar with the previous ones. Brody also began to contort letterforms, creating an endlessly mutable range of typographic solutions for headlines and story leads while leaving the body text highly accessible. He also played with the continuity afforded by the magazine, gradually deconstructing or morphing a section's title to its most abstract possibilities. Typography was mixed with graphic symbols and devices, sometimes to the point of blurring the line between text and object, creating a new visual vocabulary. Brody kept the magazine evolving, introducing computer-condensed and extended typography in 1985 and then more classic layouts toward 1986, the year he left *The Face*. Logan and Brody worked together again on *Arena* from 1987 to 1990.

THE FACE MAGAZINE / creative direction, Neville Brody / UK

Speak

Speak magazine's first issue was published in 1995 by editor Dan Rolleri, who set out to develop a quarterly package of thoughtful writing on culture, loosely covering music, fashion, literature, and art. Two years prior, Rolleri hired Martin Venezky as he finished graduate school at Cranbrook Academy of Art › 130, giving him the task of designing *Speak*'s media kit; the proposed design led editor and designer to court as they fought over design, content, wages, and, ultimately, pride. Venezky was called back when another designer failed to deliver, and he completed the media kit as well as the first issue. For the ensuing edition, however, Venezky was replaced with David Carson › 186.

Back as art director for the third issue, Venezky proceeded to establish an almost accidental aesthetic within *Speak* that stemmed from his connection to and investment in each spread as well as the minimal budget available for photography and illustration, which led to the use of found materials and hand-drawn elements. With vast detailing, methodical layering, and unexpected yet thoughtful elements, each page slowly revealed its contents by engaging the reader. Similarly, the relationship between Rolleri and Venezky proved detailed and layered as they grew and matured alongside the magazine, steering each issue into a more intellectual realm with conscious disregard for advertisers and profits. While *Speak* was acclaimed in the design community, it failed to promote itself in the editorial world, and while its loyal readers appreciated the content, the lack of advertising funds eventually led to its demise in 2001 after publishing 21 issues.

NO. 1 / **Preview issue** / **Fall 1995**

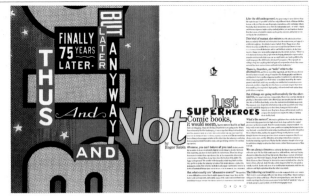

NO. 6 / **Summer 1997**

NO. 20 / **Martin Venezky** / **USA, Fall 2000**

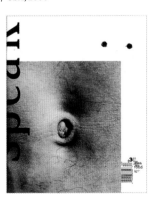

NO. 21 / **Final issue** / **USA, 2000**

NO. 9 / **USA, April/May 1998**

NO. 10 / **June/July 1998**

NO. 3 / **Fall 1996**

***SPEAK* MAGAZINE** / **Martin Venezky** / **USA**

Nest

From an experience working with a photographer on a book and an incandescent passion for interior decoration—he spent five years decorating his Baltimore apartment—Joseph Holtzman launched his own magazine focusing on interiors but, as the subsequent 24 issues proved, that would merely begin to describe the content of *Nest*. With no publishing experience, no design know-how, and certainly no defined target audience, Holtzman rented an apartment adjacent to his own in New York and with his own money created the first issue in 1997. As a testament to the controlled eccentricity that became the clarion call of *Nest*, the first cover and its related feature story showed a room wallpapered by an avid fan with fashion magazine covers of Farrah Fawcett. Whether the subject was the interiors of a submarine, an apartment covered in silver foil, or a house built out of beer cans, *Nest*'s content shared not just shock value but displays of the unique living shelters individuals create for themselves—an endless parade of individuality that *Nest* reveled in.

The magazine itself was anything but traditional, and Holtzman took pride in that he constructed every page, even though he could barely operate a computer. With graphic designer (and saxophonist) Tom Beckham as his "graphics director," Holtzman created a design aesthetic revolving around ornaments and patterns framing its extensive photography, with the typography receding to a secondary role. Physically, *Nest* changed every issue; it featured complex and costly die-cuts, trims, and production tricks that made the magazine an object of affection itself. Further establishing his own rules, Holtzman took few advertisers and relegated them to the front and back of the book, leaving the feature stories intact—and he did not hesitate to drill four holes or a cross through the whole magazine, ads included. Despite comparatively low circulation, distribution, and promotion, *Nest* enjoyed much critical acclaim. It ceased publication in 2004.

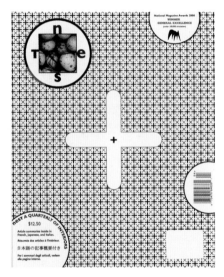
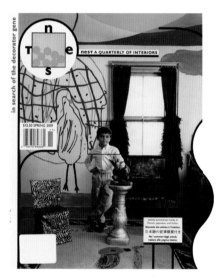

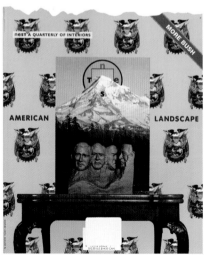

Martha Stewart Living

Following a preliminary career as a stockbroker, Martha Stewart began a successful catering business that led to her first book, published in 1982 by Clarkson Potter (and designed by Roger Black). *Entertaining* catalogued the menus and decorations of various dinner parties and receptions, effectively launching Martha's domestic design career. With the success of *Entertaining* and the growth of Clarkson Potter, its editor hired Gael Towey as art director, who worked on many books, among them Stewart's. In 1990, through a deal with Time, Inc., Stewart began developing her flagship magazine, *Martha Stewart Living (MSL)*, and hired Towey as the art director. The inaugural issue launched by the end of the year. Through its focus on beautiful photography that elicited deep yearning from any still life, whether an ear of corn or a napkin ring, and its presentation in simple and clear layouts colored in a distinctive range of pastels that never became cloying, *MSL* became irresistibly successful through the 1990s.

With success comes imitation, and when many magazines began mimicking *MSL*'s style, it was necessary to redesign. In 2000, Towey approached book cover designer Barbara deWilde to undertake the task. For the next two years, DeWilde and her design team reworked every detail of the magazine, from recipe charts to feature stories. Two of the most distinctive introductions were Archer and Surveyor, proprietary type families designed by Hoefler & Frere-Jones › 230 that, along with the photography, became the hallmark of the magazine. The redesign began to be implemented on October 2002, and it served as a balanced and nuanced purveyor for the numerous recipes, decorations, and products that dozens of stylists, editors, photographers, and art directors develop from the ground up. *MSL* is now part of a vast empire, Martha Stewart Living Omnimedia, of which its production values and philosophy permeate every single aspect, in part because of the leadership of Towey, its chief creative officer since 2005.

MARTHA STEWART LIVING MAGAZINE / USA, 1995–2003

New York

Originally published as the Sunday supplement of the *New York Herald Tribune* newspaper in 1964, *New York* had two of the most galvanizing personalities in New York's publishing industry, its editor, Clay Felker, and staff writer Tom Wolfe. When the *Herald Tribune* closed in 1968, Felker and prior collaborator Milton Glaser › 170 decided to extend the life of *New York* as a weekly magazine covering every perspective—real estate, finance, dining, fashion, politics, shopping, everything—of living, working, and playing in the city. With Felker as editor and Glaser as design director, the first issue was launched in April 1968. It rode an ascendant wave of attention and acclaim until media mogul Rupert Murdoch snatched away the publication in 1977. *New York* continued, but it was not the same without Felker, Glaser, or its art director of nine years, Walter Bernard.

Beginning in 2004, the magazine underwent big changes, hiring editor Adam Moss and design director Luke Hayman. Together they went back to *New York*'s editorial and visual origins to create a new interpretation. The result was a tightly packed magazine that managed to feel both traditional and contemporary through the combination of various ingredients: several typefaces (including the original slab serif), mixed and matched freely; Oxford (or Scotch) rules as active framing devices; dynamic charts and diagrams; bold photography; and a redrawn logo by Ed Benguiat that ties together more than 40 years of publication. Since Hayman's departure in 2006 to join Pentagram › 162, Chris Dixon has continued the evolution of *New York* as a vibrant representation of the city and the practice of editorial design.

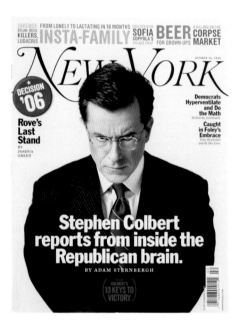

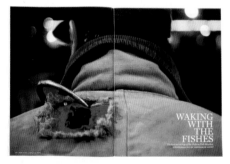

NEW YORK MAGAZINE / Pentagram: Luke Hayman / USA, 2005–2006

The New York Times Magazine

On September 6, 1896, the first printed photographs from the *New York Times* appeared in its inaugural issue of the Sunday supplement, *The New York Times Magazine*, and for more than a century it has literally supplemented the news with expanded views of the moment's most pressing matters. In the late 1970s and early 1980s, under the art direction of Louis Silverstein, the *New York Times* newspaper underwent a significant redesign, introducing the six-column format, creating new sections, and revising older ones. Silverstein hired Ruth Ansel as art director for the magazine, after she left *Harper's Bazaar* › 327, and while her interest wasn't explicitly in the inside spreads and typography, she did create striking covers. She brought assorted voices to the magazine by commissioning work from photographers like Mary Ellen Mark, Gilles Peress, and Bill King, and, from her own acquaintances, by using illustration and artwork from local up-and-comers like Andy Warhol, Roy Lichtenstein, and James Rosenquist.

Ansel left in 1981 and Roger Black, previously at *Rolling Stone* › 328, took over in 1982; he gave the magazine structure and consistency while maintaining the gravitas of the covers. Beginning in 1994, with the art direction of Janet Froelich, who had previously worked at the weekend magazine of the *Daily News*, the *Times Magazine* began to introduce a sophisticated use of white space, inventive execution of typography, and commissioned stately photography and illustration. Perhaps a representative of the magazine's astute blending of word and image is William Safire's column, "On Language," introduced in 1979. Every week Safire explores the grammar, usage, and etymology of words like *warrior*, *epicenter*, and *nuance*, and every week a designer or illustrator visualizes the word, making evident the communicative potential of writing and design, together.

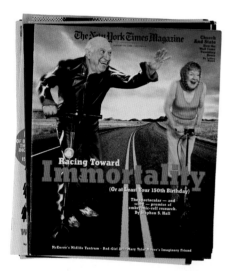

PRACTICE
In Identity

340
Logos

For many graphic designers, the logo is the ultimate expression of graphic design—a literal, figurative, or abstract icon, or a compelling wordmark that represents a product or organization and makes it instantly identifiable. Logos by themselves can't tell the complete story or describe all the attributes of a product or organization; they are beholden to the behaviors of who or what they represent and the associations triggered by their reputation. Logos are also rarely deployed alone; rather, they are accompanied by a complementary visual system (an identity program) that enhances and supports its presence. Nonetheless, there is something infinitely satisfying about a strong, memorable, innovative, and clever logo—especially one that can stand on its own.

350
Identity Programs

Building a visual language that can serve as an encompassing identity for a product or organization requires the definition of colors, typefaces, and other graphic elements and their integration in an expandable system that is consistent but adaptable to different communication needs and mediums. Identity programs range from the sparingly simple, defining a small range of colors and applications of the logo, to infinitely expandable systems, with multiple versions of a logo or a comprehensive library of imagery and graphics that acts as a kit of parts that can be assembled at the discretion of designers or vendors inheriting the program. Neither direction is better than the other, and both require a disciplined application to achieve consistency and relevance.

Detail of **UNILEVER IDENTITY AS USED ON CONSUMER PACKAGING** / Wolff Olins / UK, 2004

Coca-Cola

Pharmacist Dr. John S. Pemberton used two main ingredients in the creation of his famous beverage, coca plant and cola (or kola) nut. Frank Robinson, his partner and the company's book-keeper (chief financial officer, perhaps, in today's terms), named the drink Coca-Cola, which Pemberton introduced in 1886 at Jacob's Pharmacy in Atlanta, Georgia. Coca-Cola's first ad ran in the *Atlanta Journal* on May 29, 1886, and featured the name set in a sans serif typeface; it wasn't until a June 1887 ad that Robinson introduced the Spencerian handwriting logo he developed. Later, an oilcloth sign with the red logo on a white background was placed on the awning of Jacob's Pharmacy. More than 120 years later, the Coca-Cola logo remains true to its original. It has undergone numerous refinements over the years, and as the brand became bigger and harder to control, firms like Lippincott Mercer in the 1960s—they introduced the wave underline based on the contour of the bottle—and Landor Associates in the 1980s developed comprehensive identity programs. Whether hand-painted on a wall in a rural village or printed in corporate letterhead, the Coca-Cola logo is one of the most recognized in the world.

COCA-COLA LOGO

Ashland, Oregon, USA, 2006 / Photo: Flickr user ElektraCute

Paris, France, 2008 / Photo: Flickr user OTAILLON

Brighton, UK, 2008 / Photo: Flickr user Dominic's pics

Schenectady, New York, USA, 2007 / Photo: Flickr user roytsaplinjr

Ridgeland, Mississippi, USA, 2007 / Photo: Flickr user iboy_daniel

IBM

During World War II, International Business Machines Corporation (IBM) took its first steps toward advancing computing technologies while continuing the development of its electric typewriter. Change came in 1952 when Thomas J. Watson Sr., IBM's chief executive for nearly four decades, passed the title to his son, Thomas J. Watson Jr. Determined to position IBM as a commanding company from its products to its public appearance, Watson brought in architect and interior designer Eliot Noyes to oversee the transformation of IBM's architecture, manufacturing, product design, and visual communication. Noyes hired Paul Rand ⟩ 159, whom he knew socially, to establish a much-needed identity program for IBM in 1956. Although a simplified logo of the acronym typeset in a slab serif had been introduced in 1947, the convoluted globe logo constructed from the full name of the company that was first used in 1924 could still be occasionally seen. Rand's first change was subtle, exchanging one slab serif for another, Beton Bold Condensed for City Medium.

Slowly and delicately, Rand kept altering the logo, at one point introducing an outline version to lighten the heaviness of the letters. It wasn't until 1962 that the famous striped version was first used by Rand—it was officially introduced in 1972—as he sought to consolidate the dissonant letterforms through the unified set of lines that ran from one letter to the next. Conceptually, the stripes were spurred by the notion of the thin parallel lines used in legal documents to protect a signature from counterfeiting, alluding to a sense of authority. Rand created two versions of the logo, one that used eight lines and another 13. For nearly 30 more years, until 1991, Rand oversaw the application of the logo and the identity across all of IBM's applications, from packaging to annual reports, and instituted forceful standards for the in-house design group in documents like *IBM Logo Use and Abuse* and *The IBM Logo*, which also showed the potential flexibility and creativity of the logo. As corporate identities from the 1960s and 1970s slowly disappear, it might be a matter of time before the next version of the IBM logo has no stripes at all.

IBM, CHICAGO OFFICE / USA, 2001 / Photo: Flickr user alui0000

UPS

With bicycles and their own two feet, teenagers Jim Casey and Claude Ryan established their private delivery service as American Messenger Company in Seattle, Washington, in 1907. Six years later, the company acquired its first delivery car, a Model T Ford, and changed its name to Merchants Parcel Delivery. In 1919, it expanded service in Oakland, California, and changed the company name to United Parcel Service (UPS). The new logo introduced an eagle grasping a parcel in its claws and flying over a shield.

Around 1937, as the firm grew, another new logo was adopted, this one with the company's acronym inside a shield. After working unsuccessfully with other designers to redesign their logo, UPS approached Paul Rand ›159, who responded, to his client's surprise, with a single design solution—a simplified shield with sans-serif lettering and the outline of a bow-tied package. Rand's logo was used from 1961 until 2003, when a new logo, designed by Futurebrand, was introduced to signal the evolution of UPS from a package delivery company to a logistics company with diverse supply chain services.

UNITED PARCEL SERVICE PACKAGE CAR / Replica of the P-600 delivery vehicle / Made in Hong Kong

UPS EXPRESS ENVELOPES

FROM UNDERNEATH A NEW UPS LOGO BY FUTUREBRAND, AN OLD LOGO BY PAUL RAND EMERGES / USA, 2008 / Photo: Brandon Shigeta

FedEx

Federal Express, founded by Frederic W. Smith in 1973, inaugurated the concept of overnight delivery service by creating a hub where packages arrive and then disperse to their locations in the middle of the night. By the late 1980s, the name was synonymous with overnight shipping. Federal Express began working with Landor Associates in the early 1990s to fortify its growing brand presence. Landor's research revealed the name Federal Express was not optimal for global markets and suggested renaming the company FedEx, the way some insiders and customers already referred to it. The identity design was led by the senior design director at Landor's San Francisco office, Lindon Leader. After hundreds of design explorations and input from their clients, Leader and his team presented six possibilities to a room full of executives. Only Smith spotted Leader's typographic sculpting that revealed an arrow between the *E* and the *x*. The new logo was introduced in 1994, but people still challenge each other to find the hidden arrow.

FEDEX EXPRESS ENVELOPES

FEDEX TRUCKS AT REST / USA, 2007 / Photo: Flickr user Andrew Christensen

FEDEX MCDONNELL DOUGLAS DC-10-10(F) N361FE PLANE / USA, 2008 / Photo: Flickr user Cubbie_n_Vegas

Nike

After distributing sports shoes since the mid-1960s under the name of Blue Ribbon Sports (BRS), Phil Knight was determined to establish his own line. Looking to build an identity for it, he hired Carolyn Davidson, an art student at Portland State University. Knight requested a logo that would be as effective as the three stripes of Adidas, which were not only visually dynamic but also functional, holding the upper and lower soles together while supporting the arch. Davidson set her own fee at $35. Among her designs was a checkmark toward which Knight and his partners gravitated despite a heavy dose of skepticism. "I don't love it," Knight said, "but I think it will grow on me." It's not clear when the logo became known as the Swoosh, but one of the first shoes distributed by BRS was made of nylon, a fabric promoted in an ad as the "Swoosh fiber." The next step was choosing a name. Knight had proposed Dimension Six, to little excitement, with Bengal as another option. The day before the shoeboxes were to be printed, there was still no name. The next morning, one of his partners, Jeff Johnson, came up with Nike, after the Greek goddess of victory. "I guess we'll go with the Nike thing for now," Knight commented, "I really don't like any of them, but I guess that's the best of the bunch." Not a bad turn of events for a couple of ugly duckling choices.

NIKE PRODUCTS / USA

 RECOMMENDED READING › 390

ABC LOGO / After other designers had failed, the American Broadcasting Company (ABC) approached Paul Rand › 159. With a visually compelling acronym of three round letters, Rand drew each letter out of three perfect circles, with their counterspaces also forming three perfect circles. Over the years, ABC has attempted to replace the logo—even Peter Saville › 180 designed an alternative in 1996—to no avail. / Paul Rand / USA, 1962

NBC LOGO / Years ahead of its competitors, the National Broadcasting Company (NBC) began airing color broadcasts in 1953. Three years later, the NBC peacock strutted its colored feathers for the first time, not as a logo but as an on-air identifier to brag about the departure from black and white. After the 1975 abstract *N* logo was found to pose a trademark infringement on the Nebraska ETV Network, the peacock was embedded in the *N* in 1979. The peacock finally became the center of attention in 1986 with a simplified design by Steff Geissbuhler › 157, who trimmed the peacock's feathers from 11 to six and turning its head to face right. / Chermayeff & Geismar, Inc.: designer, Steff Geissbuhler / USA, 1986

CBS LOGO / Based on hex symbols drawn on Shaker barns to ward off evil and on a drawing of an all-seeing eye in a book about Shaker art, William Golden, creative director of Columbia Broadcasting System (CBS), devised the streamlined drawing of the eye with graphic artist Kurt Weiss. Golden intended it as a visual device for just one season, but CBS president Frank Stanton designated it the official logo. / CBS: creative direction, William Golden / USA, 1951

I ♥ NY LOGO / Hoping to boost the state's economy by increasing tourism, in 1975 the New York State Department of Commerce hired advertising agency Wells, Rich, Greene and designer Milton Glaser › 170 to develop a campaign. With the theme "I Love New York," Glaser first designed a logo that spelled out the full name, and it was accepted. While riding in a taxi, Glaser replaced the word *love* with a heart and had to convince his clients this was the better option. Of course, it was. The "I ♥ [blank]" visual trope has become one of the most imitated, parodied, and commercialized, much to the distress of the state's lawyers, who have reportedly filed approximately 3,000 trademark objections. / Milton Glaser / USA, 1975

GENERAL ELECTRIC LOGO / In 1892, Thomas Edison's The General Electric Company merged with The Thompson-Houston Company to form General Electric. The initials *GE*, in an Art Nouveau style, were used as a logo. In 1900 they were simplified, bordered by four swirling curlicues, and placed inside a circle. "[The] letters *G-E* are more than a trademark," stated a 1923 advertisement. "They are an emblem of service—the initials of a friend." That friend grew to be one of the largest corporations in the world. Despite the company's constant innovations and diversification, GE has maintained its logo—referred to as the "meatball" around the 1960s—nearly without change. A vibrant update by Wolff Olins › 206 in 2004 built a visual language around the logo, extending its life just a few more years—or centuries. / Designer unknown / USA, 1892 / Version shown: Wolff Olins / USA, 2004

BP LOGO / After the merger of British Petroleum (BP) and Amoco in 1998, an interim "BP Amoco" wordmark typeset in an italic sans serif over a swoosh was briefly used. In 2000, Landor Associates introduced the Helios, named after the Greek god of the sun. A radiant but ambiguous abstraction of a sun, a flower, a plant, or all of these was designed by the San Francisco office, led by creative director Margaret Youngblood. The Helios became the centerpiece of the identity, downplaying, in lowercase letters, the BP acronym to establish some distance from the word *petroleum*. A massive advertising campaign, "Beyond Petroleum," was created by Ogilvy & Mather. More than a decade after the merger, BP stands simply for BP. / Landor Associates / USA, 2000

CITI LOGO / Citicorp and Travelers Group merged in 1998 to form Citigroup, at the time the world's largest financial firm. Working with Michael Wolff as a consultant and Pentagram's › 162 Paula Scher › 182 and Michael Bierut › 203 as the identity designers, Citigroup gave them ten weeks to design a logo that would best represent the visual legacy of both corporations. Drawing a subtle red arc over a lowercase *t*, Pentagram created a new, abstract umbrella, the identifier for Travelers Group, that also served as a joining symbol of the two companies. The shortened name *Citi*, which was a joint recommendation by Wolff and Pentagram, was rendered in blue to carry the equity of Citicorp's logo. In her monograph, *Make it Bigger*, Scher confides that this was the first logo she sketched, but then she created other options to demonstrate that a "scientific logo exploration" was actually performed. / Pentagram: Paula Scher / USA, 1998

UNILEVER LOGO / As owner of some of the world's best-known brands in the food, beverage, and personal care industries—Ben & Jerry's, Lipton, Knorr, Dove, and Pond's, to name a few—Unilever's brand is carried in products across 150 countries. In 2004, Unilever hired brand consultancy Wolff Olins › 206 to create a new identity. Led by creative director Lee Coomber and executed by outside designer Miles Newlyn, the new logo is a rare, successful instance in corporate identity where more, as opposed to less, is more. Coming together to form a *U*, 25 individual icons represent different aspects of Unilever—for example, lips (for beauty, looking good, and taste); a bee (for creation, pollination, hard work, and biodiversity); a bowl of delicious-looking food; and particles (a reference to science, bubbles, and fizz). / Wolff Olins / UK, 2004

LONDON UNDERGROUND LOGO / When the Central London Railway and a number of private underground lines were consolidated in 1906 they formed a new company, the Underground Group. In 1907, a precedent for the now famous roundel was established: a blue bar with white lettering resting on top of a solid red circle. Frank Pick, responsible for the publicity and appearance of the Underground, commissioned typographer Edward Johnston in 1916 to design a typeface for the system—Johnston Sans—and later, in 1918, to revise the logo. Johnston changed the solid circle to a band and typeset the name in his own typeface with dashes underlining each letter between the first *U* and the final *D*. The logo was simplified in 1935 by German graphic designer Hans Schlege and revised in 1972 by the London-based firm Design Research Unit. / Edward Johnston / UK, 1918 / Version shown: Design Research Unit / UK, 1972 / Image: Courtesy of Transport for London

PENGUIN BOOKS LOGO / The affordable paperbacks of Penguin Books › 274 were first published in 1935, and it was a youthful 21-year old employee, Edward Young, who designed the iconic horizontal-striped covers and charming logo, the latter the result of a visit to the London Zoo. When Jan Tschichold › 140 was hired to standardize the design of Penguin Books in 1947, one of his contributions was to redraw Young's penguin, and Pentagram › 162 partner Angus Hyland did further modifications in 2003. While these iterations concern the main Penguin Books logo, it is common to find the black and white critter take on different shapes, styles, and accoutrements in certain collections or individual cases. A recurring version is the "Dancing Penguin" logo—or, as some call it, the "Appendicitis Penguin," with its curled stomach. / Edward Young / UK, 1935 / Versions shown, left to right: Edward Young (UK, 1935), Designer unknown (USA, 1944), Jan Tschichold (UK, 1949), Pentagram (UK, 2003), David Pearson (UK, 2007)

NORTHWEST AIRLINES LOGO / From its home airport in the Twin Cities of Minneapolis and St. Paul, Northwest Airlines (then named Northwest Airways) began as a mail carrier in 1926 and started flying ticketed passengers one year later. As its name implies, the airline flew north and west to Winnipeg, Canada; Seattle, Washington; Alaska; and, later, Tokyo, among other destinations. In 1988, Landor Associates designed a logo that was both witty and serious. Honoring the name, the logo shows an arrow pointing to the northwest as if it were a compass, with a slanted *N* on the right. Looking at the arrow and the *N* together reveals a *W* to reinforce *northwest*. By 2003, Northwest Airlines's routes had greatly expanded beyond that one direction, and it shortened its name to NWA and developed a new logo by TrueBrand. The arrow still points northwest, but the visual play lost its wings. / Landor Associates / USA, 1989

CANADIAN NATIONAL RAILWAYS LOGO / The legacy of the Canadian National Railways Company (CN) spans to the mid-nineteenth century and across more than 20,000 route-miles of track in Canada and the United States. With logos that included moose and maple leaves in its past, and an increasingly antiquated perception by customers, CN commissioned New York designer James Valkus to assess the project, and he recommended a complete overhaul. Valkus assigned the logo project to Canadian designer Allan Fleming. His solution, a single-stroke line forming the letters *CN*—Fleming suggested dropping the *R* for *Railways* to create bilingual acronym, *Canadien National* in French and *Canadian National* in English—represents "the movement of people, materials, and messages from one point to another." At the time, Fleming stated that "this symbol will last for 50 years at least." As of this book's publication date, in one more year his prophecy will come true. / Allan Fleming / Canada, 1960

The Cross · The Pulpit · The Fish · The Fire

The Dove · The Cup · The Book · The Triangle

Glass artistry, Ed Macilvane

PRESBYTERIAN CHURCH (U.S.A.) LOGO / When various divisions of the Presbyterian Church came together in 1983 to form Presbyterian Church (U.S.A.), the largest such group in the United States, they hired Malcolm Grear Designers (MGD) from a pool of 46 possible consultants. The brief to MGD indicated that the new logo should include the cross as its main element as well as fire, a descending dove, and the Bible. To add to the challenge, the contract stipulated that a committee from the Presbyterian Church was to oversee the design process, not just the selected solutions. The result is an impressively inclusive seal that incorporates all the requested iconography and then some. More remarkable is that the logo was approved by an initial committee, then a 40-member board, and, finally, a 700-member governing board. / Malcolm Grear Designers / USA, 1985

CAMPAIGN FOR NUCLEAR DISARMAMENT

Nuclear bombs were deployed by the United States on the Japanese cities of Hiroshima and Nagasaki in 1945. To the dismay of people around the world, the United States, the Soviet Union, and Great Britain continued to test such weapons even after World War II ended. One of the most vocal groups urging a stop to this was the Campaign for Nuclear Disarmament (CND), formed in London in February 1958. Two months later, in conjunction with the Direct Action Committee Against Nuclear War (DAC), the CND organized a rally on Easter Day at Trafalgar Square, followed by a 52-mile march to the atomic weapons establishment in the village of Aldermaston. Reportedly, 4,000 people marched for four days, swelling to 10,000 in its final moments, many of them bearing placards picturing a stark, black circle with a white, angled, drooping cross.

Designed by Gerald Holtom, a textile designer, the symbol was meant to combine the N and D of the semaphore flag-signaling system, used to communicate at a distance by positioning one flag in each hand in different configurations. The *N* is formed by pointing both arms downward at a 45-degree angle, while holding just one arm straight in the air forms the *D*. "I was in despair. Deep despair," Holtom later explained

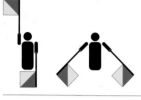

LETTERS *D* AND *N* OF THE SEMA-PHORE FLAG SIGNALING SYSTEM

POSTERS FOR THE CAMPAIGN FOR NUCLEAR DISARMAMENT / Ken Garland / UK, 1962-1966

to *PeaceNews* magazine editor Hugh Brock. "I drew myself: the representative of an individual in despair, with hands, palm outstretched, outwards and downwards in the manner of Goya's peasant before the firing squad. I formalised the drawing into a line and put a circle round it." Holtom presented this design to DAC, which embraced it as its rallying visual for the march, and afterwards CND adopted it as its official logo, putting it front and center as it hosted other rallies to Aldermaston in subsequent years. Social-minded graphic designer Ken Garland designed many of the CND's posters and flyers beginning in 1962, activating the symbol in different ways.

Attending the 1958 rally was Bayard Rustin, an American civil rights activist who is one of the acknowledged connections in bringing the symbol to the United States and separating it from its connections to the CND for use in civil rights demonstrations. It later gained popularity as a symbol to protest the Vietnam War and then became associated with the hippie subculture. Gradually, however, it became a symbol simply for peace. Because the CND never registered the symbol as a trademark, it has become the property of everyone, and in opening that ownership the symbol has gained its true strength, made ever more prevalent and meaningful as people render it in different ways and imbue it with their own personalities.

REINTERPRETATIONS, APPROPRIATIONS, AND MANIFESTATIONS OF THE PEACE SYMBOL / Photographers, from left to right: Mika Hiironniemi, CarbonNYC, Jayel Aheram, aturkus, cogdogblog, jeffpearce, dental ben, hashmil, eyeliam, normanack, NatalieMaynor, Clarita / All images uploaded to Flickr under a Creative Commons Attribution license

New Haven Railroad

Formed in 1872, the New York, New Haven, and Hartford Railroad, commonly referred to as "the New Haven," operated freight and passenger trains between New York and Boston, enjoying modest success until the beginning of the twentieth century. Then followed a string of woes over the next 70 years. The New Haven avoided bankruptcy once during World War I but succumbed to it in 1935. After resurfacing in 1947, the New Haven saw better days with Frederick Dumaine Jr. as president, but in 1954 Patrick B. McGinnis, looking to increase dividends to shareholders, took over the position. Dividends increased, but the performance of the company decreased. McGinnis was replaced less than two years later. However, he left behind an important visual legacy for both the corporate identity and railroad industries.

McGinnis worked with his wife, Lucille McGinnis, to develop a new identity in 1954. She commissioned Swiss-born Herbert Matter, a design consultant for Knoll and faculty member at Yale School of Art › 129, who created a boldly simple, single-weight slab serif of the *NH* monogram that became, literally, the centerpiece of the identity program. It was regularly printed big—sometimes even twice on the same cover—in a limited color palette of black and red on everything from timetables to brochures to the front of the train, which sported a bold paint scheme unlike any other. Matter created much of the material but, after McGinnis's departure, the responsibilities went to the New Haven, which went bankrupt in 1961 and ceased operations in 1968. Since 1990, thanks to a group of rail enthusiasts, 16 locomotives that run on New York State's Metro-North Railroad and Connecticut's Shore Line East proudly sport Matter's identity.

NEW YORK, NEW HAVEN, AND HARTFORD RAILROAD / USA, 1954 / Herbert Matter / Images: Mark J. Frattasio Collection

The New School

Since its founding in 1919 as The New School for Social Research by a group of former Columbia University professors who felt limited in the kind of courses and teachings they could offer, this New York institution has served as an alternative to higher education. Whether it was opening its doors to European intellectuals fleeing fascist regimes at the University in Exile, offering a broad range of continuing education evening classes for adults, or facing a student uprising as recently as 2008 that demanded, among other things, the resignation of its president, Bob Kerrey, The New School has consistently veered away from relative normalcy. Over the years, it has established eight major divisions, each with its own unique personality.

In 1997, the different schools came under the broad umbrella of New School University with an institutional logo by Chermayeff & Geismar › 156, but in 2005, after two years of studying the public's perception, a bold new nomenclature and identity were introduced. "The New School" was how people already referred to the university, and this was adopted as its official name. Each school name was then woven in with this basic name—for example, Parsons School of Design is now Parsons The New School for Design. Tying together all the schools was a decidedly different identity created by brand agency Siegel+Gale, headed by creative director Howard Belk. A graffiti-inspired visual system, referencing the school's urban context, provides a flexible reference point that allows the logo to change and feel as active as its faculty and student body. And as New York City has grown increasingly graffiti-less since the late 1980s, The New School stands out in this newly sanitized environment.

THE NEW SCHOOL FOR GENERAL STUDIES

THE NEW SCHOOL FOR SOCIAL RESEARCH

MILANO THE NEW SCHOOL FOR MANAGEMENT AND URBAN POLICY

PARSONS THE NEW SCHOOL FOR DESIGN

EUGENE LANG COLLEGE THE NEW SCHOOL FOR LIBERAL ARTS

MANNES COLLEGE THE NEW SCHOOL FOR MUSIC

THE NEW SCHOOL FOR DRAMA

THE NEW SCHOOL FOR JAZZ AND CONTEMPORARY MUSIC

NEW SCHOOL IDENTITY AND APPLICATIONS / Siegel+Gale: executive creative direction, Howard Belk; creative direction, Young Kim; design, Lloyd Blander / USA, 2005

MTV

Working with John Lack, the executive vice president of Warner Satellite Entertainment Company (WASEC), Robert Pittman, a successful radio programmer, helped establish a groundbreaking cable television channel: MTV, the music channel. Fred Seibert, a former jazz record producer and radio station promotion coordinator, was hired by Pittman to oversee the identity of the channel. Seibert turned to his lifelong friend Frank Olinsky, who had just established Manhattan Design with two partners, Pat Gorman and Patty Rogoff, to create the logo. The process was remarkably collaborative: Rogoff first drew the big *M* and worked with Gorman to determine its perspective; then Gorman suggested a pointy *TV* to its side, which Olinsky took and spray-painted it. Meanwhile, the *M* was subjected to productive tomfoolery, with the partners rendering it in bricks, polka dots, and zebra stripes, and suggesting the logo could be all these things.

Seibert presented the mutating logo to Pittman and Lack, and met resistance to both the solution and the firm behind it. Seibert was asked to hire a big-name designer like Push Pin Studios › 168 or Lou Dorfsman › 173 to do the logo. He did, but as the process extended and time became a problem, Manhattan Design's was approved. Seibert next focused on the station identifications for broadcast, which Pittman equaled to radio jingles, instantly recognizable and memorable. The first pool of collaborators comprised production houses like Broadcast Arts, Colossal Pictures, and Perpetual Motion Pictures, who created surreal ten-second animations that gave life to the MTV logo. For MTV's top-of-the-hour identification, illustrator Candy Kugel at Perpetual took the still images of Neil Armstrong's moon landing (available in the public domain) and colorized the MTV logo on top of the American flag. On August 1, 1981, at 12:01 a.m., to the unmistakable sound of MTV's guitar riff, this image launched a new generation of viewers, artists, designers, and citizens.

(RED)

In January 2006, Bono, the lead singer of U2, and Bobby Shriver, a philanthropist-cum-producer-cum–city councilmember, launched (RED), a new business model, to help raise awareness about the AIDS epidemic in Africa and to provide a sustainable flow of money for the Global Fund, the international financing organization that invests the money it receives to fight AIDS, tuberculosis, and malaria. (RED) partners with some of the most visible brands that license the (PRODUCT) RED brand to market specific products or services, with a percentage or a set amount of the profits going to the Global Fund. Apple has released (RED) editions of its iPod Nano and iPod Shuffle, Converse has launched a collection of Chuck Taylor All-Star shoes made from canvas sourced in Africa, and the Gap has created a (RED) collection of T-shirts and accessories. Marrying together all the products and services is a simple visual device created by Wolff Olins › 206.

For the main brand—the name was selected because red is the color of emergency, which certainly applies to AIDS—RED is rendered in a sans serif typeset within parentheses. For the license brand, (PRODUCT) RED, the logo of the partner is placed within the parentheses and RED becomes a superscript; the combination is meant to be read as, for example, "Apple to the power of RED." The simplicity of the identity barely hints at the complexity of Wolff Olins's task: finding a way to create a new, strong brand for (RED) that could be integrated with some of the best-guarded and most carefully developed brands, turning untouchable assets like Starbucks green and American Express blue to red. While consumerism and philanthropy still remain an oxymoron, (RED) demonstrates, through action and design, a possible blueprint for their convergence...well, a (RED) print for their convergence.

DESI(RED)

INSPI(RED)

PARTNE(RED)

ADMI(RED)

CULTU(RED)

(Ⓜ) RED

(★CONVERSE) RED

(GAP) RED

(EMPORIO ARMANI) RED

(AMERICAN EXPRESS) RED

INC(RED)IBLE

INSPI(RED)

ADO(RED)

(RED) IDENTITY / Wolff Olins / USA, 2006

Walker Art Center

From 1965 to 1995, the Minneapolis Walker Art Center had employed a series of sans serif typefaces—Univers ›372, Helvetica ›373, Franklin Gothic ›370, and DIN ›377—as its logo, and its overall identity displayed, as design writer Peter Hall once described it, an "unwavering adherence to the clinical International Style." In 1990, Laurie Haycock Makela joined the Walker as design director, replacing Mildred Friedman, who had held the position for 20 years, and in 1995 she introduced a remarkably different, and distinct, identity based on a new type family, Walker. Designed by Matthew Carter in collaboration with Haycock and her team, Walker is, at its barest, a sans serif just like its predecessors, but the full typographic system provides a kit of parts that can render innumerable permutations: Five styles of "snap-on" serifs can be attached to each character and selectively added to the top or bottom, left or right, or all. It also included variants for heavy rules at the top, bottom, or both; a range of connectors to create custom ligatures; and, to top it all off, italic versions of each variant. Taking the place of a typical logo, the Walker typeface unifies all the materials of the museum and gives it a highly individual identity. It also established the Walker Art Center's in-house design studio as one of the most innovative.

walker art center
1965

WALKER ART CENTER
1971

Walker Art Center
1985

Walker Art Center
1977

Walker Art Center
1990

PREVIOUS WALKER ART CENTER LOGOS / USA, 1965–1990

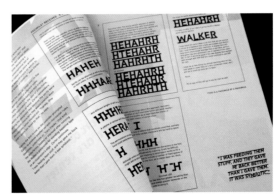

THE SPACE BETWEEN THE LETTERS, Moira Cullen for *Eye* magazine reprint / Laurie Haycock Makela, Deborah Littlejohn / USA, 1995

ABCDEFGHIJKLMNO
PQRSTUVWXYZ&ÆŒ
ꞪꞫꟷꟷꟷ1234567890
THE WALKER FONT
CONTAINS FIVE DIF-
FERENT "SNAP-ON"
SERIFS AND THREE
JOINING STROKES:

ꞪHHH ꞪHHH
ꞪHHH ꞪHHH
ꞪHHH ꞪHꞀꞀH

WALKER TYPEFACE / Matthew Carter / USA, 1995

DIANA THATER EXHIBIT INVITATION / Matt Eller / USA, 1997

WALKER DESIGN NOW INVITATION /
Laurie Haycock Makela / USA, 1996

In 1998, design educator and writer Andrew Blauvelt took on the role of design director and further developed the design studio and its output, overseeing the revitalization of the museum's identity in preparation for its momentous expansion in 2005. Still foregoing an institutional logo and looking to extend the viability of its previous approach, Blauvelt and designer Chad Kloepfer designed Walker Expanded, an expansive range of vertical striping rendered in different patterns and motifs, with bright colors that hold a series of words that, together and only when applied, form the identity. Set mostly in Avenir with select words rendered in Carter's Walker, the system is again typographic, but instead of being built around styles like italic or bold, it is arranged around groups of words and patterns and motifs. So, for example, the Peer-to-Peer "weight" includes language from within the institution, like *Film/Video*, a department name, while the Public Address "weight" contains more typical language, like *movies*. The system is complex, and it requires conscious manipulation from the designers—who benefit from a font developed by Eric Olson, who runs Process Type Foundry in Minneapolis and is a former designer at the Walker's design studio, that makes the combination of words and patterns more easily accessible. Instead of simply replacing it, Walker Expanded builds on the legacy and innovation of its former flexible identity and creates a new language—literally, visually, and metaphorically.

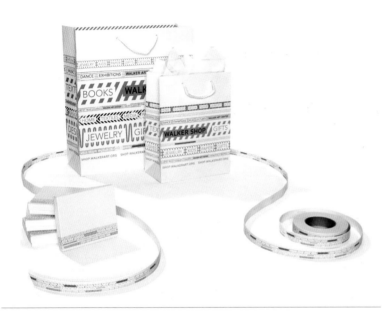

SHOPPING BAGS, BOXES, AND TAPE / Andrew Blauvelt, Chad Kloepfer / USA, 2005

Step 1 Select a font and choose a word by typing the corresponding character

 WALKER ART CENTER

Step 2 Delete space bar to overlap elements

WALKER ART CENTER

Step 3 Choose a pattern

 etc.

Step 4 Overlap the two lines by setting the leading to zero

Step 5 Repeat to create a line and customize the color

CUSTOM FONT USAGE INSTRUCTIONS / Andrew Blauvelt, Chad Kloepfer, Eric Olson / USA, 2005

No Walls, No Problem

During 2004, while the Walker's main building was closed for the expansion, the interim "Walker Without Walls" identity was introduced to maintain the visibility of the museum and acknowledge its transition. A standardized system of curves, arrowheads, and bubbles was designed to generate endless variations for short-lived collateral and could also be applied directly over existing collateral.

INTERIM WALL GRAPHICS / Andrew Blauvelt, Alex DeArmond / USA, 2004

ORIGINAL NEWS RELEASE (LEFT) WITH OVERLAID INTERIM IDENTITY / Andrew Blauvelt, Alex DeArmond / USA, 2004

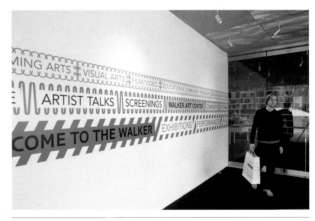

WALL GRAPHICS / Andrew Blauvelt, Chad Kloepfer / USA, 2005

Summer Olympic Games

Every four years, the world is captivated by the Summer Olympic Games. For athletes, the Olympics are the pinnacle of their dreams and aspirations; for the media, they are an endless source of stories of courage. Sponsors thrill to the sight of their logo emblazoned on billboards and skintight uniforms, and graphic designers delight in the visual revelry of the Games' graphic identity. While many of these comprehensive and extensive programs are remarkable, three of them are continually referenced as the most memorable, and one of them as the most controversial.

The heated social and political climate in Mexico City in 1968 was palpable as the world focused on the entangled country, with a student protest that ended in tragic bloodshed almost canceling the Games. But soon after, Mexico was clad in the colorful and exuberant regalia of the identity program designed by Lance Wyman (USA), Peter Murdoch (UK), and architect Eduardo Terrazas (Mexico) under the leadership of Pedro Ramírez Vásquez, chairman of the Organizing Committee, which provided a joyful and needed contrast to the events leading up to the Games. Wyman devised the logo by combining the iconography from Mexico's indigenous civilizations with Op Art, resulting in a vibrant deployment of concentric circles and lines with the number 68 as its hinge—and he was responsible for the development of most of the program, working actively with Mexican designers and design students. The identity was also designed as a system that could be molded in many ways—sometimes literally by Mexican craftsmen, who produced everything from pinwheels to jewelry, encouraging the citizens to embrace the identity as a representation of their visual culture.

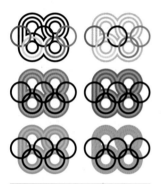

IDENTITY

UNIFORM / Julia Johnson Marshall

EVENT TICKETS / Beatrice Colle

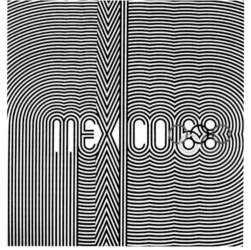

POSTER / art direction; Eduardo Terrazas, Pedro Ramirez Vásquez

PICTOGRAMS / Eduardo Terrazas, Universidad Iberoamericana students

POSTAGE STAMPS

MEXICO 1968 / Lance Wyman / Mexico, 1968

RECOMMENDED READING › 390

In 1966, at the same time Wyman was awarded the project, Otl Aicher › 166 received the commission from the National Olympic Committee (NOC) for the 1972 Games in Munich. Although they were marred by the terrorist activity that claimed the lives of 11 Israeli athletes, the Munich Games presented the opportunity to show a different Germany from the one experienced in the 1936 Berlin Games under Adolf Hitler. Aicher and his team developed a colorful identity that drew from the local Bavarian environment without crossing into pure folklore. The evocative imagery, focusing closely on the athletes, was paired with a solid grid system and the sole use of Univers › 372, which allowed flexibility and maintained consistency.

Developing the hypnotic emblem of the Games was not a smooth process: Aicher's first design was an abstract radiant garland that the committee did not consider distinctive enough to copyright; his second design, based on the letter *M*, met the same reaction. The NOC then held an open competition, yielding 2,300 entries that did not fulfill their needs. Finally, a member of Aicher's team, Coordt von Mannstein, merged the original garland with a spiral structure for the winning emblem, nearly a year after the first version had been presented. Aicher and his team also developed a cohesive set of nearly 180 pictograms for sporting events as well as services through a strict orthogonal and diagonal square grid, where all visual elements were arranged at 90 and 45 degrees. The sum of all the work was a precise and structured identity with just the right amount of warmth—succinctly embodied, perhaps, in Waldi, the geometric dachshund you could not resist petting.

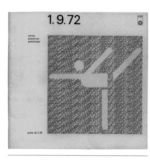

Above and Right GYMNASTICS AND SHOOTING DAILY PROGRAMS

OFFICIAL GUIDE TO THE GAMES OF THE XXTH OLYMPIAD MÜNCHEN 1972

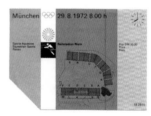

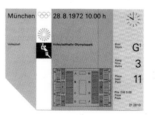

PARKING STUB

EVENT TICKETS

WALDI, THE OFFICIAL MASCOT, IN DIFFERENT COLOR CONFIGURATIONS

ATHLETICS AND GYMNASTICS REGULATIONS BOOKLET

OLYMPIC SUMMER, CULTURAL EVENTS PROGRAM

MUNICH 1972 / Otl Aicher / Germany, 1966–1972 / Images: Courtesy of Joe Miller

After the dim financial results of the 1976 Games in Montreal and the lowest country attendance at the 1980 Moscow Games since 1956, Los Angeles faced little to no competition in winning the Olympic bid; only New York challenged for the American candidacy, and in the next phase, Tehran dropped out voluntarily. With no public funding, the Organizing Committee relied on existing sports facilities and makeshift Olympic Villages at universities across Los Angeles and Southern California. Bringing together approximately 130 venues was the task of the Jerde Partnership, led by architect Jon Jerde, who collaborated with the environmental design firm Sussman/Prejza, led by Deborah Sussman. When the committee agreed to step away from a red/white/blue design approach, Jerde and Sussman developed an architectural and graphic kit of parts where a series of scaffolding structures, freestanding columns, arches, and banners was emblazoned with a cornucopia of stars, stripes, geometric shapes, and even a confetti pattern rendered in unexpected combinations of magenta, red, yellow, and aqua. The final look, dubbed "Festive Federalism," succeeded in establishing an Olympics presence where none existed; when it was dismantled, no dreaded white elephants remained.

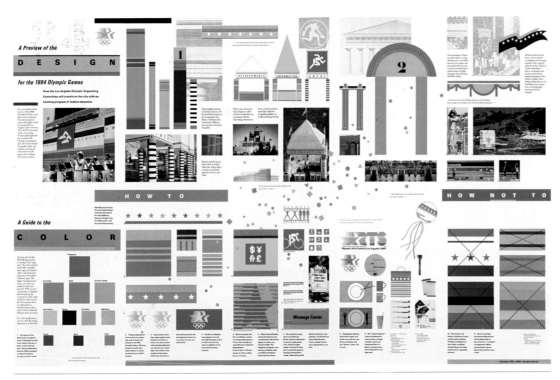

Above and Below ENVIRONMENTAL AND BRANDING APPLICATIONS

KIT OF PARTS

LOS ANGELES 1984 / Sussman/Prejza & Company, Inc.: Deborah Sussman; The Jerde Partnership / USA, 1984

In contrast to these examples, the identity for the Games that won't take place until 2012 has already cemented its place as one of the most memorable—and not for the right reasons—five years before it takes the world stage. Unveiled with momentous fanfare in June 2007 by Sebastian Coe, head of the Organizing Committee, the jagged, morphing, almost fluorescent logo met global distaste. News anchors mocked it on air, newspapers ran demeaning editorials where children could submit their own (theoretically superior) logos, and an online petition to revoke the logo gathered 48,616 signatures in 48 hours. It was designed by Wolff Olins › 206 in London, which describes the identity as "unconventionally bold, deliberately spirited and unexpectedly dissonant, echoing London's qualities of a modern, edgy city." The 2012 emblem is devised as a shape that can be filled with imagery and, in turn, meaning for everyone; it uses a kinetic visual language—so much that a launch video had to be removed from the website because some people claimed it was inducing seizures— that prepares the identity for the most widely broadcast Olympics through television, the web, and mobile devices, targeting much more deliberately a new, younger generation of viewers. Wolff Olins's work may be have been berated, but the potential to redefine the expectations of how Olympics identities should perform and adapt is undeniable.

2012 SUMMER OLYMPIC GAMES LONDON IDENTITY /
Wolff Olins / UK, 2007

OBAMA '08 PRESIDENTIAL CAMPAIGN

On Saturday, February 10, 2007, the junior senator from Illinois, Barack Obama, announced his candidacy for the presidency of the United States at the Old State Capitol building in his state's capital city, Springfield. At the front of the podium and in the glove-covered hands of attendees in the form of placards, the Obama '08 campaign logo was introduced. The glowing blue O with the red and white stripes of the flag swooping across it to form a horizon was unlike any other presidential campaign logo ever produced. This is neither hubris nor rhetoric: Until that point, campaign logos were always typographic solutions that clumsily attempted to integrate stars and flags. Obama '08 was a simple icon that could stand by itself, no differently than successful consumer brands like Nike ›343, Target, and Apple. The logo was created by Sender LLC, a Chicago-based design firm headed by Sol Sender, who was approached by motion graphics firm mo/de, which in turn had been contracted by AKP&D Message and Media, the consulting firm of David Axelrod, top campaign advisor to Obama. With two weeks to develop options, Sender and his design team, Andy Keene and Amanda Gentry, created over a dozen logo options, gradually filtering the proposals to two

OBAMA '08 LOGO IN TWO-COLOR VERSION / Sender LLC / USA, 2007

"O" LOGOMARK IN ONE-, TWO- AND FOUR-COLOR VERSIONS / Sender LLC / USA, 2007

EIGHT OUT OF FOURTEEN LOGO APPLICATIONS FOR DIFFERENT SECTORS AND CULTURES OF THE POPULATION / Obama '08 Campaign / USA, 2008

or three viable options, with the *O* rising as the most successful.

Sender delivered the identity assets to the campaign with a set of standards and guidelines to ensure consistency, as different vendors had to manufacture numerous campaign artifacts. He never expected the permutations that made the campaign's identity even more impressive. With John Slabyk as art director and Scott Thomas as director of new media, the campaign developed a broad and cohesive identity

that exploited the simplicity of the logo. To reach and connect with different segments of the population, they adapted the logo in clever ways, whether it was replacing the flag with a lined sheet of paper for students or replacing the *O* with a colored rainbow for the lesbian, gay, bisexual, and transgender community.

In addition, a cadre of creatives began interpreting the image of Obama himself and what he stood for. The most notable was Shepard Fairey, whose self-published, three-color

portrait of Obama featuring the word *hope* ignited the trend. The campaign later officially commissioned Fairey, as well as Lance Wyman, Jonathan Hoefler ›230, and Scott Hansen, among other artists, to create prints. The logo, meanwhile, at a grassroots level, took on the shape of cookies, muffins, chili dishes, and Halloween pumpkin carvings, generating a contagious creative aura. On Tuesday, November 4, 2008, Barack Obama was elected the 44th president of the United States of America.

CHANGE WE CAN BELIEVE IN **POSTERS** / Obama '08 Campaign / USA, 2008

POSTERS BY RON ENGLISH IN SAN FRANCISCO / Photo: Flickr user Jef Poskanzer / USA, 2008

POSTERS BY SHEPARD FAIREY IN WASHINGTON, D.C. / Photo: Flickr user Daquella manera / USA, 2008

OBEY LOOK-ALIKE OBAMA POSTER / Photo: Flickr user Jef Poskanzer / USA, 2008

MURAL ON THE SIDE OF THE OBAMA '08 CAMPAIGN HEADQUARTERS IN HOUSTON PAINTED BY AEROSOL WARFARE BASED ON DESIGN BY SHEPARD FAIREY / Photo: Flickr user jetherlot / USA, 2008

Lo-Res

Unlike bitmap fonts, most typefaces used on today's computers are resolution independent. They are designed at very high resolutions, making their shapes scalable to virtually any size. However, because they usually are not (or can not be) optimized for low resolutions, they are difficult to read on screen at small sizes.

In contrast, a bitmap font is designed to be optimized for a specific resolution; that is, a specific number of pixels relative to it's body.

In order to achieve perfect pixel control at small sizes, bitmap designs incorporate the pixels in their structure. The result is that the pixels remain apparent when the fonts are scaled to other sizes. (Their apparent resolution does not increase as the resolution of the output device is increased, for example, from video display to a printed page.) Therefore, each bitmap design is tied to a resolution.

For ease of use, the Lo-Res fonts are provided in outline format; as stair step outlines of the bitmap design. When used at low resolutions (when the pixels are visible to the naked eye, such as on a video display) the Lo-Res fonts are best used at their intended size, or at point sizes that are integer multiples thereof.

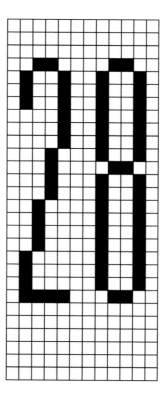

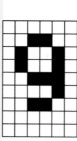

At high resolutions (when the pixels are invisible to the naked eye, such as print quality output) the Lo-Res fonts can be scaled to any size.

PRACTICE
In Letterforms

362
Classics

For all the advances in digital technology, it's humbling to consider that some of the most ubiquitous typefaces used today were designed as far back as the fifteenth century. While most have undergone necessary nip-and-tuck restorations as production methods have changed—from metal to phototypesetting to digital—they remain true to their origins, and in their familiarity and simplicity endure as classic typographic choices.

376
New Classics

Created and released after 1984—the proverbial line in the sand for design and digital technology—certain typefaces have become instant classics, offering contemporary interpretations and evolutions of the basic serif and sans serif forms or revivals of existing typefaces. Quickly put to use and widely spread through digital distribution, these typefaces have lasted beyond their initial offering, unusual among the many contemporary typefaces whose use is sustained for a limited period only.

382
Innovative

Whether they are challenged by a production method's limitations, a new technology's potential, or by curiosity, typeface designers have continued to innovate both the technical and aesthetic attributes of letterforms in the context of both client commissions and personal explorations. Successful to different degrees and affinities, these typefaces demonstrate the ample room still left for innovation in a practice that is centuries old.

386
Scorned

"There is no such thing as a bad typeface," wrote Jeffery Keedy, "just bad typography." This assessment is true, for the most part, as the best typographers and designers have always proven that even the most unpopular typefaces can perform surprisingly well in the appropriate context and execution. Nonetheless, some typefaces are handicapped by nature or by association: Certain typefaces may be poorly constructed or suffer from subjectively debatable aesthetics, while others, through their use, abuse, and misuse, become tainted and damaged goods. Regardless of cause and despite appropriate uses for these, finding alternatives is recommended.

Detail of **LO-RES CATALOG** / Emigre: Rudy VanderLans / **USA, 2001**

Garamond

DESIGNER Claude Garamond / Jean Jannon / **DATE** fifteenth and sixteenth centuries / **COUNTRY OF ORIGIN** France / **CATEGORY** Serif / **CLASSIFICATION** Garalde

If you were to ask designers today about their preferred Garamond, the answers would likely be as varied as the many cuts that have been developed by hand and digitally—featuring different serif angles, *x*-heights, and axes—over the last 100 years, usually to a confusing degree. The first revivals came in 1918 from the American Type Founders, 1921 by Lanston, and 1922 by Monotype, which all believed to have based their designs on the work of Claude Garamond in the fifteenth century—until 1926, when Beatrice Warde, the American typographer, writer, and scholar, revealed in the British typography journal *The Fleuron* that the sources were instead the work of the sixteenth-century Jean Jannon, whose work closely resembled Garamond's. The name Garamond nevertheless remained attached. The 1925 cut by D. Stempel AG was based on Garamond's work, and so was Robert Slimbach's version for Adobe › 223 in 1989. ITC's rendition in 1975 by Tony Stan is the least accurate interpretation of either Garamond or Jannon's work; it is considered by many designers the ugly duckling of the Garamonds.

YOUR NEW GLASS EYE FOR 826 VALENCIA, MCSWEENEY'S PIRATE STORE / writing, illustration, design, production, Sasha Wizansky / USA, 2002

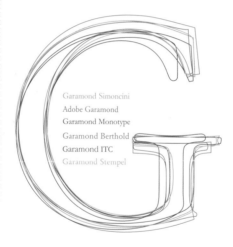

Garamond Simoncini
Adobe Garamond
Garamond Monotype
Garamond Berthold
Garamond ITC
Garamond Stempel

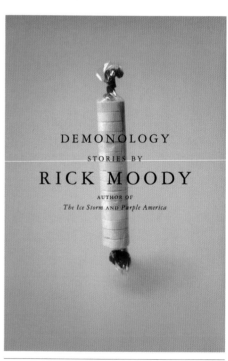

DEMONOLOGY, Rick Moody / Little, Brown / Paul Sahre / USA, 2000

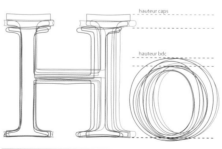

COMPARISON OF SIX GARAMONDS / Peter Gabor / France, 2006

TEKNION FURNITURE SYSTEMS *ABILITY* **PRODUCT BROCHURE** / Vanderbyl Design; Michael Vanderbyl / USA, 1997

Bembo

DESIGNER Stanley Morison / **FOUNDRY** Monotype Corporation / **YEAR** 1929 / **COUNTRY OF ORIGIN** United Kingdom / **CATEGORY** Serif / **CLASSIFICATION** Garalde

Francesco Griffo da Bologna, a typeface designer and punch cutter, was brought to Venice by the famed fifteenth-century Renaissance printer Aldus Manutius. His first project was designing a typeface for *De Aetna*, a book by the Italian Scholar Pietro Bembo—the namesake of the classic book typeface drawn by British designer Stanley Morison for Monotype. A slightly calligraphic quality is evident in Bembo, notably in the serifs, the transitional curves, and the length of its ascenders and descenders; these details have established Bembo as a favorite for large bodies of text, where it provides consistent color and texture, great legibility, and good use of space.

BARBARA BARRY INVITATION AND ANNOUNCEMENT / Vanderbyl Design: creative direction, Michael Vanderbyl; design, Katie Repine / USA, 2005

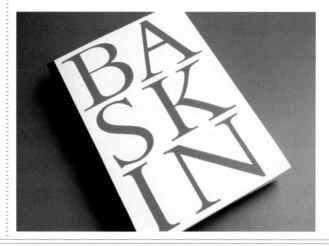

BEE SEASON, Myla Goldberg / Anchor Books, Random House / Amy C. King; photography, Barry Marcus / USA, 2001

THE HUMAN CONDITION: SELECTED WORKS BY LEONARD BASKIN, STEPHEN F. AUSTIN UNIVERSITY EXHIBITION CATALOG / Summerford Design, Inc.: Jack Summerford / USA, 1996

Caslon

DESIGNER William Caslon I / **FOUNDRY** Caslon Foundry / **YEAR** 1720–1730 / **COUNTRY OF ORIGIN** United Kingdom / **CATEGORY** Serif / **CLASSIFICATION** Transitional

The first manifestation of a Caslon style came in 1722, when William Caslon I designed Caslon Old Style. Over the following decades, through the Caslon Foundry, he released variations of Caslon that were widespread in Britain and later in the United States. Benjamin Franklin was one of its fervent admirers, using it in his printing regularly. Some of the first printings of the United States Declaration of Independence and the United States Constitution were set in Caslon.

Caslon has been subject to various revivals. In 1902, American Type Founders (ATF) released Caslon 540 and three years later Caslon 3, a slightly bolder version modified to work better with evolving printing technologies. In 1990, Carol Twombly digitized a version for Adobe › 223, and in 1998 ITC › 220 released ITC Founder's Caslon, where each size was digitized separately, just as it used to be cast separately, and ITC released it in 12-, 30-, and 42-point versions as well as a poster weight.

***THE LAB* GIG POSTER** / Graham Jones / UK, 2008

AMERICAN AURORA, Richard N. Rosenfeld / St. Martins Press / Henry Sene Yee/ USA, 1996

ANNSWERS IDENTITY / Aufuldish & Warinner: Bob Aufuldish / USA, 1999

OLD FRIENDS, Stephen Dixon / Melville House Publishing / David Konopka / USA, 2004

Bodoni

As director of the Stamperia Reale, the official press of Ferdinand, Duke of Parma, Giambattista Bodoni was in charge of printing and producing official documents as well as his own. Through this office he developed Bodoni. Toward the late 1790s, Bodoni abandoned the Old Style roman serifs, and instead of tapering the serif into the horizontal strokes, he developed a more mathematical and geometric approach emphasized by the contrast of thick strokes and thin serifs, forming upright angles. Many cuts and renditions now exist of Bodoni; Morris Fuller Benton's for American Type Founders, Inc., and Henrich Jost's Bauer Bodoni for the Bauer foundry are two of the most common. Regardless of what version of Bodoni is used, elegance, luxury, and sophistication are qualities sure to be achieved.

DESIGNER Giambattista Bodoni / **YEAR** 1790s / **COUNTRY OF ORIGIN** Italy / **CATEGORY** Serif / **CLASSIFICATION** Didone

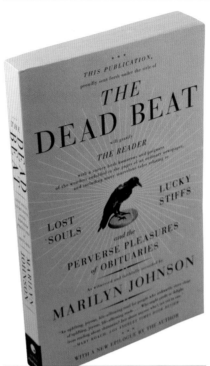

THE DEAD BEAT, Marilyn Johnson / Harper Perennial / Milan Bozic; photography, Eric Workum / USA, 2006

BLOSSA TRESTJÄRNIG PACKAGING FOR VIN & SPRIT / BVD: creative direction, Catrin Vagnemark; design, Susanna Nygren Barrett, Mia Heijkenskjöld / Sweden, 2003–2007

MARYLAND INSTITUTE COLLEGE OF ART ADMISSIONS PROSPECTUS 2004-2006 / Rutka Weadock Design: art direction, Anthony Rutka; design, Hwa Lee; major photography, Bruce Weller / USA, 2004

Didot

DESIGNER Firmin Didot **FOUNDRY** House of Didot / **YEAR** 1784 / **COUNTRY OF ORIGIN** France / **CATEGORY** Serif / **CLASSIFICATION** Didone

When designing Didot, Firmin Didot moved away from the handlettering and calligraphic characteristics of the era in search of a cleaner and more legible solution. This was accomplished with high contrast in the strokes and the use of hairlines and horizontal serifs with little bracketing. These changes personified the beginning of the modern style, and Didot became the French standard for over a century. As happens with older, successful typefaces, Didot has been redrawn many times, weathering the process of reinterpretation and new technologies; Adrian Frutiger's version for Linotype may be the best regarded; but the more modern interpretation by Hoefler & Frere-Jones › 230, designed for *Harper's Bazaar* › 327 and later made available for retail, features seven optical sizes—from 6 point to 96 point—that optimize each size to maintain the contrast and finesse deserved by the elegant Didot.

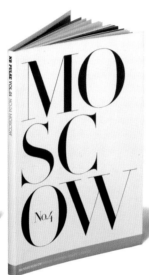
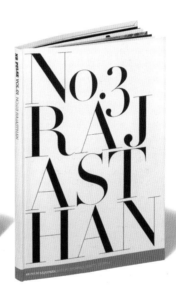

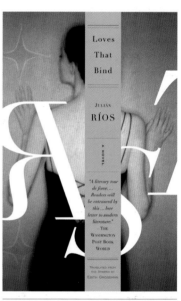

***LOVES THAT BIND**, Julián Ríos / Random House / John Gall; photography, Deborah Samuels/Photonica / USA, 1999*

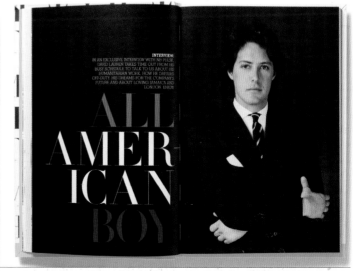

Trajan

Inspired by the capital letters found on the Column of Trajan in Rome, and later expanded with small caps, Trajan translated the chiseled manifestation of the original second-century source into a form fit for the twentieth century. Trajan's rise to fame came in its overuse for movie posters and titles, which made it nearly cliché. While it can also be found in other applications, such as book covers and TV shows, Trajan's presence in movies has unleashed a series of pleas from designers who wish to put a stop to the overexposure.

DESIGNER Carol Twombly / **FOUNDRY** Adobe Type / **YEAR** 1989 / **COUNTRY OF ORIGIN** United States / **CATEGORY** Serif / **CLASSIFICATION** Glyphic

CALIFORNIA COLLEGE OF ARTS AND CRAFTS CAPITAL CAMPAIGN / Vanderbyl Design: Michael Vanderbyl / USA, 1997

BECOMING ELECTRIC **INVITATION FOR INTERVAL** / Graham Jones / UK, 2006

EXAMPLES OF MOVIE TITLES TAKEN FROM POSTERS CREATED IN 2008 ALONE

Berthold Akzidenz Grotesk

DESIGNER N/A / **FOUNDRY** H. Berthold AG / **YEAR** 1898 / **COUNTRY OF ORIGIN** Germany / **CATEGORY** Sans Serif / **CLASSIFICATION** Lineale Neo-Grotesque

Berthold Akzidenz Grotesk has been one of the most influential sans-serif typefaces, informing many sans designed more than 50 years later—in turn, Akzidenz Grotesk was informed by 1880's Royal Grotesk. However, Akzidenz Grotesk, as it was first distributed by H. Berthold AG in the early twentieth century, was an amalgamation of typefaces created by different foundries that H. Berthold AG slowly purchased; as a result, Akzidenz Grotesk differed by point size, never quite acknowledging its varied sources or admitting any differences. Starting in the 1950s under the direction of Günter Gerhard Lange, some of the designs were unified and the family expanded to include bolder weights and condensed variations. In 2006, Berthold released Akzidenz-Grotesk Next, redrawn by Bernd Moellenstaedt and Dieter Hofrichter, to finally provide a fully unified version of this groundbreaking design.

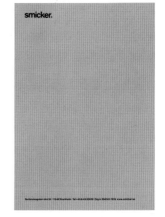

A TRIP TO SWEDEN EXHIBITION IDENTITY AND POSTER SERIES / BVD: creative direction, Susanna Nygren Barrett / Sweden, 2002

SMICKER/DUBBLERA IDENTITY / BVD: creative direction, Susanna Nygren Barrett; design, Mia Heijkenskjöld / Sweden, 2008

ULTRASILENCER SPECIAL EDITION PIA WALLÉN IDENTITY PROGRAM FOR ELEXTROLUX / BVD: creative direction, Susanna Nygren Barrett; design, Johan Andersson, Carolin Sundquist / Sweden, 2007

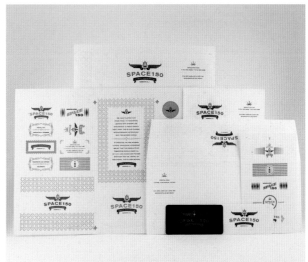

SPACE150 IDENTITY, NUMBERS 16 AND 17 / Every 150 days, Space150 changes its logo, stationery, website, and promotional materials, done either in-house or commissioned to an outside designer / Studio on Fire / USA, 2006

Franklin Gothic

DESIGNER Morris Fuller Benton / **FOUNDRY** American Type Founders / **YEAR** 1902–1912 / **COUNTRY OF ORIGIN** United States / **CATEGORY** Sans Serif / **CLASSIFICATION** Lineale Grotesque

Named—or not—after Benjamin Franklin, a single roman face was released in 1902. Over the following decade, Morris Fuller Benton added several weights and widths to the family. A popular choice in advertising, Franklin Gothic was expanded by ITC in 1980, when Victor Caruso added several weights in which he enlarged the *x*-height and condensed the lowercase forms. A decade later, David Berlow developed condensed, compressed, and extra-compressed variations, further enhancing Franklin Gothic's versatility and popularity.

LOCALMUSIC.COM IDENTITY / Volume, Inc.: Eric Heiman / USA, 2000

BLISS TRIED + BLUE TRAVEL KIT / USA, 2008

Gill Sans

DESIGNER Eric Gill / **FOUNDRY** Monotype Corporation / **YEAR** 1927 / **COUNTRY OF ORIGIN** United Kingdom / **CATEGORY** Sans Serif / **CLASSIFICATION** Lineale Humanist

Despite being a sans serif, the underlying structure of Gill Sans reveals its serif inspirations—from the Column of Trajan to Carolingian scripts. These give Gill Sans a less mechanic feel than its contemporary sans serifs, like Futura › 371. Gill Sans is undeniably reminiscent of Johnston Sans, the typeface designed for the London Underground › 346 in 1916 by Gill's mentor, Edward Johnston—and since Johnston was proprietary to the Underground, the availability of Gill Sans may have propelled it to its vast use in England. With its signature *Q*, *R*, *a*, *g*, and *t*, Gill Sans quickly became a British star, used by the BBC and Penguin Books › 274, among others. The various weights in the family provide great flexibility in its applications, small or large; Gill Sans Ultra Bold, however, stands oddly on its own with its exaggerated forms.

HIGHTEE GILL ULTRA BOLD T-SHIRT / Toko / Australia, 2008

BRAIN TONIQ LOGO AND PACKAGING / Paul Ambrose, Huc Ambrose / USA, 2007

CENTER FOR BUSINESS, ART, AND TECHNOLOGY / UK, 2008 / Photo: Fernando de Mello Vargas

THE PORTRAITS SPEAK: CHUCK CLOSE IN CONVERSATION WITH 27 OF HIS SUBJECTS, Chuck Close / A.R.T. Press / Lausten & Cossutta Design / USA, 1997

Futura

DESIGNER Paul Renner / **FOUNDRY** Bauer / **YEAR** 1927–1930 / **COUNTRY OF ORIGIN** Germany / **CATEGORY** Sans Serif / **CLASSIFICATION** Lineale Geometric

Based on geometric forms, Futura became a representative of the Bauhaus ideals of the time—even though Paul Renner was not directly involved in it—and one of the most influential geometric typefaces, inspiring others, like Kabel and Avenir. The original design's large family included Old Style figures, alternate characters, and even two display styles that did not quite resemble the rest of the family. Today, as for other early-twentieth-century typefaces, many versions of Futura exist. Adobe, URW, and Neufville Digital all have released digital versions varying in fidelity. A British foundry, The Foundry, offers Architype Renner, which features the rare alternates. Futura is most famously used by Volkswagen, epitomized by the radical "Lemon" print ad; the car company now owns a proprietary, customized version of Futura.

Far Left **ARCTIC PAPER'S** *THE GUIDE TO UNCOATED PAPER* / Shaz Madani / UK, 2008

Left *UNFOLD JAPAN: AN EXHIBITION OF CONTEMPORARY JAPANESE FURNITURE DESIGN* FOR VIADUCT FURNITURE / MadeThought / UK, 2005

FIELD NOTES, 48-PAGE MEMO BOOKS / Draplin Design and Coudal Partners: product design, Aaron Draplin / USA, 2008

MYSTERIOUS FUTURA STENCIL UNDERNEATH THE 45TH STREET BRIDGE IN THE UNIVERSITY DISTRICT OF SEATTLE, WASHINGTON / USA, 2007 / Photo: Flickr user veganstraightedge

THE CENTURY BUILDING LOGO / Eric Kass / USA, 2007

Univers

DESIGNER Adrian Frutiger / **FOUNDRY** Deberny & Peignot / **YEAR** 1954 / **COUNTRY OF ORIGIN** France / **CATEGORY** Sans Serif / **CLASSIFICATION** Lineale Neo-Grotesque

Univers was the first family to use numbers as a naming system for its various weights—21 variations when first released—built around its roman version, suited for long bodies of text, Univers 55. Based on Berthold Akzidenz Grotesk ›369, it uses optically even strokes as well as a large *x*-height

that increases legibility when used very small or as large as billboards and buildings can handle. In 1997, in conjunction with Linotype, Adrian Frutiger reworked and expanded the Linotype Univers version to include 63 fonts, and a third digit was added to the numbering system.

SELF-PROMOTIONAL AGENDA THAT EXPERIMENTS WITH THE USE OF TWO BLACK INKS / Estudio Ibán Ramón: art direction, Ibán Ramón; design, Ibán Ramón, Diego Mir, Dani Requeni / Spain, 2007

***BYPRODUCT* EXHIBITION POSTER FOR SOUTHERN EXPOSURE** / Efrat Rafaeli Design / USA, 2001

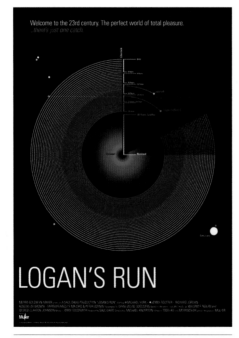

***LOGAN'S RUN* POSTER INCLUDED IN THE *NOW SHOWING* EXHIBIT BY WEAR IT WITH PRIDE** / Muller; Tom Muller / USA, 2008

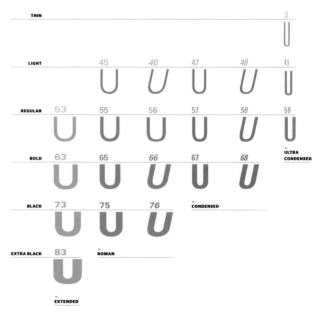

Univers utilizes a numbering system to define various widths, weights, and styles. The first digit, running from top to bottom in the table, denotes weight, with 3X the thinnest and 8X the thickest. The second digit, running from left to right, denotes width, with X3 the most expanded and X9 the most condensed. To differentiate between roman and italic styles, odd and even numbers are used respectively.

Helvetica

DESIGNER Edouard Hoffman and Max Miedinger / **FOUNDRY** Haas Type Foundry / **YEAR** 1957 / **COUNTRY OF ORIGIN** Switzerland / **CATEGORY** Sans Serif / **CLASSIFICATION** Lineale Neo-Grotesque

In 1957, under the direction of Edouard Hoffman at the Haas Type Foundry, Max Miedinger drew Neue Haas Grotesk, based on the increasingly popular Berthold Akzidenz Grotesk › 369, designed at the end of the previous century. Three years later, Linotype and D. Stempel AG redrew it to work with the Linotype machine—however, they renamed the typeface to avoid selling it with a competitor's name, first to Helvetia (Latin for Switzerland) and then to Helvetica (Latin for Swiss), on Hoffman's request.

Helvetica quickly became one of the most used typefaces in the 1960s and 1970s, specifically as a bastion for both the International Typographic Style and for corporate identity. From Switzerland to the United States, influential designers from Josef Müller-Brockmann › 152 to Massimo Vignelli › 160 exploited the neutrality of Helvetica and established it as a premier element of visual communication. Since then, Helvetica has been a polarizing choice among designers, who simply love it or hate it. In the 1990s, Dutch designers Experimental Jetset used Helvetica prominently in their work, breathing fresh air into it. In 2007, Gary Hustwit directed the documentary *Helvetica*, which traces its history and use and features its friends and foes.

1957 Haas Grotesk
ABCDEFGHIJKL
mnopqrstuvwxyz
äÇçëëïöß&§/!?,....
1234567890*

1960 Helvetica
ABCDEFGHIJKL
mnopqrstuvwxyz
äÇçëëïöß&§/!?,....
1234567890*

afPQRS5, afPQRS5.

HELVETICA: A DOCUMENTARY FILM **BY GARY HUSTWIT** / Shown: David Carson, Matthew Carter, Wim Crouwel / A Production of Swiss Dots Ltd. in association with Veer / production and direction, Gary Hustwit / © Swiss Dots Ltd.

"EVERYTHING IS OK" TAPE / A social design experiment in subversive positivism / **MINE™:** creative direction, Christopher Simmons; design, Christopher Simmons, Tim Belonax / USA, 2006–ongoing

Left **LETTERPRESS SET-UP AND POSTER COMPARING SAMPLES OF NEUE HAAS GROTESK AND HELVETICA AT 72 POINTS** / Switzerland, 2008 / Photos: Sam Mallett

Avant Garde

DESIGNER Herb Lubalin / **FOUNDRY** International Typeface Corporation / **YEAR** 1970 / **COUNTRY OF ORIGIN** United States / **CATEGORY** Sans Serif / **CLASSIFICATION** Lineale Geometric

Herb Lubalin › 167 had worked with the controversial publisher Ralph Ginzburg on the magazines *Eros* and *Fact:* in the 1960s before launching *Avant Garde* › 322, featuring a masthead set in what later became Avant Garde, the typeface. Originally conceived and designed by Lubalin and his partner, Tom Carnase, as an all-uppercase alphabet with a jovial set of ligatures, it was meant to be used solely on the magazine as art directed by Lubalin. In 1970, when Lubalin founded ITC › 220 with Aaron Burns and Ed Rondthaler, the foundry released ITC Avant Garde, which was quickly appropriated by design and advertising agencies—not always to great effect. The misuse of the ligatures and the overuse of the typeface was reportedly a sore (and sour) issue for Lubalin, who considered its use by others flawed.

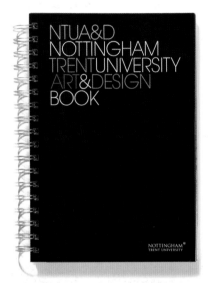

THE SCHOOL OF VISUAL ARTS POSTER / art direction, Silas H. Rhodes; design, Paul Sahre / USA, 2006

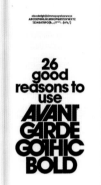

AVANT GARDE TYPE SPECIMEN / ITC / USA, 1970

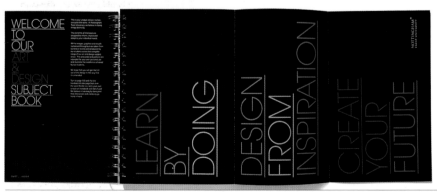

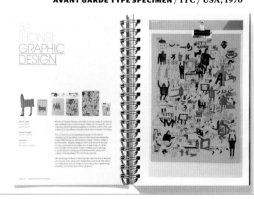

NOTTINGHAM TRENT UNIVERSITY ART AND DESIGN PROSPECTUS / Un.titled / UK, 2007

Clarendon

In the early nineteenth century, with the advent of the industrial revolution in England, typography experienced an expressive spurt in support of the production of large posters and advertisements in the form of bold (really bold, sometimes) and decorative typefaces. Clarendon was born in this period. It was bold and complemented both sans-serif and serif typefaces. Robert Besley was able to register Clarendon in 1845 under the Ornamental Designs Act of 1842, which protected his design, but the protection lasted three years only, and his design was quickly and broadly pirated. The friendly contour of Clarendon—achieved by the soft curve that joins the slab serifs with the stems—along with its varied weights, has maintained designers' interest for more than 150 years.

DESIGNER Robert Besley / **FOUNDRY** Fann St. Foundry / **YEAR** 1845 / **COUNTRY OF ORIGIN** United Kingdom / **CATEGORY** Slab Serif / **CLASSIFICATION** Egyptian

HAROLD LEE MILLER IDENTITY / Eric Kass / USA, 2007

CLARENDON METAL TYPE, FROM THE COLLECTION OF TYPORETUM / UK, 2008 / Photo: Justin Knopp

PART OF PROJECT M'S BUY-A-METER PROJECT / T-shirt sold for $425 to raise funds for households in need of fresh water in Hale County, Alabama / Project M / MINE™: design, Christopher Simmons / USA, 2007

OLD STYLE WOOD TYPE, A PRECEDENT FOR CLARENDON, FROM THE COLLECTION OF TYPORETUM / UK, 2008 / Photo: Justin Knopp

Copperplate Gothic

While it is officially categorized as a sans serif and has *Gothic* in its name—another way of saying sans serif—Copperplate Gothic features some of the industry's finest, sharpest, tiniest serifs, suggestive of stone carving. Designed in all caps, its intended use was for personal stationery—a realization that still stands, as Copperplate Gothic is usually offered in templates from print shops and online business card printers. Nonetheless, Copperplate Gothic has been used properly and poorly in every imaginable context: food packaging, film titles, corporate identities, and flyers around the world. Despite having no lowercase, Copperplate is readable at small sizes and longer bodies of text because of its wide structure.

DESIGNER Frederic W. Goudy / **FOUNDRY** American Type Founders / **YEAR** 1901 / **COUNTRY OF ORIGIN** United States / **CATEGORY** Sans Serif / **CLASSIFICATION** Decorative

PANIC ROOM TITLE SEQUENCE / Columbia Pictures / director; David Fincher / Picture Mill: William Lebeda; production, CafeFX; visual effects, Kevin Tod Haug / USA, 2002

RALPH LAUREN'S RUGBY STOREFRONT IN NEW YORK / USA, 2008

FF Meta

DESIGNER Erik Spiekermann / **FOUNDRY** FontShop International / **YEAR** 1991–1998 / **COUNTRY OF ORIGIN** Germany / **CATEGORY** Sans Serif / **CLASSIFICATION** Humanist

In 1985, Sedley Place Design was charged with redesigning the identity for the Deutsche Bundespost (the West German Post Office). The design team was convinced that neither Helvetica › 373 nor Univers › 372 would work, so they commissioned Erik Spiekermann › 226 to develop a corporate typeface that would withstand usage in postage stamps, livery, and documents. The result was PT 55, a narrow typeface with a large *x*-height and a distinctive style. Despite the work that went into it, the typeface was not used and was shelved.

In 1989, as Spiekermann launched FontShop International › 227, he and Just Van Rossum updated the PT 55 drawings to create FF Meta— named after the studio Spiekermann founded in 1979 (and left in 2001)—it was released in 1991 under the FontFont label. Over the next years, more weights, along with small caps, were released. The typeface's quirky ruggedness and versatility in text and display settings made it a popular selection in the 1990s. In 2007, after three years of collaboration with Christian Schwartz › 231 and Kris Sowersby, Spiekermann released FF Meta Serif, finally giving FF Meta a worthy serif companion.

DOCUMENTING MARCEL EXHIBITION POSTER / Skolos-Wedell: design, Nancy Skolos, Thomas Wedell; photography, Thomas Wedell / USA, 1996

***60* BOOK, CELEBRATING THE SIXTIETH BIRTHDAY OF BUSINESSMAN WINFRIED ROTHERMEL** / Anja Patricia Helm / Germany, 2006

FF DIN

DESIGNER Albert-Jan Pool / **FOUNDRY** FontShop International / **YEAR** 1995 / **COUNTRY OF ORIGIN** Germany / **CATEGORY** Sans Serif / **CLASSIFICATION** Grotesque

DIN stands for Deutsche Industrie Norm (German Industrial Standard), the standards established since 1917 by the German Institute for Standardization in Berlin in agreement with the German Federal Government. For example, DIN 25449 sets the standards for design and construction of concrete components in nuclear facilities, and DIN 1451 is the standard for typography used in transportation and administrative documents of the German Government, as established in 1936. Within DIN 1451, two typefaces are defined: DIN Mittelschrift and its condensed companion, DIN Engschrift. While many variations resemble and precede DIN 1451, it was DIN Mittelschrift that Albert-Jan Pool used to design FF DIN for FontFont—a type family that now counts approximately 30 weights. Its austere look and friendlier contours than those of other sans serifs have made FF DIN one of the most pervasive typefaces since the late 1990s, establishing it as a contemporary typeface with German engineering—not a bad combination.

"NEWBORN" SCULPTURE, DESIGNED TO COMMEMORATE THE 2008 DECLARATION OF INDEPENDENCE OF KOSOVA / Ogilvy Kosova, Kosova, 2008 / Photo: Valdet Bujupi

THE "NEWBORN" SCULPTURE SITS IN FRONT OF THE YOUTH CENTER IN PRISHTINA—ITS TEAM CELEBRATES AMONG ITS NOOKS AND CRANNIES / Ogilvy Kosova, Kosova, 2008 / Photo: Jeton Kacaniku

MISSISSIPPI FLOODS: DESIGNING A SHIFTING LANDSCAPE, Anuranda Mathur, Dilip Da Cunha / HVADesign: Henk van Assen / USA, 2001

UNIVERSITY OF WUPPERTAL COMMUNICATION DESIGN DEPARTMENT *DIPLOMA* EXHIBITION POSTER / Uwe Loesch / Germany, 2006, 2007

MY GOD'S BETTER THAN YOUR GOD **SELF-PUBLISHED PROTEST POSTER** / The Design Consortium: design, Ned Drew / USA, 2006

Gotham

DESIGNER Tobias Frere-Jones / **FOUNDRY** Hoefler & Frere-Jones / **COMMISSIONER** *GQ* magazine (2000) / **YEAR** 2002 / **COUNTRY OF ORIGIN** United States / **CATEGORY** Sans Serif / **CLASSIFICATION** Geometric

In 2000, the men's lifestyle magazine *GQ* approached Hoefler & Frere-Jones › 230 with a clear brief: to design a proprietary sans-serif typeface with a geometric structure that felt fresh and masculine. Armed with extensive photographic research of New York vernacular lettering, Tobias Frere-Jones developed Gotham, into which he translated the more engineered language of the signage found across the city. While Gotham is based on all-uppercase signage, Frere-Jones designed a range of weights that go from thin to black and include lowercase and italics. In 2002, after *GQ*'s exclusivity came to an end, Gotham was released for retail purchase. It instantly became a favorite of designers, who praised its adaptability to any number of projects and industries. In other words, Gotham is like a good pair of jeans: It looks good with anything.

Top and Right GOTHAM SKETCH AND FINAL RENDITION / Hoefler & Frere-Jones / USA, 2000

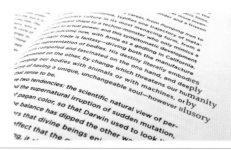

UNEASY NATURE EXHIBITION CATALOG FOR THE WEATHERSPOON ART MUSEUM / Volume Inc.: Eric Heiman / **USA, 2006**

RIGHTS, CAMERA, ACTION BROCHURE FOR THE AMERICAN CIVIL LIBERTIES UNION / Hyperakt: creative direction, Julia Vakser; design, Julia Vakser, Matthew Anderson, Deroy Peraza / UA, 2008

SYRACUSE INTERNATIONAL FILM FESTIVAL IDENTITY AND MARKETING MATERIALS / Hyperakt: creative direction; Julia Vakser, Deroy Peraza; design, Matthew Anderson, Jonathan Correira / USA, 2007

HEATH CERAMICS BOOK COVER AND IDENTITY / Volume Inc.: Eric Heiman / USA, 2004, 2006

Knockout

DESIGNER Tobias Frere-Jones / **FOUNDRY** Hoefler & Frere-Jones / **YEAR** 2000 / **COUNTRY OF ORIGIN** United States / **CATEGORY** Sans Serif / **CLASSIFICATION** Grotesque

During the mid- to late nineteenth century metal-cast typefaces were replaced with heavily condensed and expanded wood type lettering manufactured in large sizes taking shape as decorative alphabets as well as slab and sans serifs. These were commonly used for printing posters, typically associated with traveling entertainment shows. From this tradition, Tobias Frere-Jones designed the 32 styles of Knockout, ranging from the ultra-condensed and light to the generously extended and black. Foregoing the typical nomenclature and structure of type families (i.e., regular, italic, bold, bold italic), Knockout features a numbering system similar to that of Univers › 372, where the first digit defines the style and the second the weight— these are accompanied by matching boxing weight class names, from Junior Heavyweight to Ultimate Sumo. Knockout is based on Frere-Jones' previous work for *Sports Illustrated*'s proprietary typeface Champion Gothic.

THE LANGUAGE OF PASSION, Mario Vargas Llosa / Farrar, Straus and Giroux / Kathleen DiGrado / USA, 2003

WEST SIDE STORY POSTER / Sandstrom Partners: creative direction, Marc Cozza; illustration, Howell Golson / USA, 2006

KNOCKOUT / Hoefler & Frere-Jones / USA, 1994

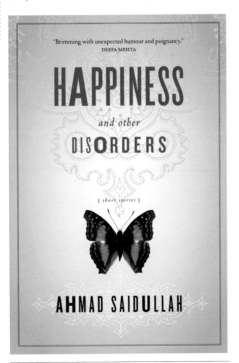

HAPPINESS AND OTHER DISORDERS, Ahmad Saidullah / Key Porter Books / Ingrid Paulson Design; photography, Prill Mediendesign & Fotografie/istockphoto / USA, 2008

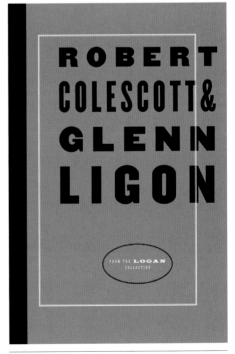

THE ROBERT COLESCOTT & GLENN LIGON EXHIBITION CATALOG FOR THE UNIVERSITY OF DENVER VICTORIA H. MYHREN GALLERY / Aufuldish & Warinner: Bob Aufuldish / USA, 2004

FF Scala

DESIGNER Martin Majoor / **FOUNDRY** FontShop International / **YEAR** 1988–1990 (Scala); 1993 (Scala Sans) / **COUNTRY OF ORIGIN** Netherlands / **CATEGORY** Serif, Sans Serif / **CLASSIFICATION** Humanist

Frustrated with his limited typographic choices—a mere 16 typefaces using PageMaker 1.0, running on one of the first Macintosh computers—while working at the Vredenburg Music Centre in Utrecht, Martin Majoor decided to develop a typeface to suit his needs, including small caps, ligatures, and Old Style numbers. He named the typeface after the Teatro alla

Scala in Milan. In 1990, FontShop International ›227 released FF Scala, the most serious text face at that point released under the FontFont label. FF Scala Sans was released three years later; it cemented FF Scala's popularity through its consistent versatility and one of Majoor's drivers: "Two typefaces, one form principle."

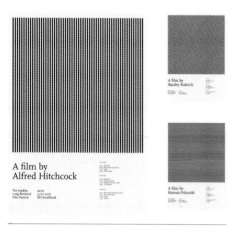

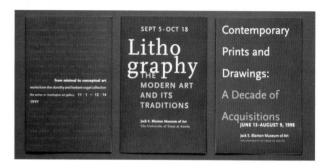

2007 HORROR FILM FESTIVAL POSTER SERIES / Thomas Brooks / UK, 2007

JACK S. BLANTON MUSEUM OF ART EXHIBITION INVITATIONS / HVADesign: Henk van Assen / USA, 1998

Left **REDUCING CRIME: WHAT'S NEXT? AMERICA WORKS PROGRESS REPORT** / Kym Abrams Design: creative direction, Kym Abrams; design, Eric Czerwonka; writing, Valjean McLenighan / USA, 2002

Hoefler Text

DESIGNER Jonathan Hoefler / **FOUNDRY** Hoefler & Frere-Jones / **YEAR** 1991 / **COUNTRY OF ORIGIN** United States / **CATEGORY** Serif / **CLASSIFICATION** Transitional

In the late 1980s and early 1990s, type foundries began translating their most important typefaces to digital fonts at a time when the technology was not highly advanced nor the processes perfected—with "the world's greatest typefaces," as Jonathan Hoefler notes, "quickly becoming some of the world's worst fonts." Hoefler began work on an expanded family that strived to establish a standard for what typeface design and development in the digital age could be.

Included in the ambitious family are roman, bold, and black weights, each featuring roman and italic small caps, swash and alternate swash italics, alternate ligatures, and engraved capitals, among many other characteristics inspired by fine printing. Apple became aware of Hoefler's work and turned to him to apply it to their TrueType GX format, a technology for the creation and use of fine typography in their operating system. TrueType GX did not fully succeed, but a limited family of Hoefler Text has been included as part of the Macintosh's Operating System since OS7 in 1991. It now remains to be seen if this typeface's wide availability will turn it into the next Times New Roman.

HOEFLER TEXT / Hoefler & Frere-Jones / USA, 1991

STEP INSIDE DESIGN 24, NO. 1 / MINE™: Christopher Simmons; art direction, Michael Ulrich; editing, Tom Biederbeck / USA, January/February 2008

HOEFLER TITLING, THE DISPLAY-SIZE COUNTERPART TO HOEFLER TEXT, SET IN A VISCOUS AND CAFFEINATED MILKY SUBSTANCE / Gemma O'Brien / Australia, 2008

Mrs. Eaves

DESIGNER Zuzana Licko / **FOUNDRY** Emigre Fonts / **YEAR** 1996 / **COUNTRY OF ORIGIN** United States / **CATEGORY** Serif / **CLASSIFICATION** Transitional Serif

The notion of revival in typeface design typically entails redrawing existing letterforms to better fit the moment's printing processes and technologic advances. With Mrs. Eaves, Zuzana Licko › 225 set out to reinterpret an old classic, designed for today's readers, while embedding her own aesthetic in it. Licko's choice was Baskerville, a typeface designed by John Baskerville in the 1750s. His work had been seriously criticized at the time for poor legibility due to its high contrast in thicks and thins. Baskerville, who was also a printer, developed a deep black ink and smooth, glossy papers previously unseen; these may have accounted for his work's exalted contrast but they did not aid his popularity.

Wanting to retain the lightness and openness characteristic of the source and stemming from the controversial, misunderstood contrast, Mrs. Eaves features a smaller *x*-height that compensates for the reduced contrast. With its roman, italic, bold, small caps, and petite caps weights and its wide range of ligatures, Mrs. Eaves became an instant choice for designers. Its elegance and versatility made it ubiquitous in the 1990s, as it stood apart from the grunge and display typeface craze of the time. In 2002, Emigre Fonts released Mrs. Eaves in OpenType, making the endless options of ligatures and number styles easily available with 1,150 glyphs.

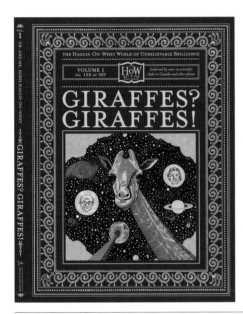

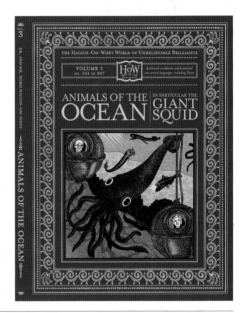

THE HAGGIS-ON-WHEY WORLD OF UNBELIEVABLE BRILLIANCE **BOOK SERIES** / Plinko: art direction, Dave Eggers, Plinko; illustration, Michael Kupperman / USA, 2003–2006

COLD WATER CANYON
Indigenous Shrubs of Santa Monica
PLANOGRAPHIC
YUMMY YUCCA CALCULATOR
PRINTING
sliding aluminum doors
KITCHENETTE
environmentally sound recycled paper
Bakersfield, California
QUALITY

MRS. EAVES / Emigre Fonts; Zuzana Licko / USA, 1996

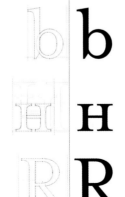

FOR THE RELIEF OF UNBEARABLE URGES, Nathan Englander / Vintage / Barbara deWilde / USA, 1999

SYNERGY V3 LINE PACKAGING FOR SYNERGY WORLDWIDE / Moxie Sozo; Leif Steiner / USA, 2008

Bell Centennial

DESIGNER Mathew Carter / **COMMISSIONER** AT&T / **YEAR** 1976–1978 / **COUNTRY OF ORIGIN** United States / **CATEGORY** Sans Serif

In 1976, AT&T turned to Mike Parker, director of typographic development at Linotype, who then commissioned Matthew Carter › 221 to update Bell Gothic, the typeface designed by Chauncey H. Griffith and used in the company's phone books since 1937. The requirements for the new typeface were demanding: Fit more characters per line, reduce the need for abbreviations, and increase legibility at very small sizes printed on very light newsprint. Matthew Carter's design slightly condensed the characters and increased their x-height while incorporating more open counters and deep ink traps into the family's four styles: Name and Number, Address, Sub Caption, and Bold Listing. Its success is certainly proven in its use and performance in phone books, and Bell Centennial enjoys an alternate life in the hands of designers enthralled with the way the ink traps and other peculiarities look at larger sizes.

Bell Centennial
Name & Number
ABCDEFGHIJK
LMNOPQRSTU
VWXYZ&1234
567890abcdef
ghijklmnopqrs
tuvwxyz.,-:;!?

BELL CENTENNIAL NAME & NUMBER /
**Commissioned by AT&T / Matthew Carter /
USA, 1976–1978**

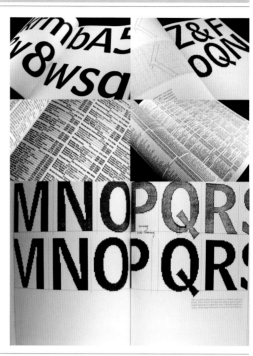

TYPE AND TECHNOLOGY MONOGRAPH NO. 1 BY THE CENTER FOR DESIGN AND TYPOGRAPHY, THE COOPER UNION / Matthew Carter / USA, 1982

Template Gothic

DESIGNER Barry Deck / **FOUNDRY** Emigre Fonts / **YEAR** 1990 / **COUNTRY OF ORIGIN** United States / **CATEGORY** Display

Inspired by an old hand-drawn laundry sign that Barry Deck took home after it had been replaced by a new one, Template Gothic was designed to look "as if it had suffered the distortive ravages of photomechanical reproduction," Deck explains. At the time, he was a student at CalArts › 131, where Ed Fella › 185 and Jeffery Keedy were promoting type experimentation. After a class trip to Emigre › 224, Rudy VanderLans asked Deck if they could release Template Gothic—and it soon became a praised and scorned representative of the experimental 1990s.

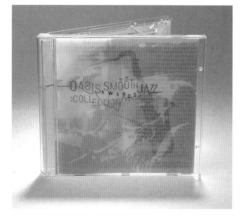

COLD WATER CANYON
CALIFORNIA
Chromolithography
AMERICAN
Indigenous Shrubs of Santa Monica

TEMPLATE GOTHIC / Emigre Fonts: Barry Deck / USA, 1990

OASIS SMOOTH JAZZ AWARDS COLLECTION, various artists / Native Language / Infinite ZZZ: art direction, Joel Venti; design, Jawsh Smyth / USA, 2000

EVERY GOOD BOY LIVE SHOWS POSTER / Emigre: Rudy Vander-Lans / USA, 1993

FF Blur

DESIGNER Neville Brody / **FOUNDRY** FontShop International / **YEAR** 1991 / **COUNTRY OF ORIGIN** United Kingdom / **CATEGORY** Display

FF Blur was developed in a period of enthusiastic technological experimentation. Neville Brody took the opportunity to explore how typography and technology could be bridged through messaging and perception. Using Photoshop's Blur filter and Autotrace feature, exaggerated contours and emphasized bitmaps were obtained and three weights released: light, medium, and bold, each with its own unique effect. FF Blur, like other experimental typefaces of the 1990s, allowed for a new kind of visual aesthetic enabled by the broadening embrace of the computer.

FÉRIA BY L'OREAL PARIS / USA, 2008

GRAPHIC ARTS MESSAGE **EXHIBITION SEMINAR WORKSHOP POSTER FOR TOO CORPORATION** / Research Studios / Japan, 1992

LIFT OFF **BROCHURE FOR UNISOURCE** / Pressley Jacobs Design, Inc. / USA, 1997

Lo-Res

DESIGNER Zuzana Licko / **FOUNDRY** Emigre Fonts / **YEAR** 1985; 2001 / **COUNTRY OF ORIGIN** United States / **CATEGORY** Bitmap

From the first editions of the Macintosh in 1984 and 1985, typefaces could be designed in their coarsest resolution only and, without the aid yet of Adobe's PostScript language, resulting in bitmap fonts. In these early days of digital type, Zuzana Licko ›225 developed a range of bitmap typefaces and supplied them to Rudy VanderLans for use in the first editions of the influential *Emigre* magazine ›100. At the time, the layouts and fonts met with mixed feelings, but their uniqueness blossomed in the context of Emigre's font business ›224. Originally released as Emigre, Emperor, Oakland, and Universal, these fonts were repackaged as the Lo-Res family in 2001. These bitmap fonts are designed for specific sizes, based on the vertical number of pixels of the grid, and are best scaled onscreen by full integers—for example, Lo-Res 9 must be set at 9 points to look sharp, and its next optimized size is 18 points. The Lo-Res family ranges from 9 to 28 and features narrow, serif, and sans-serif options. In the twenty-first century, these groundbreaking designs now exude nostalgia.

Emperor 8
Oakland 8
Emigre 10
Universal 19

LO-RES / Emigre: Zuzana Licko / USA, 1985 and 2001

LO-RES CATALOG / Emigre: Rudy VanderLans / USA, 2001

THE AGE OF INTELLIGENT MACHINES, Raymond Kurzweil / The MIT Press / USA, 1992

Bello

DESIGNER Akiem Helmling, Bas Jacobs, and Sami Kortemäki / FOUNDRY Underware / YEAR 2004 / COUNTRY OF ORIGIN Netherlands / CATEGORY Script

After design and typeface development became highly mechanized by the computer, a slow movement to bring back the hand-drawn and handmade—produced through the computer nonetheless—started to emerge in the early 2000s. One of the catalysts broadly embraced was Bello Pro, a brush script rendered by hand and perfected on the computer. Taking advantage of the blooming OpenType font format, Bello Pro was able to produce a convincing script where every single character connected with the other, regardless of the combination—something past script typefaces could not anticipate or address fully—by providing contextual characters that re-acted to what was beside them. Bello Pro features a sturdy small caps companion that complements the free-flowing nature of the script, as well as beginning and ending swashes and more than 60 ligatures that add flair as well as mimic a more natural script.

IS NOT MAGAZINE / Mel Campbell, Stuart Geddes, Natasha Ludowyk, Penny Modra, Jeremy Wortsman / Australia, 2005–2008

BELLO / Underware / Netherlands, 2005

Ed Interlock

DESIGNER Ken Barber, Ed Benguiat, Tal Leming / FOUNDRY House Industries / YEAR 2004 / COUNTRY OF ORIGIN United States / CATEGORY Display

As head of the publishing department of Photo-Lettering, Inc. (known as PLINC), a New York-based phototypesetting shop that provided headline and display lettering to advertising agencies in the 1930s until it closed in the 1980s, Ed Benguiat drew nearly 500 alphabets. Some were digitized by ITC › 220, but the majority live only in the film-based archives of PLINC, purchased by House Industries › 228 in 2003. Working with Benguiat, Ken Barber, House Industries' typography director and lettering expert, selected a range of styles to develop as OpenType typefaces that would do justice to Benguiat's fluid hand-lettering. The Ed Benguiat Collection, launched in 2004, features Ed Script, Ed Gothic, Ed Roman, Ed Brush, and Ed Interlock—and while they all take advantage of the versatility of OpenType, it is Ed Interlock that wildly exploits the technology.

As the name implies, Ed Interlock's appeal is its ability to lock one letter to the next in a complex way usually achieved only by hand as drawn for a specific application. With 1,400 ligatures, Ed Interlock reacts to the letters being set and proposes the best and most interesting lock-up; in addition, it maintains a visual balance between top and bottom lock-ups. Programmed by Tal Leming, a type technology specialist, House Industries cheekily calls this "Artificial Edtelligence."

ED BENGUIAT FONT COLLECTION PACKAGING / House Industries / USA, 2004 / Photo: Carlos Alejandro

ED INTERLOCK NOTES AND ANIMATION OF CONTEXTUAL SUBSTITUTION ROUTINES / House Industries: design, Ken Barber / USA, 2004

ED BENGUIAT FONT COLLECTION MAILER / House Industries / USA, 2004

Times New Roman

Version A **DESIGNER** Stanley Morison and Victor Lardent / **COMMISSIONER** The *Times* / **FOUNDRY** Monotype / **YEAR** 1931 / **COUNTRY OF ORIGIN** United Kingdom / **CATEGORY** Serif / **CLASSIFICATION** Garalde
Version B **DESIGNER** Starling Burgess / **FOUNDRY** Lanston / **YEAR** 1904 / **COUNTRY OF ORIGIN** United States / **CATEGORY** Serif / **CLASSIFICATION** Garalde /

In 1931, the *Times* of London commissioned Stanley Morison, a typography consultant to the Monotype Corporation, to oversee the production of a new typeface for the newspaper. Drawn by Victor Lardent, a draftsman in the *Times*' publicity department, and based on Robert Granjon's Plantin, the typeface made its debut in 1932.

While this is the prevailing assumption of its origins, the type historian and director of typographic development at Mergenthaler Linotype Co. in the 1960s and 1970s, Mike Parker, tells a different story. In a 1994 article called "W. Starling Burgess, Type designer?" for *Printing History*, the journal of the American Printing History Association, Parker wrote that it had been Starling Burgess, a Boston aeronautical engineer and naval architect with an interest in typography, who in 1903 designed the roman version that preceded Morison's design for the Lanston type foundry. Burgess'

work found its way to Monotype's archives in London, where Frank Hinman Pierpont, an American type designer who headed the matrix factory and drawing office, produced what would become Times New Roman. Morison presented Pierpont's design to the *Times* without crediting him and downplaying his involvement.

What is clear is that Times New Roman is one of the most pervasive typefaces—perhaps to a fault. With time and its inclusion as a default font in both PC and Macintosh computers and in Microsoft's Office products, used in an inconceivable amount of documents issued by government organizations, schools, libraries, grocery stores, dentists, and anyone with a computer, Times New Roman's gravitas has diminished.

5,0 ORIGINAL BEER PACKAGING / feldmann+schultchen design studios: André Feldmann, Arne Schultchen, Florian Schoffro, Inge-Marie Hansen, Kati Lust, Edgar Walthert / Germany, 2007

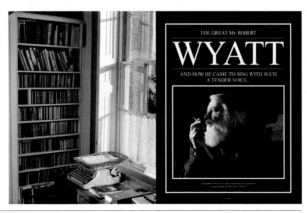

FANTASTIC MAN **MAGAZINE NO. 3** / Top Publishers / Netherlands, 2006

NIKE, INC., FORM 10-K / USA, 2008

Arial

Arial, or Sonoran San Serif, as it was first named, was originally designed and used for Xerox and IBM's truck-sized xerographic (laser) printers in the 1980s. Based on the Monotype Grotesque series, it sports softer curves and diagonally cut strokes to increase legibility but, just as well, it dubiously features the same proportions as Helvetica. Microsoft, which tapped Monotype to provide TrueType fonts, added Arial to its Windows 3.1 operating system in 1992, and it instantly and globally became the type du jour for PowerPoint presentations, Word documents, and websites across the world, much to the chagrin of designers who consider it Helvetica's bastard child.

DESIGNER Robin Nicholas, Patricia Saunders / **FOUNDRY** Monotype Imaging / **YEAR** 1982 / **COUNTRY OF ORIGIN** United States / **CATEGORY** Sans Serif / **CLASSIFICATION** Neo-Grotesque Sans Serif

HELVETICA VS. ARIAL, A PLACE TO STOMP ON ARIAL AND RELEASE YOUR FURY / engage studio / UK, 2003

ARIAL OR HELVETICA? A QUIZ TO TEST YOUR RECOGNITION SKILLS / I Live On Your Visits: Derren Wilson / UK, 2003

Papyrus

Inspired by the ancient Middle East, imagined as what 2,000-year-old vernacular would look like set on papyrus, and hand-rendered as calligraphy on textured paper, Papyrus was acquired by Letraset after ten other type companies passed on it. Over a six-month period, Papyrus was created by hand using traditional materials such as Rapidographs, French curves, and Wite-Out. Papyrus' popularity increased when it was bundled with Apple's Mac OS X in 2001. Its handwritten feel made it a darling for designing tea packaging, yoga studio identities, film opening titles, CD covers, real estate advertising, newsletters, lingerie stores, personal business cards, anything organic, and much more.

DESIGNER Chris Costello / **FOUNDRY** Letraset (1983) / **YEAR** 1982 / **COUNTRY OF ORIGIN** United States / **CATEGORY** Display

SALVAGGIO'S PACKAGING FOR NINO SALVAGGIO INTERNATIONAL MARKETPLACE / Goldforest: creative direction, Michael Gold, Lauren Gold; design, Carolyn Rodi / USA, 2006

Comic Sans

DESIGNER Vincent Connare / **COMMISSIONER** Microsoft Corporation / **YEAR** 1994 / **COUNTRY OF ORIGIN** United States / **CATEGORY** Display

Comic Sans is constantly under criticism and scrutiny by designers who are appalled by the design and its wide use across the globe. First designed as a support typeface for the interface of Microsoft Bob—a friendlier alternative to interacting with Windows 95—it was never intended for public release. Yet, Comic Sans *was* released as part of Windows 95 alongside Trebuchet, Webdings, and Verdana. Today it can be found in almost every street in the world and online, whether as a conscious choice, a default selection, or in disdain, as in the efforts of bancomicsans.com.

Photos: Rani Goel

Photo: Rani Goel   Photo: Dan Raynolds   Photo: Jan-Anne Heijenga   Photo: Ben (Crouchingbadger) Ward

COMIC SANS IN USE

Fajita

DESIGNER Noel Rubin / **FOUNDRY** Image Club / **YEAR** 1994 / **COUNTRY OF ORIGIN** United States / **CATEGORY** Display

Based on the typeface Sarah Elizabeth, found in one of the many Dan X. Solo type compendia, Fajita was developed in two weights, Mild and Picante, that include different accented characters. Since its release, Fajita can be found on awnings and menus across the country that specialize in Mexican or TexMex food—slowly blending them all into one simple stereotype. While Fajita may not be the greatest typographic accomplishment, its impact in visually pigeonholing the food industry for a specific demographic is worth noting.

IMAGE CLUB CATALOG / Splorp: Grant Hutchinson / Canada, 1993   **MOCK-UP SAMPLES OF FAJITA IN USE** / Splorp: Grant Hutchinson / Canada, 1993

COOPER BLACK

Seeking a career in illustration, in 1899 Oswald Bruce Cooper enrolled in Chicago's Frank Holme School of Illustration, where one of his teachers was Frederic W. Goudy, one of the most prolific American type designers. Cooper eventually steered into lettering and design away from illustration, himself becoming a teacher at Holme. Fred Bertsch, who ran an art service business next door, became friends with Cooper, and in 1904 they established Bertsch & Cooper, combining Bertsch's business savvy and Cooper's talent. Beginning with local clients, they created lettering for advertising and soon found themselves with bigger commissions for national campaigns. With the wider exposure, the Barnhart Brothers & Spindler (BB&S) type foundry took notice of Cooper's work and approached him to design a type family based on his lettering. Apprehensive at first, Cooper agreed, and in 1918 he designed a roman typeface with rounded serifs that was simply called Cooper and later renamed Cooper Oldstyle. Two years later, he designed Cooper Black, taking the rounded serifs of the original typeface to their broadest extreme to create the heaviest typeface to date, both literally and figuratively: As a metal font at 120 points, the full alphabet weighed

EASYJET LIVERY / © easyJet airline company limited / USA

COOPER BLACK TYPE SPECIMEN / USA, 2007 / **Photo: Matthew Desmond**

CACAHUATES, INC., IDENTITY / Tea Time Studio; developed with aBe / Spain, 2004–2006

COOPER BLACK AT HOME / Francis Chan / Canada, 2007

more than 80 pounds, and, when typeset, it unequivocally commanded attention with its sheer mass.

Cooper Black became the best-selling typeface of BB&S, and it spurred a trend in black typefaces from its competitors, including an eerily derivative design, Goudy Heavyface, by Cooper's former teacher. Cooper Black also became a de facto selection for advertising, with its exuberant friendliness and boldness. In 1924, Cooper designed the italic companion to

his original roman and, two years later, Cooper Black Italic further popularizing Cooper's type designs. Cooper Black and its italic counterpart enjoyed success through the 1930s, but other bold typefaces like Futura ›371, Univers ›372, and Helvetica ›373 gradually replaced them through the 1960s and 1970s. The Cooper typefaces were briefly resurrected in advertising in the latter decades, but they eventually became a default choice for store signs, flyers, and other dull applications. At the turn of the century, Cooper

Black and its italic enjoyed a resurgence, first with revivals like Oz Black by Patrick Giasson in 1999 and Rosemary by Chank Diesel in 2000, and second by oozing a sense of advertising nostalgia unto graphic designers. Used ironically and with a knowing wink, Cooper Black has reappeared not just in advertising but in books and magazines, motion graphics, and even corporate and brand identities.

COOPER BLACK, AS FOUND IN THE STREETS OF CHICAGO AND NEW YORK / USA, 2004–2006

FAT PIG, Neil LaBute / Faber and Faber, an affiliate of Farrar, Straus and Giroux / Charlotte Strick / USA, 2004

RECOMMENDED READING

4AD › 301

Vaughan Oliver: Visceral Pleasures, by Rick Poynor and Vaughan Oliver, Booth-Clibborn Editions, 2000

ABSOLUT › 307

Absolut Book: The Absolut Vodka Advertising Story, by Richard W. Lewis, Journey Editions, 1996

Absolut: Biography of a Bottle, by Carl Hamilton, Texere, 2002

AICHER, OTL › 166

Otl Aicher, by Markus Rathgeb, Phaidon, 2007

BASEL SCHOOL OF DESIGN › 128

Swiss Graphic Design: The Origins and Growth of an International Style, 1920–1965, by Richard Hollis, Yale University Press, 2006

Graphic Design Manual: Principles and Practice, by Armin Hofmann, Arthur Niggli, 2001

The Road to Basel: Typographic Reflections by Students of the Typographer and Teacher Emil Ruder, by Helmut Schmid, Helmut Schmid Design, 199

BEALL, LESTER › 146

Lester Beall: Trailblazer of American Graphic Design, by R. Roger Remington, W.W. Norton, 1996

BLACKLETTER › 68

Blackletter: Type and National Identity, by Peter Bain and Paul Shaw, Princeton Architectural Press, 1998

Mexican Blackletter, by Cristina Paoli, Mark Batty Publisher, 2006

Fraktur Mon Amour, by Judith Schalansky, Verlag Hermann Schmidt Mainz, 2006

Fraktur: Form und Geschichte der gebrochenen Schriften, by Albert Kapr, Verlag Hermann Schmidt Mainz, 1993

BLUE NOTE RECORDS › 298

Blue Note Records: The Biography, by Richard Cook, Charles & Co., 2004

Blue Note: The Album Cover Art, edited by Graham Marsh, Felix Cromey, and Glyn Calligham, Chronicle, 1991

The Blue Note Years: The Jazz Photography of Francis Wolff, by Michael Cuscana, Charlie Lourie, and Francis Wolff, Rizzoli, 2001

BRODOVICH, ALEXEY › 143

Alexey Brodovitch, by Kerry William Purcell, Phaidon, 2002

Alexey Brodovitch, by Gabriel Bauret, Assouline, 2005

BROWNJOHN, ROBERT › 155

Robert Brownjohn: Sex and Typography, by Emily King, Laurence King Publishing, Princeton Architectural Press, 2005

BUBBLES, BARNEY

Reasons to Be Cheerful: The Life and Work of Barney Bubbles, by Paul Gorman, Adelita, 2008

CARTER, MATTHEW › 221

Typographically Speaking: The Art of Matthew Carter, by Margaret Re, Princeton Architectural Press, 2003

CATO PARTNERS › 208

Design by Thinking, by Ken Cato, HBI, 2005

Ken Cato: The Dimensions of Designs, by Ken Cato, Images Publishing, 2006

CHANTRY, ART › 184

Some People Can't Surf: The Graphic Design of Art Chantry, by Julie Lasky, Chronicle Books 2001

COCA-COLA › 308, 340

For God, Country, and Coca-Cola: The Definitive History of the Great American Soft Drink and the Company That Makes It, by Mark Pendergrast, Basic Books, 2000

COLOR › 56, 57

Complete Color Harmony Workbook, by Kiki Eldridge, Rockport 2007

DORFSMAN, LOU › 173

Dorfsman and CBS, by Dick Hess and Marion Muller, American Showcase, 1987

EATOCK , DANIEL › 211

Daniel Eatock Imprint: Works 1975–2007, by Daniel Eatock, Princeton Architectural Press, 2008

EMIGRE › 100

Merz to Emigre and Beyond: Avant-Garde Magazine Design of the Twentieth Century, by Steven Heller, Phaidon, 2003

FLETCHER/FORBES/GILL › 161

The Art of Looking Sideways, by Alan Fletcher, Phaidon, 2001

Alan Fletcher: Picturing and Poeting, by Alan Fletcher, Phaidon, 2006

Graphic Design as a Second Language, by Bob Gill, Images Publishing, 2004

FOSSIL › 310

Tinspiration: The Art and Inspiration of the Fossil Tin, by Fossil, Fossil Partners Ltd., 2006

HERSHEY'S CHOCOLATE › 309

Hershey: Milton S. Hershey's Extraordinary Life of Wealth, Empire, and Utopian Dreams, by Michael D'Antonio, Simon & Schuster, 2007

HIPGNOSIS › 302

For the Love of Vinyl: The Album Art of Hipgnosis, by Storm Thorgerson and Aubrey Powell, PictureBox, 2008

Comfortably Numb: The Inside Story of Pink Floyd, by Mark Blake, Da Capo, 2008

Taken by Storm, by Storm Thorgerson and Peter Curzon, Vision On, 2007

HOUSE INDUSTRIES › 228

House Industries, by House Industries, Die Gestalten Verlag, 2003

JOHNSON, MICHAEL › 209

Problem Solved: A Primer in Design and Communication, by Michael Johnson, Phaidon, 2004

KENT, SISTER MARY CORITA › 172

Come Alive! The Spirited Art of Sister Corita, by Julie Ault, Four Corners Books, 2006

M&CO. › 183

Tibor Kalman, Perverse Optimist, by Michael Bierut, Peter Hall, and Tibor Kalman, Booth-Clibborn Editions, 1998

INDEX

Page numbers in bold refer to topic's individual entry

CONTRIBUTOR INDEX AND DIRECTORY